# TEACHING AND LEARNING MATHEMATICS IN MODERN TIMES

**Dr. R.N. PATEL**

**B.Sc. (Hons.), M.A., M.Ed., Ph.D.**
**Former Principal,**
**Kapila Khandvala College of Education,**
**Santa Cruz, Mumbai.**

HPH

Himalaya Publishing House

MUMBAI • DELHI • NAGPUR • BENGALURU • HYDERABAD •
BHUBANESWAR • CHENNAI • PUNE • INDORE • AHMEDABAD
LUCKNOW • ERNAKULAM • KOLKATA • GUWAHATI

**First Edition : 2012**

---

**Published by** : Mrs. Meena Pandey for **Himalaya Publishing House Pvt. Ltd.,**
"Ramdoot", Dr. Bhalerao Marg, Girgaon, **Mumbai - 400 004.**
Phone: 022-23860170/23863863, Fax: 022-23877178
**E-mail: himpub@vsnl.com; Website: www.himpub.com**

**Branch Offices** :

**New Delhi** : "Pooja Apartments", 4-B, Murari Lal Street, Ansari Road, Darya Ganj, New Delhi - 110 002. Phone: 011-23270392, 23278631; Fax: 011-23256286

**Nagpur** : Kundanlal Chandak Industrial Estate, Ghat Road, Nagpur - 440 018. Phone: 0712-2738731, 3296733; Telefax: 0712-2721215

**Bengaluru** : No. 16/1 (Old 12/1), 1st Floor, Next to Hotel Highlands, Madhava Nagar, Race Course Road, Bengaluru - 560 001. Phone: 080-32919385; Telefax: 080-22286611

**Hyderabad** : No. 3-4-184, Lingampally, Besides Raghavendra Swamy Matham, Kachiguda, Hyderabad - 500 027. Phone: 040-27560041, 27550139; Mobile: 09390905282

**Chennai** : No. 8/2, Modley 2nd Street, Ground Floor, T. Nagar, Chennai - 600 017. Phone: 044-28144004/28144005; Mobile: 09345345051

**Pune** : First Floor, "Laksha" Apartment, No. 527, Mehunpura, Shaniwarpeth (Near Prabhat Theatre), Pune - 411 030. Phone: 020-24496323/24496333; Mobile: 09370579333

**Lucknow** : Jai Baba Bhavan, Church Road, Near Manas Complex and Dr. Awasthi Clinic, Aliganj, Lucknow - 226 024 (U.P.). Phone: 0522-2339329, 4068914; Mobile: 09307501550

**Ahmedabad** : 114, "SHAIL", 1st Floor, Opp. Madhu Sudan House, C.G. Road, Navrang Pura, Ahmedabad - 380 009. Phone: 079-26560126; Mobile: 09377088847

**Ernakulam** : 39/176 (New No: 60/251) 1st Floor, Karikkamuri Road, Ernakulam, Kochi - 682011, Phone: 0484-2378012, 2378016; Mobile: 09344199799

**Bhubaneswar** : 5 Station Square, Bhubaneswar - 751 001 (Odisha). Phone: 0674-2532129, Mobile: 09338746007

**Indore** : Kesardeep Avenue Extension, 73, Narayan Bagh, Flat No. 302, IIIrd Floor, Near Humpty Dumpty School, Indore - 452 007 (M.P.). Mobile: 09301386468

**Kolkata** : 108/4, Beliaghata Main Road, Near ID Hospital, Opp. SBI Bank, Kolkata - 700 010, Phone: 033-32449649, Mobile: 09883055590, 07439040301

**Guwahati** : House No. 15, Behind Pragjyotish College, Near Sharma Printing Press, P.O. Bharalumukh, Guwahati - 781009, (Assam). Mobile: 09883055590, 09883055536

**DTP by** : Sudhakar Shetty (HPH Pvt. Ltd., Mumbai)

**Printed at** : M/s. Aditya Offset Process (I) Pvt. Ltd., Hyderabad. On behalf of HPH.

# PREFACE

Mathematically, it can be said that Life – Mathematics = Zero. Utility of mathematics in our life is extremely high.

This book is written with the sole purpose of helping the student-teachers in particular and the teachers' world at large, in their study of mathematics. Reading this book they will love mathematics.

This book covers a wide range of issues in the teaching of mathematics and offers supporting tasks to students to enable them to translate theory into practice.

Large paragraphs have been converted into small paragraphs so that the readers can understand and remember the contents well for a longer period. Last chapter of this book contains a variety of recreational items involving mathematics for the readers to enjoy.

I take this opportunity to acknowledge my hearty thanks to Prin. Dr. P.N. Chavda, Thakur Shyamnarayan College of Education and Research, Kandivali and Prin. Dr. Vandana P. Maheshwari, KKCE, Santa Cruz and Prin. Shri Japanbhai Desai, Sardar B.Ed. College, Amroli (Surat), for their timely help in providing reference books which were really useful in my undertaking. My hearty thanks to Mrs. Krupa R. Patel, a teacher, for extending her hand of co-operation by providing suitable matter for this book. I cannot help acknowledging my hearty thanks to three students, Kshitij M. Patel, Vismay M. Patel and Devang P. Sailor for donating many recreational items included in the last chapter.

Constructive criticism and comments on this book are welcomed.

**R. N. PATEL**

# CONTENTS

# 1 MATHEMATICS EDUCATION — WHO DECIDES?

To teach mathematics is a high calling. The truth of mathematics is real and fundamental and it is right for all pupils to study mathematics throughout all of their compulsory schooling.

But here the questions arises: What is mathematics? Why does mathematics deserve its place in the curriculum? Why is mathematics education important? What mathematics will it be appropriate to learn in the 21st century? How can mathematics be best learnt by each individual pupil? How is mathematics best taught and learnt?

As you, student-teacher, learn to teach mathematics, you will need to seek answers to these key questions. There are no simple answers. There is often much disagreement about the issues raised above. The issue is not — what is the best way to teach mathematics?, but what is mathematics really all about?

Teaching cannot be resolved without confronting problems about the nature of mathematics. Your time spent as a student-teacher can provide opportunities to develop your understanding of the ideas that underlie these controversies. You will then be better prepared to making teaching decisions in the best interest of your pupils.

## 1.1 Mathematics and you

You are about to begin learning how to teach mathematics. But in reality, you are not a beginner. You already have a wealth of experience of mathematics education. Whether you have studied mathematics at degree level or not, you would have spent many hours of your life engaged in learning and using mathematics.

The teacher's view of mathematics is shaped to a very large extent by his/her own mathematical experiences as a student and they will also influence your personal philosophy about mathematics education. To grow and develop as a mathematics teacher you will need to go on reflecting about mathematics, about education and about your place in relation to both.

## 1.2 Mathematics and Education

While you are learning to teach mathematics, you should consider somewhat abstract issues of the nature of mathematics and the purpose of education.

### The nature of mathematics

Is the nature of mathematics a controversial issue? Surely. Everyone has a fairly clear idea of what the subject is and consequently what should be taught in schools.

Mathematics can mean different things to different people:

Paul Halmos (1986) — 'It is security — certainly, truth, beauty, insight, structure, architecture. I see mathematics, the part of human knowledge that I call mathematics as one thing — one great glorious thing.'

Philip Davis and Reuben Harsh (1986) — 'Mathematics does have a subject matter and its statements are meaningful. The meaning, however, is to be found in the shared understanding of human beings, not in an eternal non-human reality. In this respect, mathematics is similar to an ideology, a religion or an art form, it deals with human meanings and is intelligible only within the context of culture. In other words, mathematics is a humanistic study. It is one of the humanities.'

You might conclude that although the responses of these people are different, they are nonetheless still talking about the same thing. However, there is a significant difference between these two views and it is rooted in different understandings of human knowledge.

For Paul Halmos, mathematics seems a fixed objective body of true ideas, independent of culture. For Davis and Hersh, mathematics is a fallible, yet correctable product of human thought rooted in human culture.

Developing your standpoint on the nature of mathematics is important because it will influence the values about mathematics that you convey to your pupils.

## 1.3 The aim/purpose of Education

Aims express intentions of individuals or groups, they are not just abstract ideas. As with the nature of mathematics, there is no universal agreement on aims of education. This is, because different groups can and do have different sets of values which are in turn rooted in their different world views of belief systems.

There are some broad categories that help to illuminate the area of educational aims. They are—

(1) Academic development (2) Vocational development

(3) Personal development (4) Social development

*1. Academic development:* Education should help pupils to develop a thorough knowledge and understanding of the subject matter. At the same time, pupils should be encouraged to form appropriate attitudes towards the subject of mathematics.

The desired outcome is sufficient people inducted into the academic community, including an adequate supply of good teachers at all levels. This is in order that subject's place within our cultural heritage and its future development are guaranteed.

2. *Vocational development:* Education should provide with the relevant knowledge and skills that they need in the world of work.

The desired outcome is a suitably equipped workforce ready to adapt to the needs of a growing economy.

3. *Personal development:* Education should provide opportunity for the all around development of the individual.

The desired outcome is autonomous people who have a well developed self awareness and who continue to grow and mature in adult life.

4. *Social development:* Education should provide the forum within which peoples can develop socially and find their roles within society.

The desired outcome is individuals who will be confident in their interpersonal relationships and in their role as critical citizens.

Society has many misconceptions about mathematics education and its role in our world. *e.g.,*

(1) Mathematics is a collection of rigid rules and mysterious procedures that seem to be unrelated to each other and require total mastery with little or no understanding.

(2) Mathematics is difficult and demanding. It is a subject in which it is socially acceptable to do poorly.

(3) The widespread role of mathematics is underestimated in both — the world of work and the world of everyday living.

(4) The school mathematics is irrelevant and unnecessary. It is unrelated to the pupils in their professional and personal lives.

These false perceptions and regrettable attitudes about mathematics have a significant and negative impact on mathematics education. These attitudes about mathematics can be changed only if our pupils become knowledgeable about mathematics and are prepared to become lifelong learners and users of mathematics.

Each of these four areas of development has (at some time within the history of mathematics education) been the focus of concern for different groups. Considering your aims for education, is a further, important part of clarifying the values that will inform your mathematics teaching.

### Further Issues

Perspectives on the nature of mathematics and on the aims of education come together to form aims for mathematics education.

Having established the purpose of mathematics education (*i.e.,* a sense of 'why'), there remain the further questions 'what' and 'how'. The way in which one answers these questions will be strongly connected to one's aims.

## 1.4 Competing Influences on the Mathematics Curriculum

Below are descriptions of the mathematical perspectives of four different social groups:

1. The mathematical purists
2. The industrial pragmatists
3. The progressive educators
4. The social reformers

These groups are not real organised associations of people, but instead represent a catagorisation offering a framework for exploring the competing influences within mathematics education. The origins of much current practice in mathematics education have their roots within the opinions attributed to one of these four groups.

## 1. The Mathematical Purists

This group is primarily concerned with the academic and some aspects of personal development of pupils.

Its members strongly reject any utilitarian emphasis on work or the application of mathematics for the justification as a school subject. They also assume that it is obvious that mathematics education has no role in the social development of young people.

The tradition of emphasising the importance of mathematics as a subject for the improvement of the mind continues to be maintained by some today.

The mathematical purists consider mathematics to be an objective form of knowledge, a complex hierarchical structure of ideas linked together through proof and rational thought. They celebrate its significant contribution to our cultural heritage, identified it more as an art than a science and believe it to have aesthetic qualities.

The Cambridge mathematician G.H. Hardy (1940) wrote — 'The mathematician's patterns, like the painter's or the poet's, must be beautiful; the ideas, like the colours or the words, must fit together in a harmonious way. Beauty is the first test: there is no permanent place in the world for ugly mathematics.'

They see the role of the teacher as enabling the effective transmission of this body of knowledge and encouraging particular qualities in the pupils, such as concern for rigour, elegance and precision.

This group supports major competitions for pupils, partly because these help identifying the next generation of mathematicians.

## 2. Industrial Pragmatists

This group is primarily concerned with the vocational development of pupils through mathematics. There is some recognition of the need for social development but only in as far as it prepares young people for the world of work. Academic development is acknowledged to be relevant for a few, but the dominant focus of mathematics eduction must be on the great mass of ordinary people.

Everybody needs an adequate mathematical education, so that they can contribute to the development of a successful economy.

Members of this group are most likely to be found amongst employers in industry or leaders of technical and scientific profession. There is a tradition of this group trying to influence mathematics education from the last century. At that time, their argument was mainly with the mathematical purists.

According to Prof. John Perry (1901) — 'The study of mathematics began because it was useful, continues because it is useful and is valuable to the world because of the usefulness of its results, while the mathematicians, who determine what the teacher shall do, hold that the subject should be studied for its own sake.'

This group has grown considerably in numbers and strength throughout the 20th century and was arguably the most influential at the end of the century.

The industrial pragmatists see mathematics as an established collection of very useful techniques and skills that can be applied to a large range of technical and scientific contexts. They recognised that there is a body of knowledge to be learnt but consider that it is only to be learnt in order to be applied.

There is, however, sometimes a tension within this group as to which areas of mathematics are most important. Some advocate a strong emphasis on Arithmetic and basic numeracy while others require pupils to learn mathematics most helpful for them to function in a rapidly changing technical society. So, they welcome an increased emphasis on the use of calculators and especially computers.

They see the role of the teacher as being to instruct the pupil in skills and to motivate them by the use of real work contexts.

Learning requires thorough practice and pupils benefit from doing practical and possibly experimental work. At a higher level, pupils should learn the skills for applied problem-solving and modelling.

Assessment has a dual function for the industrial pragmatists. On one level, it acts as a simple aid to selection for a particular job. It also ensures that core skills have been developed and verified.

## 3. Progressive Educators

This group is primarily concerned with the personal development of pupils with the individual child as focus of attention. It rejects the adult-oriented nature of vocational development and supports social and academic development only to the extent that these are supportive of personal development.

Members of this group have, like the industrial pragmatists, grown in prominence during the 20th century.

According to Jean-Jacques Rousseau (18th century) — 'Teacher's first duty is to be humane.

> Love childhood. Look with friendly eyes on its games, its pleasures, its amiable dispositions. Which of you does not sometimes look back regretfully on the age when laughter was ever on the lips and the heart free of care? Why steal from the little innocents the enjoyment of a time that passes all too quickly?

Here, we find a concern to put the child, not the future adult, at the centre of the educational project.

This group is much more interested in the process of learning and rejects any attempt to impose mathematics on the pupils. It believes that pupils should be supported in exploring and discovering the subject for themselves. There is a concern for the child to remain motivated and to have positive feelings and attitudes.

Learning mathematics should build up children's self-esteem and help them to become confident and autonomous. They are encouraged to pursue their own open-ended investigations, to engage in projects related to personal interests and to find their own ways of expressing and communicating their own mathematics.

They see the role of the teacher as coming alongside the pupils and acting as a guide in the pupils' journey of discovery. This means that it is the responsibility of the teacher to create an appropriate learning environment, both in terms of stimulating resources and supportive social dynamics.

Mathematical educators within this group have been influential in developing mathematics equipments. Computers and calculators are considered important for offering new environments within which mathematical exploration can happen.

There is also an emphasis on developing caring, supportive relationships in the classroom with children being shielded from significant social conflicts.

Children are to be treated as individual and allowed to learn at different rates. It is important to recognise and celebrate their success. So records of achievement and criteria based assessment are to be welcomed. External examinations are not considered helpful as they have the potential for bringing discouragement and disappointment to the child. They are also seen as skewing the curriculum towards short-term goals.

## 4. Social Reformers

This group is primarily concerned with the social development of pupils, in the sense that education should empower the individual to participate fully and critically in a democratic society. Consequently, aspects of personal development are considered important. Encouraging vocational and academic development is appropriate only through negotiation with the pupil.

Members of this group have only relatively recently begun to influence mathematics education but the origins of this group within education can be traced back to the 19th century. In more recent times, social reformers have had more influence in the emerging education structures of developing countries.

Julius Nyerere (1991) has pointed out — 'The people have to be able to think for themselves, to make judgements on all the issues affecting them, they have to be able to interpret the decisions made through the democratic institutions of our society.'

The other stimulus to the work of the group of social reformers has been the need to work towards equality of opportunity for all within education. Within mathematics education, significant work has been done in the field of gender issues — multicultural and anti-racist mathematics.

Ernest (1991) opined — "Mathematics is seem to be a social construction: tentative, growing by means of human creation and decision-making, and connected with other realms of knowledge, culture and social life.'

This offers a much wider definition of mathematics than is the norm and challenges the mathematical purists' exclusive ownership of 'real mathematics.'

They see the role of the teacher as facilitating pupils in both posing and solving their own problems. This requires the teacher to set conditions (*a*) in which pupils can participate in decisions about their learning and (*b*) in which they feel able to question their mathematics course and its associated teaching methods.

Resources need to be socially relevant and include authentic materials such as newspaper and sources of real data. Discussion is central to the learning process and conflicting ideas are welcome in promoting greater understanding.

Any form of assessment must be seen to be fair to all pupils and should not disadvantage any social grouping. This requires a greater variety of modes of assessment; and so project work and the on-going assessment of course work is highly valued.

## EVALUATE YOURSELF

1. What is the aim or purpose of Education?
2. Give in detail the description of the mathematical perspective of any two different groups.
3. Write short notes on with respect to mathematical perspectives:
   (1) The nature of mathematics
   (2) Mathematical Purists
   (3) The industrial Pragmatists
   (4) The progressive Educators
   (5) The social Reformers
4. Discuss the broad categories that help to illuminate the area of educational aims.

'One inevitable result of this explosive development of mathematics has been the creation of new subject matter. Such fields as mathematical logic, probability and statistical inference, topology and modern abstract algebra are largely or wholly the product of recent mathematical research.'

— ***Report of Commission of Mathematics***

# 2 WHAT IS MODERN MATHEMATICS?

The concept of 'modern mathematics' became widespread in India in the 'seventies' of 20th century. Then it was new approach to mathematics and was called 'new/modern mathematics.' Before that, now we can say that it was 'old mathematics.' Now, when 30-40 years have passed in teaching modern mathematics in schools and colleges, it is of no use to address it as 'modern mathematics.' So, henceforth when we say 'mathematics', it should be understood as 'modern mathematics.'

To understand what mathematics is, some definitions of mathematics will be quite helpful.

## 2.1 Some useful definitions

***New English Dictionary:*** 'Mathematics, in a strict sense, is the abstract science which investigates deductively the conclusions implicit in the elementary conceptions of spatial and numerical relations.'

***Webster's Dictionary:*** 'Mathematics is the science of numbers and their operations, interrelations, combinations, generalisations and abstractions and of space configuration and their structure, measurement, transformations and generalisations.'

***Galileo:*** 'Mathematics is the language in which God has written the universe.'

***Benjamine Peirce:*** 'Mathematics is a science that draws necessary conclusions.'

***Bertrand Russell:*** 'Mathematics is the subject in which we never know what we are talking about nor whether what we are saying is true.'

***Locke:*** Mathematics is a way to settle in the mind a habit of reasoning.'

***Marshal H. Stone:*** 'Mathematics is the study of abstract system built of abstract elements which are not described in concrete fashion.'

***Roger Bacon:*** 'Mathematics is the gateway and key of all sciences... Neglect of mathematics work injury to all knowledge, since who is ignorant of it cannot know the other sciences or the things of the world. And what is worse, men who are thus ignorant are unable to perceive their own ignorance and so do not seek a remedy.'

***Courant and Robbins (1941):*** 'Mathematics as an expression of the human mind reflects the active will, the contemplative reason and the desire for aesthetic perfection. Its basic elements are logic and intuition, analysis and construction, generality and individuality.'

***National Policy of Education (1986):*** 'Mathematics should be visualised as the vehicle to train a child to think, reason, analyse, articulate logically. Apart from being a specific subject, it should be treated as a concomitant to any subject involving analysis and reasoning.'

***Prof. Voss:*** 'Our entire civilisation depending on intellectual penetration and utilisation of nature, has its real foundation in mathematics and mathematical sciences.'

## 2.2 Meaning of Mathematics

The above mentioned definitions throw light on the concept and meaning of mathematics as below:

1. Mathematics is the science of (*a*) numbers, (*b*) space and direction, (*c*) measurement, (*d*) magnitude, (*e*) quantity, and (*f*) logical reasoning and calculation.
2. Mathematics is an accepted science which deals with (*a*) quantitative facts and relationships, (*b*) relationship between magnitudes of quantitative and qualitative facts, (*c*) problems involving space and form, and (*d*) quantitative aspect of our life and knowledge.
3. Mathematics is the important means of generalisation and means to draw conclusion and judgement.
4. Mathematics is the method of progress of various subjects.
5. Mathematics is an applied science for the expression of other sciences.
6. Mathematics is the perfection of generalisation.
7. Mathematics is the systematised, organised and exact branch of science which is the by-product of our empirical knowledge.
8. Mathematics is an inductive and experimental science.
9. Mathematics is a tool especially suited for dealing with abstract concepts of any kind.
10. Mathematics is an exact and progressive branch of science which plays and important role in various walks of human life.
11. Mathematics is the queen of all sciences and backbone of civilisation. It is no exaggeration to say that the history of mathematics is the history of civilisation.
12. Mathematics is basic to a large number of branches of human knowledge.
13. Mathematics involves man's high cognitive powers. It is an exact science involving high cognitive abilities and powers.
14. Mathematics in itself is neither a physical nor an experimental science in the sense that the natural sciences are.
15. Mathematics is a distinct field of study in its own right.

Thus, the term 'mathematics' has been interpreted and explained in various ways. This is due to our empirical knowledge and various types of experiences. But, ultimately all types of explanations conclusively end at some kinds of relationship with number and space. Therefore, it may be concluded that mathematics is the numerative and calculative part of human life and knowledge.

These definitions of mathematics may be put into some specific categories to explain the concept and meaning of mathematics. *e.g.*

1. Mathematics as the science of logical reasoning.
2. Mathematics as a science of quantity, magnitude, numbers and space.
3. Mathematics as an important means of generalisation and as the perfection of generalisation.
4. Mathematics as an applied science for the expression of other sciences.
5. Mathematics as the means to draw conclusion and judgement.
6. Mathematics as the method of progress of various subjects.

The definition under the first category is most accepted and widely used.

## 2.3 Mathematics as the Science of logical reasoning

The question arises – what is logical or rational reasoning?

Reasoning is based on previous established facts. To establish a new fact or truth, it should be put it on the test of reasoning. If the new fact agrees with the previously established facts, it is called logical or rational.

In the process of logical reasoning, we never approach anything without a question-mark in our mind. For each question we frame a hypothesis and test the same empirically or theoretically with the help of previously established facts.

Logical reasoning is beyond subjectiveness. Thus, by process of reasoning we move to a higher level and work out mathematical results at the abstract level.

## 2.4 Nature of Mathematics

A discipline, by virtue of its nature, distinguishes itself from another discipline of knowledge. Every discipline has its own specific structure which is the basis of its identity. This structure determines the predictive value of the subject. The degree of true prediction signifies the strength of the structure of the subject. Mathematical predictions are almost accurate and cent per cent true. This is due to strong structure of mathematics based on sound foundation.

The nature of mathematics can be described as below:

1. In schools, the subjects included in the curriculum have certain aims and objectives. In school curriculum, mathematics holds a strong, stable and important position as compared to other school subjects.
2. If the structure of a subject is weak, its truthfulness, reliability, validity and prediction also decreases in the same proportion. On the basis of this specific structure, the nature of each subject is determined and accordingly the place is given in the school curriculum. All subjects do not have same structure. Mathematics has its unique nature on the basis of which one can compare it with other subjects.

3. Mathematics involves conversion of abstract phenomena or concepts into concrete form. Thus, abstract concepts are explained and understood with the help of mathematics.
4. Mathematics does not leave any doubt in the minds of the learners about concepts, principles, laws, theorems, etc. It provides response like yes or no, right or wrong.
5. Mathematics is an exact science. Mathematical knowledge is exact, clear, systematic and logical as they may be easily understood. Once it is captured it can never be forgotten.
6. Mathematical rules, principles, laws, formulae, etc. are universal and that can be verified at any place and time. They are not changeable.
7. Mathematics has its own well-defined, useful and clear language. It means that mathematical terms, concepts, symbols and notations, formulae and principles, theorems, operations develop a specific language. Some examples of this language: (*a*) $5 \in A$ (*b*) $\tan \theta$ (*c*) $\Delta$ ABC (*d*) $30 \div 6$.
8. Mathematics has its own tools like intuition, analysis, construction, logic, reasoning, generality and individuality.
9. Mathematics has its own mode of operations like addition, subtraction, multiplication, division, square, square root, cube, cube root, etc.
10. Mathematics is a science of measurement, quality, space and magnitude. These concepts, first of all, were developed in mathematics and afterwards in other branches of knowledge.
11. It is numerical and calculation part of human life and knowledge.
12. Mathematics is like a chest filled up with so many tools concerning with the operations like measuring, counting, weighing, etc.
13. Mathematics deals with quantitative facts and their relationships as well as with problems involving space and form. It also deals with relationship between magnitudes.
14. Mathematics enables the man to study various phenomena in space and establish different types of relationships between them.
15. Mathematics is that science which is the by-product of our empirical knowledge.
16. Mathematics draws numerical inferences on the basis of given information and data.
17. Mathematics has been originated from numbers and number-system is a special field of it from which other branches of mathematics are developed.
18. Mathematics is related to all the subjects and provide basis for the development of each discipline of human knowledge. The development of all sciences depends on the progress of mathematics as its knowledge is applied to them very frequently.
19. Mathematical knowledge is applied in the study of different branches of science, *e.g.*, Physics, Chemistry, Biology and other sciences.
20. Mathematics is related with each aspect of human life.
21. Mathematics is a science of logical reasoning. It involves inductive and deductive reasoning and can generalise any proposition universally.
22. Mathematics is a science of abstract form. By the process of reasoning one moves to the higher level and work out mathematical results at abstract level.

23. Mathematics involves a peculiar type of reasoning which possesses a number of characteristics, *viz.*, simplicity, accuracy, certainty of results, originality, similarity to the reasoning of life and verification.
24. From our observations of physical and social environment, we form certain intuitive ideas or notions called 'postulates' and 'axioms'. Mathematical propositions are based on postulates and axioms.
25. The Vedang Jyotish (1200 BC) gives mathematics the highest place of honour among the sciences which form 'Vedang'. It reads as — "As are the crests on the heads of peacocks, as are the gems on the heads of snakes, so is the 'Ganit (*i.e.*, mathematics) at the top of the sciences called 'Vedang.'"

## 2.5 What is Modern Mathematics?

What is new or modern in 'modern mathematics' is explained below:

### 1. New Content

There is a huge knowledge-explosion. It is said that mathematics is doubling every ten years. There is much new to be studied in terms of discovered new content. Since, 17th century, several new discoveries have been made in the field of mathematics. As a result, many entirely new branches of mathematics and major applications of mathematics have been largely developed. For example:

Set-Theory, Linear programming, Topology, Functional Analysis, Axiomatic method as a method of study in mathematics, Geometrical Transformation, Measure Theory, Game Theory, Quality Control, Computer mathematics, etc.

The earlier study of various developed topics in mathematics is an important part of most of the new mathematics programmes, the approach being changed.

### 2. New Language

Mathematics applies the 'principle of brevity', which is the soul of wisdom, in its language. Mathematical language is free from verbosity. It is empowered to put the ideas or things pinpointedly. Mathematical language cuts short the lengthy and complicated statements and expresses ideas or statements in exact form by using notations, symbols, formulae, etc.

For example, 'the difference of the squares of two terms or numbers is equal to the product of their sum and their difference' — may easily and shortly be written as $a^2 - b^2 = (a + b)(a - b)$ where a and b are the two terms or numbers.

Modern mathematics speaks a different language from its predecessors. It uses what is called 'set language' and 'set notations.' Set Theory was developed during the later half of the 19th century. Now, all of mathematics right from Arithmetic to the most advanced topics, is based on 'set theory.' Thus, set theory has become the unifying theory for mathematics.

The mathematical ability is inherent in man. Therefore, he is able to assign notations and symbols to ideas and objects. Mathematical results in their symbolic form help us in solving various complicated problems easily.

The progress of mathematics depends on the extremely large use of mathematical language and symbolism. In teaching of mathematics, the teacher has to develop in learners the ability to employ mathematical language and symbolism. It is the duty of the teacher of mathematics to create in them an interest towards its language and symbolism.

A good pupil of mathematics must be in a position to appreciate the precision, brevity, logic sharpness and beauty of its peculiar language. To comprehend these, some important symbols are given here:

| *Word Form* | *Symbolic Form* | *Word Form* | *Symbolic Form* |
|---|---|---|---|
| Therefore | $\therefore$ | correspondence | $\longleftrightarrow$ |
| Since/as/because | $\because$ | belongs to | $\in$ |
| Greater than | > | subset | $\subset$ |
| Less than | < | universal set | U |
| Congruency | $\cong$ | summation (Sigma) | $\Sigma$ |
| Similarity | $\sim$ | frequency | $f$ |
| Union | $\cup$ | line AB | $\overleftrightarrow{AB}$ |
| Intersection | $\cap$ | ray AB | $\overrightarrow{AB}$ |

Students are expected to be very familiar with these symbols.

Lindsay remarked — "Mathematics is the language of physical science and certainly no more marvellous language was ever created by the mind of the man."

Galileo said — "Mathematics is the language in which God has written the universe."

Most of the results of scientific inventions and discoveries are stated in the language of mathematics.

## 3. New Structure

The new structure of modern mathematics is based on logical reasoning. In modern mathematics, what is to be taught in mathematics has been reorganised along more logical lines. Greater stress has been laid on the study of mathematics structure and the role of postulates, axioms and definitions. It is accompanied by more use of logic and more emphasis on the foundations of mathematics.

The pupils of mathematics, instead of looking for unrelated tricks he is expected to memorise, looks for basic structure and general principles.

## 4. New Approach

In the teaching of traditional *i.e.*, old mathematics, rote repetition was considered as the most efficient method of learning. Old approach was advocating memorising and repeating. The students were expected to respond the whole theorem or problem verbatim.

In modern mathematics, understanding and not memory is placed at premium. Greater stress is laid on concepts and problem analysis. The new approach advocates discovering and inventing. Thus, modern approach is more meaningful, more enjoyable, more adaptable, more systematic, logical and up-to-date. In its new approach, more emphasis is placed upon students thinking and less relying on teacher's instruction and students' memorisation.

There has been a change in the methodology of teaching mathematics. Discovery method *i.e.,* Heuristic method probably is the most important feature of modern mathematics programmes. With its standard and universal terminology, common symbols, sound structure and logical approach, it helps the pupils to do and understand more mathematics in less time.

Considering the demands of modern science, technology, industry, trade and agriculture, modern mathematics is quite adequate.

### What to understand with Modern Math?

1. Understanding the nature and role of deductive reasoning in algebra as well as in geometry.
2. Understanding the language of sets which penetrates all the different structures of mathematics.
3. Understanding mathematical structures like —
   (*a*) Basic arithmetical structures describing properties of natural, rational, real and complex numbers.
   (*b*) Basic algebraic structures describing groups, rings, fields and vector spaces.
   (*c*) Basic geometrical structures describing Euclidian and non-Euclidian geometries, topology, etc.

## 2.6 Types of Reasoning used in Modern Mathematics

The prominent types of reasoning used in modern mathematics are:

1. Inductive Reasoning
2. Deductive Reasoning

### 1. Inductive Reasoning

Human knowledge, generally, arises from observations and experiences. In the beginning, mathematics also arose out of practical applications and it was intuitive. From our observations and experiences, we come to know that some particular properties hold good in the sufficient number of cases. By this, we may conclude that these properties will also hold good in all other similar cases. We can verify it also. This type of logical reasoning is called "inductive reasoning.'

Here 'inductive' means a particular statement/proposition/theme/theory/rule/formula is induced from general observations and experiences.

Thus, in inductive reasoning, one proceeds from several particular examples to a general agreement. In mathematics, this type of reasoning is mostly used.

### 2. Deductive Reasoning

This reasoning consists in comparing the statements and drawing a conclusion therefrom. Thus, here we deduce the solution or proof for a particular problem or statement on the basis of general premise. Here, a particular statement or proposition is proved using already established general rules. We proceed, here, from general to specific, *i.e.* from a premise to specific.

Deductive reasoning is based on self-evident truth, established facts, postulates, axioms, etc. In mathematics, the inductive reasoning is useful for beginners but afterwards mostly deductive reasoning goes on more and more fruitful.

Whitehead — "Mathematics in the widest sense is the development of all types of deductive reasoning."

Mathematics in the making is not a deductive science, it is an inductive, experimental science.

## 2.7 Essentials/Fundamentals of Deductive Reasoning in Mathematics

The following are the essentials or fundamentals of deductive reasoning in mathematics:

(1) Undefined Terms (2) Defined Terms (3) Postulates (4) Axioms (5) Theorems/Propositions

### 1. Undefined Terms

Definition makes a 'term' meaningful and clear. But in every branch of knowledge, one may get certain terms for which no definition could be given. The terms which cannot be defined are termed as 'undefined terms.' In mathematics also there are some undefined terms. *e.g.,*

In Geometry the terms 'point', 'line' 'plane (surface)' are undefined terms. In Algebra the terms 'set', 'number', 'variable' are undefined terms. In Arithmetic the terms '0', 'number', 'successor (in the sense that a + 1 is the successor of a)' are undefined terms.

In Euclidian Geometry the term 'point' is defined as 'that which has no length, breadth and depth.' Line is defined as 'that which has length but has no breadth and depth.' This is simply confusion. These definitions are far from clear in themselves. To avoid confusion, in modern mathematics, these terms are taken as 'undefined terms.'

### 2. Defined Terms

In each discipline including mathematics there are many technical terms which are well-defined. These are defined with the help of undefined terms, other defined terms and by using non-technical language.

*e.g.,* In Geometry, 'circle' is a well-defined term. It is defined as 'A circle is the union of coplanar points, equidistant from a fixed point in the same plane.'

Here the technical term 'circle' is defined with the help of (*i*) undefined terms 'point' and 'plane' (*ii*) defined term 'equidistant', (*iii*) the set operation 'union' and (*iv*) other non-technical terms like from, fixed, same, etc.

### 3. Postulates

There are two types of basic assumptions on which mathematical reasoning is based. They are: Postulates and axioms. They frame the entire structure of mathematics.

Generally, while proving a theorem, the help of some already proved theorem or theorems is taken. If we go backward, there must be a theorem for which we have no previous theorem to help us. In proving this very first theorem, we have no other way but to accept certain statements or propositions as they are without stressing on these proofs. These initial propositions are assumed to be true without any necessity of proof as if they are self-evident truths.

The statements which are accepted as true in a particular disciple or system without stressing on their proofs are known as 'postulates.' They are unproved first principles.

Every system has its own selection of postulates. Postulate should be totally independent. The only thing to be remembered is that there should be no internal inconsistency, *i.e.,* in a system a statement should not be proved at the same time, both false and true, with the help of its postulates.

Thus, postulates are those assumptions or first principles, beyond the principles of logic, by which a particular mathematical discipline may be defined. Postulates make it possible to prove several theorems and with no reference to any figures or drawings.

*Examples of some postulates:*

(1) Every natural number has its unique successor.

(2) '0' is not a successor of any natural number.

(3) Two numbers having the same successor are identical.

(4) Two distinct points determine one and only one line.

(5) Given a line, there are at least two points on it.

(6) A plane contains at least three distinct non-collinear points.

(7) Three non-collinear distinct points determine one and only one plane.

(8) If a = b and b = c then a = c

(9) All right angles have the same measure.

(10) '0' is a number.

## 4. Axioms

An axiom is a mathematical fact to be accepted without proof. It may be considered as a self-evident truth.

Euclid regarded initial assumptions as axioms and called them 'common notions.' Those were accepted as true because of their conformity with common experience and sound judgement. Thus, axioms are axioms of logic or 'common notions.'

*Examples of some axioms:*

(1) The whole is greater than any of its parts.

(2) The whole is equal to sum of its all parts.

(3) Things equal to the same thing are equal to one another.

Some mathematicians, now-a-days consider the terms 'postulates' and 'axioms' as synonymous. But it is better to maintain distinction between them. Keep the term 'axiom' for the axioms of logic or common notions and use the term 'postulate' for those assumptions or first principles for a particular mathematical discipline. In short, axioms may be applied to *any* branch of knowledge while postulates may be applied to a *particular* branch of knowledge.

## 5. Theorems

The basic elements in any system of modern mathematics are: (*i*) undefined terms, (*ii*) postulates, and (*iii*) definitions. Their collection and build up helps in proving the truth of the various statements or propositions called 'theorems' in a particular system.

*Examples of some theorems:*

(1) Prove that the sum of measures of the angles of a triangle is 180°.

(2) Prove that if two lines intersect, they intersect in one and only one point.

(3) Prove that if $\frac{a}{b} = \frac{c}{d}$ then $\frac{a+b}{b} = \frac{c+d}{d}$ where a, b, c, d $\in$ R and b $\neq$ 0, d $\neq$ 0.

(4) Prove that $A \cup (B \cup C) = (A \cup B) \cup C$ where A, B, C are non-empty sets.

What is to be proved as true or untrue depends upon the already selected undefined terms, postulates and definitions. One cannot manipulate the proving of a theorem at one's will.

A theorem consists of three parts: (*i*) Given or Data, (*ii*) To prove, and (*iii*) Proof. In proving a theorem, two types of proofs are in use: Direct proof and Indirect proof.

For proving 'If p then q', if we start with p and end with q through a series of steps using logical reasoning, then the proof is called a direct proof. When one is unable to prove a proposition directly, the technique 'indirect proof' is used.

## 2.8 Methods of Study Mathematics

Every discipline has its own methods of study. Any discipline uses various specific devices, processes, steps, techniques, strategies, etc. in its developmental sequence. The various integrated sets of these activities are termed as 'methods.' Mathematics has its own specific methods of study, which can be put into two categories: Axiomatic methods and Genetic methods.

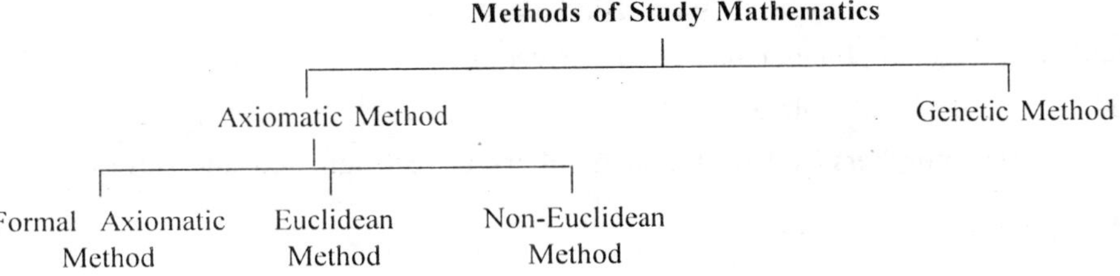


Axiomatic methods include (*i*) Formal Axiomatic Methods, (*ii*) Euclidean Method, and (*iii*) Non-Euclidean method.

### (i) Formal Axiometic Method

In this modern method, deductive structure is fixed but differences occur in the undefined terms involved in the postulate. Here, theories are formulated using postulates without giving meaning to the undefined terms. The theories or principles thus formulated may be applied to the objects of any system and undefined terms may be given desired and appropriate meanings accordingly. Therefore, in this method the undefined terms are meaningless as they do not have any certain meaning.

In this method, there are some hidden assumptions which are presented in the form of postulate, *e.g.*, A postulate presented by Hilbert is —

If a line *l* which intersects the side AB of a ΔABC, does not pass through A, B, or C, then it will necessarily intersect side AC or side BC of ΔABC.

### (ii) Euclidean Method: [Please refer to Ch. No. 3]

### (iii) Non-Euclidean Method: [Please, refer to Ch. No. 3]

### (iv) Genetic Method

The genetic method of the study of mathematics is also called 'Arithmetical Analysis Method'. The other important method that comes under the category of genetic method is 'cardinal numbers and set theory.'

The term 'genetic' is taken from Biology and Hilbert gave this method the name of 'genetic method'. Like axiomatic method, in this method also the obvious properties of mathematical system of objects are enlisted in the form of postulates. The unobvious properties of system of objects are expressed by means of these postulates. This process also follows deductive method like other methods.

The delivery of natural numbers occur in the order 1, 2, 3,..., n, n + 1,.... The properties of natural number system were enlisted by Givppe Piano, an Italian mathematician (1889 AD) in the form of five postulates, *viz.*,

(1) Closure Property
(2) Commutative Property
(3) Associative Property
(4) Distributive Property
(5) Identity Element

This number-system initiated Arithmetic as the theory of natural numbers and other similar number-systems.

In the set of natural numbers, 0 is included. Thus, the set of whole numbers has been derived.

$N = \{1, 2, 3, 4, \ldots\}$ $W = \{0, 1, 2, 3, 4, \ldots\}$

From whole numbers the set of Integer has been derived.

$I = \{\ldots, -4, -3, -2, -1, 0, 1, 2, 3, 4, \ldots\}$

In this sequence, rational numbers and irrational numbers were originated and developed.

$$Q = \left\{\frac{a}{b} \mid a, b \in I, b \neq 0\right\}$$

Further in this order real numbers, imaginary numbers and complex number systems came into existence.

It is said that before the evolution of numbers, a primitive man, while taking out sheep, one by one, for grazing out of the enclosure, he was marking on a stone, one sheep one mark. While coming back, he was crossing the mark, entry of one sheep one mark was to be crossed. In this way, he was able to know how many sheep were missed/lost or surplus sheep from other herd of sheep.

In mathematics this is known as one-to-one correspondence. 1-1 correspondence originated concept of number, set and set theory.

## 2.9 Scope of Mathematics

Mathematics is so widespread that the demarcation of its scope is an extremely difficult task, say next to impossible. According to the definition, 'Mathematics is the science of all sciences and provides basis to all the disciplines', two main categories of mathematics are:

(1) Pure Mathematics
(2) Applied Mathematics

## [A] Pure Mathematics

The theoretical aspect of mathematics is known as 'Pure (Basic) mathematics.' It treats only theories and principles. It takes no notice of their applications to the concrete situations. It involves systematic and deductive reasoning.

It consists of all those assertions of the kind that if such an such proposition is true of anything, then such an such proposition is certainly true of that thing. For example, if $a^2 - b^2 = (a + b)(a - b)$ is true then $(a + 1)^2 - (b - 1)^2 = (a + 1 + b - 1)(a + 1 - b + 1) = (a + b)(a - b + 2)$ is also true.

It is developed on an abstract self-contained basis without any consideration to the possible practical applications that may follow.

### Sub-branches of pure mathematics

(1) Algebra : It includes arithmetic, algebraic structure, elementary and multivariate algebra, linear multivariate algebra, etc.

(2) Geometry : It includes Euclidean and non-Euclidean geometry, analytic geometry, trigonometry, projection, co-ordinate geometry, differential and algebraical geometry, etc.

(3) Modern Mathematics : It includes the following topics —

(*i*) Set Theory — Origin and definition, fundamental concepts of set, set theory, postulates of axiomatic set theory, the present status of axiomatic set theory, etc.

(*ii*) Topology — General topology, topological groups, differential topology, algebraic topology, etc.

(*iii*) Algebraic Systems — Groups, Rings, Fields, Vector spaces, etc.

(4) Analysis : It includes real and complex analysis, Functional analysis, Differential equation, Theory of Probability, Vectors, etc.

(5) Combinatorics and Number System : It includes combinatories, combinatorial geometry and Number System.

## [B] Applied Mathematics

The applications of pure mathematics in developing the various means to serve the human and humanity is known as 'Applied Mathematics'. It takes into account those parts of mathematic theories that have certain direct and practical application to objects or actions in the material world. Thus, while pure mathematics is simply theoretical, the applied mathematics is practical.

Principles of applied mathematics have been used to investigate phenomena such as heat, light, electricity, sound, magnetism, mechanics, astronomy, navigation, etc. Applied mathematics helps in solving very complicated problems of physical or real world.

Applied mathematics also has various sub-branches. The sub-branches of it are given below:

(1) *Calculatory science:* It consists of numerical notations, calculatory aspects of Algebra, Geometry and Trigonometry, calculatory use of tables and graphs, Geometrical aids, mathematical models, analogic computation, digital computation, etc.

(2) *Statistics:* Fundamental principles, estimation, hypothesis, testing structures, etc.

(3) Numerical Analysis

(4) Mathematical Theory of Optimization

(5) Automation Theory

(6) Information Theory

(7) Mathematical Aspects of Physical Theories — It includes:

(*i*) Mechanics of solids, mechanics of fluids, mechanics of particles and other systems

(*ii*) Quantum Mechanics

(*iii*) Statistical Mechanics

(*iv*) Electromagnetic Theory

(*v*) Theory of Relativity

(*vi*) Dimensional Analysis

(*vii*) Riemanian Geometry

## Relation between Pure and Applied Mathematics

The relationship of pure and applied mathematics has been beautifully illustrated by Dantzigs — 'Applied mathematics is like wine which becomes pure in course of time.'

Thus, applied mathematics has its roots in pure mathematics and pure mathematics is flowering into applied mathematics.

In the beginning the mathematical concepts developed in human mind. They were originated through mathematical structures as found in his environment. The abilities of systematic and deductive reasoning inherent in human being, turned into abstraction in due course of time. For example, in the beginning man learnt how to count with the help of concrete objects. Then he developed number-words for counting without using concrete objects. Ultimately, this led to the invention of abstract numerals 1, 2, 3, 4, ...

At the time of invention of many theories and structures of pure mathematics, their applications in various fields were unknown. For example, the complex numbers, one of the inventions of pure mathematics is now widely and intensively applied in electricity, radio, and other related fields of Physics and Engineering.

Thus, applied mathematics acts as a bridge to link pure mathematics on the one hand, with physical, biological, social sciences, etc. on the other hand. It acts and reacts on science and technology as well as on pure mathematics. *e.g.,* space dynamics, fluid dynamics, ballistics, mathematical economics, mathematical biology, etc.

Let us see the wonders of applied mathematics. By using only pen and paper, mathematically we can (*a*) weigh the planet Earth, (*b*) determine the orbits of planets (*c*) prepare for any space flight, (*d*) solve complicated problems of trade and commerce.

Archimedes once remarked — 'Give me a sufficient strong and long stick, acting as a lever. And I will lift up the Earth from its position.'

## 2.10 Some Suggestions to pupils on Studying Mathematics

- There is abundant evidence that pupils often employ wasteful and inefficient procedures in studying mathematics.
  - They allow their attention to be distracted and their work interrupted.
  - They are careless in their reading, listening and written work.
  - Many times they do not recognise that the specific procedures involved in the study of some parts of mathematics are not necessarily involved in the study of some other parts of mathematics.
- They do not analyse their assignments to determine what particular procedures will contribute most efficiently to the mastery of the work in hand.
- They fail to form a habit of depending upon themselves.
- They are unsystematic and do not take time for deliberate reflection before starting their work.
- The following list of suggestions may help the pupils in studying mathematics:

1. Form the habit of —
   (*a*) studying mathematics at a regular time, in a regular place.
   (*b*) getting down to work *at once.* Do not delay.
   (*c*) paying concentrated and sustained attention to your work after you start.
   (*d*) listening all new words and concepts and learning them *at once.*
   (*e*) using the index and the reference tables in your books as sources of information about new words, formulae, numerical values, etc.
   (*f*) expressing verbal statements in symbols.
2. Work —
   (*a*) as rapidly as you can after you start.
   (*b*) by yourself for the most part.
   (*c*) carefully.

   It is easier to avoid mistakes than to find and correct them after they are made.
3. Do not allow avoidable interruptions after you start.
4. Take plenty of time to think. Do not start to solve a problem or to give a proof until you have clearly in mind exactly what is given and exactly what is required and have developed a plan for doing what is wanted.
5. At the preparatory stage, get the assignment clearly in mind.
   - Recall the teacher's explanation. If necessary study again the sample exercises and the explanation in your text.
6. Read the problems and exercises carefully. Be sure that you understand clearly what is given and exactly what you are expected to do to find or to prove.
   - Read thoughtfully and reflect as you read. Superficial reading in mathematics is generally just a waste of time.

7. Plan your work for the work period you start.
   - If you do not know how to begin, consult textbook and try to recall the explanations which your teacher has given.
   - Try to find our just where and what your difficulty is. Do not give it up.
8. If you are to copy an exercise or a problem, be sure that you copy it correctly.
9. Try to write out the questions that bother you, making them very clear and specific. Often the answer will suggest itself.
10. Memorise important rules, formulae and facts. Be sure that you understand their meanings and can use them correctly.
    - It is easier and better to memorise statements and formulae as wholes than to memorise them by parts.
    - In memorising formulae, it helps to read them *aloud*.
    - Mnemonic devices are often helpful in memorising.
    - In order to fix rules and formulae in your mind, use them as soon as possible after you have learnt them.
11. Write neatly, put down figures in neat columns and rows.
    - Small, round, vertical writing is most legible.
12. Never use scrappy, dog-eared paper. Use scratch paper as little as possible.
13. Remember that every symbol has a definite meaning.
    - Always read meanings into the symbols you use.
14. An exercise is frequently made up of series of steps. Do one step at a time.
    - Compare exercises in Algebra with similar types of exercises in Arithmetic.
    - Sometimes, this will give you a cue/suggestion that will be helpful.
    - When the time permits, check your work and your answers.
15. Sketch diagrams/graphs when you can. This makes it easier to understand problems.
16. In numerical problems, form the habit of making a preliminary *estimate* to serve as a rough check on your work.
17. In preparing for a recitation, spend some time in organising the lesson in a logical form in your mind.
18. Replace large numbers by approximations in planning the solutions of problems.
19. Listen in the class with your whole attention. Do not have books opened or pencil in hand unless specifically asked to do so.
20. Be mentally alert, active and aggressive.
21. Be critic of all statements made. Be specifically critical of statements that are not adequately supported by reasons.
22. Enjoy overcoming hard mathematical obstacles.

23. It may be confidently expected that deliberate, organised and systematic attention to the improvement of study habits will in fact return very substantial and gratifying dividends.
24. Plan out the proof of the materials to be understood and digested.

## EVALUATE YOURSELF

1. What is the meaning of mathematics?
2. What is Modern Mathematics? Why is it named as 'Modern' or 'new'? Discuss.
3. Justify: 'Mathematics is the Science of logical reasoning.'
4. Explain fully the Nature of Mathematics. Explain its fundamentals with the help of appropriate examples.
5. What types of reasoning is used in Modern mathematics? Explain the types.
6. Which are the fundamentals of Deductive reasoning in mathematics? Explain each of them.
7. Name the methods of study mathematics. Explain one of the methods.
8. Explain the relation between Pure Mathematics and Applied Mathematics.
9. What are undefined terms? How do they provide the starting point for deductive reasoning in mathematics? Give examples.
10. What are postulates and axioms in mathematics? Give some examples of them.
11. Write short notes on:
    (*a*) Postulates and axioms
    (*b*) Scope of mathematics
    (*c*) Inductive and Deductive reasoning
    (*d*) Genetic method of study mathematics.
    (*e*) Pure and Applied Mathematics
    (*f*) Nature of Modern Mathematics.
12. Explain with illustration the new language of modern mathematics.
13. What should the students keep in mind while studying mathematics?

'Mathematics is a living, growing subject. The vitality and vigor of present day mathematical research quickly dispels any notation that mathematics is a subject long since emblamed in text books. Mathematics today is in many respects an entirely different discipline from what it was at the turn of century. New developments have been extensive, new concepts have been revolutionary. The sheer bulk of current mathematical development is staggering.'

— ***Report of Commission of Mathematics***

# 3 EUCLIDEAN AND NON-EUCLIDEAN METHODS OF STUDY GEOMETRY

## 3.1 Euclidean Method of Study Geometry

Euclid wrote several books. His most important work is 'Elements', a collection of thirteen volumes. The Euclidean Geometry has drawn its content as well as methodology directly from the work 'Elements.'

The basic elements of Euclidean methods are — definitions, postulates and axioms. Euclid was very much systematic and methodical in his work. The steps of this method are as under:

### Presentation of Fundamental Concepts

(1) He begins with the definitions of some basic terms like point, line, plane (surface), circle, etc.

| | | |
|---|---|---|
| Point | : | A point is that which has no parts. |
| Line | : | A line is that which has length but no breadth and no depth. |
| Plane | : | A plane is that which has length and breadth only |
| Plane Surface | : | A plane surface which lies evenly with the straight line on itself. |
| Circle | : | A circle is a plane figure contained by one line such that all the straight lines falling upon it from a point within the circle, are equal to one another. |

These definitions were presented by using primitive terms like parts, length, breadth, depth, evenly, following, etc. These primitive terms are not defined and they need not be defined.

(2) On the basis of definitions of fundamental concepts, Euclid has laid down some of his common assumptions. Five of them be named as postulates and the other remaining five as 'common notions or axioms.' They are given below:

### *Postulates*

(*i*) A straight line can be drawn from any point to any other fixed point.

(*ii*) A finite straight line can be produced continuously in a straight line.

(*iii*) A circle may be described with any centre and any distance.

(*iv*) All right angles are equal to one another.

(*v*) If a straight line, falling on two straight lines, makes the interior angles on the same side, less than two right angles, the two straight lines produced indefinitely meet on that side which are angles less than two right angles.

Postulates are accepted true as they are self-evident truth. These were concerned with the physical world.

### *Common notions/Axioms*

(*i*) The things which are equal to the same thing, are equal to one another.

(*ii*) If equals be added to the equals, the wholes are equal.

(*iii*) If equals be subtracted from equals, the remainders are equal.

(*iv*) Things which coincide with one another are equal to one another.

(*v*) The whole is greater than any of its part.

Those are also considered as self-evident truth.

(3) Considering all these ten assumptions as self-evident truth, he at once starts the work on propositions which are known as 'theorems.'

Euclidian geometry consists in proving these propositions or theorems with the help of definitions, postulates, axioms and previously proved truth and employs a process of logical reasoning. These three steps are shown below:

Definitions of primitive terms ⟶ Postulates and axioms ⟶ Theorems having logical proofs

Thus, Euclid had tried carefully to utilise definitions and assumptions in deriving so many geometrical conclusions and had arranged them in a systematic and geometrical sequence. Euclid's work has ruled the study of Geometry for not less than 2000 years in the schools spread all over the world.

Euclidean geometry has served as a good model for mathematicians and non-mathematicians to follow in presenting ideas systematically and with logical reasoning.

As the time passed, many flaws are found in the 'Elements' especially in the 20th century. Consequently, Euclidean Geometry is completely out-of-date now-a-days. At present, Euclidean Geometry is completely replaced by non-Euclidean Geometry.

## 3.2 What is wrong with Euclidean Geometry?/Shortcomings of Euclidean Geometry

### 1. Every term cannot be defined

Euclid apparently tried to define everything which is not possible. Every definition should be unambiguous and convincing. In this context, a German mathematician Felix Klein remarks —

'Euclid begins with the definition of all sorts of geometric concepts such as point, line, straight line, surface, plane, angle, circle, etc., …The meaning of these definitions is wholly obscure, all sorts of meaning be attached to it … In any event, it has not been possible to find an unambiguous interpretation for Euclid's definition of the straight line and likewise for many of his other definitions.'

Thus, Euclid had tried to give intuitive descriptions of the undefined objects in his system. The Non-Euclidean Geometry now accepts some of the basic terms like point, line, etc. as 'undefined terms.'

### 2. Unprecisely stated axioms

Euclid's many of the axioms are stated unprecisely. Stephen S. Willoughby (USA) rightly remarks — 'Some of his axioms were not stated precisely. *e.g.,* 'it is possible to extend a finite straight line continuously in a straight line.' Suppose a finite straight line is extended half of its length, then one-fourth of the original length, and then one-eighth of the original length and so on. Does this constitute extending it *continuously*? Since zero had preceded him, it is surprising that Euclid was not precise enough about his postulate to avoid this sort of interpretation… In mathematics we say what we mean.'

### 3. Incomplete assumptions

Mathematicians of the world have found out the most important flow in Euclid's set of incomplete assumptions. As a result, many troubles have been created in understanding what he wants to prove. With the help of his set of assumptions, many times it is not possible to prove the theorems he enlisted in his 'Elements.' Sometimes, many false results are proved true, using his assumptions. Such situations arise due to following shortcomings in his set of assumptions:

#### *(a) Superimposition required many new assumptions*

Euclid proved first few theorems on congruency by the process of superimposition, *i.e.,* to pick up a triangle and place it on another triangle and to verify whether they exactly coincide. How can one pick up a triangle from a surface? How can one carry it? How can one drop it on another triangle? To answer these questions, a series of assumptions are required which allow motion of geometrical figures. No such assumptions are found in 'Elements.'

#### *(b) Non-existence of the concept 'betweenness'*

Many proofs in Euclidean Geometry depend on 'betweenness.' In its absence, a number of fallacies/paradoxes arise. *e.g.,*

(1) All obtuse angles are right angles. (2) All triangles are isosceles.

These can be proved if the concept of 'betweenness' does not exist.

### (c) *No real numbers used*

Euclid did not used real numbers in his assumption as irrational numbers were unknown to him. Lack of these assumptions is responsible for the incompleteness of the proofs related to the theorems on proportion.

## 4. Trustworthiness on figures

Euclid depended too much on the figures while proving theorems. This is because of the incompleteness of the set of assumptions.

For example, as given in 'Elements', while constructing an equilateral triangle with a given side AB, a circle is to be drawn, in turn, with A and B as centres and AB as the radius. If these two circles intersect in C, then ABC is an equilateral triangle.

But is there any guarantee that these two circles will definitely intersect? No assumption of Euclid says so. Can one say that it is obvious from the figure? A figure is not to be used as a part of the proof. Only logical reasoning and assumptions are to be used.

Similarly, one of the Euclid's proposition is that one and only one perpendicular can be drawn on a line from a point outside it. He did not try to prove it simply on the ground that it is very much obvious from the drawing.

## 5. Improper use of terms and symbols

Terms and symbols as used in Euclidean Geometry is not in their right perspective. *e.g.*, Equality is shown by the symbol =. It is alright when we say that $5 + 4 = 6 + 3$. But when Euclidean Geometry says $\Delta ABC = \Delta PQR$ when both of them are distinct, it is not proper, as both the triangles are not the same. (we now say that $\Delta ABC \cong \Delta PQR$)

What we denote as a line-segment to day, Euclid denoted it as a line. This is improper use of the term 'line', because 'line-segment' and 'line' are different concepts.

The above-mentioned five shortcomings of Euclidean Geometry compel us either to correct it or to replace it.

According to Bertrand Russel — 'His definitions do not always define, his axioms are not always demonstrable, his demonstrations require many axioms of which he is quite unconscious. A valid proof retains its demonstrative force when no figure is drawn but very many of Euclid's earlier proofs fail before this test... The value of his work as a master piece of logic has been very grossly exaggerated.'

## 3.3 Non-Euclidean Method of Study Geometry

Non-Euclidean Geometry emerged under the criticism of Euclidean Geometry by prominent mathematicians like Guass, Lobachevlki, Reisman and Bolyai. Hilbert (1862-1943) a renowned mathematician attempted to correct and strengthen Euclid by supplying the group of postulates as under:

Group I : Postulates of connection

Group II : Postulates of order

Group III : Parallel postulates

Group IV : Postulates of congruency

Group V : Continuity postulates

Group VI : Completeness postulates.

## Group I: Postulates of Connection

These postulates help (*i*) in connecting undefined terms and (*ii*) in emphasising the existence of some minimum points. These postulates are —

(*i*) Two distinct points determine one and only one line.

(*ii*) A line is a set of points containing at least two points.

(*iii*) Three distinct non-collinear points determine one and only one plane.

(*iv*) A plane contains at least three distinct non-collinear points.

(*v*) If a plane contains two distinct points of a line, it contains the whole line.

(*vi*) If two planes contain a point in common, they have another point in common.

(*vii*) A line contains at least two points, a plane at least 3 non-collinear points, and a space at least four non-coplanar points.

## Group II: Postulates of Order

These postulates emphasise the existence of the concept of 'betweenness.'

(*i*) If A, B, C are collinear points, such that A–B–C, then one can say C–B–A also.

(*ii*) If A and C are two distinct points on a line, then at least one point B lies between A and C. Also, there exists a point D such that A–C–D.

(*iii*) Among three points lying on a line, only one point may lie between the other two.

(*iv*) A line may contain four points A, B, C and D such that A–B–C as well as A–B–D and A–C–D as well as B–C–D.

(*v*) If A, B, C are three non-collinear points and if $l$ is a line on the plane of these points but not passing through them, and if $l$ passes through a point of the line-segment $\overline{AB}$, then it passes through a point on either line-segment $\overline{BC}$ or $\overline{AC}$.

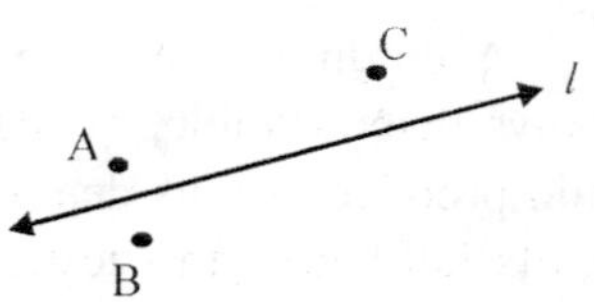


## Group III: Parallel Postulates

Guass was the first to prove that the Euclid's postulates of parallels are not genuine. One of the Euclid's postulates of parallels is as below:

'If a straight line falling on two straight lines makes the interior angles on the same side, less than two right angles, then the two straight lines if produced indefinitely meet on that side on which are angles less than two right angles'.

Guass challenges this postulate as there is no mention of the 'same plane.' Some other postulates of parallels were also criticised and disproved which led to Non-Euclidean Geometry. The Non-

Euclidean method of geometry was propounded independently by Bolyai of Hungery in 1825 A.D. and Russian mathematician Lobechevlki in 1826 A.D. respectively.

One of the Euclid's postulates of parallels is: Through a point not on a straight line, there is one and only one straight line parallel to the given line.' In Non-Euclidean Geometry this postulate reads as: 'if there is a line $l$ in a plane and a point P lies in the same plane but not on the line $l$, then in this plane at least two lines can be drawn through the point P and not intersecting the line $l$ anywhere.' (This is because the plane may be spherical.)

Thus, Non-Euclidean postulates are true for spherical surface of the earth while Euclidean postulates are confined to only plane surface. This makes considerable difference in the concepts, terms and propositions of Geometry.

## Group IV : Postulates of Congruency

1. If $\overline{AB} \cong \overline{CD}$ and $\overline{AB} \cong \overline{EF}$, then $\overline{CD} \cong \overline{EF}$.
2. If AB is a line and C is a point on another line, then a point D can be plotted on another line such that AB = CD i.e., $\overline{AB} \cong \overline{CD}$.
3. A line contains two line-segments $\overline{AB}$ and $\overline{BC}$ on the opposite side of B and another line contains two line-segments A′B′ and B′C′ on the opposite side of B′, then if $\overline{AB} \cong$ A′B′ and $\overline{BC} \cong$ B′C′, then $\overline{AC} \cong \overline{A'C'}$

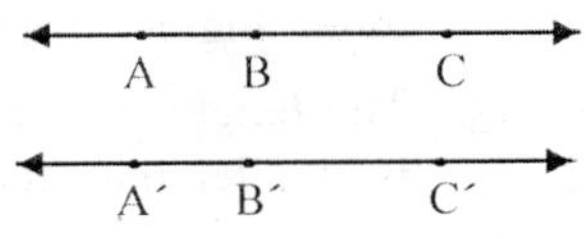


4. If $\angle ABC \cong \angle PQR$ and $\angle ABC \cong \angle DEF$, then $\angle PQR \cong \angle DEF$.
5. $\angle ABC$ is given. $l$ is a line in the plane which contains $\overrightarrow{OC'}$. Then on one side of $l$, $\overrightarrow{OA'}$ can be plotted such that $\angle ABC \cong \angle A'OC'$.

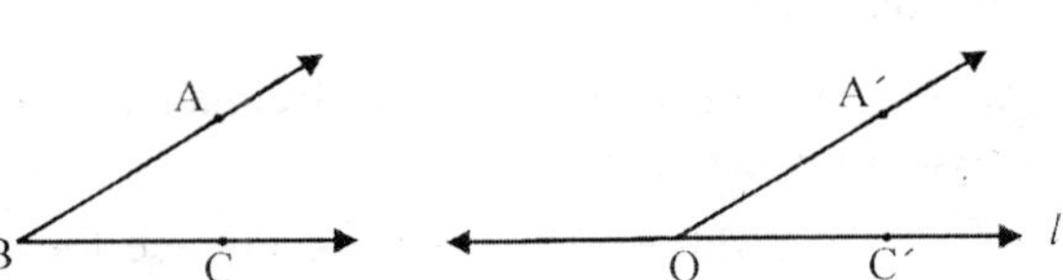


6. In triangles ABC and A′B′C′ if $\overline{AB} \cong \overline{A'B'}$, $\overline{AC} \cong \overline{A'C'}$ and $\angle A \cong \angle A'$, then $\overline{BC} \cong \overline{B'C'}$, $\angle B \cong \angle B'$ and $\angle C \cong \angle C'$.

## Group V : Continuity Postulates

Point $A_1$ lies between two points A and B of a line. If we take points $A_2$, $A_3$, $A_4$,... on the same line such that $A-A_1-A_2$, $A_1-A_2-A_3$, $A_2-A_3-A_4$ and so on and also if $\overline{AA_1} \cong \overline{A_1A_2} \cong \overline{A_2A_3} \cong \overline{A_3A_4} \cong \ldots$ then there exists a positive whole number n such that $A - B - A_n$.

## Group VI : Completeness Postulates

Hilbert – 'Mathematical system does not permit the entry of new points, lines or planes without following the postulates of the groups I to V given above.'

Hilbert, in this way, tried to modify Euclidean Geometry by amending its errors with the help of above postulates. The study of Geometry in our schools now-a-days is made mostly in the modified form suggested by Hilbert.

## 3.4 Forms of Non-Euclidean Geometry

It is interesting to have the glimpses of the forms of Non-Euclidean Geometry, *viz.* (1) Hyperbolic Geometry and (2) Elliptical Geometry and (3) Spherical Geometry.

### *(1) Hyperbolic Geometry*

Hyperbolic Geometry differs a lot from the Euclidean Geometry in so many aspects. Some of the theorems which are not true in Euclidean Geometry but are true in Hyperbolic Geometry are given below:

(1) The sum of the measures of the angles of a triangle is less than 180°. [The sum of the measures of the angles is different for different types of triangles.]

(2) The sum of the measures of the angles of a quadrilateral is less than 360°.

(3) Similar triangles are congruent. If three angles of a triangle are congruent to the respective three angles of another triangle, then the triangles are said to be congruent.

(4) The length of the line-segment determined by the midpoints of the two sides of a triangle is smaller than that of the third side.

(5) The parallel lines converge in the direction of parallelism.

(6) The measure of the angle constructed in the semi-circle is not equal to 90°.

In Hyperbolic Geometry, there is no existence of squares.

### *(2) Elliptical Geometry*

An outstanding mathematician Reiman in one of his famous lectures on 'the hypotheses of Geometry' pointed out that —

> 'Although through experience the unboundedness of space is almost certain, yet it does not make us to conclude that a line is infinite.'

Euclidean Geometry and Hyperbolic Geometry assumed that line is infinite in length. But it is not so with Elliptical Geometry. For example, if we imagine two-dimensional world of the surface of a sphere, we come to know that no lines are parallel on this surface. So, we conclude, 'To any given line, from a point outside the line, no parallel line can be drawn.' The geometry constituted such ideas is called an Elliptical Geometry.

Thus, two postulates — (1) the negation of the parallel postulate and (2) infinite like postulate, have given birth to Elliptical Geometry.

Some of the important and interesting results arrived in Elliptical Geometry are given below:

(1) Lines are not infinite in length.

(2) There is no existence of parallel lines.

(3) The concept of 'betweenness' does not hold in the system of this Geometry.

(4) It is not true that one and only one perpendicular can be drawn on a line from a point not on the line.

(5) A triangle may have two right angles.

(6) It is not true that, 'The measure of any exterior angle of a triangle is equal to the sum of the measures of its interior opposite angles.'

### *(3) Spherical Geometry*

Vismay wants to measure the area of his farm. He may use the formulae of Euclidean Geometry but theoretically 'Spherical Geometry' is being used by him since his measurements are made on the spherical surface of the Earth. But for a small area, the surface of the earth is almost plane. So, the postulates of Non-Euclidean Geometry may be used in Euclidean Geometry for a specific purpose and in some specific situations.

In the spherical geometry every line has a finite length equal to the length of half a great circle on the sphere.

Some interesting results of spherical geometry:

(1) Every line has a finite length.

(2) There can be an infinite member of straight lines through two distinct points.

(3) The sum of the measures of the angles of a triangle is greater than 180° and it approaches 180° when the area of the triangle approaches zero.

(4) In this type of geometry, Pythagoras Theorem does not hold true. It becomes true only when the area of the right triangle approaches zero.

(5) There is no line, through a point not on the given line, parallel to the given line.

- The evolution of Non-Euclidean Geometries, brought about a radical change in the concepts of postulates. Now, these are considered as basic assumptions in most of the mathematical systems. This makes Euclidean Geometry more clear and exact by making the efforts to remove the shortcomings of Euclidean Geometry.

## EVALUATE YOURSELF

1. Discuss the Euclidean Method of study Geometry.
2. What are the foundations of Euclidean Geometry?
3. Explain fully the shortcomings of Euclidean Geometry.
4. Write short notes on:

   (1) Hyperbolic Geometry (2) Elliptical Geometry (3) Spherical Geometry

   (4) Postulates of order (5) Parallel postulates
5. Bertrand Russel — 'The value of Euclid's work as a masterpiece of logic has been very grossly exaggerated.' Justify the statement.
6. Explain the forms of Non-Euclidean Geometry.
7. Differentiate between Euclidean and Non-Euclidean Geometrics.

8. Describe the essential features of Hilberts modifications of Euclidean Geometry.
9. Should the teaching of Euclidean Geometry be totally excluded from our syllabus of Mathematics? Justify your answer.
10. How does modern geometry differ from the Euclidean?

* * *

'That the whole is greater than its parts is not an axiom, as that eminently bad reasoner, Euclid, made it to be .... Of finite collections it is true, of infinite collections false.'

— ***G.S. Peirce***

# CURRICULUM IN MATHEMATICS

Most of the human activities are objective-centred. Schooling is an important human activity. So, it must be purposeful affair. There are some definite motives of schooling. The major considerations for which a child is sent to school may broadly be stated as the acquirement of knowledge and skill; intellectual habits and power, desirable attitude and ideals, development of social virtues and good citizenship. These may be termed as 'aims of schooling.'

Therefore, now, it is the sole responsibility of the schools to contribute towards the attainment of these aims. It requires some means through which the specified aims can be realised. These means may be termed as 'curriculum of the school.' So, whatever can contribute towards the attainment of aims of schooling must be included in the curriculum.

It is very essential for a teacher to have a good knowledge about the different aspects of curriculum.

## 4.1 What is Curriculum? Definitions and Meaning

Some important definitions will be helpful in arriving at the meaning of curriculum.

**Definitions:** Some important definitions are presented below:

According to Cunningham: 'The curriculum is a tool in the hands of artist (teacher) to mould his material (pupils) according to his ideals (objectives) in his studio (school).'

According to P. Samuel : 'The curriculum is the sum total of the experiences of the pupil that he receives through the manifold activities that go on in the school, in the classroom, in the laboratory, in the library, on the playground, in the workshops and seminars, and in the numerous informal contacts between teacher and pupils.'

According to Secondary Education Commission (1952-53) (Mudaliar Commission Report): 'Curriculum does not mean only the academic subjects traditionally taught in the schools, but it includes totality of experiences that a pupil receives through the manifold activities that go in the school, in the classroom, library, laboratory, workshop, playgrounds and in the numerous informal contacts between teachers and pupils. In this sense, the whole life of school becomes the curriculum which can touch the life of the students at all points and helps in the evolution of the balanced personality.'

According to Froebel : 'Curriculum should be conceived as an epitome of the rounded whole of the knowledge and experience of human race.'

In the words of Bent Kronenberg : 'Curriculum is the systematic form of subject matter which is prepared to fulfil the needs of the pupils.'

According to Crow and Crow — "Curriculum includes all the learners experiences, in or outside school that are included in a programme which has been deviced to help him to develop mentally, physically, socially, emotionally, spiritually and morally."

According to Shane H.G. and Meswian E.J. — "The physical curriculum is the sum of experiences, the learning skills, habits and attitudes that the child has made a part of himself and that governs his behaviour as a result of the environment provided by school."

According to Saylor and Alexander — "The curriculum is the total effort of the school to bring about desired outcomes in the school and out of the school situation."

## Meaning

Curriculum is a Latin word which means 'to run' or 'race course' or 'race ground' or 'course to run.' So, curriculum is a course or path which a pupil has to run for reaching a certain goal. Curriculum is a path which has to be followed by a teacher for realising the aims of education. Curriculum is a means through which aims of education are attained.

It is a logical sequence of subject matter to be imparted as a new knowledge and experience to the learners for their development of personality.

Like the term 'education', curriculum has also two meanings — traditional and real.

### 1. *Traditional Meaning*

More often what is taught in a classroom is taken as the curriculum of that class. It is very limited and narrow interpretation of the term curriculum. It is confirmed to only school education or bookish knowledge. Again, traditional curriculum has been defined as a group of subjects or fields of study arranged in a particular sequence.

It has been imagined as the subject matter *i.e.,* content to be employed in instruction. Such a narrow and shallow interpretation of the meaning and function of curriculum has led to a lot of defects and consequent failure to attain the real objectives of education.

The traditional meaning of curriculum suffers from following defects:

*(1) Narrowness:* This meaning has confined the curriculum to only subject matter arranged and preserved in the form of books. Only the content of academic interest is involved here. It neither includes nor solves the day-to-day problems of society. It is inadequate in the sense that subjects after subjects are added and provision for co-curricular activities goes on increasing.

*(2) Abstractness:* The traditional curriculum is dominated by abstract and isolated studies and skills. As a result, it lacks realistic experiences.

(3) *Irrelated Items:* Traditional curriculum is nothing but a collection of irrelated items based on psychology of learning prevailed in olden times. It emphasised that learning by parts is better than learning in wholes. So, it is naturally resulted in recitation without understanding and rote memorisation.

(4) *Rigidity:* Traditional curriculum is resulted into rigidity and inflexibility. Quantitative standards and same text for years make the curriculum rigid. Pupils achievement is measured in only quantity.

## 2. *Real Meaning*

According to real or broader meaning of curriculum it is the means that the school adopts to discharge effectively and meaningfully its fundamental social responsibilities. So, it includes the whole programme of the school and not merely a group of subjects or studies. Thus, curriculum is more than only teaching some subjects within the four walls of a room.

It is a series of activities and experiences which the older generation plans for the younger generation, and tries to execute the plans through school programmes, so that the pupils become ideal members of society. Thus, curriculum is the means of realising the aims and objectives of education.

This meaning of curriculum considers the nature of the child and the requirement of the community at large as two main determinants of the curriculum. Some educationists emphasise the nature of the child more, while others emphasise the requirement of community.

According to first view, the curriculum should be framed according to the vital interest of the child. The child should be given ample opportunities for self-experience and personal activities so that his individual personality is fully developed.

According to the second view, the curriculum should not be only child-centred but also community-centred. The ideals and values of the society should also be considered by the framers of the curriculum. The supporters of this view say that the child is to grow in the way society likes him to grow. So, the ideals and requirements of the society should determine the curriculum. This view emphasises that the child is to be taught what is needful for his present as well as future life.

Hence, the curriculum should concentrate on the experiences of the human race as a whole. In brief, the purpose of the school is to reflect civilisation itself and the curriculum is the epitome of human knowledge, skills and experiences.

The world is changing very fast creating new needs and new values and hence, the mathematics curriculum which suited during our grandfather's time is not necessarily capable of meeting the present needs of pupils and the society.

The *what* and *how* of mathematics have always been determined by its *why*. These objectives are fundamentally important to guide curriculum framers, textbook writers, teachers and other education officers and administrators.

Thus, the meaning of curriculum can be summarised as:

(1) Curriculum is a set up of study and experiences through which the aims and objectives of education are realised and the behaviour of learner is changed in the desirable direction.

(2) Curriculum includes subject matter and textbooks, and involves the totality of experiences on the part of the pupils.

(3) Curriculum has a very wide scope.

(4) In the educational process, all the three — teachers, learners and curriculum have equal importance.

(5) Curriculum is a means which gives right direction to the teachers, learners, authors and administrators.

(6) It includes learners attitude, aptitude, interest and experiences, in or outside school and help the pupil to develop mentally, physically, socially, emotionally, spiritually and morally.

(7) Hence, organisation of learning experiences in a planned and systematic manner, keeping the child in centre may be called curriculum.

(8) It is flexible, varied and progressive in the sense that it tries to meet the needs of the pupil as well as the current demands of even ever-changing society.

(9) Curriculum is a well-planned scheme of studies and experiences of imparting education to the child. The curriculum of mathematics is the part of the total curriculum. It helps and contribute its maximum towards the realisation of the aims and objectives of education.

## 4.2 Purposes of Curriculum

John Dewey emphasised that education takes place in and through the society in which the teacher and the taught both live. Thus, it is the society which determines the aims and objectives, subject matter or content and curriculum and methods of teaching. Therefore, the process of education contains three poles — the teacher, the child and the society. As a matter of fact, education consists in the interaction of these three factors. Yet, curriculum has a greater importance because in the absence of curriculum, neither the teacher will be able to impart knowledge effectively nor the learner will be able to learn anything correctly and logically.

Some important purposes of curriculum are enlisted here:

(1) To make pupil capable of understanding their national heritage and having trust in it.

(2) To evoke feeling for honour of an individual.

(3) To develop —

(*i*) all round personality and individuality of a pupil.

(*ii*) appropriate mental, emotional, cultural points of views and desired habits.

(*iii*) knowledge and various skills in a child according to his interest and abilities.

(*iv*) a unique judgement ability so that they may find differences in good and evil, right and wrong, essential and non-essentials.

(*v*) interest and abilities in child for research.

(*vi*) the thinking researching understanding and decision-making abilities of a child for moral development.

(*vii*) appropriate social and economical relations so that the child may successfully lead life in family, school and society.

(*viii*) vocational skills so that he can stand on his own.

(4) To lay foundation for rich, useful and effective moral life so that he may contribute for social welfare and social prosperity.

(5) To promote various constructive and creative abilities of child in conformity with the different stages of his development.

(6) To promote national and international outlook and a sense of international peace, fraternity and brotherhood in the child.

(7) To provide the child knowledge, skills and economic and cultural relations of human society.

(8) To indicate an aesthetic and artistic expression and appreciation in a child.

(9) To create —

(*i*) new values for themselves by means of their resourcefulness, courage, behaviour and scientific attitude and aptitude.

(*ii*) faith in child for Indian Republic.

(*iii*) feeling of pride to make the child aware with citizens' rights and responsibilities.

## EVALUATE YOURSELF

1. What do you mean by 'curriculum'? Discuss the meaning of curriculum with few definitions.
2. Explain the traditional meaning of curriculum.
3. Discuss the real or broader meaning of curriculum.
4. Enlist the purposes of curriculum.
5. 'Curriculum has a very wide scope' — Justify.
6. Bring out the meaning that can be attached to the term 'curriculum of mathematics.'

'Mathematics is the Queen of Sciences and Arithmetic, the Queen of Mathematics.'

— ***C.F. Gauss***

'I have taught Mathematics to almost every kind of student. In my experience, there is hardly any man who may not become a discoverer, an advancer of knowledge and the earlier the age at which you give him chances of exercising his individuality the better.'

— ***John Perry***

# 5 CONSTRUCTING CURRICULUM IN MATHEMATICS

## 5.1 Need for Planning of Curriculum

The main and common motto of every school is — 'To make the child a complete and perfect man.' This is because he may be able to lead his life in a better way than he is today and may be quite helpful to society in its every front.

In formal education, the curriculum is a major means of imparting knowledge and skills. In the present age, the needs of people and that of society are widening and changing very rapidly. Today's need may become outdated tomorrow. For example, today one needs a scooter but tomorrow it becomes useless and one may need a four-wheeler. And thus, one's needs go on increasing.

The rapid social, scientific and technical changes do have influenced significantly the man's outlook on life. Therefore, the philosophy of life is going on changing. As a result, naturally, the aims and objectives of education also go on changing. So, it needs a dynamic approach to curriculum construction. It is not desirable to pull on with a static curriculum.

In mathematics too, if the instruction is to be worthwhile it must be systematically planned. The revision of curriculum in mathematics after appropriate time is an important aspect in its planning and it should be a continuous process. The revision of the present curriculum helps the removal of the shortcomings of the existing subject matter.

It is suggested that every year experts in mathematics must confer and conclude about any modification to be made in curriculum. For such modifications, there must be thorough and wide discussion and consensus. The revision in the curriculum of mathematics should take place within at most five years.

## 5.2 Constructing curriculum in Mathematics

Following are the five main stages of framing curriculum in mathematics:

I. Formation of objectives of curriculum.

II. Selection of contents *i.e.,* subject matter or topics.

III. Organisation of contents.

IV. Suggesting appropriate learning experiences.

V. Suggesting suitable methods and techniques for evaluation.

## 5.3 Formulation of Objectives of Curriculum

Curriculum construction, as it is a very important task, must have certain aims and objectives. These objectives are basically important as a guide to curriculum framers, text book writers, teachers and administrators of schools.

The educational values of the subject provide the basis to formulate the objectives of curriculum of that subject. Mathematics has educational values, so as a subject, it is an essential part of school education. These values or aims of teaching mathematics have to be realised through the curriculum. Thus, the educational aims and objectives of teaching mathematics are, in a way, also the objectives of its curriculum.

Young has proposed three major educational values of the study of mathematics. They are:

(1) Practical or Utilitarian values,

(2) Mathematics as a mode of thoughts,

(3) Development of attitudes, habits and ideals.

Blackhurst suggested that the educational values of mathematics are related to attitudes, concepts and informations.

Schorling classifies them as: (1) attitudes, (2) concepts, and (3) abilities.

Breslich classifies the chief aims of study of mathematics as:

Development of (1) understanding (2) skills (3) problems and methods
(4) appreciations (5) attitudes (6) habits.

Mimick has classified these values into four categories. They are:

(1) Practical Values (2) Preparatory Values
(3) Cultural Values (4) Disciplinary Values

This classification is more comprehensive. These values can be taken up as the fundamental criteria to assess the suitability of content to be incorporated in the curriculum.

These objectives can also be classified into important broad categories like Knowledge, Understanding, Skills, Application, Attitude, Appreciation and Interest.

These objectives should be expressed in specific terms with respect to the expected changes in the pupils' thought, feeling and action with the help of content in mathematics.

The final statement of objectives and their specifications should necessarily be included in the proposed draft of the curriculum.

In the absence of the formation of specifications of educational objectives or objectives of curriculum one cannot proceed properly in the right direction towards one's goal. Without ascertaining the objectives, the selection and organisation of subject matter may become vague, wasteful and ineffective.

## Chief Advantages of the Formation of Objectives of Curriculum

They are mentioned below:

(1) It provides —

(*a*) definite direction to educational activities

(*b*) criteria for selection of suitable content.

(*c*) basis to planning and organising the educational programmes.

(*d*) basis to evaluate the progress and achievement of the learners.

(*e*) clarity and significance to curriculum.

(2) It helps —

(*a*) in presenting the educational activities in a systematic way.

(*b*) in ascertaining the priorities.

(*c*) in establishing balance between different aspects of educational programmes.

(*d*) in the standardisation of evaluation and learning experiences.

(*e*) in creating appropriate learning situations.

(3) It makes —

(*a*) possible the differentiation in different aspects of learning.

(*b*) the learning functionals.

(4) It determines the nature of educational activities.

(5) On the basis of objectives the educational process can be well-defined.

## 5.4 Selection of the Content/Topics

The selection of the content or subject matter or topics for the curriculum of mathematics and for the particular stage or level is a very important yet difficult and tedious task.

One should remember that the objectives of curriculum form the core of criteria for the selection of content. The objectives laid down or behavioural changes anticipated can be realised only if suitable contents and topics are properly selected and organised.

In this selection the principle of utility, principle of preparation for higher studies, principle of disciplinary value, principle of cultural value, principle of child-centredness, principle of community-centredness, principle of flexibility, principle of correlation and integration, principle of teachers' views and experiences, and principle of modernisation and emerging trends can play a decisive role.

The selection of content should be carried out on the basis of the following principles which are also termed as 'Principles of Curriculum Construction.'

## 5.5 Principles of Curriculum Construction w.r.t Selection of Content

### 1. Principle of Utility (Practical) Value

In the present materialistic age, the significance of any subject matter lies in its practical utility. The knowledge and skills which are applicable in daily life is everybody's necessity. The difficulty here arises: 'Which should be considered as useful or useless for the learning of its inclusion in mathematics curriculum?' Sometimes we consider the topics having practical applications in day-to-day life as useful topics and the rest is useless.

Of course, this is a very narrow interpretation of the term 'utility.'

According to this principle or criteria 'only those topics should be included in the curriculum which are useful in our day-to-day life as well as in future life, too.'

The learners intend to acquire that knowledge and skills with ease and pleasure which seem to be useful for them now or in future. Therefore, the planners and framers of curriculum of mathematics must have to keep in mind the utilitarian aspect of the content/topics before its inclusion in the curriculum. From this point of view, there are certain topics of mathematics which are indispensable for everyone. For example,

Four fundamental operations of simple calculation, profit and loss, average, percentage, simple an compound interest, concept of length, weight and capacity and their larger and smaller measurements, coinage, area, taxes, tables and graphs, household accounts, simpler notation of statistics, simple and common geometrical figures and their properties, etc. are the most useful content for elementary and middle stage.

Giving a little broader meaning to the term *utility*, this principle may be interpreted with wider meaning. A topic should be included in the curriculum if it is useful —

(*i*) in everyday life.

(*ii*) in the study of other subjects now or in future.

(*iii*) in understanding the scientific and technical progress.

(*iv*) in providing common ground for a fairly good number of vocations.

(*v*) in understanding and appreciating the role played by mathematics in the development of civilisation in its various aspects in commerce, trade, heavy industry, engineering, physical and social sciences and other branches of knowledge.

(*vi*) in the realisation of the artistic and aesthetic value of the subject of mathematics.

(*vii*) in inspiring the students by acquainting them with the biographies of mathematicians and the history of discoveries and inventions in mathematics.

(*viii*) in rendering help for the future research work in the field of mathematics and sciences.

## 2. Principle of Preparatory Value

According to this principle, the content of the curriculum in mathematics —

(1) should be helpful to prepare the pupils for leading their future life smoothly, and

(2) it should also prepare them for further advanced education.

Therefore, the content should be so selected that it should be —

(1) a terminus for those who prepare to enter in actual life giving up their studies, and also

(2) for those who prepare for higher education.

The majority of pupils intend to give up their studies at a particular level and enter into real life such as domestic, occupational, business, government service, farming, etc., and only a small percentage of pupils have a will to acquire higher education. So, it is realised by educationists and the educational planners that in the curriculum of secondary education the content related to preparatory course of higher education should not be given too much weightage.

After every stage of education some pupils leave the school and prefer to enter in family life or to choose any vocational stream, and others go in for higher education. Therefore, the curriculum should be such as to be able to prepare both types of students adequately. The curriculum framers should keep in mind that those who leave the school for one reason or the other are as fully equipped as possible for life.

Generally every child aims to go higher and higher on the education ladder. So, the education at a particular stage must aim to prepare the child for the education at the higher stages. It is certainly true that the child may not need the study of certain topics at the present stage, *e.g.,* the study of the measures of central tendency in statistics in Std. VIII, but it is equally true that the ignorance of these topics may become a major handicap in achieving knowledge in the higher classes. Therefore, the curriculum of mathematics at any level or stage must cater to the future needs of the higher classes.

If we collect statistics with regards to wastage and stagnation in education, we will come to know that the pupils who would like to go for higher studies or who would choose mathematics as the subject for specialised learning are very few. Believing that the preference should go to majority, *i.e.,* equipping school learners with all the essential knowledge of mathematics to live a balanced life, yet the useful and important topics forming the firm base for the higher studies in mathematics should be necessarily incorporated in the curriculum.

Considering the needs of community, the needs of the pupils, the curriculum framers should take into account the views of the teachers and give them due importance in any programme of curriculum construction in mathematics.

## 3. Principle of Disciplinary Value

Mathematics has disciplinary value as it disciplines and trains the faculties of mind like faculty of reasoning and thinking, faculty of imagination, concentration, memorisation, inventiveness, etc.

In the past, there was too much emphasis upon this value. As a result, so many useless topics and contents were included in the curriculum which only proved a burden to the pupils.

For example: Simplify $\dfrac{(56)^2 \times (134)^3 \times \sqrt{2209}}{0.00072 \times \sqrt[3]{922373}}$ [The students do not know Logarithms]

It is futile to increase the load of the curriculum by including a topic merely for the sake of its disciplinary value. But to discipline the mind is not the only function of education. The education must be meaningful, useful and functional.

Thus, the disciplinary value of a topic cannot become the criterion for the inclusion of it in the curriculum.

The real useful problems indeed train the mind in a much better way than the unreal formal problems. Thorndike rightly remarked —

> 'Teach nothing merely because of its disciplinary value but teach everything so as to get, what disciplinary value it does have.'

Training of mind depends largely on methods of teaching adopted by the teacher. If a topic is taught in an effective, logical and psychological manner, it will definitely create some mental habits. So, one can conclude that the adoption of suitable methods of teaching mathematics is much more useful, important and practical than the content which one may assume that it will discipline the minds of pupils.

## 4. Principle of Flexibility

Now-a-days our society is no more rigid. It is very much dynamic. As a result, the aims of education go on changing very fast as they depend on the changing needs of dynamic society. So, a rigid and inelastic curriculum is unable to meet the requirements of the present day mini-societies *i.e.,* schools.

The development in the subject and the research reports on this field also accept the necessity of periodical changes in the curriculum of mathematics. Thus, the curriculum should be flexible enough in accordance with the needs of the changing society.

The curriculum should also be reviewed and modified frequently so as to shape it according to the latest developments of the subject and to the changing requirements of a dynamic society.

## 5. Principle of Cultural Value

Mathematics has played an important role in the advancement of culture and civilisation. Some topics of mathematics are very helpful in the development of habits having cultural value. For example, habits of logical reasoning and thinking, co-operation with others, sympathy towards needy, accuracy in any work, tolerance and appreciation of pieces of mathematical literature and other artistic things. Such topics should be included in the curriculum.

Such topics are no less important than those which claim to be useful in solving the problems of day-do-day life.

There are certain ideas and facts of mathematics that form an integral part of modern culture and civilisation of our society. Therefore, while selecting topics for curriculum of mathematics, the cultural value of the content should be taken into account and be given due weightage to them.

## 6. Principle of Child-centredness

In the curriculum construction, the framers should give proper weightage to the needs and requirements of the child for whom the curriculum is constructed. From the psychological point of view also it must be so, because the school and the curriculum are meant for the child and not the child for the school and curriculum.

In the past, of course, the education was totally subject-centred but now-a-days more and more weightage is given to make it child-centred in each activity of educational programmes. In short, everything has to be made to suit the child.

In the selection of topics or subject matter to be encompassed in the curriculum, the child's needs, interests, age level should be kept in view.

In any scheme of curriculum construction, the needs, ability, interest and other developmental characteristics of the children of a particular age, his capacity and interest should be kept in mind.

In child-centred curriculum greater importance is given to the child in place of subject, activities and experiences. Such type of curriculum is constructed according to the child's present and future needs, abilities and capacities, attitudes, interests and hobbies, his difficulties at physical as well as mental level.

Thus, it helps in harmonious development of personality of the child. Kinder-Garten, Montessori, Project and Heuristic methods, etc., are the examples of child-centred curriculum. Thus, it is constructed on the basis of psychological principles and theories.

## 7. Principle of Community-centredness

The curriculum should be approximately linked with community life. So, the social life outside and inside the school must have some bearing on the activities to be taken up in the school. This will bring the child into closer contacts with some of its significant and important activities.

It is no less important to remember that the needs of the society determine the aims of schooling which, in turn, becomes the determining factor for selection of content. Thus, the curriculum is to be socialised so that the child does not feel alienation from organised human life.

A curriculum should serve the community of a particular region by educating the children according to the needs, aspirations and ideals of that community. And therefore, it should be framed and shaped for the welfare and upliftment of the local community.

In the present dynamic community, the curriculum should be elastic enough to be adapted to local needs and situations. Therefore, in the curriculum of mathematics all such topics should be incorporated which take care of the needs of the society in particular and community at large.

## 8. Principle of Correlation and Integration

A new piece of knowledge is not an isolated fragment. The divisions of the curriculum are made only for the sake of convenience for the authors and teachers. There is a close connection between the different branches of knowledge and between the different branches of the same subject. This connection may be horizontal as well as vertical. Therefore, there is an urgent need to correlate the various topics of a subject and various subjects of study. Since mathematics has a good positive correlation with all other subjects, it will be easier to correlate its content with other subjects.

The knowledge of mathematics is also indispensable for human life. So, it can quietly be related with community life and all human activities.

The report of Secondary Education Commission has also pointed out —

> 'The curriculum should not stultify its educational value by being split up into a number of isolated, unco-ordinated water-tight subjects. Subjects should be interrelated and within each subject the content should, so far as possible, be envisaged as '*broad fields* units which can be correlated better with life rather than narrow items of information.'

Seemingly an isolated fragment of a new piece of knowledge is related with what is already there in the manifold structure of the mental content. So, knowledge is not to be imparted in isolated units but it should take place through a well-integrated and interlinked process.

According to Perry — 'Mathematical study began because it was useful, it continues because it is useful and it is valuable to the world because of the usefulness of its results.'

The correlation in the curriculum aims at realising and acquiring the unity of knowledge through which the different needs of a particular stage and at different stages can be fulfilled.

Correlated curriculum is more a methodology rather than a type of curriculum construction. This signifies the intimate connection and correlation of various subjects in the curriculum. Correlated curriculum emphasises that instead of presenting knowledge in segments (parts), it should be presented as an integrated whole through integration and correlation.

*Types of Correlation:* The correlation can be of the following types:

(1) Correlation of mathematics with nature and life-activities of the pupils.

(2) Correlation of mathematics with other subjects.

(3) Correlation among the different branches of mathematics.

(4) Correlation among the different topics of mathematics.

(5) Correlation of mathematics with crafts and work-experience.

(6) Correlation of mathematics with theoretical and practical studies.

In order to correlate teaching of mathematics, the teacher is expected to know —

(1) physical, social and cultural environment of the pupils,

(2) day-to-day life-activities of the pupils,

(3) nature and structure of other subjects and possibilities of seeking correlation with them,

(4) nature and structure of the topics/contents of the different branches of mathematics,

(5) nature and structure of the topics of the same branch of mathematics,

(6) nature of the projects undertaken by the pupils.

## 9. Principle of Modernisation

The mathematics curriculum should be traced according to the latest developments of the topics in the field of mathematics and in accordance with the modern world. This is a must for the curriculum makers so that we may not lag behind in the scientific and technological race. For this purpose, the views of the specialists in mathematics should be sought.

New thinking and emerging trends in school mathematics should be allowed to play its due role in the choice of contents for the mathematics curriculum. Some of these are mentioned below:

(1) The time spent on Arithmetic should be saved by not including it as a separate entity.

(2) The branches of mathematics should pay more attention to the nature of mathematics. Generally, the teachers teach mathematics as a tool. He pays greater attention on developing skills in computation or in mechanical manipulation. They expect the pupils to apply some fixed rules in computation.

But now it is necessary to emphasise the basic properties of number-systems, formal properties of fundamental operations, axiomatic exposition, rules of deduction and more precise definitions. Also, the use of clearly defined terminology and the employment of precise and appropriate symbolism. For this, the language of sets should be accepted.

(3) At present too much time is spent on a large number of complicated and unnecessary sums in Algebra, requiring only mechanical manipulations such as expansion and factorisation, HCF and LCM, square roots and cube roots, ratio and proportion, surds and indices, etc.

Not that these concepts and computation should be totally discarded. Only the elementary ideas involving less mechanical manipulations should be introduced. Emphasis should be given on basic ideas such as variables, function and relation, equalities and inequalities, equations and inequations, etc. More emphasis should be given on the development of an appreciation of the structures of Algebra stressing the number systems and their properties like closure, commutative, associative, distributive, existence of identity element, binary operation, law of trichotomy, etc.

(4) At present the Euclidean geometry has been seriously questioned. So, greater emphasis may be put on the axiomatic structure, logical reasoning and the nature of proof.

No sharp distinction is advisable between algebra and geometry. Analytical method should be used throughout the geometry.

(5) Whenever and wherever possible, plane and solid geometry should be treated together.

(6) Some important fundamental ideas such as symmetry, similarity, congruency, inductive discovery and deductive proof; meaning of at least, at most, if, if and only if, one and only one; converse of a theorem or a statement, definitions and postulates, etc. should be emphasised in keeping with the modern spirit of mathematics.

(7) Trigonometry should be related to Algebra and Geometry. Much of the work on identities should be eliminated. Instead, the problems on height and distance should be given due weightage. Greater stress should be given to the study of trigonometric functions.

(8) The idea of co-ordinates and co-ordinate geometry should be introduced as much early as possible. Work in algebra and geometry needs to be integrated through the use of co-ordinates and their graphic representations.

(9) Statistical notions such as averages, mean, median, mode, dispersion, variability, normal probability curve, etc. should be introduced, considering their growing usefulness in our life.

## 10. Principle of Teachers' Views and Experiences

In the tri-polar process of education, teacher is one of the three important poles. It is the most important but unfortunately most neglected criterion for the selection of the subject matter or content.

In the real sense, he is the real person who has to deal with the curriculum. So, teachers' views and experiences must be given due consideration in framing the curriculum.

An experienced teacher knows well the abilities, interests, needs, aptitudes and mental abilities, capacities and levels of pupils of a particular stage. So, he knows the suitable content which should be taught to them.

But mostly it happens, unfortunately, that he is given least opportunity in the selection of curriculum and sometimes he is not consulted at all! The curriculum is imposed on him and he is unaware about the significance of changes in the curriculum, if any. Though few teachers are included in the curriculum committee to represent the teachers' world but their selection is arbitrary rather than academic specialities.

The teachers must have definite say in the selection and organisation of curriculum material. There should be a good representation, participation and contribution of experienced and academically well equipped teachers in the whole process of curriculum construction.

## Young's Views on Selection of Content for the Curriculum of Mathematics

The world famous mathematician J.W.A. Young has expressed his views regarding the selection of content for the curriculum of mathematics. According to him, the following important points should be kept in view while selecting the content or topics of curriculum of mathematics:

1. To exhibit most clearly and to the best advantages the mathematical type of thoughts.
2. To help a better understanding of the Laws of Nature.
3. To bring out clearly the mathematical relationships that exist (*a*) in the social organisms and (*b*) in the activities of modern life. And therefore, to exhibit how mathematics helps in solving their day-to-day problems.
4. To impart sufficient skill in the actual performance of mathematical processes so as to meet the future requirements of the pupils.
5. To allow the organisation of selected material into a homogeneous whole, meeting the demands of pedagogy.

## 5.6 Organisation of Content/Topics

The third stage of curriculum construction is the organisation of subject matter. After the selection of topics/subject matter, it requires proper order and arrangement. The arrangement of topics demands some questions to be seriously answered:

1. When and where should a particular topic be introduced?
2. What topic would be most suitable after a particular topic?
3. How much portion of a topic should be taught keeping in view the (*a*) particular level/stage of pupils and (*b*) the age-group of pupils?
4. What should be done before and after a topic?

These requirements can be satisfied through a psychological, logical and scientific way. So, the subject matter should be organised on the basis of certain psychological principles. The following principles and methods may be helpful in organising and arranging the curriculum material:

## 5.7 Principles of Curriculum Construction w.r.t. organisation of Content/Topics

### 1. Principle of Logical and Psychological Order

For the organisation of the contents/topics in mathematics, there are two different, but can easily be integrated, view points — one is psychological and the other logical.

The psychological organisation considers the organisation according to the development of the mind of the pupil — his needs, interest, abilities, etc. The logical organisation takes into account the systematisation of knowledge more important than the pupil. It demands that the topics of mathematics should be taught in a logical order depending upon the modes of thinking and fundamental processes.

For example, what is first — ratio and proportion or variation? Logic demands and recommends that variation should be taught after studying ratio and proportion. But practically, variation is easier than ratio and proportion. Not only easier but its utility value is also more than that of ratio and proportion. So, psychologically it is proper to teach variation first and then ratio and proportion. Of course, we cannot do away with logic since the systematic organisation of the subject cannot be sacrificed.

Teacher has to find out the 'golden mean' between these two ways of teaching. He needs to organise the contents and topics in such a way that he can follow psychology and logic at one and the same time.

It is the psychology that decides what type of logic is suitable for the pupils of a certain age and of a certain level and their abilities, interest, etc., and what kind of topics will be most suitable for the development of such logical thinking. Psychology is more concerned with the learners and learning processes while the content of mathematics by its very nature requires logical treatment for its further development.

Though both approaches are seemingly different but an experience teacher can easily integrate them as both are not diagonally opposite to each other. Their integration ultimately benefits the pupils a lot in their understanding of the mathematics.

The logical reasoning maintains proper sequence of topics while psychological reasoning throws light on the power of understanding of the pupils at a certain level and practical utility of the topic in their daily life. Of course, the combination of both these approaches make the content more interesting and understandable.

## 2. Principle of Activity

Modern education emphasises activity-centred teaching, as the child is active by Nature. The children show more interest in any type of activity and concrete form of the subject matter rather than in passive learning and abstract form of the subject matter. Children learn through direct experiences more than the indirect experiences. So, they should be given more opportunities for using concrete things in order to have experience of learning skills and acquiring useful knowledge. Therefore, topics which give greater scope of practical work should be included in the curriculum.

Organisers of curriculum should explore more and more possibilities for such type of activities and propose opportunities for it as and when possible.

In activity-centred curriculum, various activities are emphasised in a specific manner. In a support of this John Dewey expressed his views emphatically that 'by means of activity-centred curriculum a child will develop interest in useful and purposeful activities which will promote his developments to the fullest extent possible.'

A topic which carries a greater scope for practical work should be given preference for inclusion in the curriculum. Only at the higher level, topics carrying a greater scope for abstract form should be included. This approach helps in developing interest and positive attitude towards mathematics.

In mathematics, the activities like counting, computing, measuring, weighing, drawing graphs, tabulating, constructing geometrical figures, should be included in the curriculum. The practical works related with home activities, recreational activities, vocational activities, social and community life activities should also be given due place in the curriculum.

With these activities, the content should be arranged according to the needs and tastes of the pupils. These activities also provide a better ground for abstract principles of mathematics.

## 3. Principle of Individual Difference

There are individual differences in children. The same type of content may not be desirable for all. Varied content material should be included for different categories of pupils. The duration of course is another factor to be kept in view.

Generally, curriculum is framed for the needs of group as a whole or for the purpose of class teaching. To a certain extent, it is a good approach as the teacher has to teach the pupils in a group. But, at the same time, psychology shows that no two individuals, even if they are twins, are alike. There are wide differences in their interests, aptitudes, intelligence, abilities, capacities and experiences. The class teaching system does not cater for the individual's needs and interests as the rigid syllabus may not suit all the pupils. It proves that there should be some scope of individual teaching in the curriculum to satisfy the needs of individual pupils.

Of course, the requirements of the group as a whole should have priority over the individual requirements, but it cannot be entirely neglected. Thus, the syllabus must be helpful in dealing with the individual needs. For this, the ideal situation is 'one teacher for one child' or 'one syllabus for one child.' This may be taken as ultimate goal. Looking at the present situation of Indian economy and schools, it is not feasible. It will be worth pointing out that in olden days, in Nalanda and Taxshila learning-centres the ratio of teachers and students was 1 : 6. For sixty thousand students, there were ten thousand teachers!

There are suggestions in this regard:

(1) The content of curriculum should be so arranged that the difference in the abilities of the pupils may not be ignored. There should be ability-grouping of the pupils. The pupils of almost the same intelligence and abilities may be kept in one group.

(2) There may be grouping of topics in the curriculum.

(3) Provision of differentiated assignments.

(4) Provision of individual teaching. If this is not possible then the teacher-pupil ratio be kept 1 : 30 or at most 1 : 40.

## 4. Principle from Empirical to Rational

According to this principle, the most evident and familiar things should come in the beginning of the topics. General ideas and theories should be rationalised later on. It is similar to proceed 'from known to unknown' or 'from particular to general' or 'from concrete to abstract.'

It is always a safe approach to begin with what we see, feel and experience than with what we argue, generalise and explain. The learning of mathematical knowledge begins from observation, experience, intuition and induction. It is accomplished gradually through deduction. Thus, first of all, the child gains the knowledge empirically. He feels the rational basis for any knowledge much later the experiences gained in his day-to-day life.

Therefore, the curriculum should be so organised that the pupils are able to acquire facts through intuition, experience, observation and induction on first hand and thereafter its basis of rationality.

## 5. Principle of Gradual Increase in Difficulty Level

In the organisation of content the maxims 'from easy to difficult' and 'from simple to complex' should be followed.

The organisers of the curriculum have to keep in mind the mental level, age level, abilities and capacities of pupils in the arrangement of topics/content material of curriculum. It should suit the mental capacity and development of the age group of that class. It means that the topics in the curriculum should neither be too easy nor too difficult.

But here the problem arises. What is simple for a mathematics teacher may not necessarily be simple for the pupils. It is not an easy task to decide what is really easy and what is really difficult for the learner. So, there should be a constant watch on the difficulties realised by the pupils. In every case, the difficulty level of a topic must be judged from the point of view of the pupils. The experiences of mathematics teacher will be most suitable means for the judgement of the difficulty level of a topic.

In this regard 'Cultural Epoch Theory' may also be followed. According to this theory — 'The order in which the human race developed is the best order for the organisation of content material of curriculum.'

Thus, the content/topics which were discovered or developed earliest of all, must be the easiest of all. The topics discovered or developed later on are mostly in order of growing difficulty. But this theory can be over-ruled by the criterion of utilitarian or psychological arrangements. In short, this theory should be used only as a guideline to determine the difficulty level.

In the organisation of curriculum for any particular level or grade, only those topics should be included which are within the comprehension of learners, in order of their difficulty level.

## 6. Principle of Correlation

## 7. Principle of Teachers' Views and Experience

[For both of these principles, please, refer to Principles of Curriculum Construction w.r.t selection of Content/Topics]

## 8. Principle of Topical Arrangement

Topical arrangement is based on the unity of the topic, *i.e.,* a topic is taken as a unified unit. It implies that a topic should be completed in all respect at one stage *i.e.,* at a stretch. It should be finished, with its all possible aspects, entirely before the next topic is taken.

This approach is based on the principle that the topic is an unbreakable unit and it is to be taught and learnt as a whole. It emphasises on continuous and elaborate teaching of a specific topic.

Generally, here, a topic is selected as the basis of many other topics. For example, 'Unitary method' may be taken as the basis for the teaching of simple interest, compound interest, average, percentage, time and work, etc.

### *Merits of Topical Arrangement*

1. It provides thorough knowledge of a topic to the pupils.
2. It facilitates the learning process since a topic is treated as a centre of correlation for other topics.
3. All the abilities and capacities of learners can be utilised to learn the topic thoroughly.
4. There exists a natural link and sequence in the continuous teaching of a topic for a long time.

5. The continuous teaching of a topic may ensure full and whole-hearted concentration of pupils on the subject matter.
6. It will be easier for the teacher of mathematics to set the question-paper for the evaluation of the efficiency of the pupils.

### *Demerits of Topical Arrangement*

1. This approach does not possess any significant advantage.
2. It enforces the pupils to study the topic in its much details which are of no immediate importance to them.
3. If a topic is taught and learnt for a long time, the interest of the pupils may become less and less after some time.
4. A topic takes quite a long time to be completed, so only very few topics will find place in the syllabus of a particular class.
5. It deals with all types of problems, simple as well as complex, related to different aspects of a topic in the same class which is unpsychological. Therefore, the learners of lower age are unable to comprehend and grasp them.
6. It does not provide opportunity for revision of the knowledge learnt in the previous class. So, most of the knowledge acquired earlier is likely to be forgotten.
7. It is an unnatural, unpsychological and impracticable arrangement of subject matter.
8. In this age of 'knowledge explosion' when the knowledge of mathematics gets double within ten years, it is impossible to include the latest aspect of a topic in the syllabus. However, some simple and easier topics may be finished at one stage.
9. This arrangement may be replaced by 'Spiral Arrangement.'

## 9. Principle of Spiral (or Concentric) Arrangement

This arrangement is based on the assumption that knowledge extends and widens just as a spiral or concentric circles. Thus, beginning from a nucleus, the horizon of knowledge goes on widening.

While organising topics/contents of a curriculum it is to be thought that whether we should cover a topic as a whole in a particular grade (topical arrangement) or we should spread it over to different grades by covering easier portion in lower grades and the difficult ones in the higher and higher grades (concentric or spiral arrangement).

Principle of spiral arrangement accepts that any subject mater cannot be given an exhaustive treatment at the initial stage of learning. Therefore, in this arrangement, at the first stage the subject is presented in a very simple form like the centre or the nucleus of a circle and further knowledge is imparted subsequently in the form of wider and wider circles in the following stages.

In this system, an elementary knowledge is given in the introductory years, something more is taught in the next year, again something more is added in the subsequent years and so on. This process goes on from year to year and from class to class. Thus, the knowledge of a topic is given for sufficient number of years with more and more, deeper and deeper content continuously in a progressive manner.

The spiral arrangement should be followed in the following manner:

(1) The subject matter of every topic should be divided into a number of smaller independent units or parts or portions.

(2) These parts should be graded in a systematic manner according to their difficulty value of the content.

(3) Each part should be introduced when the pupils have attained the proper stage of development, the power of comprehension, appropriate age group for its introduction.

The spiral arrangement implies that a topic should be split up into different parts and these parts should be spread over different grades according to their easiness and complexity. A part of the topic should be introduced when a sufficient background has already been prepared for it.

Here, everything is done at its proper stage. It also provides an opportunity for revision as the complex portions cannot be taken up without introducing the previous things for that topic. Therefore, spiral arrangement should be preferred while organising the subject matter of the curriculum.

Here, the study of a topic is spread over a number of years. For example, expansion, factorisation, equations, statistics, trigonometry, HCF, LCM, rational expression, etc. Their complexity goes on increasing every year.

Mathematical development is based on the number-system and four fundamental operations, *viz.* addition, subtraction, multiplication and division. Number-system and these operations reappear everywhere, now and then, in simple or complicated forms. This repetition of fundamental ideas and concepts in building of structure and development of mathematics is known as a 'cyclic development' of the subject.

Therefore, in the organisation of curriculum of mathematics, adequate provision should be made for 'cyclic arrangement' of the subject matter. It leads ultimately to natural spiral arrangement in mathematics.

### *Merits of Spiral Arrangement*

1. As spiral arrangement is a psychological approach, it is certainly a good arrangement.
2. It is psychologically sound system, as simple and concrete aspect of a subject matter is dealt at the introductory stage and complex and abstract concepts are taken up subsequently at further stages.
3. It is suitable system of arrangement of subject matter of mathematics because it proceeds from simple to complex and from concrete to abstract.
4. This system becomes more successful if a teacher deals mathematics independently to the pupils of an introductory class and teaches continuously same subject to the same pupils in the successive classes.
5. It enables the teacher to cover a portion according to the receptivity and grasping power of the learner and if he finds any gap of knowledge, that can be filled up year after year.
6. Interest of pupils remains alive since the new knowledge is associated with previous knowledge. So, new problems are taken up with new interest and solved at ease.
7. The knowledge of mathematics acquired by this arrangement is more lasting because the same topic is learnt over many years with some additional content in each year.

8. It involves the revision of content learnt in the previous year or class which provides a strong basis to proceed further for the acquirement of new, more complex and wider knowledge of mathematics.

### *Demerits of Spiral Arrangement*

This system may become unsuccessful and harmful if —

1. the division and arrangement of different portions of a topic of mathematics is not according to age level and abilities of the learners.
2. a teacher in a class becomes over-ambitious and discusses most of the content to be given in subsequent years.

### *Conclusion*

1. Spiral arrangement should be preferred to while organising the subject matter of mathematics curriculum, as it has more merits and quite less demerits.
2. For its successful implementation the teacher of same pupils and same subject should be assigned to one teacher throughout their schooling for a certain stage as far as possible.
3. Topical arrangement cannot be entirely discarded. There are certain topics which can be taken up entirely as a unit and be finished at a stretch.

Thus the particular arrangement will depend on the length and complexity of the topic.

## 5.8 Suggesting Appropriate Learning Experiences

After formulation of objectives, and selecting as well as organising content/topics, the fourth major step in the development of curriculum is to list suitable learning experiences.

The listing of learning experiences depends upon —

(1) needs of a particular society or community,

(2) abilities, capacities and interests of the learners,

(3) the facilities available in the school.

These factors usually differ from place to place.

In the light of these factors a few suggestions for the introduction of suitable learning experiences are incorporated. They only indicate a few simple activities which probably cause effective learning and help in achieving the set objectives.

Following criterions may be helpful in judging the validity of the learning experiences selected in any curriculum. Consequently, the subsequent changes thereon should be brought in by the teacher as to meet his own requirement.

Learning experience should be —

(1) practicable

(2) adequate

(3) effective

(4) suitable for the concerned content area or topics

(5) appropriate to the desired behavioural changes defined under objectives.

## 5.9 Suggesting Suitable Methods and Techniques for Evaluation

'Curriculum' and 'Evaluation' are not regarded as distinct and separate functions. On the contrary, they are regarded as closely related parts of the same education process. Without laying down some basic principles of evaluations, no curriculum can be planned and executed.

The teacher should evaluate properly what has been done with his pupils and by his pupils, in order to meet the set objectives of teaching mathematics at a particular stage. Therefore, in the development of curriculum, all the important points regarding evaluation of the pupils' progress in mathematics should be definitely pointed out in the attached guidebook of curriculum.

### Critical Analysis/Evaluation of Syllabus in Mathematics

In Mathematics, the required syllabus for a particular stage/class is set for the realisation of the set objectives of teaching mathematics at that stage.

The State Board of Education formulates its own syllabus in mathematics for different stages/grades according to the needs of the society, availability of the local resources and the facilities available in its schools.

Critical study and analysis of a syllabus is carried out to a certain extent for knowing the competency to carry out the task for which it has been set. This critical analysis should be as objective as possible. The following criteria may render help in this task:

#### (1) *Criteria related to the objectives of teaching mathematics*

(*a*) The syllabus should indicate sufficient and adequate objectives of teaching mathematics at a particular stage.

(*b*) The objectives should be properly classified into specific categories.

(*c*) They should be clearly defined in terms of expected behavioural changes.

(*d*) The syllabus should lay emphasis on realising set objectives.

#### (2) *Criteria related to selection and organisation of the contents of mathematics*

(*a*) The contents/topics should be well-graded.

(*b*) The content should cater the needs of advanced studies in mathematics to a great extent.

(*c*) The content/topics should be related to the criterion of utility.

(*d*) The syllabus should greatly consider the needs, interest, age level, abilities, capacities and other psychological aspects of the pupils.

(*e*) The organisation of the contents/topics should be according to spiral arrangement.

(*f*) The selection and organisation of the contents/topics should follow the principle of integration and correlation.

(*g*) The syllabus should have adequate scope for oral work, written work, drill work and home assignment.

### (3) *Criteria related to learning experiences/situations*

(*a*) The syllabus should suggest —

(*i*) a list of suitable learning experiences for the realisation of expected proposed objectives.

(*ii*) a variety of teaching aids or learning materials.

(*iii*) activities, experiences and practical work for the teachers.

(*iv*) text books, reference materials and books for further study.

(*b*) The syllabus should have —

(*i*) some indication regarding teaching plan and teaching materials.

(*ii*) useful suggestions for the authors of the text books in mathematics.

(*c*) The syllabus should —

(*i*) recognise and cater for the individual differences in pupils.

(*ii*) leave scope for independent individual projects or hobbies.

(*d*) A sufficient time should be allotted per week for the contents in the syllabus.

### (4) *Criteria related to the evaluation plan*

(*a*) Syllabus should discuss the evaluation plan for assessing the pupils' progress.

(*b*) The methods and techniques suggested in syllabus should fulfil the objectives of evaluation in mathematics.

(*c*) Syllabus should mention —

(*i*) the distribution of marks according to the division of mathematics into branches.

(*ii*) qualifying passing marks in mathematics.

(*iii*) the mode of examination — home or public — at the end of each session.

## 5.10 Shortcomings of Existing Curriculum of Mathematics

Following are the main shortcomings of existing curriculum of mathematics:

1. It is subject-centred and not child-centred.
2. It is having topical arrangement.
3. It does not give any place to practical work in mathematics.
4. It puts more emphasis on examinations.
5. It is rigid and not flexible.
6. It is devoid of mathematical activities like mathematics club, hobbies, etc. There is no creative activities.
7. There is no conformity with the aims, objectives and learning experiences of teaching mathematics.
8. The approach in curriculum construction is not objective and pragmatic.
9. It is not constructed according to the social and cultural values of teaching mathematics.
10. In mathematics curriculum there is no place with social progress.

11. Separate content written for Arithmetic, Algebra and Geometry shows that they are not correlated with each other.
12. The curriculum of primary, upper primary, secondary and higher secondary stage are not adequately and carefully correlated.
13. So many principles, concepts, rules and problems are not related with our daily life.
14. At primary stage only Arithmetic is included in the curriculum.
15. A lots of topics and problems included in the mathematics curriculum are dull, uninteresting, and useless especially for gifted children.
16. Teaching of Geometry is not according to psychological principles.
17. It does not cater for commercial and technical training to the pupils. So, they are unable to utilize their knowledge at he higher stage.
18. There is main emphasis on exercise and revision. It is not highlighted that which parts of the content require revision.
19. The capabilities, interests of different age groups are not taken into consideration.
20. Thus, critical evaluation/study of mathematics curriculum clearly shows that the present curriculum is simply bookish, theoretical, over-crowded and unpsychological. It is not child-centred, activity-centred and practical.

So there is a need for its improvement. According to Secondary Education Council (1952-53) Report, the defects in the then mathematics curriculum were:

1. It is (*a*) narrow in conception, (*b*) bookish and theoretical, (*c*) not related to daily life of children, and (*d*) examination ridden.
2. Its content is voluminous but not rich and significant.
3. It has lack of technical and vocational subjects.
4. The individual differences of children are not taken into accounts.
5. There is no attention towards interests and needs of the children as well as society in the curriculum.
6. The construction of curriculum is unpsychological.
7. The execution of curriculum is not effective.

Kothari Commission (1964-66) enlisted the defects in the curriculum as below:

1. Present curriculum is inadequate as it does not consist all experience of pupils.
2. It is not useful as there is lack of creative activities.
3. It is over-packed.

In this way, the critical assessment of existing mathematics curriculum may be made on the basis of following points:

1. Formulation of objectives and specifications
2. Selection and organisation of subject matter
3. Relation between teaching objectives and contents/topics
4. Comprehensiveness of the content

5. Child-centredness and community-centredness of the content
6. Theoretical and practical aspects of the content
7. Correlation in subject matter
8. Utility of content in relation to examination and evaluation of pupils

## 5.11 Improving Mathematics Curriculum/Reforming Steps

The existing curriculum of mathematics has many shortcomings. It has failed in its task of promoting complete and harmonious development of the child. It needs an early reorientation on the lines suggested below:

1. The aims and objectives of teaching mathematics should be given due importance.
2. While determining the objectives all the three domains — cognitive, affective, and psychomotor — must be thoroughly considered.
3. The learning experiences should be organised in order of difficulty, *i.e.,* from simple to complex.
4. There should be provision for practical work so that 'learning by doing' may takes place in learning mathematics.
5. Content should be organised in logical as well as psychological order.
6. It should include content which helps in the appreciation of the work and contribution of great mathematicians.
7. Curriculum should consist of variety of physical and intellectual activities, necessary for proper adjustment to the physical and social environments.
8. Curriculum should be flexible and should fulfill the varying needs of the child and the society.
9. Child's needs, interests, abilities and capacities should be considered well.
10. It should solve the problems of livelihood of the child.
11. Oral work and home work should be given due importance with written work and drill work in mathematics.
12. Various topics and activities should form an integrated whole and should not remain isolated.
13. It should provide education for useful and meaningful utilisation of leisure time of the pupil.

The Kothari Commission (1964-66) suggested some important recommendations to eradicate the defects of the then existing curriculum. They are:

1. There should be periodical revision of curriculum.
2. School curriculum should be upgraded through research and advancement. University Department of Education, Training Institutions, Boards of School Education and State Institute of Execution should undertake it.
3. Schools should be given freedom to devise and experiment now curriculum which suited to their needs and interest.
4. The Subject Teachers' Association (STA) in different school subject should be formed so that it may help to stimulate experimentation and upgradation of the curriculum.

5. The preparation of text books and teaching material should be undertaken on a large scale.
6. Orientation programmes for teachers should be organised for revising the curriculum.
7. Curriculum should be child-centred and should develop the natural interest, aptitudes and capacities of child and satisfy his needs.
8. *At the Primary Stage*

   At present mathematics is divided into Arithmetic, Algebra and Geometry. This involves unnecessary repetition in teaching of fundamental operations with numbers. It is, therefore, most desirable and appropriate that the course in Arithmetic and Algebra be integrated and emphasis be placed on the principles and laws of mathematics and logical and psychological thinking.

   The syllabus should include development of number-system, system of numeration and notation, equations, groups and functions. Geometry course should be reorganised in a more rational manner.
9. *At the Secondary and Higher Secondary Level*
   (*a*) At present, mathematics syllabi are divided in the traditional manner into Arithmetic, Algebra, Geometry, Trigonometry, Statistics and co-ordinate Geometry. This needs to be revitalised and brought up-to-date.
   (*b*) The entire Arithmetic course as well as the basic operations in Algebra can be completed by the end of the primary stage.
   (*c*) There is considerable room for eliminating out-dated material from the syllabus. For example, simplification, factorisation, finding HCF and LCM, etc.
   (*d*) Trigonometry should be related to Algebra and may not be treated as a separate subject. Much of the work as trigonometrical identities, complicated problems on height and distances can be considerably cut down.
   (*e*) The emphasis on memorising the theorems and exercises in Geometry should be given up. The approach to the teaching of Geometry should be entirely changed. An axiomatic and systematic treatment be adopted.
10. Set language may be used in defining the basic terms in Geometry and operations with number-systems. Because, it is the set language which adequately integrates Arithmetic, Algebra and Geometry. Use of notations for lines, line-segments, rays, measures of angles, etc. provides for more precision in language. So, they should be adopted.

NCERT Document (2000) has also suggested a number of recommendations to improve the curriculum. Some of the major recommendations are given below:

Information and Communication Technologies (ICT) have begun to challenge what, all over the world, schools try to teach and also the whole basis of assessing the knowledge and skills that pupils acquire.

The process of education can no longer neglect the social and psychological impacts of the ICT. These technologies affect many people think and learn. This has been widely recognised.

Therefore, integration of ICT into schools is a natural sequence in the evolution of the schooling process. But this integration has several implications which clearly make the following demands:

1. The educational planners should update plans for education in an electronic environment and expand their design, so that the computer becomes more than a subject of study.

2. The educators should accept the following general principles:

(*a*) Creation of framework for enhancing learning opportunities that are offered by computer-based learning material and accessible resources.

(*b*) Flexible curriculum models which would embrace interdisciplinary and cross-disciplinary thinking.

(*c*) Development of attitudes that are value-driven and not technology-driven.

(*d*) Access to professional development opportunities for teachers which would enable them to act as facilitators of learning.

3. The curriculum framers should re-define their role. All innovative experiments in the areas of media production, interactive video and multimedia computer software help curriculum development processes.

4. The teacher should adopt an instructional design that helps learners to master heuristic and algorithmic strategies for using the computer and communication technologies, wherever possible.

5. The educators should evolve a method of evaluation of what students learn in ICT-rich environment supported by the computer and communication technologies.

For this, environment is going to bring awareness in the teaching world and it also is going to bring significant changes from:

(*a*) traditional learning atmosphere to a climate of values that encourages exploration, problem-solving and decision-making.

(*b*) traditional classroom teaching to participatory interactive group learning.

(*c*) competency in fixed body of knowledge to understanding a web of relation between the parts of a whole.

(*d*) collection of information to processing of information that leads to knowledge management skills.

6. A sound programme of vocational education requires extensive and broad-based preparation through work-education and pre-vocation education during the first ten years of formal schooling.

7. The management system for vocational education has to be developed in strength, structure and task delineation.

8. The teacher has to assume his/her new role as a facilitator of learning and implement and maintain innovations in the classroom. The new courses should help teachers to acquire skills of using information technology as well as making the best use of computer in curriculum transactions.

## EVALUATE YOURSELF

1. What is the need for the planning of curriculum?
2. What are the major stages of curriculum construction? Discuss their significance.
3. Explain the formation of objectives of curriculum.
4. What are the chief advantages of the formation of objectives of curriculum?
5. Enlist the principles of curriculum construction with respect to the selection of content. Discuss the principle of utility (practical) value.
6. Write short notes on:
   (*i*) Principle of logical and psychological order
   (*ii*) Principle of individual differences
7. Enlist the principles of curriculum construction with respect to the organisation of content. Discuss the principle of activity.
8. Explain the principle of topical arrangement. Discuss its merits and demerits.
9. Explain fully the principle of spiral arrangement. Discuss its merits and demerits.
10. Discuss the criteria of critical study and analysis of syllabus for a particular class.
11. What are the shortcomings of existing curriculum of mathematics?
12. Suggest the reforming steps of improving mathematics curriculum.
13. What procedure would you bear in mind while framing a curriculum of Mathematics as a member of the curriculum committee? Discuss.
14. Suggest some points to be kept in mind while critically evaluating a syllabus. Discuss fully.
15. 'The present day school curriculum in Mathematics has outlived its utility.' — Justify.
16. Does the present high school syllabus in your state come up to your ideals? What changes do you propose in it?
17. As a curriculum framer, what do you prefer — principle of topical arrangement or principle of spiral arrangement? Justify your views.

'Substantial changes in mathematical curriculum are long overdue. But a mere change of subject matter is not sufficient. A poor curriculum well taught is better than a good curriculum badly taught. A good curriculum well taught is the only acceptable goal.'

— ***Report of Commission of Mathematics***

# 6 THE CURRICULUM CONSTRUCTION: PROBLEMS, BASES, TYPES

## 6.1 Problems

Problems are indispensable in the study of mathematics. One cannot think of mathematics without problems. The teaching of any topic of mathematics cannot be completed successfully without dealing with problems connected to that topic. Therefore, while organising the curriculum of mathematics, the problems should be given their due place.

Mathematics, due to its nature, differs from other school subjects. Its study is meant for the development of logical thinking and reasoning. Problem-solving is a very good means to evoke and train logical thinking and reasoning. This will produce and overcome difficulties. The efforts to solve problems provide an opportunity of better understanding and also the application of learnt knowledge.

The presentation and arrangement of problems is the next step after the organisation of curriculum or syllabus. These problems should have bearing (*a*) on the subject matter, and (*b*) on the human life activities.

The practice in solving problems helps in developing —

(*a*) mathematical skills,

(*b*) habit of doing work with speed and accuracy, and

(*c*) the ability to apply mathematical facts in different types of situations.

The training in problem-solving enables the pupils to attack the problem in a right direction.

## 6.2 Types of Problems

There are various types of problems as given below.

### 1. Real Problems

Real problems are those which are true to life and are directly related to the actual life situations. The solving of real problems helps in training the child to face successfully various new and even unexpected situations in different walks of life.

In mathematics, real problems occupy a very important place. They help in the achievement of the aims and objectives of mathematics. Therefore, such type of problems be allotted a major share in the curriculum of mathematics, so that the opportunity of adequate practice may be available to the pupils.

*A few examples of real problems:*

1. Divide ₹ 120 between Krupa and Mira such that Krupa gets ₹ 10 more than what Mira gets.
2. The printed cost of a saree is ₹ 3,200. If the seller gives 15% discount, what will be the actual cost to be paid by Mrs. Kiran to the shop-keeper?
3. Find out the simple interest on ₹ 2,500 for 2 years at 8% per annum.
4. Gopal bought a cow for ₹ 4,500. Later on, as he needed some money, he sold it to Govind for ₹ 4,000. Find out Gopal's loss percentage.

## 2. Unreal Problems

The problems which have no relationship with real life situation and are presented only for the use of mathematical processes are called 'unreal problems.' The informations contained by such type of problems are false, misleading and do not happen in actual life situations.

So, the inclusion of such problems in mathematical is without any sound base. Yet, these are presented in mathematics as a test of comprehension of mathematical ideas and concepts. So, it is assumed that they are somehow helpful in the development of mathematical reasoning.

*A few examples of unreal problems:*

(1) If $\sin^2\theta + \cos^2\theta = 1$, prove that $\tan^2\theta + 1 = \sec^2\theta$

(2) If the cost of 3 sofas is the same as that of 2 chairs and that of 5 chairs is the same as that of 6 tables. If the cost of 5 tables is ₹ 10,000 then find the cost of a chair and the cost of a sofa.

(3) Divide ₹ 180 among Kishan, Kiran and Kshitij such that Kiran gets ₹ 10 more than what Kishan gets and Kshitij gets ₹ 50 more than what Kiran gets.

(4) Find three consecutive natural numbers whose some is 25.

## 3. Puzzle Problems

The problems which may puzzle the pupils' mind are known as 'puzzle problems.' The solution of these problems can be found out after much taxing of brain. Therefore, their solution demands much time, energy and patience. But their complication helps in maintaining the curiosity of the pupils.

These problems also offer an opportunity of drill in the mechanical operations of mathematics. Therefore, puzzle problems may be included in small numbers alongwith other types of exercises as some enthusiastic pupils will certainly show more interest in this type of problems.

These puzzle problems also serve the purpose of recreation and pass time because it is definitely difficult and also time taking in finding out their solution. Of course, puzzle problems cannot be made an integral part of mathematics, but for the development of interest and skills in mathematics, a few puzzle problems, for the recreation purpose may be included in the exercise work.

'Lilavati', the famous mathematics book written by great Indian mathematician Bhaskaracharya includes puzzle problems in great numbers.

### *A few examples of puzzle problems :*

*1. From Lilavati:* Two monkeys were sitting on a tree at a height of 100 ft. There was a tank at a distance of 200 ft. from the bottom of the tree. One monkey went to the tank after coming down vertically from the tree. The another monkey, after jumping some height above the tree, jumped on the tank in the direction of hypotenuse. If the distance covered by both the monkeys to reach the tank was the same, find out the height jumped by the second monkey above the tree. (*Ans: 50 ft.*)

2. *Magic Square:* Prepare a magic square of $3 \times 3$ with the numbers 11 to 19 such that the sum of the numbers in each column, each row and each diagonal is the same (*i.e.,* say 45).

## 4. Catch Problems

These problems whose solution can be achieved by catching or understanding the meaning of certain word(s) given in them, are called 'Catch Problems'. This means that these problems involve jugglery of words. If the pupil is able to catch or understand the hidden meaning of these words, he succeeds in solving the problem.

In catch problems the purpose is to test the mental alertness of the pupils. Therefore, to some extent catch problems are similar to puzzle problems. But they differ also in many ways.

### *Differences between puzzle problems and catch problems*

1. In a puzzle problem the pupil knows its nature and he understands that his mathematical skills are being tested through the complicated problems. But in a catch problem he is unaware of its exact nature. The pupil can solve the problem only when he could catch the meaning of the key words involved in the problem.
2. Puzzle problems are intricate, difficult and somewhat long, while catch problems are less intricate, less difficult and somewhat short.

### *Advantages*

1. The catch problems are more helpful in achieving objectives of teaching mathematics.
2. They are good for mental gymnastics and amusement.

### *Conclusion:*

This type of problems are useful if they are included in a limited numbers in mathematics.

### *A few examples of catch problems:*

1. Kshitij has triple money than what Vismay has. If Kshitij has ₹ 500 more, than what Vismay has, find the total money with them.
2. A pillar is 10 m high. An insect tries to go to the top of the pillar. But at a time it goes up 2 m and comes down 1 m. How many trials will it need to reach the top of the pillar?

## 6.3 Criteria for the Selection and Formulation of Problems

All the four types of problems — real, unreal, puzzle and catch — can be included in mathematics in proper proportions according to the needs and age-level of the pupils. But, sometimes unreal and undesirable problems occupy a greater proportion in mathematics due to ignorance of importance of types and nature of problems.

Therefore, while formulating the problems, the following points should be kept in mind by the teachers, book-writers, curriculum planners and mathematicians:

1. The problems should be —
   (*a*) real, interesting and enjoyable,
   (*b*) related with human life situations and activities,
   (*c*) helpful in the achievement of general aims of education,
   (*d*) in accordance with the levels of the pupils,
   (*e*) capable of realising the objectives of teaching mathematics,
   (*f*) presented in simple and understandable language,
   (*g*) based on historical background.
2. They should have some practical, social and environmental value.
3. They should pose a challenge to the intellect of pupils but they should be rational and capable of being solved with reasonable efforts.
4. They should form an indispensable basis for higher studies in mathematics and other vocations in future life.
5. Some problems may be borrowed from other subjects so that the correlation of these subjects can be established with mathematics.
6. In the presentation of problems, the maxim of 'simple to complex' should be followed.
7. There must be some provision of oral problems to be presented by teachers in the curriculum.

## 6.4 Important Bases of Curriculum Construction

There are four important bases of curriculum construction. They are:

### 1. Philosophical Basis

The construction of curriculum is done for realising aims and objectives of education. It should be according to the following philosophies:

(*1*) *Realism:* The philosophy of realism includes those activities in the curriculum through which knowledge can be obtained in real situations of life. In realistic curriculum subjects dealing with day-to-day activities are included. It is developed according to utility and needs of the pupils and the society.

(*2*) *Idealism:* The chief aim of curriculum assumes thoughts, eternal values and ideals of mankind. Idealism provides principal place to literature, art, music, etc., in curriculum. So, in idealistic curriculum humanistic subjects are emphasised.

(3) *Naturalism:* One of the major aims of education is 'the free development of individuality of child.' So, naturalists are supporters of providing unlimited freedom to the child for self-expression. In naturalistic curriculum science subjects occupy main place.

(4) *Pragmatism:* The main principle of construction of pragmatic curriculum is *utility*. It is based on subjects of utility. The construction of pragmatic curriculum is done according to interests of the child. The framers of curriculum build curriculum of elementary classes on the basis of curiosity, practical interest, sophisticated expression and mutual exchange of thoughts.

### 2. Psychological Basis

Psychological basis emphasises that —

(*a*) the child is the centre of education so both education and curriculum is meant for the child.

(*b*) the education of the child should be based upon psychological methods and principles.

According to this base, formulation of curriculum should be done according to the child's interest, natural tendencies, requirements, abilities and capacities. Hence, child should be imparted education according to his abilities and capacities.

### 3. Sociological Basis

The main aim of social tendency is to develop society and to make it progressive. According to this base, those subjects and activities are included in the curriculum which provide help in developing appreciation of sociability. This tendency emphasises inclusion of social qualities in children so that they contribute their best to social welfare, upliftment and advancement.

### 4. Scientific Basis

According to this base, more importance is given to the scientific subjects in the curriculum. Its supporters hold the view that it is only after the study of scientific subjects that the whole mankind can lead a complete life. It promotes scientific attitude towards life and society. So, naturally, it opposes literary education. It proposes practical and useful knowledge.

## 6.5 Types of Curriculum in Mathematics

There are various types of curriculum in mathematics. Some important ones are discussed below:

### 1. Subject-centred Curriculum

(1) It is based upon a clear specific ideology of education and sociability. But it is unpsychological in nature as it pays no consideration to the needs, interests, abilities, capacities and attitude of the child.

(2) It gives more emphasis on subject matter instead of the child. Only subject matter is the primary thinking. Thus, it emphasises bookish knowledge and learning. Its content is definite, fixed and predetermined.

(3) It can achieve an effective correlation among various subjects. It facilitates testing and examination. But it cannot lead to wholesome development of the personality of the child.

## 2. Experience-centred Curriculum

(1) In experience-centred curriculum, experiences of the child are regarded as more important for the development of a child in comparison with emphasis on subject-matter and activities.

(2) It is flexible and progressive. Its base is democratic. Therefore, it is psychological in nature as it also takes into consideration the needs, interests, abilities and capacities, attitude, etc. of the child.

(3) It can establish a close relationship between the school and the society. It also develops a sense of self-discipline and qualities of leadership. But this can be done only when the teachers are very capable and intelligent for the implementation of this type of curriculum. No doubt, its evaluation is comparatively difficult.

## 3. Craft-centred Curriculum

(1) In this type of curriculum, emphasis is given on the training of various crafts, like spinning, weaving, woodwork, leather work, paper work, etc.

(2) Our country is the most significant example of craft-centred curriculum.

## 4. Core-Curriculum

(1) In core curriculum some subjects are grouped together as essential and compulsory subjects and many other subjects are kept optional.

(2) Study of compulsory subjects is necessary for all children and out of the optional or elective subjects, a child is free to select one or more subjects according to his needs, interests and abilities.

(3) The core-curriculum is child-centred and gives practice and experiences to solve social problems. Thus, it aims to develop both — the individual and the society.

(4) Thus, according to it so many subjects are taught together and the child becomes dynamic, efficient in work and socially useful individual.

## 5. Activity-centred Curriculum
## 6. Child-centred Curriculum
## 7. Correlated Curriculum

[For detail, please, refer to Ch. No. 5]

## EVALUATE YOURSELF

1. Which are different types of problems in the study of mathematics?
2. Explain the real problems and unreal problems with giving suitable examples.
3. What do you mean by puzzle problems? Give suitable examples.
4. Explain he criteria for the selection and formulation of problems.
5. Discuss fully the bases of curriculum construction.
6. Explain the various types of curriculum in Mathematics.

❊ ❊ ❊

# THE PLACE OF MATHEMATICS IN SCHOOL CURRICULUM

## 7.1 Why to learn Mathematics?

The knowledge of mathematics is indispensable for us. It is impossible to achieve success in life without the knowledge of mathematics, mathematical approach and application. The scientific and technological progress is totally based on the progress of mathematics.

John Becon has very clearly pointed out — 'Mathematics is the gate and key of the sciences.... He who is ignorant of it cannot know the other sciences.'

Hoghen stated — 'Mathematics is the mirror of civilization.' This clearly indicates the place of mathematics in human life.

Kothari Commission also remarked — 'Science and mathematics should be taught on a compulsory basis to all students as a part of general education during the first ten years of schooling. In addition, there should be provision of special courses in these subjects at the Secondary Stage for students of more than average ability.

## 7.2 The Place of Mathematics in Ancient Period

From ancient period too, mathematics has got a higher and valuable place in educational system of all the countries of the world.

Plato, a Greek philosopher and mathematician, had put a board on the gate of his residence with a note — 'Let no one destitute of Geometry enter my doors.'

In India, mathematics has found a place in curriculum. During Vedic period, post vedic period and period of Buddhism, mathematics had a higher position among the various subjects of the education of that time.

Mahaviracharya, a great Indian Jain mathematician rightly remarked in his book 'Ganit Saar Sangraha' — 'Mathematics is very useful in all public, vedic and social acts. It is widely used in economics, science of cooking, music, dramatic, arts, architecture, ayurveda, sexology, poetics, prosody, logic, grammar, astronomy, astrology, etc.... existence of anything in this universe is not possible without mathematics.'

In medieval period also mathematics was a compulsory subject in the process of education. During British Rule in India, teaching of mathematics was compulsory. Now-a-days it is a compulsory subject for all the pupils upto SSC Examination. Thus, mathematics was always a part and parcel of school curriculum.

## 7.3 Why is Mathematics an Important School Subject?

Without mathematics nothing could be existed. It is the result of the efforts of great mathematicians philosophers, thinkers, logicians and educationists that mathematics has got a highest status.

The following are the main reasons why mathematics should be an important school subject.

### 1. *Relation with Human Life*

Mathematics is related to every aspects of human life. For example, food, clothes and shelter are the three fundamental needs of man. To fulfill these needs a person seeks activities and vocations. Some larger vocations like engineering, banking, accountancy, architecture, business, etc., are directly linked with mathematics. Other smaller vocations like tailoring, carpentry, farming, vendoring, etc., make a wide use of Arithmetic and Geometry. What to say, even housewives prepare monthly budget or daily marketing. For that, knowledge of mathematics is a must. Our modern civilization is, indeed, based on mathematics.

### 2. *Bases of All Sciences*

Mathematics is the bases of all sciences. Modern age is the age of science and technology. The advancement of science and technology and also that of fine arts (music, dancing, painting, etc.), economics, psychology, social sciences and literature is due to progress of knowledge and skills of mathematics.

In Biological researches also Bio-statistics is used. Without mathematics all these sciences do not exist.

### 3. *An Exact Science*

Mathematics is a very exact science. The interpretation and conclusions of mathematics are always definite, clear, precise and exact. For example,

(1) In ten-based system the sum of 3 and 4 is always 7, no more no less.

(2) Two perpendicular lines intersect always at $90^o$.

(3) tan 45 is equal to 1, and no other number.

(4) Triangle is always a closed figure.

### 4. *Promotes Logical Thinking*

Mathematics develops logical thanking. In mathematical disposition, every step has its logical reason. For example,

(1) $4a + a = 5a$ as $4 + 1 = 5$

(2) $a \times a = a^2$ as $1 \times 1 = 1$ (*i.e.*, $1^2$)

(3) $a^3 \times a^2 = a^5$ as $(a \times a \times a) \times (a \times a) = a^5$

(4) $3 \times 2 = 6$ as 3 times $2 = 2 + 2 + 2 = 6$

$2 \times 3 = 6$ as 2 times $3 = 3 + 3 = 6$

The logical thinking helps in the mental development of the child. The logical thinking also provides a definite way of thinking which involves a definite sequence of truth. For example, in Geometry while proving a theorem not only logical thinking but a definite sequence also is necessary.

### 5. *Bright Future*

Those who understand and can do mathematics well, will have significantly enhanced opportunities and options that will open gates to productive bright future. Those who lack mathematical competence and skills will find many gates closed and they will find their future unproductive and unsuccessful.

## 7.4 Mathematics as a Compulsory Subject

Everybody needs some knowledge of mathematics to lead his life successfully. Of course, for an ordinary man the mathematical knowledge of primary and middle school level may be quite sufficient to cope with his needs.

So, there is no dispute to make mathematics a compulsory subject upto middle school curriculum. But there is a great controversy among the educationists over making it compulsory at high school and higher secondary stage.

Why should mathematics be compulsory or optional at high school stage? There are various arguments in favour and in against of both.

## 7.5 Arguments against Mathematics as a Compulsory Subject

There has been wide criticism of making mathematics a compulsory subject upto S.S.C. Examination. Some of the arguments are presented below:

### 1. *Difficult subject*

One of the most used argument about mathematics is that it is an exceptionally difficult subject. The students having average ability are unable to grasp it and assimilate it.

The pass percentage of high school examination in mathematics is very low compared to other subjects of the school curriculum.

It is a belief — wrong or right — that every pupil does not have the competency to learn it successfully because its study requires high IQ (Intelligence Quotient) and special abilities. So, why should everybody be burdened to learn it as a compulsory subject?

Therefore, this exceptionally difficult subject should be optional at each level for every pupil.

### 2. *Disciplines the mind — A myth*

It is not the correct view that the study of mathematics disciplines the mind and helps in developing mental powers. In support of this view, one can argue that the students studying subjects other than mathematics have not always inferior mental faculties compared to those who study mathematics. Most of the Principals of high schools are Arts graduate! How can one dare to say that the poets and poetesses like Ragindra Nath Tagore and Sarojini Naidu and the authors of novels and short stories and philosophers like Radhakrishnan and many of the spiritual thinkers have non-disciplined minds?

### 3. *Base for Future Studies — A false belief*

It is a wrong belief that the study of mathematics helps in learning other subjects at school stage and proves a base for their learning in future. Its study has no correlation and if any, then negative coefficient of correlation with other subjects except Science and Technology. As far as its study is concerned, no transfer of training is possible for learning other subjects.

Mathematics is useful to those students who desire to study higher mathematics or sciences at post-school stage. But those who would like to study Politics, History, Sociology or languages in future should not be forced to study mathematics at the high school stage.

### 4. *No Bread and Butter Value*

On the basis that mathematics has bread and butter value, it cannot be made compulsory. Of course, the study of mathematics is useful in some vocations like engineering, banking, statistical methods, accountancy, surveying, computer science, astronomy, astrology, etc., but only a little percentage of students opt for these specialised courses, or these professions. There are only few highly specialised courses which need advanced-level knowledge of mathematics.

Then, why should all the students be bothered and burdened by making mathematics a compulsory subject?

### 5. *No Utility in Day-to-Day life*

There is no doubt that the mathematical knowledge is required for our day-to-day transactions of money. But is it necessary to study mathematics upto SSC Examination? For our day-to-day purpose, mathematical knowledge upto seventh standard is quite sufficient. And that can be achieved in a few years of schooling. But what we learn upto SSC Examination, much of its mathematical knowledge is divorced from our actual life. What is the use of learning expansion, factorisation, HCF. LCM, quadratic equations, etc. in our day-to-day life?

### 6. *Dull and Boring Subject*

Generally, students regard mathematics as a dull and boring subject. Only a very few students have natural aptitude and genuine interest in mathematics. So, it is unpsychological to make mathematics compulsory to those who do not at all wish to study it.

### 7. *Cause of Stagnation and Wastage*

If one studies and analyses the problem of stagnation and wastage in the high school stage, one will find that most of the students stagnate in SSC Examination due to compulsory mathematics as they have no interest and ability to study mathematics required for it. It will be interesting to know the number of students appearing at SSC Examination and the number of those joining the eleventh standard.

### 8. *Policy of Developed Countries*

In most of the developed countries of the world, mathematics is compulsory only upto middle school stage. Then, why in India, a developing country, should we make mathematics compulsory upto SSC Examination?

In short, mathematics should be an optional subject at the high school stage.

## 7.6 Arguments in Favour of Mathematics as a Compulsory Subject

An intensive study and analysis of the above arguments can reveal their absurdity. The following arguments are in favour of keeping mathematics as a compulsory subject at high school stage:

1. Mathematics is not at all a difficult subject. How can a discipline which is closely related to every aspect of human life and which induces logical thinking, which provides a definite way of thinking and which is exact in its nature, be difficult?

   Perhaps it is a pre-made terror and disgust by parents and others which adversely affects the child's attitude towards mathematics. Actually mathematics is not difficult but has been imagined difficult by the teacher's wrong methods of teaching and the faulty arrangement of the curriculum in mathematics by the curriculum framers.

   Actually, mathematics should be presented as a recreational activity for the child from the very beginning. For example, generally, the teacher asks the students to memorise $3 \times 2 = 6$ (multiplication tables). Actually the teacher should say — 'dear pupils, suppose you have 3 shirts of different designs and 2 pants of different designs. In how many different ways can you wear them so that no two ways should be the same?' The pupils will enjoy and remember the fact and will not find mathematics a difficult subject.

2. Mathematics is the art of all arts and science of all sciences. The plea that those who are going to study or use mathematics at the post-school stage should only be made to study it at the high school stage, is also incorrect. How can one decide, who is going to become engineer, lawyer, politician or statistician in his life, quite so early after passing middle stage examination?

   So, it will be unwise to block the path of one's progress by making the study of mathematics optional at the high school stage.

   It is better to keep open all the gates of knowledge by making the study of mathematics compulsory at the entire school stage, so that pupils may get a broader scope for the choice of subjects and vocations for him and not to experience or feel regret for his early choice.

   Specifically in our country where most of the parents are illiterate it is not worthwhile and justifiable to seek diversification at the middle school stage.

3. It is also argued that every high school student is not going to become an engineer, or lawyer or statistician, etc. But at an early stage, it is very difficult to know who is going to become an engineer, a lawyer, a pilot, etc. Then why should the student be deprived of the opportunities to get for the wide choice of vocations or the higher studies? So, upto at least high school stage, mathematics should be a compulsory subject.

   The ignorance of mathematical knowledge may prove a great handicap in the advanced studies of various subjects which may create a hurdle in the progress of a pupil.

The exclusion of mathematics at the high school level will make it incomplete and in comprehensive. At this level, there is no substitute for mathematics.

4. Mathematics does help in training and disciplining the mind. It develops the power of thinking and reasoning. It also gives mental exercises for strengthening the faculties of the mind.

   Young rightly remarks — 'Mathematics is the only subject that encourages and develops logical thinking. It enables the pupils to discriminate between essentials and non-essentials.

5. One cannot deny the bread and butter value of mathematics. Mathematics helps everybody in earning and also in wisely spending.

   In the modern era of science and technology, almost all the vocations have been dominated by the knowledge and skills of science and technology. Mathematics helps in learning this essential knowledge and skills. Thus, its study earns a valuable place in one's life.

6. To some extent it is justified that school mathematics is divorced from actual life. What we teach in a school has a little practical value.

   But, it is quite unfair to blame the subject for such sort of affairs. Our defective methods of teaching and inadequate approaches are mainly responsible for divorcing it away from the necessities of life. To a certain extent, the curriculum framers are also no less responsible for such situation.

   It is also unwise to say that all what we need in our life in terms of mathematical knowledge can be easily learnt by studying mathematics upto middle school stage. Today life has become more complicated, so we need more mathematics to understand and adjust to the demands of life.

7. Mathematics is not dull and uninteresting. No subject is dull and uninteresting in itself. Much depends upon –

   (1) the will and interest of the learner,

   (2) the teachers, the prescribed curriculum and methods of teaching.

   Those who love mathematics take it as a very interesting and pleasant subject. It is difficult, dull and uninteresting to only those who simply do not want to study it or cannot work regularly and systematically.

   For example, how interesting the number-systems are! Take the perfect square numbers. They are 1, 4, 9, 16, 25, 36, 49, 64, 81, 100, 121, ... Have you ever studied the differences between the two consecutive perfect numbers? They are 3, 5, 7, 9, 11, 13, 15, 17, 19, 21, ... All odd consecutive numbers! The pupils will really find mathematics a very interesting subject. It depends upon the teacher. If he brings such wonderful things to the notice of the pupils, they will really enjoy mathematics.

   Mathematics by virtue of its artistic and aesthetic value is quite interesting and useful.

8. The argument that the study of mathematics requires specific ability and intelligence seems to be irrelevant. Because abilities can be achieved and trained and 'intelligence' has not yet been accurately defined. 'Intelligence' is an undefined term in Psychology.

Psychologists from the whole world, once, gathered at Paris in a symposium to accurately define the term 'intelligence.' After rigorous discussion, for hours, at last a psychologist stated — "Intelligence is what intelligence is!"

There is a dictum that — "It is not intelligence but industry that makes a man genius." And mathematics certainly helps students to be industrious.

9. The emphasis of our basic education is on the learning of 3 R's *i.e.,* reading, writing and arithmetic. This combination reflects on the needs of human life. This means arithmetic (mathematics) is not less important than the other two types of learning.

   In fact, there can be no true schooling without mathematics.

10. One common notion which is frequently repeated is that mathematics should be optional for girls at high school stage. This has been accepted and implemented by most of the Indian States.

    The argument behind this notion is that in future most of the girls have to indulge in the role of housewives. After middle school education they should be given the education of home science, tailoring, knitting, drawing, music, painting, toy-making, etc., in place of mathematics. No doubt, these subjects are suitable by nature for girls but these subjects do not have their end at high school stage. The above cited subjects require a good knowledge of mathematics for their study and expertness. So, they should be given an important place in higher education.

    It will be more useful for girls if they are equipped with the knowledge of mathematics at least upto high school stage. It should be compulsory even for girls.

11. Let us not blindly imitate foreign countries. In those countries, mathematics is compulsory only upto 8th standard. But the standard of mathematics teaching is quite higher than that in our country. What their students study upto 8th standard is more than what our students study upto 10th standard.

    There are also more adequate facilities and opportunities for guidance and counselling in those countries. Parents of the pupils are also well educated. So, in those countries after middle school stage, the pupils enjoy greater advantages in choosing the subject and planning for their career in comparison to our country.

## Conclusion

Now-a-days educationists feel that for minimum requirements of common people, education of mathematics, upto middle school stage is quite insufficient. Therefore, general compulsory education must be extended upto SSC course. This extension includes more content in compulsory disciplines like literature, social sciences, science and technology and mathematics.

Thus, mathematics should be given a prominent place and its study should be made compulsory upto SSC course in 10 + 2 system of education.

## EVALUATE YOURSELF

1. 'Mathematics should be a compulsory subject upto high school level' — How far do you agree with this statement?
2. What is the place of mathematics in the present day school curriculum?
3. 'Mathematics is an important school subject.' — Justify this statement.
4. Comment on — 'Should mathematics be a compulsory or optional subject in our high school classes?'
5. Write short notes on:
   (1) The place of mathematics in ancient period.
   (2) Mathematics — as an interesting subject.
6. Why is mathematics an important school subject? Explain.
7. Discuss the arguments against mathematics as a compulsory subject at high school stage.
8. Discuss the arguments in favour of mathematics as a compulsory subject at high school stage.
9. 'Mathematics is not at all a difficult subject.' — How far do you agree with this statement?
10. 'It is not intelligence but industry that makes a man genius.' — Comment in support of this statement.

'Mathematics is the predominant science of our time, its conquests grow daily, though without noise, he who does not employ it for himself, will one day find it employed against himself.'

***— J.F. Herbart***

# TEACHING MATHEMATICS

## 8.1 What is Teaching Math?

Teaching mathematics in schools is an extremely difficult task. It will challenge the best efforts of the best teachers. It requires much more than a thorough knowledge of the content of mathematics.

For professionally prepared mathematics, teacher two aspects are equally important. They are:

(1) Significant knowledge of mathematics, and

(2) Suitable and effective technology for teaching mathematics.

So, a truly functional programme of professional preparation must emphasise on —

(1) The acquiring of knowledge of mathematics, and

(2) The acquaintance with and use of the more efficient technologies of teaching mathematics.

Teaching of mathematics demands skill in the technique of teaching each particular topic or aspect of the subject in —

(1) developing generalised concepts,

(2) co-ordinating generalisation with applications,

(3) discriminating between essential and non-essential matters within the subject,

(4) knowing where to place emphasis and where to anticipate difficulties,

(5) detecting difficulties when they do occur and sensing their precise nature,

(6) knowing how to help the pupils to avoid or overcome their difficulties.

The analysis of the instructional problems involved in the teaching of any topic in mathematics divides logically into the following considerations:

(*a*) Background of experiences of the pupils before he starts to study the topic.

(*b*) Understanding expected from the pupils before he starts to study the topic.

(*c*) Particular understanding or abilities the pupils should acquire or strengthen through the study of the topic.

(*d*) Activities and procedures that enable the pupils most effectively to gain the desired understanding and abilities.

(*e*) Specific difficulties to be expected from the pupils to encounter in his effort to acquire these understanding and abilities.

(*f*) Specific suggestions, devices and procedures that help the pupils most effectively to overcome these specific difficulties.

(*g*) Materials and procedures related to the particular topic that will best stimulate and maintain the pupils' interest.

According to J.B. Show (1918) — There are four significant methods of teaching mathematics. They are —

(1) *Scientific Method:* Leading to generalisations of widening scope.

(2) *Intuitive Method:* Leading to an insight into subtler depths.

(3) *Deductive Method:* Leading to a permanent statement in rigorous form.

(4) *Inventive Method:* Leading to an ideal element and creation of new realms.

## 8.2 Purposes of teaching mathematics

(1) Mathematics is one of the compulsory subjects of Primary and Secondary Education. The main aim of teaching mathematics at the primary and secondary level is —

(*i*) to train the mind, and

(*ii*) to develop the power of understanding and critical thinking among the pupils.

(2) According to National Committee on Mathematical Requirements —

> 'The primary purpose of teaching mathematics should be to develop those powers of understanding and of analysing relationships of quantity and space which are necessary: (*a*) to have an insight into and a control over an environment, (*b*) to have an appreciation of the progress of civilisation in its various aspects, and (c) to develop habits of thought and of action which will make these powers effective in the life of an individual.'

## 8.3 Processes of teaching mathematics

Current researches clearly points out that 'How mathematics is taught is more important than the mathematical concepts being taught.'

A deep conceptual understanding is the foundation upon which mathematical proficiency, factual knowledge and procedural skills are built.

National Council of Teachers of Mathematics identified five procedures that highlight ways of acquiring and using knowledge of mathematical content. They are: (1) Problem solving (2) Reasoning and proof (3) Communication (4) Connections (5) Representation.

## 1. *Problem Solving*

The teacher should —

(1) Select and use appropriate methods of computing. *e.g.*, mental computation, estimation, paper and pencil, calculator or computer, etc.

(2) propose detailed analysis and assessment, and value alternative approaches to solving problems.

(3) extend mathematical knowledge by considering the thinking strategies of others.

(4) reflect and evaluate mathematical thinking processes used in solving problems.

(5) utilise different problem solving strategies like drawing a diagram, choosing an appropriate operation, eliminating possibilities, guessing and checking, etc.

(6) develop clarification and understanding of new mathematical concepts, processes and vocabulary.

(7) solve a variety of multi-step, non-routine, complex problems including puzzles, applications, open-ended or extended problem-solving projects.

(8) estimate solutions to problems and determine the reasonableness of answers by relating them to the estimates.

## 2. *Reasoning and Proof*

The teacher should —

(1) link problem solving to the sequence of steps in a proof and draw reasonable conclusions.

(2) explain and justify problem-solving procedures.

(3) examine patterns and note regularities and irregularities in various types of problems.

(4) make and investigate mathematical incomplete/unproven information.

(5) formulate counter examples.

(6) use a variety of formal and informal proofs appropriate to the course.

(7) identify information as necessary, sufficient or extraneous and conclusions as valid or invalid.

## 3. *Communication*

The teacher should —

(1) express mathematical ideas coherently and clearly.

(2) employ precise language and notation of mathematics to express mathematical ideas clearly.

(3) organise and consolidate mathematical thinking using communication methods like group discussion, oral presentations, written reports, etc.

## 4. *Connections*

The teacher should —

(1) formulate real-world situations that require extended investigations, solve them and justify answers.

(2) establish connections among mathematical expressions, real-world situations, physical models, pictorial representations.

(3) find applications of mathematical concepts in newspapers, magazines, TV, radio, etc.

(4) explore historical and multicultural contributions to mathematics.

(5) recognise and apply mathematical ideas and relationships in areas outside the mathematics classroom, *e.g.,* art, science, other curricular areas and everyday life.

*5. Representation*

The teacher should —

(1) use a variety of visual representations like graph papers, patty paper, dot paper, models, etc., to explore and formulate conjections related to mathematical concepts being studied.

(2) represent mathematical concepts using physical models, visualisations, appropriate symbolic notations, etc.

(3) represent problem situations verbally, numerically, graphically, geometrically or algebraically.

## 8.4 Importance or Value of Teaching Mathematics

Why should everybody learn mathematics? Why should it be a compulsory subject in school curriculum? What is the advantage of doing so much labour in teaching and learning mathematics? The following pages will give the answers of these questions.

Teaching of mathematics has the following values:

### 1. Utilitarian/Practical Value

(1) Mathematics is an important subject in school curriculum. No other subject of school curriculum can surpass mathematics as far as the utilitarian value of mathematics is concerned.

(2) It is more closely related to our daily life as compared to other subjects. Mathematics is needed by all of us — big or small, rich or poor, younger or older, man or woman — in every sphere of our life. Our daily life and bahaviour is totally dependent on mathematics. Not a single aspect of our life is free from its use. Every one of us uses some mathematics directly or indirectly in every form of our life. *e.g.,*

(*a*) One has to get up at right time to be able to join his duties at the right time. All such things need measurement (such as distance-speed-time) which can be possible only through mathematics.

(*b*) A house-wife also needs mathematics for: (*i*) preparing good dishes, (*ii*) looking after her house, (*iii*) preparing monthly family budget and estimates, (*iv*) writing various expenses, and (*v*) noting down so many household transactions.

(*c*) Right from the big industrial houses, traders, business firms, engineers and bankers — mathematics is utilised even by petty shopkeepers, small carpenters, labourers, humble coolies, workers, drivers, vendors, salesmen, housemaids, not only for earning the livelihood but also to spend wisely and save for future, however little the amount may be.

(*d*) We need the knowledge of mathematics (*i*) in classifying and understanding every fact, (*ii*) in our daily routine in house, outside market, income-expenditure, etc.

(3) Mathematics has bread and butter value, too. The vocations now cease to be empirical, handled down from one generation to another. One has to choose and train oneself in one or the other vocation. With the advent of modern technology, mathematics has been a live wire for one's contact to an occupation.

The base of any vocation, however big or small it may be, is essentially economical or mathematical. Therefore, the knowledge of mathematics is capable of opening new gates to so many vocations.

(4) Mathematics is the base of all the essential knowledge and progress in science and technology. It is not only useful for different branches of science but also helps in their progress and organisation. Knowledge of mathematics is an essential prerequisite to the study of other sciences.

Bacon has rightly said, "Mathematics is the gate and key of the sciences."

Guilford (1954) observed, "The progress and maturity of a science are often judged by the extent to which it has succeeded in the use of mathematics."

What we enjoy today in our life as a result of scientific inventions, has only been possible with the aid of mathematics. So, there is a greater weight in Young's (1937) saying,

> "Whenever we turn in these days of iron, steam and electricity, we find that mathematics has been the pioneer, were its backbone removed, our material civilisation would inevitably collapsed. Modern thought and belief would have been altogether different, had mathematics not made the various sciences exact."

In the report of Education Commission (1964-66) it is rightly pointed out that the study of mathematics plays a prominent role in modern education:

> "One of the outstanding characteristics of scientific culture is quantification. Mathematics, therefore, assumes a prominent position in modern education. Apart from its role in the growth of the physical sciences, it is now playing an increasingly important part in the development of biological sciences. The advent of automation and cybernetics in this country marks the beginning of now scientific industrial revolution and makes it all the more imperative to devote special attention to the study of mathematics. Proper foundations in the knowledge of the subject should be laid at school."

We cannot safely and economically use scientific inventions without the aid of mathematics.

(5) Our calendars and watches will be helpless if mathematics ceases to work for them. Our cartographers will not be able to draw maps and our meteorologists will not be able to foretell rain and weather conditions in case they give up mathematics.

(6) Mathematical knowledge is indispensable in understanding and controlling the forces of Nature. Even the stars, the sun, the planets, the moon are bound to move as mathematics directs. This view point is shared by John Perry (1902) when he says —"In these days, all men ought to study natural sciences. Such a study is practically impossible without the knowledge of higher mathematical methods."

(7) Mathematics found its way into agriculture and the production in the farm output has shot up. To achieve self-sufficiency in food and other farm-products in the highly specialised fields like geometric survey, aerial mapping, communication and machine designs, mathematics has placed an essentially important part.

(8) In the absence of mathematics, any sort of accounts, insurance, banking and entire business systems would be paralysed. All engineering will come to a halt. We would not have houses to live in, bridges to cross the river, dams and tunnels for watering the fields and producing electricity.

Thus, mathematics is responsible for giving us a system organisation and essential abilities for leading a successful life. We would remain too much handicapped in our life, in case, we remain ignorant of mathematics.

(9) Economics, Philosophy and many other areas are mathematically oriented. Political Science and Logic are regarded as sciences only in so far as they are mathematical.

(10) Mathematics is the indispensable tool of precision in measures involving quantity, time and space. The ultimate concept of space travel, the harnessing of hidden sources of energy from other space, newer and greater use of atomic energy, automation, electronic devices and such other developments serve only a few illustrations of the greater demand for scientific and mathematical advent.

(11) Its importance is next to that of mathematics teaching. People can go along without their mathematics teaching but not without calculation. Mathematics is responsible for the advent of instruments such as calculators, computers, etc.

- The knowledge of fundamental processes of mathematics and the skill to use them are the preliminary requirement of a human being in any society of modern time.
- One cannot lead his daily life activities very well without basic knowledge of mathematics.

⏩ A common man can do well various activities without learning how to read and write but he can never pull on without learning how to count and calculate.

(12) The study of mathematics helps —

(*i*) in giving accurate and reliable knowledge,

(*ii*) in solving problems of our life,

(*iii*) in disclosing the realm of Nature,

(*iv*) in proper understanding of the Nature's work and complicated problems of life by converting them into the language of signs and symbols,

(*v*) in acquisition of desirable attitudes and ideals,

(*vi*) in acquisition of knowledge and skills,

(*vii*) in imbibing so many virtues and good habits.

(13) Study of mathematics is useful to inculcate all values of life such as utilitarian, social, moral, aesthetic, intellectual, disciplinary, cultural, international values.

## 2. Social values

(1) Mathematics is a subject of great social value. There is never been a greater need to be mathematically literate than in our more rapidly expanding society and economy. Mathematics plays a vital role in the economic and social development of a country because it is the basis for all sciences and technology.

(2) The harmony, law and order and dynamicity prevailed in our society are all because of mathematics.

(3) The world transactions, exchange, commercial trades and business depend on mathematics.

(4) Mathematics is essential to citizenship competence.

(5) One can lead a normal social life only when he is able to adjust himself in the existing social set up. Today our social set up is totally governed by the scientific and technical knowledge which can be attained only by study of mathematics in the democratic society like ours, it is very important that a citizen be competent in making wise decisions.

(6) The economy of any state or society, business, administration, transportation, agriculture, exchange, commercial trades, communication and so many scientific inventions and discoveries that have knitted the world into a family owe their existence to mathematics.

The famous great Napoleon once stated, "The progress and improvement of mathematics is linked to the prosperity of the State."

(7) The history of mathematics openly reveals that whenever a country has given due weightage to the teaching of mathematics, it has made a tremendous progress. Whatever progress and development in the world are, all due to mathematics.

(8) Mathematics throughout the ages has been claimed as a factor in the development of human personality.

(9) In the present social set up, mathematics is more important for the common man. In this age of rates, taxes, insurance premia, savings and interests, rents and propaganda, only a person with good mathematical background can be reasonably sure that he is getting his due.

(10) Mathematics helps in the proper organisation and maintenance of our social structure. Society is the result of the union of individuals. It needs various laws, morals and traditions for its existence.

(11) The journey to moon has been possible only through the concrete principles of mathematics.

(12) Mathematics helps in developing the child into social and intellectual citizens.

In this connection Kothari Commission (1964-66) suggested, "Science and mathematics should be taught on a compulsory basis to all pupils as a part of general education during first ten years of schooling."

## 3. Moral values

(1) Study of mathematics does help in character formation and moral development. What is needed in a man of strong character is not only germination but also nourishment through the teaching of mathematics.

(2) The qualities like self-confidence, self-reliance, self-respect, truthfulness, self-control, honesty, cleanliness, justice, punctuality, dutifulness, patience, purity of thoughts, respect for other's opinion, discrimination between good and bad, brevity and simplicity in the expression of thoughts, observation of rules, belief in the systematic organisation and arrangement, preciseness, firmness, etc., which definitely contribute towards a strong character are automatically inculcated through the teaching of mathematics.

(3) Gradually, the study of mathematics bring such changes in the pupil of mathematics that he becomes almost free from vices of hatredness, envy, jealousy, telling a lie, contempt towards other's views, etc.

(4) It helps in developing proper moral attitudes as there is no place for prejudiced feeling, biased attitude, doubtfulness and half-truths in the solutions of problems in mathematics.

(5) Metzler rightly remarked — "Work must be either right or wrong and if wrong, the mistake must be discovered."

In mathematics right is right and wrong is wrong forever. It cannot be both — right and wrong at the same time.

(6) Dutton rightly said, "Mathematics does furnish the power for deliberate thought and accurate statements and to speak the truth... Gossip, flattery, slander deceipt — all speak from a slovenly mind that has not been trained by mathematics."

## 4. Aesthetic/Artistic Value

(1) Who says that mathematics is a dry, hard, laborious and uninteresting subject? Only those, who have heard from their elders and have got no proper opportunities to study mathematics, say so.

In reality, for the lover of mathematics, there is all beauty, art, music and fineness in mathematics. Mathematics is the creator, nourisher and saviour of all the arts. What we enjoy in the arts like drawing, painting, dancing, music, architecture, etc., is all due to mathematics.

(2) The fundamental of any music is in the systematisation of octave (sā, re, ga, ma, pa, dhā, ni, sā) which requires the knowledge of mathematics. Music is nothing but mathematically organised and systematised sound. All the musical instruments are played on the set rules of mathematics.

According to Leibnitz — "Music is the modern hidden exercise in Arithmetic of a mind unconscious of dealing with numbers."

(3) Even the poetry is not enjoyable without mathematics. In poetry, the formation of 'metre' is totally based on mathematics. Different types of metre have different but certain numbers of letters with their specific weight in each step.

(4) One finds a huge treasure of pleasure after getting success in solving a mathematical problem. It was the reason why Archimedes, Pythagoras, Ramanujan and many other mathematicians got feeling of ownership and self-confidence when they succeeded after a long struggle in a mathematical problem.

(5) Mathematical regularity, symmetry, similarity, order and arrangement play a leading part in beautifying and organising the work of these arts.

The secret of beauty of a garden or an ornament or a flower-pot lies in the hands of the arrangement made with the help of mathematics.

(6) In dancing too, one has to take care of mathematics in taking steps and responding the tunes.

(7) Mathematics also entertains us with its own riddles, puzzles, games, etc.

(8) Mathematics helps in developing the sense of appreciation among children.

## 5. Intellectual Value

(1) The study of mathematics develops all our intellectual powers like concentration, precision, originality, observation, memorisation, innovation, imagination, invention, creativity, logical thinking, systematised reasoning, etc.

(2) No research can be carried out without the knowledge of mathematics. It is the basis for all scientific and technical researches.

Indian Education Commission (1966) has pointed out — "we cannot overstress the importance of mathematics in relation to science education and research. This has also been so, but at no time has the significance of mathematics being greater than today.... It is important that deliberate effort is made to place India to the world map of mathematics, within the next two decades or so."

Compte (1964) stressed mathematics as the foundation of scientific education — "All scientific education which does not commence with mathematics is necessarily defective at its foundation."

(3) Every problem in mathematics is an open challenge to the faculties of the mind and a systematic organised exercise for one's mental health.

Plato once said — "Mathematics is the subject which provides an opportunity for training of the mind to close thinking, stirring up a sleeping and uninstructed spirit."

(4) Every problem in mathematics passes through a process that trains an individual in the scientific method of thinking and reasoning, *i.e.,*

(*a*) to know what is given and what is to be found out,

(*b*) to collect all the relevant facts and techniques concerning the solution of the problem,

(*c*) to analyse them carefully and sorted out for choosing the most suitable ones,

(*d*) with the help of these, to reach on some conclusion,

(*e*) to verify the derived conclusions and accept only when they prove true.

(5) Mathematical knowledge, it is said, is doubling every ten years. So, the important thing is, not to acquire such ocean of knowledge but to learn *how* to acquire knowledge, *i.e.,* one should aim to acquire the power of acquiring knowledge. This knowledge is useful only when we know how to apply it in solving our problems.

Prof. Schultze rightly said — "Mathematics is primarily taught on account of the mental training it affords and only secondarily on account of the knowledge of facts it imparts."

Therefore, the power of acquiring knowledge and skill to apply it at the hour of need — is only aimed through the teaching of mathematics.

(6) Hubsch — "Mathematics is like a wheatstone and by its study one learns to think distinctly, consecutively and carefully."

(7) Mathematics provides opportunities for the intellectual gymnastics of man's inherent powers and mental abilities.

(8) Mathematics helps —

(*a*) in drawing necessary conclusions,

(*b*) in interpreting various ideas and themes with useful meaning,

(*c*) in developing the ability of induction, deduction and generalisation,

(*d*) in developing scientific attitude among children,

(*e*) in giving the training of scientific methods to the children,

(*f*) in acquisition of intellectual habits of reasoning and thinking.

## 6. Disciplinary Value

(1) Disciplinary value of mathematics is a broader form of intellectual value. Learning of mathematics makes a person disciplined in his life. It equips a person with proper intellect, reasoning and seriousness needed to lead a responsible life. Therefore, the mind trained through the study of mathematics is more capable of leading a well-disciplined life.

(2) Mathematics by its very nature helps the pupils to imbibe so many virtues and good habits like simplicity, exactness, accuracy, concentration, hard working, punctuality, regularity, neatness, cleanliness, orderliness, certainty of results, originality, verifiability of results, habit of paying attention, etc.

(3) These habits go on a long way to train the pupils in leading a life, full of self-restraint and reasoning. Thus, a mind trained by mathematics is more disciplined than that not being trained by mathematics.

(4) Mathematics helps in constructive discipline. Every pupil of mathematics is habituated to think without prejudices and biases.

(5) A pupil of mathematics can discriminate what is good and what is bad, what is right and what is wrong, what is essential and what is non-essential, what is desirable and what is undesirable.

He does not take decision through his emotion but tries to apply logic and intellect. He does not believe hearsaying but tries to investigate the thing before reaching it.

(6) Discipline of mind generates the peculiar power of thinking, reasoning, innovating and decision-making in the learner which enables him to face any new situation in future in a disciplined manner.

## 7. Cultural Value

(1) Cultural value aims at the understanding of culture, civilisation and the world, in a mathematical way. In the development of our civilisation, mathematics has played a major role.

Mathematics is developed according to the necessities of human beings and, in turn, helped them to overcome difficulties in the way of their progress. Thus, the prosperity and cultural advancement of a society has been mostly depended upon the progress of mathematics.

Hogben has rightly remarked — "Mathematics is the mirror of civilisation and the emperor of the whole academic world."

(2) By culture of a state/nation/society we mean the mode of living of its inhabitants. The culture is reflected through how they live, behave, eat, drink and maintain their mutual social relationship.

(3) The scientific discoveries are to a great extent responsible for bringing changes in the mode of living of human being. And those discoveries owe their roots in mathematics. Thus, the progress and improvement of mathematics has continuously influenced the culture, *i.e.,* the progress in culture and civilisation is due to that in mathematics.

(4) Mathematics acquaint us with the culture and civilisation and helps in its preservation, promotion and transmission to the coming generation.

Thus, knowledge of mathematics increases our cultural heritage which is passed to the younger generation through the teaching of mathematics. So, our precious and valued heritage *viz.,* ancient painting, architecture, sculpture, classical music, poetry, drawing and design-making have been preserved in the form of mathematical knowledge.

(5) Mathematics shapes the culture. The advancement of various occupations such as engineering, medicine, industry, transportation, communication, agriculture, etc. builds up our culture due to the progress of mathematics.

The modern materialistic attitude of individuals in our country is also the outcome of impact of mathematics on human life and culture.

Books are the chief sources of acquainting us with the past achievements of one's race and culture of humanity at large. Math text books also contain treasure of our culture that can only be known by laying emphasis on Math teaching.

(6) Mathematics is the backbone of our culture and civilisation. What we have in our modern culture and civilisation owes its debt to science and technology which in turn depend upon mathematics.

The history of mathematics portrays culture and civilisation of different countries at different periods. The greatness of Indian culture is once reflected through the glory of Indian mathematicians.

(7) Newsom (1951) rightly stated — "I believe that mathematics when conceived in its broadest sense, is an indispensable tool in a complex world. Our citizens, specially in a democracy must posses competence in making wise decisions. They must understand the origins of the existing knowledge and expansion of that knowledge."

The mathematics has been a pioneer in adjusting with the progress of culture and civilisation and also in its advancement.

## 8. International Value

(1) Mathematics has international value as it is helpful in creating international understanding and brotherhood. Mathematics has made it self-sufficient for its existence and progress.

(2) What we have in mathematics today is the result of the combined efforts of all the nations and races in the world.

(3) We all human beings — the inhabitants of all nations, the followers of all the religions and members of all the races — are the same, as far as the potential of knowledge and intellectual development is concerned. And therefore, it is unwise to think superior or inferior to any of the other race, culture or nation.

(4) All mathematicians, whatsoever may be their caste, colour or creed, have generously contributed to the progress of mathematics.

(5) There is a continuous flow of teachers, researchers and mathematicians from one nation to another for the exchange of scientific and mathematical ideas. The research magazines, journals and periodicals as well as books on mathematics are exchanged and circulated among almost all the nations of the world.

(6) A new idea brought in the field of mathematics does not take much time to become an international property.

## 9. Economical Value

(1) A person should be economical in different walks of life. The art of economical living should not be confined only to financial matters. In the modern age, economy of time is the most valuable. We should not waste our time in gossiping, wandering uselessly, attending useless ceremonies for hours or days, joining rallies and processions aimlessly. Studying mathematics saves us from all these useless activities and keeps us busy in useful and meaningful work.

(2) Mathematics helps to a great extent in developing the art of economical living. It is the most suitable subject for inculcating the spirit of economy in matters of money, time, speech and thought. Mathematics helps in developing the attitude of economical living. The learning of art of economical living is a by-product of the learning of mathematics.

## 10. Scientific Value

(1) Scientific and technological progress entirely depends upon extensive use of mathematics. The creative powers of mind is developed by solving complicated problems of mathematics, and is used for further study.

(2) Higher mathematical studies lead towards new innovations and develop attitude of discovery and invention among the pupils. No new scientific work or discovery of invention can be had without the knowledge of mathematics. No scientific research is possible without the application of the knowledge of mathematics.

## 11. Concentrative Value

(1) Study of mathematics require high concentration. Without wholehearted concentration mathematics cannot be learnt, as it needs attention at every step. It induces concentration in the mind of learner.

(2) Concentration is a habit of mind. Continuous practice helps in acquiring it. Mathematics develops this habit.

Hamilton rightly stated — “The study of mathematics cures the vice of mental distraction and cultivates the habit of continuous attention.”

## 12. Expressive Value

The study of mathematics develops the habit of expressing ideas in clear, brief, precise, accurate and exact manner. Such expression has a great importance in our day-to-day life.

The knowledge of mathematics insists a person to be extremely careful and attentive in expressing his ideas by selecting and using appropriate words, phrases and terms.

## EVALUATE YOURSELF

1. What do you mean by teaching mathematics?
2. What are the processes of teaching mathematics?
3. Why should be mathematics taught and learnt?
4. Write short notes on:
   (*a*) Utilitarian value of teaching mathematics.
   (*b*) Disciplinary value of teaching mathematics.
   (*c*) Cultural value of teaching mathematics.
5. 'The study of mathematics is of great value for every common man of modern age.' — Discuss it from utilitarian point of view.
6. 'Mathematics is the gateway and key to all sciences.' — Explain with examples.
7. 'From a great businessman to an humble coolie, everybody makes use of mathematics, directly or indirectly.' Comment.
8. 'For the lover of mathematics there is all beauty, art, music and fineness in mathematics' — Discuss this statement from the aesthetic value of teaching mathematics.
9. Explain the social values of mathematics.
10. 'All scientific education which does not commence with mathematics is necessarily defective at its foundation.' — Comment.
11. Discuss in detail the disciplinary value of mathematics.
12. What is the cultural value of mathematics? Explain fully.
13. How does mathematics help in establishing international relationship? Discuss.
14. Explain the importance of mathematics in daily life.
15. Write short notes on:
   (1) Nature of mathematics
   (2) Moral values of mathematics
   (3) Economical values of mathematics.

> 'We must not treat mathematics as a game of manipulating arbitrary symbols but as a product of human societies whose members co-operate socially to advance civilisation and culture. This means that mathematics has sociological, psychological, pragmatic and empirical aspects besides the synthetical aspect with which alone the positivists seem to be concerned.'
>
> — ***Jagjit Singh***

# AIMS & OBJECTIVES OF TEACHING MATH

- All the subjects taught in the schools have their own identity, importance and educational values.
  - The educational value of a subject is established by goals/aims (both are taken as synonymous terms) which are achieved by through the study of the subject.
  - This means, each subject has certain goals/aims of teaching.
  - The achievement of goal is ascertained by testing the pupil's performance at the end of the course/session.
  - Thus, goal/aim is a target situated somewhere at a distance *i.e.,* in future.

## 9.1 Aims of Teaching Mathematics

- On the basis of educational values of mathematics, the aims of teaching of mathematics can be easily established.
  - There are three main aims of mathematics teaching:

    (1) Utilitarian aim, (2) Disciplinary aim, (3) Cultural aim.
  - There are some general aims of teaching mathematics also:

    (1) Aesthetic aim (2) Moral aim (3) Social aim (4) Intellectual aim (5) Vocational aim (6) Psychological aim (7) Self-learning aim (8) Pre-preparational aim (9) International aim (10) Recreational aim.

## 9.2 What are Objectives

- An objective is a point or an end-view of the possible achievement in terms of what a pupil is to be able to do when the whole educational system is directed towards educational aims.

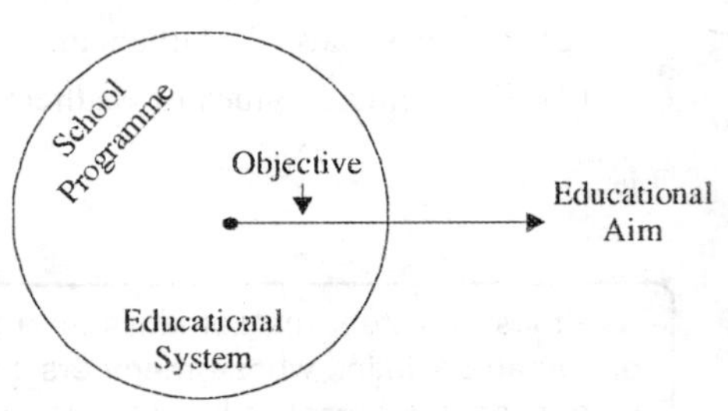

- An objective is a point or an end-point or end-views towards which an action is diverted. It is a planned change sought through any activity, what we set out to do.
- The statement of objective contains a non-behavioural (non-active) verb, such as understand, appreciate, etc.
- The term 'specifications', 'specific objective' and 'behavioural objective' are synonymous.
- The statement of specification contains a behavioural (action) verb, such as write, read, draw, etc.

## 9.3 Relation between Aims and Objectives

| *Aims* | *Objectives* |
|---|---|
| 1. Aims are the directions in education. | 1. Objective is an end-view of the possible achievement. |
| 2. Achievement of aims is beyond the scope of school programme | 2. Objectives can be achieved during school programme. |
| 3. They are subjective. | 3. They are objective. |
| 4. They are formal | 4. They are informal and informative. |
| 5. They cannot be changed for subject to subject | 5. They may be changed for subject to subject. |
| 6. Aim is a broader and comprehensive term and has a wider range. | 6. Objective is a narrower term and has limited range. |
| 7. So, aims do not help in selecting the appropriate content of the subject. | 7. So, objectives help in selecting the proper contents and proper day-to-day activity. |
| 8. Aims are to be realised with the help of objectives. | 8. Objectives originated from aims. |
| 9. Being broader and wider, they become meaningless in day-to-day work | 9. Being specific and narrower, objectives become meaningful. |
| 10. Social philosophy is the source of aims. | 10. Psychology is the source of objectives. |
| 11. Aims includes objectives. | 11. Objectives are a part of aims. Objectives help to reach up to the aims. |
| 12. They can be achieved after a long period. | 12. They can be achieved in a short-period. |
| 13. Educational aims are concerned with all subjects taught to the child. | 13. Teaching objectives of different subjects may be different. |
| 14. Aims are not very clear and definite. | 14. Objectives are clear and definite. |
| 15. School, society and nation are accountable for achievement of aims. | 15. Teacher is accountable for achievement of objectives. |
| 16. They are theoretical and indirect. | 16. They are direct and concerned with the teaching-learning process. |
| 17. They are related with whole educational system and whole curriculum. | 17. They are related with the teaching of any specific topic. |
| 18. Aims are very difficult to evaluate. | 18. Objectives can be easily evaluated. |

## 9.4 Objectives of Mathematics

### (A) Classroom Instructional Objectives

1. The pupil acquires *knowledge* of mathematical terms, concepts, facts, symbols, definitions, laws.

### Specifications

(*i*) The pupil *recognises*...

the names of the parts of a triangle, Pythagorean law, the diagram of a circle, definition of an angle, the members of a set, commutative property.

(*ii*) The pupil *recalls*...

(*a*) definitions such as finite set, parallel lines, similarity, congruence, equation, open sentence;

(*b*) the names of concepts such as LCM, set, number, line, plane, betweenness;

(*c*) the names of parts of a triangle, polygon, polyhedron;

(*d*) the names of properties like commutative, associative, and properties of adjacent angles; etc.

2. The pupil develops an *understanding* of mathematical terms, facts, definitions, concepts, properties, laws, relationships, theories, procedures.

### Specifications

(*i*) The pupil *discriminates between*...

(*a*) an acute angle and an obtuse angle;

(*b*) a linear equation and a quadratic one;

(*c*) a finite set and an infinite one;

(*d*) a prism and a cylinder.

(*ii*) The pupil *sees a relationship*...

(*a*) between similarity and symmetry;

(*b*) between indices and logarithms;

(*c*) between sin $\theta$ and cos $\theta$.

(*iii*) The pupil *selects*...

(*a*) appropriate instruments to draw a triangle of given measures;

(*b*) an appropriate method to factorise a given expression;

(*c*) an appropriate property to solve an example.

(*iv*) The pupil *compares*...

(*a*) parallel lines and skew lines;

(*b*) equal sets and equivalent sets;

(*c*) the properties of natural numbers with those of real numbers.

(*v*) The pupil *classifies...*

(*a*) the given points into interior points and exterior points with respect to a given triangle;

(*b*) the given sets into convex sets and non-convex sets;

(*c*) the angles into alternate angles, corresponding angles and interior angles.

(*vi*) The pupil *cites illustrations...*

(*a*) of symmetric figures;

(*b*) of open sentences;

(*c*) of equal sets;

(*d*) of a binomial.

(*vii*) The pupil *detects errors...*

(*a*) in statements like "Similar figures are always congruent";

(*b*) in wrongly presented venn diagrams;

(*c*) in formulae; *e.g.*, area of a rectangle = $l/b$;

(*d*) in a given example; *e.g.*, factorise: $(x - y)^3$

(*viii*) The pupil *rectifies errors...*

in a given statement, diagram, formula, example; *e.g.*, Area of a rectangle = $l + b$.

(*ix*) The pupil *generalises...*

(*a*) that profit = S.P. – C.P.

(*b*) that the sum of the measures of the angles of a triangle is 180;

(*c*) that the modulus of a number is always a positive number.

(*x*) The pupil *verifies...*

(*a*) the answer by substituting the values in a given problem or equation;

(*b*) the answer by drawing a graph.

(*xi*) The pupil *uses an appropriate method...*

(*a*) to work out a problem;

(*b*) to solve a rider.

3. The pupil *applies his knowledge and understanding* in new and unfamiliar situations.

## Specifications

(*i*) The pupil *analyses...*

(*a*) the given example into what is given and what is to be found out;

(*b*) the given enunciation of a theorem into what is given and what is to be proved;

(*c*) the given problem or rider into a sequence of steps to be followed.

(*ii*) The pupil *formulates hypothesis...*

(*a*) that "if congruent figures are always similar, then similar figures may always be congruent".

(*b*) that "a circle is a convex set."

(*iii*) The pupil *collects*...

relevant data about a hypothesis; *e.g.*,

(*a*) What are the properties of congruent figures? of similar figures? Are they the same?

(*b*) What is a circle? Does the segment determined by two points of a circle entirely lie on a given circle?

(*iv*) The pupil *selects*...

relevant data, *i.e.*, facts and principles for a particular situation; *e.g.*, when the measures of two sides of a right triangle are given, he selects the Pythagorean principle to find out the measure of the third side.

(*v*) The pupil *judges*...

the adequacy of data or procedure or apparatus; *e.g.*,

(*a*) to draw a triangle, he needs at least three measures;

(*b*) to find out the volume of a cylinder one has to have its height;

(*c*) to locate a point on a plane, its *x*-coordinate and *y-coordinate* are required.

(*vi*) The pupil *verifies*...

a hypothesis, based on collected data:

(*a*) the answer by substituting values in a given problem or equation;

(*b*) the answer by drawing a graph.

(*vii*) The pupil *suggests*...

(*a*) an appropriate figure to solve a rider;

(*b*) a new illustration of a non-convex set;

(*c*) a new method of solving a problem or a rider;

(*d*) how to locate an irrational number on a number line.

(*viii*) The pupil *predicts*...

(*a*) that a triangle having two obtuse angles is an impossibility;

(*b*) that in a triangle, if $l$ (AB) = 8, $l$ (BC) = 10, $l$ (CA) = 6, then, the triangle is a right-angled triangle.

(*ix*) The pupil *solves*...

new problems on factorisation, new riders, new constructions.

(*x*) The pupil *gives reasons*...

for every step; *e.g.*,

(*a*) $5 + 3 = 3 + 5$ (commutative property);

(*b*) $\Delta ABC \cong \Delta DEF$ (SAS)

(*c*) $a + 0 = 25$

$\therefore$ $a = 25$ (0, additive identity).

(*xi*) The pupil *interprets*...

a given chart, table; *e.g.*,

(*a*) a chart showing the multiplication of two negative numbers on a number line;

(*b*) a logarithm table;

(*c*) a graph of simultaneous equations;

(*d*) a graph of $2x - 3 > 10$.

(*xii*) The pupil *translates*...

(*a*) verbal statements into mathematical terms, symbols and functions; *e.g.*, five, when added to three, makes eight. $3 + 5 = 8$;

(*b*) a given truth set into a graph;

(*c*) a given problem into an equation.

4. The pupil develops the *practical skills* required in the study of Mathematics.

## Specifications

(*i*) The pupil *checks*...

mathematical instruments before he uses them;

(*ii*) The pupil *rectifies*...

the defects in the instruments; *e.g.*,

(*a*) the leg of a pair of compass;

(*b*) the setting of the apparatus; *e.g.* setting protractor for measuring angles, setting ruler for measuring segments.

(*iii*) The pupil *sets up*...

appropriate apparatus for drawing parallel lines, measuring lengths of segments, drawing a circle.

(*iv*) The pupil *measures*...

with reasonable accuracy, the height, the radius, the circumference.

(*v*) The pupil *reads*...

(*a*) graphs of equations;

(*b*) a pie-diagram showing the proportion of colours in the white ray;

(*c*) the abbreviations of trigonometrical ratios; *e.g.*, tan $\theta$ is tangent $\theta$.

(*d*) the mathematical symbols such as $\cong$, $\subset$, $\phi$, correctly;

(*e*) the logarithmic and trigonometric tables correctly.

(*vi*) The pupil *records*...

the observations accurately and neatly.

(*vii*) The pupil *makes accurate observations* ...

while reading graphs, tables.

(*viii*) The pupil *uses the data*...

which is relevant; *e.g.,* To find the area of the floor of a room whose length is 4 m., breadth 3 m. and height 2.5m., the height is not to be used.

(*ix*) The pupil *sketches*...

(*a*) simple diagrams involving directions and distances;

(*b*) diagrams of problems involving directions, distances and trigonometric functions.

(*x*) The pupil *draws*...

(*a*) a number line;

(*b*) graphs: linear, parabola;

(*c*) figures for theorems and riders.

(*xi*) The pupil *summarises observations*...

after an experimental approach; he summarises: "The sum of measures of the three angles of a triangle is 180°."

## (B) Personality Objectives

5. The pupil develops an *interest* in Mathematics.

## Specifications

The pupil, *on his own*...

(*i*) *reads*...

(*a*) funny stories, problems concerned with Mathematics;

(*b*) books, magazines, newspapers, etc., giving mathematical information; *e.g., Mathematics Today;*

(*c*) journals of research articles on Mathematics;

(*d*) biographies of mathematicians;

(*ii*) *visits*...

places of mathematical interest and importance; *e.g.,* an observatory, laboratories, statistical departments;

(*iii*) *participates*...

in activities like talks, debates, mathematical projects in or outside the school; *e.g.,* "Modern Mathematics — A Necessity," "Mathematics and Life";

(*iv*) *collects*...

pictures, stamps, specimens, photographs, data, etc., of mathematical importance; *e.g.,* specimens of leaves having symmetry, photographs of mathematicians, a picture of pyramid;

(*v*) *prepares*...

models, charts, pictures, having a mathematical significance, *e.g.,* a chart showing how to locate irrational numbers on a number line, models of polyhedrons, such as prisms, cubes, etc., graphs showing SSC results of previous years;

(*vi*) *contributes exhibits...*

concerning mathematical matters for a display organised in or outside the school; *e.g.*, exhibits showing clock arithmetic, charts showing various base systems, various types of sets, venn diagrams;

(*vii*) *writes...*

articles, news items, etc., pertaining to the subject-matter of Mathematics; *e.g.*, writes on "Logical approach in Modern Mathematics", "Why Modern mathematics?"

(*viii*) *prefers to attend to...*

programmes concerned with mathematics released on TV, radio;

(*ix*) *takes up hobbies...*

of a mathematical nature; *e.g.*, forming magic squares, gathering a quiz related to mathematics;

(*x*) *meets...*

scholars of mathematics whenever possible;

(*xi*) *helps...*

in the maintenance of a mathematics laboratory, museum.

6. The pupil develops a positive mathematical *attitude*.

## Specifications

The pupil,

(*i*) *respects...*

(*a*) research findings or new approaches contrary to the existing theory; *e.g.*, a circle and its circumference are not the same; a 'point' is an undefined term; set theory; topology;

(*b*) statistical information and interpretation;

(*ii*) *accepts...*

only those suggestions which are based on conclusions derived from mathematical calculations and logical reasoning;

(*iii*) *expresses...*

(*a*) his ideas by using mathematical examples clearly and precisely;

(*b*) his ideas in a logical sequence;

(*c*) his arguments giving reasons for each one of them;

(*iv*) *arrives at judgements...*

after weighing all possible evidences carefully and dispassionately;

(*v*) *considers...*

(*a*) new ideas, discoveries, inventions, free from prejudice;

(*b*) quantitative aspects of a given problem;

(*vi*) *reconsiders...*

his own judgements and beliefs in the light of new knowledge and theories;

(*vii*) *cooperates...*

with others in arranging mathematical models, charts, apparatus, materials, etc., in their proper places while working in the mathematics laboratory;

(*viii*) *faces...*

problems with full confidence.

7. The pupil *appreciates* the contribution of mathematics in all fields of knowledge and life.

## Specifications

The pupil,

(*i*) *expresses...*

(*a*) his realisation of the importance of mathematics in the progress of sciences and human culture;

(*b*) his appreciation of man's effort to conquer nature and natural forces;

(*c*) his appreciation of discoveries and inventions in any part of the world;

(*d*) his pride in man's heritage, mathematics being a legacy of the past and a gift of the present.

(*ii*) *recognises...*

(*a*) the contribution of mathematicians to the fund of knowledge of mathematics;

(*b*) the work of international agencies in this field;

(*c*) the mathematical aspects evident in the nature;

(*iii*) *derives a sense of pleasure...*

(*a*) in understanding the achievement of mathematics; *e.g.*, interplanetary travel, atomic energy and explosion, computers and their control of satellites, contribution of mathematics to the advancement of science and technology;

(*b*) when considering the underlying mathematical principles;

*e.g.*, Nature's arrangement of symmetry in the shape of leaves, in the shape of the butterflies;

(*c*) in understanding the beauty of similarity, congruency, symmetry and balance in figures, decorations and in the natural set-up;

(*d*) in the company of students who are good at mathematics.

## EVALUATE YOURSELF

1. State the objectives of teaching mathematics. Specify each objective in terms of at least three specifications.
2. Establish the relationship between aims and objectives.
3. What is the utility of knowledge of objectives to a mathematics teacher?

4. Write short notes on:

   (1) Objectives of mathematics (2) Specifications of objectives of mathematics.
5. What is the need of writing objectives in behavioural terms?
6. What are the major aims of teaching mathematics in schools?
7. Illustrate how the objectives of a particular topic of instruction in mathematics can be expressed in terms of behavioural changes.
8. State the objectives of teaching the following topics in mathematics and specify each objective in terms of at least three specifications.

   (*a*) Parallel lines (Std. VIII) (*b*) Similarity (Std. X) (*c*) Congruency (Std. IX).
9. 'The pupil develops an interest in Mathematics' — Give at least three specifications.

The universe is a product of a Thinker, thinking mathematically.

***— Ford Kelvin***

# 10 PLANNING FOR EFFECTIVE TEACHING AND LEARNING

## 10.1 Why to Plan?

- No part of the work of mathematics teacher is of more importance than the planning of his work.
- Teaching in mathematics aims at certain outcomes/objectives.
  - The likelihood of attaining the objectives will depend, in large measure, on how well it is planned.
- It is not altogether unnatural that many teachers give far too little attention to careful planning because the heavy instructional load which most teachers carry, together with the various co-curricular responsibilities, leave them with little time for reflective consideration of anything but the pressing demands of the moment.
  - Careful planning is the only insurance which teachers can provide against waste and inefficiency in their work.
- The establishment of a sound programme of mathematical education involves both general and specific considerations.

  (1) If the broad general aims are to be realised, comprehensive long-range planning must be done.

  (2) On the other hand, actual teaching takes place in individual classroom and this requires specific and detailed planning day-by-day.
- There are three main levels/stages of planning:

## I. Long-range Planning

- Actually planning for the mathematical education of the pupils begins with the planning of the curriculum.

    - Here, decisions are made at least w.r.t. due courses which are to be offered and here policies are established for the counselling and guidance of pupils w.r.t. the courses offered.

- The teacher of mathematics should have a voice in the decisions which are reached at this stage of planning.
    - They should be given the privilege and responsibility of making recommendations. Weight should be given to their recommendations.
- Mathematics teacher, better than anyone else, can be aware of the educational implications of various programmes. Mathematics courses and their well-considered judgements can be influential in the establishment of sound mathematical programmes in the school.
- Long-range planning also includes rough lay-out of the work for an entire year/semester. This involves —

    (1) a survey of all the work to be covered,

    (2) the organisation of this work in terms of chapters/units,

    (3) the assembling of these into what appears to be the most appropriate sequence,

    (4) the determination of approximate time allotments, and

    (5) allocation of time for review and tests,

    (6) the formulation of a general testing programme for the year/semester.
- A general broad layout of this nature is valuable because —

    (1) it necessitates the consideration of the various units of the subject matter from the standpoint of their relative values, and

    (2) it provides an approximate schedule for the work, by means of which progress may be regulated and a balanced emphasis maintained.
- In the absence of such a schedule an unusually large amount of time is sometimes spent on the earlier parts of a course and the later parts of the work are likely to receive hasty and superficial treatment.
- The plan for the year/semester should generally include the list of units to be studied, with the time schedule given by weeks.
    - Such an outline provides the teacher with a standard of reference at all times, and by frequently checking actual progress against this reference schedule it is possible to maintain a fairly uniform and balanced rate of progress.

## II. Provision for Individual Differences (as a stage in planning)

- It is axiomatic that if instruction is to be really effective, it must reach the individual pupils and promote their learning as individuals and individuals differ greatly in their interest and abilities.
- The problem of adapting instruction to individual differences has existed whenever and wherever the group receiving instruction has consisted of more than one pupil.
- The problem itself has become much more acute and pressing than it was before.

- The always questionable practice of giving identical instruction to all pupils in an unselected group has become more questionable than ever.
- If the instruction for the group is geared to a level which will challenge the abilities of the better pupils than pupils of mediocre ability will miss much of it and will tend to lose interest or will resort to memorising, while the inferior pupils will soon fall hopelessly behind and become discouraged.
- On the other hand, if the instruction in adapted to the limited abilities of the slow learner, then the superior pupils will soon lose interest because the work will not challenge their best efforts.
- In either case, the situation will result in inefficient instruction and it may easily become a fertile breeding ground for serious disciplinary problems, discontent and loss of interest, because the work will not challenge their best efforts.

- It is now recognised that the only effective method of meeting this educational dilemma is through differentiation of instruction and requirements to provide learning activities appropriate to the capacities of the pupils.
- This attempt to provide for individual differences among pupils through approximately differentiated courses represents a phase of planning. Indeed, it touches all stages of planning.
  - It finds its broadest manifestation in the long-range considerations that guide curriculum planning.
- This attempt to provide for individual differences has taken a number of forms such as —

  (*a*) Ability (or homogeneous) grouping

  (*b*) Differentiated assignment

  (*c*) Directed (supervised) study

  (*d*) Programmed learning

  (*e*) Micro-teaching

  (*f*) Individual instruction

## (a) *Ability (or Homogeneous) Grouping*

- The plan which most people have come to associate most readily with provision for individual differences is the arrangement generally called 'Ability (or Homogeneous) grouping.'
- As the name implies, it consists essentially in grouping the pupils in such a way that disparities in the abilities/interest within a given group will be reduced as far as possible.
- The great objection to the traditional miscellaneous grouping has been that instruction generally becomes geared to some one level of ability, to the consequent disadvantage of all pupils whose abilities are either above or below that particular level.
- There have been numerous adaptations of the plan but the basic principles and *modus operandi* (way of doing something, way of operating) are well-defined.
- Increasing reliance is being placed upon supplementing these indexes of general intelligence by other considerations, such as the expressed desires of the pupils and their parents,

prognostic tests, marks in previous courses in mathematics, reading ability and teachers' estimates of probable success in subsequent mathematics courses.

- Certainly the employment of any pattern of homogeneous grouping would represent a phase of planning and would require a great deal of careful thought.
- Specific objectives and units of study would have to be agreed upon and set up.
- Time allotments would have to be established.
- The criteria that would govern the placement of pupils in various courses/sections would have to be worked out.
- Thus, pre-planning is importantly involved here all along the line w.r.t. policy and administrative procedures as well as to the objectives and details of the various courses/ sections.

## *(b) Differentiated Assignments*

- The foregoing discussion has centred on long-range/broad scale plans for providing appropriate learning activities for varying interests and abilities.
- The devices of differentiated curriculums and homogeneous grouping represent means through which, at least in parts, the attainment of this objective may be facilitated.
- One method of adapting instruction to individual capacities and interest within a class is the use of differentiated assignment for pupils whose abilities and rates of work are not alike.
- This plan has met with favour because —

  (1) it can be used even in schools which are too small to permit homogeneous grouping.

  (2) it has much to commend it from the standpoint of instructional effectiveness.
- Two methods of providing differentiated assignments, which are in common use may be called —

  (1) the contract type of assignment

  (2) the multiple-level type of assignment.

## *(1) The Contract Type of Assignment*

- Under the contract type of assignment, each unit of work is organised in such a way that the accomplishment required for a bare passing grade is specified as the minimum contract which all pupils are required to execute.
- Other contracts containing additional work of a more difficult nature are set up as requirements for successively higher marks.
  - Each successive contract being gauged to a higher level of accomplishment than the preceding one.
- The contract plan is exceedingly definite in specifying the requirements for each grade/ mark, so pupils can know at any time about where they stand.

### *Disadvantages*

(1) Superior pupils are generally required to execute all the details of the minimum contract before passing on to the higher ones and often much of the work of the minimum contact

is rather simple and monotonous/uninteresting routine which fails to interest/challenge the more capable pupils.

(2) The preparation of the various contracts in suitable form for the pupils to use and the large amount of record keeping which is necessary, place a severe burden of extra-work on the teacher and may thus impair his effectiveness in the actual instructional work.

### (2) *The Multiple-level type of Assignment*

- The contract plan is but one method of providing for individual differences within a class.
- Another method which is somewhat less stereotyped but which is used more widely is the 'multiple-level' type of assignment.
- This approach emphasises quality and caliber of achievement rather than more quantity.
  - Its aim is not so much to provide detailed specifications of requirements for the various marks as it is to provide assignments appropriate in nature and difficulty to the abilities of the individual pupils.
  - In most cases, it is easier to administer than the contract plan. And it avoids some of the objections to that plan.
- There is much to be said in favour of this method of differentiated assignments and most of the recent text-books in secondary school mathematics recognise its potential value by including numerous topics, problems and exercises designated as being optional but suitable for pupils of more than average ability.
  - Some text books go so far as classify all the exercises and problems into three categories of difficulty, to correspond to the three-way classification customarily employed in homogeneous grouping.

### (c) *Directed Study & Individual Differences*

- Directed study offers a third means of providing for individual differences among pupils.
- This is one of its functions and it operates towards this end in two ways:

  (1) It provides a means through which all pupils may work at their own individual optimum rates whereby conditions are provided that are favourable to the exercise and development of initiative and of individual abilities for independent work.

  (2) It provides conditions under which those pupils who find themselves in need of help may secure such help at the time when they need it and directly from the teacher.
- There are enough experimental evidences that the less capable pupils are generally benefitted under a programme of direct study. But the brighter pupils tend to do less well than they do under the traditional plan.
- The whole movement for taking care of individual differences, of which direct duty is a part, has been from the beginning, primarily concerned with the welfare of the weaker pupils.
- The technique of directed study as it is generally conducted is a technique which stresses assistance by the teacher.
  - Be keep in mind continually in order that the superior pupils as well as those who are less capable should profit under the plan.

- If the plan is to work successfully for all, it will be necessary to administer it through differential techniques adapted to the needs of pupils of different degrees of ability.

## *Other Plans for providing for Individual Differences*

- The use of the enrichment units, for superior pupils, contribute materially towards attainment of the objectives for which they are designed.
    - They, at the same time, do not interfere with mastery of the basic material of the course.
- The group of superior pupils, using the enrichment units, show better achievement than the group of superior pupils who do not have the enrichment units.
    - Even the non-superior pupils show higher achievement in the classes, where the superior pupils are given enrichment units, than the non-superior pupils do in classes where the enrichment units are not used.
- This kind of special provision for superior pupils is administratively feasible and it can operate to the advantage of all the pupils.

## *(d) & (e) For programmed learning and micro-teaching refer to Ch. No. 24, 25.*

## *Role of Prognosis and Diagnosis in providing for Individual Differences*

- General problem of providing for individual differences, deserve special consideration.
    - This is a pre-determination or rather pre-estimation of the probable success of pupils in their mathematical work and the consequent guidance of these pupils in the selection of courses.
    - The subsequent identification of difficulties and the provision of remedial measures designed to obviate or minimise these difficulties and to set the pupils on the way to successful accomplishment.
    - The role of prognosis has been implied in part in the discussion of ability grouping, but the whole discussion of providing for individual differences would be incomplete if it do not include specific consideration of the functions of both — prognosis and diagnosis — under their implied techniques of guidance and remedial work.
    - Students often are enrolled in courses in which their expectation of real success and profitable achievement, at the outset, is doomed by lack of ability.
    - On the other hand, pupils often are permitted to avoid courses for which they have ample ability and from which they could derive substantial benefit.
    - Either of these situations represent educational wastage and stagnation and could be prevented by means of wise guidance based on careful prognosis.
    - A proper guidance programme should be regarded as an important *phase* of providing for individual differences because it implies the salvaging of interest, the conservation of personality values and the prevention of education waste.
- A systematic programme of diagnosis and approximate remedial work must be regarded as of extreme importance.

- Such a programme, if systematically carried on, can do a great deal —
  (1) toward the prevention of scholastic delinquency and discouragement, and
  (2) toward the maintenance of interest and the promotion of success.
- Frequently it is possible to trace maladjustment and failure due to particular causes such as —
  (1) Poor reading ability
  (2) Lack of motive
  (3) Excessive absorption in other interests
  (4) Inadequate mastery of technical vocabulary
  (5) Erroneous fundamental concepts, etc.
- It is expected that the schools of the future will insist diagnostic and remedial work go hand in hand with prognosis and guidance in the efforts to achieve an optimum adjustment between the individual pupil and his work.

## III. Planning a Schedule for a Course

- The layout plan for a course may best begin with a days-and-pages schedule.
  - The main use of such a device is to provide a schedule which will ensure that no principal part of the proposed coverage will be omitted from the course.
  - In making such a schedule, the course as represented in the text book, should first be laid out into the main chapters/units that are to be included.
  - Opposite to this will be set the total number of days available for the course.
  - Then these two layouts must be fitted/matched to each other so that, at least on paper, all the work to be included in the course can also be included in the number of days available.
- In laying out a time schedule for a course, there is always the likelihood of losing a few days as far as instruction is concerned during the year/semester.
  - Unscheduled interruptions and delays are almost certain to occur.

    *e.g.,* football games, illness, special meetings, unexpected holidays, etc. may cause dismissal of classes.
  - Experienced teachers operating under well-planned schedules encounter some necessary slowdowns during the course.
  - These considerations imply and emphasise the importance of leaving a few buffer days or catch-up days in the time schedule for the course.
  - They also imply the importance of weighing the different units and the different parts of each unit on the scale of relative importance. So, teachers can have enough time even for all the things of prime importance in the course.

### *Detailed Planning of Separate Unit of Work*

- Each planning of a unit may cover one day or several days or may be several weeks.
- The planning of such a unit requires —
  (1) careful and detailed analysis of the material.
  (2) the formulation of the general and specific objectives for the unit.
  (3) the selection, rejection and arrangement of topics and activities.
  (4) the provision for necessary tests.
  (5) the establishment of suggestive, though not specifically binding, time schedule.
- The actual preparation of the plan for each unit of work will do much —
  (*a*) to clarify in the teacher's mind the functional goals which he wants the class to attain.
  (*b*) to help the teacher to view the entire unit as an *organised* body of the subject matter rather than a mere assemblage of more or less unrelated details.
  (*c*) to force the teacher to compare the different topics and details within the unit w.r.t. their relative importance, thus, giving a basis for wise selection and approximate emphasis of the subject matter to be included within the unit.
  (*d*) to compel the teacher to take into consideration the relative difficulty of the various parts of the subject matter, and in this way facilitates the preparation of differentiated assignments in adjusting the requirements of the course to different levels of ability among the pupils.

### *Advantages*

(1) One of the greatest advantages of planning a unit as a whole is that this procedure makes the effective presentation of the unit.

(2) With the work definitely planned and organised, the pupils can be given a coherent preview of the entire unit.

(3) This, in turn, makes the developmental work more meaningful and adds understanding, interest and motive to the activities of the pupils during the subsequent periods of assimilative study.

## 10.2 Planning the Daily Lesson

- A daily lesson planning consists mainly —
  (1) of the teaching points,
  (2) of specifications to be achieved,
  (3) of the organisation of an orderly sequence of learning activities designed to contribute directly to the attainment of specifications,
  (4) of the actual test items to which pupils are to be exposed.
- It implies attention to such things as —
  (1) objectives and specifications,
  (2) effective and economical classroom management and routine,

(3) special drill, review, testing activities,

(4) developmental work, making assignments, directed study,

(5) any special activities to be carried on during the class period. *e.g.,* Laboratory or field work, projects, etc.

- It is perhaps even more important than the other two stages of planning, because —
  - (*a*) it has to do directly with the immediate activities of the class period,
  - (*b*) it is mainly upon the successful prosecution of these activities that ultimate success depends,
  - (*c*) the daily lesson plan for a class determines just what learning activities will go in that class during that period.
- The daily lesson planning often needs to be modified to take the advantage of unforeseen circumstances or to adapt the work to unavoidable delays.
- Lesson have sometimes been classified according to the aims or the types of activities to be carried on, *e.g.,* the developmental lesson, the drill lesson, the review lesson, the testing lesson, etc.
  - Such classifications can be helpful by bringing into focus the main objective of the day's work and the kinds of activity which seem most likely to attain the objective.
- There still remains the need to decide upon the details of the period's work and the ordering of these details.
  - The number of kinds of activity which may be included in the teaching-learning situations would be included in the following list:
    - (1) Testing for any of several purposes
    - (2) Explaining/Discussing new concepts/procedures
    - (3) Drilling/Reviewing
    - (4) Directing the students' work at chalk-board or laboratory works
    - (5) Assigning work to be done by the pupils.
- Each of these kinds of activity requires detailed planning if it is to serve its purpose.
- The essence of good daily plan lies in two things:
  - (1) The careful estimation and selection of those activities which give the most promise of good dividends in terms of the immediate objectives, and
  - (3) The arrangement of these activities into a properly ordered schedule with approximate time allotments, so that the period may be used to best advantage.
- It is possible to use a general outline form which will be objective enough to serve as a careful guide in planning, at the same time, sufficiently flexible to permit adaptation of the lesson plan to any class situation.
- A daily lesson plan is confined to only one period.
- In a daily lesson, plan the content is presented in the form of teaching points and is serialised in a psychological and logical sequence.

- In a daily lesson plan, the learning activities are shown in detail.
- In a daily lesson plan the actual test items to be exposed to the pupils are a pre-requisite.
- The test items may be in the form of an essay or a short answer or an objective type of questions.

## 10.3 Practical Hint on Planning the Daily Lesson

- To make the daily lesson plans fit a long-range schedule, the teacher needs to give careful attention each day to the relative importance of the ideas presented in the portions of the text book which is assigned for that day.
- In planning each day's lesson, it is important is highlight only the key concepts or relations and save most of the time for them.
- Frequently, the most effective teaching may be accomplished through spontaneous teacher reaction to unexpected students' problems and unpredicted teaching situations.
- Daily lesson plan should be made in the context of the overall unit plan and should be continuous from one day to the next.
    - The work of each day should be, in a way, an extension and continuation of the previous day's work.
    - Daily lesson plan should not be fragmentary or inefficient.

### EVALUATE YOURSELF

1. Why should a teacher plan?
2. Mention the three main levels of planning. Give an account of the 'Long-range Planning.'
3. What provision should be done for individual differences, as a stage in planning? Give only one form of provision for individual differences.
4. Explain 'Homogeneous Ability Grouping.'
5. Write short notes on:
   (1) Differentiated Assignments
   (2) The Contract type of Assignments
   (3) Multiple-level type of Assignment
   (4) Practical hints on Planning the Daily Lesson.
6. How does Directed study offers a means of providing for individual differences among pupils?
7. Explain in detail the role of prognosis and diagnosis in providing for individual differences.
8. 'Planning a schedule for a course is necessary.' — Comment.
9. Give an account of the detailed planning of separate unit of work.
10. Bring out the importance of 'Planning a Daily Lesson.'

# 11 PRINCIPLES OF EFFECTIVE AND MEANINGFUL LEARNING IN MATH

## 11.1 What is Learning?

- Learning is the permanent changes or modifications brought out in behaviour.
    - Learning is a dynamic process.
    - It takes place through so many activities and avenues.
- According to R.S. Wordworth — 'An activity may be called learning in so far as it develops the individual in any way, good or bad and makes his environment and experiences different from what it would otherwise have been.
- Learning of mathematics involves various activities such as reading, writing, computing, comparison, analysing, integrating, thinking, questioning, working with material objects, etc.
    - In all these activities, reasoning and logical thinking is common.
    - A child gets developed and his experiences are enriched through learning.
    - There are definite changes brought about in his behaviour and realm of experience.
    - These changes in development may result in good or bad depending upon the circumstances. Hence, development may follow positive or negative direction.
    - Learning may not be termed as a useful activity in all situations.
    - The child may also pick up meaningless knowledge, undesirable skills and habits, unsocial or criminal attitude and interest, through some learning.
- Learning is a life long process. Right from his birth, child always learns something or the other through direct or indirect experiences.
    - In school this learning continues and the child gains experiences of so many subjects and activities.
    - Is all such learning useful and meaningful?

## 11.2 What is Meaningful Learning?

- (Definition): 'The learning which is helpful in developing the innate powers and abilities of children in a right direction and makes them a useful member of the society may be termed as 'meaningful learning.'
- It is an accepted psychological fact that every learning has some meaning or significance.
  - No normal being does or learn a thing without any purpose.
  - In a way, whatever is learnt in any subject of experience through any activity carries some meaning and has the right of being called meaningful.
  - But in true sense the learning in any subject may be called meaningful only when it helps in the realisation of the aims and objectives of that subject and provides proper opportunity to a child to develop his potentialities for becoming a useful and productive member of the society.
  - Pupils need positive development through useful and meaningful learning.

### Meaningful Learning in Math

The learning in mathematics may be termed meaningful if it helps in —

(*i*) the development of mental and intellectual powers,

(*ii*) the learning of other subjects,

(*iii*) building base for the future learning in mathematics,

(*iv*) solving problems related to life activities,

(*v*) earning livelihood or preparing for useful and productive vocation,

(*vi*) developing positive attitude towards mathematics,

(*vii*) inculcating interest or motivating pupils for self-learning and independent research in mathematics.

## 11.3 What is effective learning?

- The effective learning is a product of effective teaching.
  - Effective teaching induces effective learning.
- It is very difficult to give a specific formula for effective teaching, but certain measures and techniques can be adopted to make the teaching effective.
- Some important suggestion in this regards may be as under:
  (1) Select and organise the content of mathematics according to age and mental level of pupils.
  (2) Make very clear the aims and objectives of teaching mathematics and its particular topic.
  (3) Adopt simple and interesting method for presenting the content.
  (4) Provide sufficient opportunities for exercises and practice.

(5) To avoid forgetting, provide frequent application of knowledge and skills learnt by pupils.

(6) Make provision for individual differences in the instructional procedure.

(7) Make efforts for transfer of learning to other fields.

(8) In view of organisation and application, mathematics is a cumulative and continuously expanding subject.

(9) While presenting a new content, the teacher should help the pupils —

(*i*) in achieving the initial understanding of new concepts and their relations,

(*ii*) in making the threshold understanding into a sound and comprehensive understanding,

(*iii*) in maintaining the attained knowledge and skills,

(*iv*) in preparing the background for significant transfer of attained knowledge and skills to their physical, social and intellectual environment.

## 11.4 Principles of Effective and Meaningful Learning in Mathematics

- Useless and meaningless learning is of no use. Hence, attempts should be made for arranging meaningful learning to the pupils.
- Meaningful learning is constructive, productive, purposeful and progressive in nature.
- Learning should be fruitful to the pupils so that they can use it as and when needed.
- Teacher should set the process of teaching and learning on right footing.
- There are some principles which should be followed for effective and meaningful teaching and learning in general and specifically in mathematics:

### 1. *Principle of Definite Aim*

- For effective learning, there should be some definite aims, as aims provide direction to the learning. So, the aims and objectives of teaching every topic or lesson should be made definite and clear to the pupils.
  - Definiteness of the aims makes learning interesting and purposeful.
  - Aimlessness encourages meaningless learning while definite aims and objectives help pupils in realising them through learning mathematics.

### 2. *Principle of Interest and Attention*

- Interest helps in capturing the attention of the pupils.
  - The students will remain attentive as long as their interest retained in the learning of mathematics.
  - Nothing could be learnt uninterestingly.
- Mathematics teacher should try to make his teaching and classroom activities as interesting as possible.
  - He should made efforts to arouse strong interest and whole-hearted attention to mathematics and its learning.

- Anyhow, the teaching should be child-centred.
  - For that, the pupils should be actively involved in the process of teaching and learning.
  - This will result in the smooth learning of mathematics and the pupils will be able to use effectively the product of their learning.

## 3. *Principle of Motivation*

- Motivation is the key factor in the process of learning.
  - Motivation has placed a great role in learning, discoveries and inventions.
- Motivation results in the inculcation of interest and interest helps in capturing the attention of the pupils.
- If the learning of mathematics is based on the inner urges and motives of pupils, then and then only their learning will be meaningful.
  - Therefore, the mathematics teacher should spare no efforts to bring motivation in the fore-front in the learning of mathematics.
- Teaching is causing others to learn and it cannot take place unless a learning situation has been created and pupils are motivated to learn.
- Things which satisfy the motives of pupils, appeal to them most and become contributory to their learning and picking it up easily and quickly.
- Properly motivated pupils are well set for learning.
- Providing motivation is not an easy job. It requires training and experience.
  - A sense of preparedness on the part of the teacher is very much essential.
  - The teacher should see the hygienic conditions of the classroom and choose material of real value to the pupils.
- The following points may be helpful to the teacher to motivate the learners:
  (1) Be sensitive to consider their moods and purposes.
  (2) Try to locate the intrinsic interest of mathematics for the pupils.
  (3) Capitalise the individual and group enthusiasm of the pupils.
  (4) Exhibit your own enthusiasm and communicate it to the pupils in a most sympathetic and affectionate manner.
  (5) Make a good provision for learning material as far as possible.
  (6) Extrinsic motivation damages their learning. Avoid the use of unreasonable rewards and punishment.
  (7) Appeal their senses and take care not to discourage them by assigning tasks beyond their physical and mental capacity.
  (8) See that the physical, social and intellectual environment is conducive to learning.

## 4. *Principle of Proper Methodology*

- According to the psychology of teaching and learning the most efficient, economical, meaningful and effective method of teaching and learning knowledge and skills are inducto-deductive, analytico-synthetic, problem solving, heuristic, project and laboratory methods.

- Approaches like self-effort, understanding, problem solving, intelligent practice are very useful to the pupils.
- It is the duty of the mathematics teacher to choose an appropriate method for teaching a specific piece of content, knowledge and skill.
- He should guide his students to select most suitable ways and means of learning the desired knowledge and skill.
- Proper methodology of teaching and learning mathematics certainly helps in the achievement of aims and objectives of teaching mathematics.
  - This makes the study of mathematics most meaningful.
- But all other principles of effective and meaningful learning are defeated if the teacher fails to adopt befitting methods of teaching and learners on their parts also fail to adopt suitable methods of learning.
  - So, for the teachers and the pupils both, it is very necessary to select suitable method and to use it adequately.

### 5. *Principle of Utility of Mental Powers*

- To make the learning of mathematics meaningful, pupils should utilize their mental powers as much as possible.
  - Their reasoning and thinking powers, power of imagination, power of observation, power of discrimination, power of judgement, should be properly utilised in the process of teaching and learning mathematics.
  - The knowledge and skills achieved by them through exercising their mental powers become a permanent and valuable asset to them.
  - Such learning is always meaningful and effective and therefore, the mathematics teacher should always try for the active involvement of the pupils' mental faculties.
- If the pupils realise in the very beginning that the subject matter, they are going to learn, will have wide application in their day-to-day life and in various fields of study and vocations, then their learning will be need-based and hence meaningful

### 6. *Principle of Logical Thinking*

- When the pupils work systematically and scientifically and proceed with logical thinking, the learning is meaningful.
  - The knowledge and skills, achieved by systematic process of logical thinking and reasoning, become permanent and valuable asset to the pupils.
- The crammed facts are meaningless in actual situations of life.
  - Therefore, emphasis should be made to the pupils to exercise fully their thinking and reasoning powers in learning the content instead of craming and rote, blind memorisation

### 7. *Principle of Activity*

- It is the human nature that we care or attend to those things easily which matter us most
  - These things are not only learnt efficiently but remembered for a long time, too.

- The value of these learning activities do make them meaningful.
- So, a teacher should try to acquaint his pupils with the importance of the topic or learning activities beforehand.
- This will result in making the learning of mathematics meaningful.

- Pupils love activity and wants to satisfy their curiosity. They learn best through the self-activity.
  - So, the teacher should develop mathematical ideas and principles with the active co-operation of pupils.
- When pupil is made active physically as well as mentally, learning becomes effective and meaningful.
  - Teaching is ineffective, if the pupils do not actively participate in the learning process.
- A good teaching causes others to learn. This process can be much facilitated if the pupils put their hands (physical efforts) and head (mental abilities) together. This means, they actively participate in it and learn while actually manipulating the things to be learnt.

## 8. *Principle of Heuristic and Problems Solving Attitude*

- In mathematics, the already discovered knowledge is not power. The basic things are to prepare pupils for (1) discovering knowledge, and (2) finding ways and means of solving the problems.
- The development of heuristic and problem solving attitude is very much essential for realising the aims and objectives of teaching mathematics and making its learning as meaningful and effective as possible.
- Teacher has to extract out maximum information from the pupils by proceeding on heuristic lines.
- If problem solving attitude is developed in the pupils from the very beginning, they surely enjoy the learning of mathematics.

## 9. *Principle of Integration of Theory with Practice*

- Mathematics is a theoretical as well as practical subject. It has much utilitarian and practical value. But mainly it is composed of abstract ideas and concept.
  - For effective and meaningful learning there should be a close integration of theory with practice.
  - Mathematics cannot be effectively learnt only through discussion — theoretical or practical.
  - The facts and principles of mathematics should be practically linked with the activities of life.
- Teacher should try to teach mathematics, keeping practical life situations in fore-front.

## 10. *Principle of Correlation*

- The pupils are not interested in these topics of mathematics which have no bearing on life.
  - The knowledge learnt must be vitally connected with life.

- Mathematics should be correlated with its other branches, with other subjects and with life of the pupils.
- The knowledge learnt must be functional and in its proper context. It should not be in its fragments.
  - So, efforts should be made to direct the pupils' learning towards meanings, relationships and organisations.
- There should be association and correlation of mathematical ideas.
- Every new knowledge in mathematics should be based on the previous knowledge and it should provide clue and give support to the future learning.
- The curricular, co-curricular and work-experience activities of the pupils must be properly correlated with the learning of mathematics.

### 11. *Principle of Exercise/Practice*

- Practice (Drill) is extremely significant in the learning of mathematics.
  - For effective learning a regular, persistence and continuous practice is a must.
  - It develops self-confidence and insight in the pupils.
- The law of use and disuse works significantly in the learning of mathematics.
- Mathematics needs sufficient practice (Drill) work for the fixation of knowledge and skills.
- 'Practice makes a man perfect.' Practice makes use of the facts and principles as effectively and meaningfully as possible.

### 12. *Principle of Revision*

- Many pupils are unable to understand the various abstract concepts, etc., during initial teaching. They require further clarification to understand certain steps of a sum or theorem, etc.
  - Therefore, the teacher should revise the topic. Then it becomes easier for the students (slow learners) to learn it. During the revision they will grasp it.
- Thus, revision has an important role to play in effective and meaningful learning.

### 13. *Principle of Creation and Recreation*

- Good teaching is a source of joy both to the teacher and the learners.
  - Good teaching awakens the urge for creativeness in the children and they become very eager to operate upon the material learnt.
- The effective teaching engages the whole child and also proves to be a source of enjoyment.
- By awakening the pupils' desire to be creative, they should be stimulated to activity.

### 14. *Principle of Diagnosis and Remedial Teaching*

- If the previous lesson has not been comprehended by the pupils, it is absolutely useless to proceed on with another lesson.
- Effective learning needs remedial teaching to remove the difficulties of learners.

- ▸▸ So, the teacher should diagnose the difficulties of pupils. An effort should be made to remove them as far as possible.

- ▸ Pupils should be encouraged to express themselves whenever and wherever they experience some difficulty.

## Conclusion

- ▸ Learning can be effective if above mentioned principles are adopted by the teachers as well as pupils.
- ▸ The job of the teacher lies in creating an atmosphere for effective learning through interaction and inspiring them to proceed on themselves.
  - ▸▸ In this process the teacher's personality is also an important factor.
  - ▸▸ Pupils are generally influenced by teacher's own personality and his abilities.
  - ▸▸ Besides mastery over mathematics, he should have a sense of humour, imagination, friendliness, patience, enthusiasm, self-confidence, etc.
  - ▸▸ The teacher's ability to relate the subject to life situations helps to a great extent in arousing interest in the pupils for mathematics.
- ▸ Meaningful learning in mathematics can consist of those mathematical experiences which—
  - (1) are helpful iin mental, emotional and social development,
  - (2) are useful in learning higher and advanced aspects of mathematics,
  - (3) are helpful in proper learning of other subjects,
  - (4) have utilitarian, practical and behavioural values,
  - (5) stimulate and maintain interest in mathematics and which lead to development of proper attitude towards mathematics.

## EVALUATE YOURSELF

1. Explain — What is learning? What is meaningful learning? What is effective learning?
2. Enumerate the principles of effective and meaningful learning in mathematics. Discuss in detail any two of them.
3. Write short notes on:
   - (1) Principle of Definite Aim
   - (2) Principle of Interest and Attention.
   - (3) Principle of Logical Thinking
   - (4) Principle of Utility of Mental Powers
   - (5) Principle of Correlation
   - (6) Principle of Creation and Recreation.
4. How far motivation is useful in effective and meaningful learning in Mathematics? Discuss.
5. Give an account of the principle of proper methodology in effective and meaningful learning in mathematics.

6. How far do you agree with the principle of activity in learning mathematics? Justify your answer.
7. 'Principle of Heuristic and Problem-solving attitude help in learning Mathematics to a great extent.' — Comment.

'Even in the mathematical sciences, our principal instruments to discover truth are induction and analogy.'

— ***Laplace***

'And I cherish more than anything else the Analogies, my most trustworthy masters. They know all the secrets of Nature and they ought to be least neglected in Geometry.' — ***Kepler***

# 12 MEANS OF EFFECTIVE INSTRUCTION

- Schools exist for the primary purpose of promoting learning. Teachers of mathematics have as their primary objectives the promotion of learning in mathematics.
- Two things vary from grade to grade:

  (1) The content to be learnt

  (2) The maturity of the students

  - The pupils may not all learn content in the same ways or at the same speed or with the same facility and competence.
  - It is necessary that a teacher have a good understanding of the desirable mathematical objectives and of the ways to which pupils learn mathematics.
  - He has to consider carefully the instructional means and the devices which he plans to use and to adopt them for optimum effectiveness in enabling the pupils to attain the desired objectives.

## 12.1 Important Considerations

Some of the import considerations for the teachers with respect to the instruction of mathematics are suggested below:

1. The problem of instruction is that of promoting learning.
   - Since, the learning must be done by the pupils, the problem of instruction becomes that of guiding the activities of the pupils in such a way that proper learning takes place.
   - The teacher who gives thought to ways in which pupils learn mathematics will be more likely to attain effective results than the one who does not.
   - Some important considerations w.r.t. how mathematics is learnt should be set forth at the outset.

2. Learning is an active process. It is attained not in any single way but through a variety of activities and is approached through a variety of avenues: reading, writing, listening, observing, drawing, asking questions, working with material objects, comparing, analysing, interpreting, computing and so on.
   - The one thing which all these activities need to involve is *thinking*.
   - These activities need to be so planned that they bring the learner along the path toward understanding and mastery of the subject at his level of advancement.
3. Effective instruction cannot be guaranteed by any single simple formula.
   - If instruction is to be really effective, the content must be selected and organised in such a way as to make it appropriate and suited to the age and intellectual development of the pupils.
   - The subject matter must be presented in an understandable and interesting way and there must be provision for sufficient practice.
   - Skills and concepts once developed must be maintained through reapplication and not allowed to deteriorate through disuse.
4. Since pupils do not learn with equal facility or at equal rates, there must be provision for individual differences.
   - If the instruction is to attain a maximum of usefulness, it must be carried on with the deliberate purpose of securing a maximum of transfer and in such a way that the relation of mathematics to other fields of learning and activity is made manifest.
5. All these considerations involve careful planning and adequate testing of outcomes.

## 12.2 Four Fundamental Problems of Instruction of Mathematics

- Mathematics is a cumulative and a continuously expanding subject in both — its organisation and its application.
- With every new topic the teacher is confronted with four basic instructional problems:

  Helping the students —

  (1) to acquire initial *understanding of new* concepts and relationships;

  (2) to *strengthen and deepen* these concepts and relationships, well beyond the point of mere 'threshold understanding;:

  (3) to *maintain* understandings and skills already attained; and

  (4) to build the background for significant *transfer* of those skills and understandings to their physical, social and intellectual environment.
- These four phases of teaching should be interwoven as far as possible into a unified instructional programme but their implications are essentially distinct and supplemental rather than identical.

## I. Instructing Mathematics for Understanding

- Teaching of new material is that phase of instruction which makes the heaviest demand upon the skill and artistry of mathematics teacher.

- The primary jobs are to explain, to make clear, to challenge, to guide to discovery, to develop understanding.
- In order to meet these responsibilities, the teacher must consider the logical relationships involved in the unit/topic. He must also be keenly aware of the relation of the new concepts to the experiential background of the pupils.
- He must be able to anticipate probable difficulties and detect and clear up actual difficulties as they occur in the course of the development.
- He must be able and continually willing to view the unfolding and unfamiliar (for the students) subject matter not merely through his own experienced eyes but from the standpoint of immature pupils to whom it is all new and strange.

## Pre-view

- When a new work is taken up with a class, it is usually assumed that the pupils are wholly unfamilar with the new material, but this is not always the case.
    - Effective instruction requires that time shall not be wasted and that interest shall be stimulated and conserved.
    - It does not infrequently happened that the pupils will already have acquired some acquaintance with certain part of the material presented in the text books.
    - In some cases, pupils will be found to have a fair degree of mastery of the supposedly new concepts and procedures.
    - It is both wasteful of time and deleterious to the maintenance of interest to go through the motions of teaching pupils, things with which they are already familiar. Consequently,
        (1) they become restless and impatient,
        (2) their attention wanders,
        (3) disciplinary difficulties are likely to be created,
        (4) the whole atmosphere of the class situation is rendered unfavourable to effective teaching and learning.
- Before planning the work of a new course/unit, it is desirable that the teacher finds out in the beginning, as much as he can, about the pupils' background w.r.t. such abilities and information as will be required in the new work.
    - By means of a preliminary investigation of this nature, the teacher will be in a position to proceed intelligently in building up necessary backgrounds and in presenting the new work to the class in an effective manner.
    - This need not take long. It can sometimes be done by a well-organised short talk of by a few well-chosen questions. In some cases brief written inventory tests are more useful.
    - Sometimes the information secured may save time and be of significant help to the teacher in planning and conducting the work.
- In presenting a new unit of work, it is well to give the pupils an overview of the unit as a whole in order that they may see the main concepts and principles in their relations to each other and to previous part of the work.

- A pre-view of this sort not only gives meaning and relevance to the larger ideas of the unit but also gives significance and motive to the detailed study which must make up most of the pupils' work in mastering the unit.
  - The importance of this has not always been recognised by teachers.
  - Too often the new work is simply taken up, detail by detail, with little thought of relating the details to the structure of the unit as a whole.
  - This is partly responsible for much of the current dissatisfaction with the mathematics courses in our schools.
- During this preview the pupils should be mainly in the role of listeners.
  - Interruption and questions should not be prohibited, but for the most part pupils should be urged to postpone their questions until the conclusion of the teacher's discussion in order to avoid interrupting the continuity of thought which is a most important feature of this phase of instruction.
- The pre-view offers great possibilities for stimulating the curiosity and interest of the pupils and for helping them to cultivate the art of being good listeners.

## Teaching New Material

- It is a common fault of teachers to employ too extensively the method of 'telling' or of giving a coherent discussion of a topic and then proceeding as if on the assumption that the discussion has been followed and completely understood by the pupils.
  - This assumption is almost never justified.
  - Points of difficulty will inevitably arise and unless they are cleared up promptly, they will fail to register with the pupils. This may easily result in blocking the understanding of the subsequent parts of the discussion.
- This does not mean that telling is always and entirely out of place. On the contrary, there are many times, when judicious telling/explanation may be not only proper and valuable but absolutely necessary, *e.g.,* in making clear the meaning of new terms and concepts.
  - Such use of the telling/lecture method should generally take the form of explanations/ illustrations.
- The discussion should not be one-sided. It should be diversified at intervals with frequent questions by the teacher, who should also strive to elicit questions and contributions from the class.
  - It is not always easy to get pupils to raise questions, because all the difficulties arised too often in their minds are not well-enough defined to enable them to put them into words.
- Many students are quite sensitive about appearing slow of perception, in the eyes of their classmates and rather than run the risk of embarrassment, they commonly let these matters pass in silence.
  - As a result, pupils will frequently allow statements to go unchallenged even though they do not understand them.

- Such barriers to freedom of inquiry on the part of the students can be broken only by tact and sympathetic encouragement. Pupils should be given every encouragement to raise questions at any time that they are unable to follow the discussion clearly.
- The teacher must anticipate such difficulties as far as possible and be always alert to detect them as they become apparent.
- This can often be done by noting pupils' puzzled expressions even if they may not actually raise questions.

- The teacher should check the understanding of the discussion by means of questions addressed to the pupils.
- By well-chosen questions pupils can be led to discover facts/relationships for themselves. This makes the pupils more active participant in the learning process.

**Laboratory work in Mathematics**
**Heuristic Approach in Mathematics**
**The Genetic Approach**

} Please refer the chapter No. 14

- Skillful use of the heuristic method tends to develop an attitude of mind which is the most favourable to successful work in mathematics.
- A variation of this procedure (sometimes called the Genetic Method) aims to retain its spirit and advantages, and at the same time, to remove some of its limitations by having the questions directed to the entire class/group instead of merely to one individual.
  - Thus, the intention is that the class will be guided toward discoveries as a co-operating group rather than as separate individuals.
- It is, in fact, a combination of several procedures — questioning, explaining, guiding, giving information as and when needed, eliciting pupils participation, illustrating, stimulating and evoking interest and curiosity and continual checking of the understanding and the reactions of the pupils.
  - Those activities keep the teacher closely in contact with the entire class situation and keep the members of the class in contact with each other and with the teacher, at all times.
- It is probably the most difficult of all methods of teaching mathematics because it cannot be stereotyped.
  - The teacher, in addition to possessing a broad and deep competence w.r.t. subject matter, must be not only a technician but also a skilled artist at the job of teaching.
- In the hands of trained and skillful teacher, this method may be expected to achieve excellent results and in such hand it is perhaps better adapted in general to the successful development of new material with classes than is any other single procedure.
  - In the hands of an unskilled teacher this method is likely to degenerate into random discussion from which little will be gained and in the course of which much time may be wasted.

## Developmental Teaching

- Developmental teaching is an art. It can neither be standardised nor stereotyped.
  - Procedures which are used successfully by one teacher may prove to be unsuccessful when tried by another or perhaps by the same teacher under different circumstances.
  - Much depends upon —
    (1) the personality of the teacher;
    (2) his enthusiasm, tact;
    (3) understanding of pupils;
    (4) teacher's ability to sense intuitively the procedure which will serve best to capitalise the psychological classroom situations of the moment or modify it in such a way that it may be made to contribute most powerfully in the drive toward the set objectives.
- That teacher will be most successful in developmental work who has at his command various methods of procedure and who uses them in such a way as to make them supplement each other most advantageously as occasion may indicate.
- One of the greatest mistakes which many teachers make is to try to cover too much ground in a given period of time or to try to cover a given amount of material in too short a period of time.
  - This nearly always results in superficial learning or in no learning at all.
- Particularly in the developmental teaching of new material the teacher should avoid forcing the process too rapidly.
  - The development of new concepts or principles is a slow process and it always requires a certain amount of discussion and so, lecturing should be avoided.
- When it is feasible to guide pupils into exploratory activities through appropriate questioning or laboratory exercises so that they may discover things for themselves, it should be done.
- When it is necessary for the teacher to give direct information, it should be given briefly and concisely and should be checked by pointed and searching questioning.
- New understandings as they are developed should be given permanence, clarity and interest by means of adequate illustrations and applications.
- Developmental work, in order to be successful, requires continuous interaction of the pupils' best efforts with those of the teacher.
- The aim, at all times, is to develop in the pupils a broadening background of mathematical understanding and foster a continuing interest in mathematics to the end.
  - The teacher must plan and direct the activities of the class toward these goals.
  - He must strive to secure the highest possible degree of co-operative effort on the part of the pupils.
  - He must be tactful and sympathetic, helping when necessary, encouraging, guiding, checking and always stimulating the pupils to put forth their own best efforts.

- Such a programme of developmental teaching may be expected —
  (1) to yield highly satisfactory results,
  (2) in building up an added appreciation of mathematics,
  (3) in developing an increasing ability to independent mathematical thinking,
  (4) in stimulating interest in the pursuit of future mathematical study.

## II. Instruction for Assimilating Understanding

- Pupils will not be able to make much independent progress toward the assimilation of concepts, principles and relationships of which they have not even gained a basic understanding.
- Adequate developmental teaching is an absolute pre-requisite to successful assimilative study in mathematics.
- Before the pupils are set to independent study of new material, measures be taken to test their understanding of the ideas which the teacher has tried to develop with them as a preliminary basis for their work during the assimilation period.
- Concepts/Principles/Processes are not ultimately mastered
  (1) without many illustrations in varied contexts,
  (2) without repeated application,
  (3) without extensive practice,
  (4) without prolong and sustained intellectual effort on the part of pupils.
- The purpose of developmental teaching is to give the pupils adequate basis of understanding and appreciation and motive upon which to build, but the process of mastery can, by no means, be thought of as ending with this step.
  - On the contrary, this is merely a beginning which must be followed by an extensive period in which the pupil must devote himself to the task of assimilation and fixation of the ideas, principles and processes which have been brought out in the developmental work.
  - It does not mean that the activities of the assimilation work will necessarily be divorced from discussion, illustration, demonstration, experimentation and other developmental work.
- Assimilation can take place through many avenues, although the principal one is individual directed (*i.e.,* supervised) study.
- 'Directed study' refers to a type of classroom activity rather than method of teaching. It is to be thought of as a *phase* of teaching rather than a method.
- A part of a class period can be devoted to developmental work on new concepts or processes and a part of the same period be given to assimilation work on these or previously developed ideas.
- In the developmental phase of the work, the principal aim is to produce 'threshold understanding' of new material. In the assimilation phase, the aim is to produce fuller and deeper insights, greater familiarity and improved facility.

- In short, the aim is to produce real mastery and a comfortable sense of feeling at home and at ease with the material.

- The teacher necessarily has a somewhat active role in, at least, some part of the developmental work.
  - In the assimilative stage, the situation is different.
  - The pupils and their activities now occupy the centre of the stage, while the teacher serves as a sort of promoter and director operating from the wings.
- In the process of assimilation through directed study, the pupils themselves are the main participants so far as overt activities are concerned.
  - The talk of the teacher now should be that of —

    (*i*) guiding and directing pupils' work,

    (*ii*) stimulating pupils,

    (*iii*) encouraging them,

    (*iv*) helping them over hard spots,

    (*v*) evaluating their progress, and

    (*vi*) striving to get them to put forth their best efforts to achieve a permanent and functional mastery of the material upon which they are working.

## Directed Study in Mathematics

- In directed study in mathematics, it is true that the teacher's role is much less prominent that it is in developmental teaching, but is hardly less important.
- If directed study is to be more effective, the teacher must be continually in touch with the work of each individual pupil.
  - This requires repeated inspection and quick sizing up of the difficulties and needs of the various pupils.

[For further characteristics refer to 'supervised study' Ch. 16]

## Making Directed Study more Effective

The following suggestions may be helpful to teachers in conducting directed study in mathematics:

1. Be sure that the preliminary developmental work has been clearly understood by the pupils before allowing them to begin their study.
   - This work provides the basic foundation and framework w.r.t. which the subsequent assimilative study is oriented.
   - That is, it provides the initial understandings which are to be assimilated, amplified, organised and made permanent through subsequent study.
   - Directed study can play its part in this process only if these preliminary understandings have been satisfactorily developed.

[For further suggestions refer to 'supervised study' Ch. 16]

## III. Instruction for Permanence

- The developmental and assimilative phases of instruction represent essentially the stages during which actual learning of new material takes place.
- Any subject matter, however, is likely to be forgotten, no matter how well it has been initially mastered, unless it is maintained by repeated application and practice.
  - This is particularly true of mathematical skills and relationships.
  - Skills need to be perfected and maintained through systematic drill. Concepts and relationships must be reviewed and applied at frequently recurring intervals.
  - The instructional effort which is directed toward these ends may well be called 'teaching for performance.'
  - It is generally involves material already learnt rather than new material.
  - Its importance as a means of strengthening and maintaining learning commensurates with the importance of the developmental and assimilative phases of instruction as means of acquiring new knowledge.
  - Its avenues are drill, review and application.

[For drill work and review, refer to 'Techniques and Strategies of Teaching Mathematics. Ch.15, 16]

## Maintenance

- A planned programme of cumulative drill and review work is designated a 'maintenance programme.'
- The fundamental requirement of a satisfactory mathematics programme is that it shall operate to prevent the forgetting of facts, concepts, relationships and anticipate and prevent the disintegration of skills.
- Planning of an adequate mathematics programme must be built upon the following principles:
  1. The materials to be included should be selected from the point of view of relative values.
     - The programme should not be covered/filled with trivial things.
     - Only significant skills, concepts, relationships, principles and problems situations should be included.
  2. In accordance with established principles of drill and review, the items should be distributed throughout the programme in such a way that practice upon any particular element will not be too greatly concentrated but will occur at increasing intervals and in decreasing amounts.
  3. The mathematics programme should be diagnostic, preferably self-diagnostic so that each pupil may be able to discover his own weaknesses.
  4. Supplementary practice material be provided for remedial work on the various particular elements included in the mathematics programme.
     - This supplementary material can be used most effectively if it is keyed with the diagnostic record.

5. The different sets of exercises in the mathematics programme should be comparable in terms of some uniform scoring or rating schedule so that each pupil may keep a record of his general achievement and his progress.
   - This will be of great value in stimulating pride, effort and genuine interest in maintaining skills and principles after the original interest due to their newness has worn off.

- Numerous text books published in recent years recognise the need for systematic maintenance work and make provision for it through sets of drill exercises, diagnostic inventory tests, cumulative reviews and the like, placed at strategic points in the text.
  - In some cases those exercises have evidently been prepared hastily and with little attention to their validity and suitability.
  - In other cases, their organisation and arrangement have been based upon extensive and painstaking study and upon well-established principles of the psychology of learning.
  - These same comments are equally applicable to the multitude of drill books and work books and sets of practice exercises which are now commercially available to supplement text books.
  - Some practice books are valuable aids to the teacher in carrying on an adequate mathematics programme.
  - Scientifically planned and prepared materials serve at least three useful purposes:
    (1) They make the economy of time and labour and so for efficiency in instruction.
    (2) They provide a strong motive to achievement, since they foster the pupils' continued study of their own performances, and
    (3) They provide the best possible insurance against forgetting and against the deterioration of skills and understandings.

## IV. Instruction for Transfer

- The idea and the term 'transfer of training' stem from the old theory of formal discipline which held that mind is made up of several *faculties* such as memory, reasoning and those can be strengthen in a general sense by exercise.
- It once was held that since mathematics is largely concerned with reasoning, the study of mathematics would automatically strengthen the *logical faculty* as a whole and that this faculty would then inevitably operate more effectively than before in every kind of situation.
  - Evidences indicate that considerable carry-over (transfer) is possible and in fact is often attained.
- Transfer of training is usually taken to denote the functioning in a new situation of certain aspects/structures/relations which were learnt in an original situation.
- Competent psychologists are now agreed that under favourable conditions transfer can and does occur.

## *The objects of Transfer*

1. It is desirable that all those elements of mathematical training which most people have occasion to *use* shall be taught in such a manner that they *can* be used whenever occasion demands.

   This category includes such things as —

   (1) The fundamental properties, combinations, skills, operations and concepts of arithmetic.

   (2) The laws and formulae involved in mensuration of the common geometrical figures.

   (3) The interpretation of commonly used statistical conventions and devices.

   (4) Some understanding of what is meant by the structure of a number system.

   (5) The construction and interpretation of straight line, circle and bar-graphs.

   (6) The ability to read pictographs intelligently.

   (7) The fundamental meaning of a formula.

   (8) The ability of evaluate formulae, etc., practically all the understandings and abilities.

- It is desirable that the generality of their application be emphasised so that the pupil will not be at loss when occasion requires their use in new situations.

2. The fundamental concepts, formulae and skills of elementary algebra are desirable objects of transfer.

- Every proposition constitutes a link in the immediate chain of development and to this extent the very consciousness of its relation to the preceding and subsequent parts of the development involves a measure of transfer.
  - Some of the propositions constitute extremely important generalisations which had wide application in the subsequent mathematical courses and other fields of study such as engineering and physical sciences.
  - Such important and widespread generalisations as the Pythagoras Theorem, the angle-sum relationship, the proportionality, the line-segment in similar figures, the sine and cosine laws, the metric properties of circles, various area-formulae, are cases in point.
- The foregoing list of objects of transfer may be grouped into two categories:

  (1) Things to know and understand

  (2) Things to be able to do.

3. The third object of transfer which has probably received more emphasis in writings on mathematical education than in actual teaching. This is the acquisition of a mathematical manner of thinking.

- Under this broad interpretation the desirable transfer values of mathematical study may be thought of as involving potentially such values as —

  (1) Awareness of and insistence upon precision,

  (2) Facility and confidence in the use of fundamental skills,

  (3) The establishment of self-reliance and self-imposition of responsibility for information, procedures and results,

(4) Perseverance to face difficulties,

(5) Habitual insistence upon the precise use of languages, clarity and precision in definition and statement,

(6) The ability to discriminate between a mere assertion and an inference,

(7) The habitual testing of inferences for consistency with known/given conditions,

(8) Awareness of the nature of postulational reasoning, the arbitrary nature of hypothesis, definitions and the inevitable but contingent nature of conclusion,

(9) The ability to —

(*i*) discriminate between sound and spacious argument, between valid and unwarranted inference,

(*ii*) build a consistent argument,

(*iii*) generalise relationships and apply generalisations,

(*iv*) eliminate emotional or prejudicial factors from an argument,

(*v*) generalise meanings, symbols, relationships, processes,

(*vi*) apply such generalisations to new situations,

— all these represent the transfer of the most genuine and vital sort.

## *How to secure Transfer?*

1. It is now agreed that transfer is possible but is neither automatic nor inevitable in its desirable forms.
2. Meaning plays a most important role —

   (*i*) in the process of transfer

   (*ii*) in the theories of generalisation

   (*iii*) in structuring of knowledge.

   This subsequently represents the avenues through which positive transfer of higher mental functions take place.
3. It is the act of recognition of similar elements which really constitutes transfer at the higher levels and which alone characterises all functional and rational thinking and sets it apart from mere specific identifications and mechanical rule-of-thumb procedure.
4. The problem of teaching for transfer would seem to resolve itself into the problem of teaching pupils —

   (1) to recognise similarities between new situations and other situations with which they are already familiar,

   (2) to form the habit of consciously being on the look out for these similarities.
5. Students who will readily factorise $a^2–b^2$ may fail to recognise such expressions as $m^2 – 121$ or $x^2 – 2xy + y^2 – 25z^2$ as being of precisely the same type and so, may be unable to factorise the later expressions.

6. In connection with verbal problems, the difficulty is almost never in solving the equations to which the problems give rise but rather in translating the verbal problems into symbolic forms.
7. In some cases, the similarities or identities in different situations are simple and obvious. In such cases transfer is fairly well-assured.
8. In many cases, the similarities are obscured by other more prominent elements. In such cases, it is often necessary to make careful analysis in order to disclose them.
   - Pupils will not learn to make these analyses unless they are systematically trained to do so.
   - They must have much practice under carefully supervised conditions in order to master the technique of how to make these analyses.
   - They should form the habit of deliberately instituting a search for elements of relationships in the problem in hand which are similar to corresponding elements or relationships in other situations with which they have already had experience, whenever such similarities are not apparent at the outset.
   - If such a procedure is constantly followed, the transfer of mathematical processes and techniques will be facilitated.

## 12.3 Some non-traditional patterns of math instruction

- The customary arrangement for organised instruction in mathematics is one in which each teacher works with one moderate-size class at a time and in which the teaching procedures are largely those of explaining, discussing, questioning, directing the classroom study of the pupils and testing to determine the results of the instruction.

  This is the *traditional* pattern of instruction.
- Non-traditional instructional patterns/devices deviate substantially from the traditional pattern.
- Now-a-days in India, certain unconventional or non-traditional patterns of instruction in mathematics have attained some prominence.
  - Among these can be mentioned the use of such AV devices as films, film stripes, team teaching, instruction by TV, individual projects, the use of open- or closed-circuit TV(CCTV), use of so called teaching machines, micro-teaching, programmed learning, etc.
  - These devices have come into being —
    (*a*) partly in response to the unprecedental and increasing number of pupils taking mathematics with the consequent shortage of qualified teachers.
    (*b*) partly to provide feasible ways of improving or expanding existing instructional facilities, and
    (*c*) partly because of advances in the psychology of learning.
  - Undoubtedly these are plausible argument that can be advanced w.r.t. the potential effectiveness and advantages of all these instructional media.

- Some teachers welcome these newer avenues of instruction with enthusiasm, others view them with skepticism.

### 1. *Instruction by Films & Filmstrips*

- The use of mathematical films and film strip is not new. Some films were available as early as about half a century ago and the number has increased significantly since then.
    - Some have been superior to others in conception, treatment and technical excellence.
    - Invariably they have been topical and intended for use as supplementary material.
- Opinions as to their usefulness has been divided: Following are some limiting factors:
    (1) Many classrooms are not well-adapted to the use of projection equipment.
    (2) Many teachers are not skilled in the use of such equipment.
    (3) Difficulties of scheduling films at appropriate times and of getting prompt delivery are important practical considerations.
- These limiting factors will probably diminish as time goes on.
    - More and better films are ceratin to become increasingly accessible.
    - Many new classrooms are being equipped for the use of projection equipment.
    - This equipment itself is being improved all the time.
    - As the number and range of selection of available films and film strips increase, the problems of scheduling and delivery should become less acute.
- All things considered, these devices will probably play a larger and more important role in mathematical instruction in the future than they have in the past.

### 2. *Instruction by TV*

- The use of TV presents another non-traditional avenue for instruction in mathematics which although it is still in the experimental stage, may come to have important possibilities.
    - CCTV has been and is being used with apparent success in a number of educational institutions for instruction in mathematics.
    - Another variant of the use of this medium in presenting courses is found in airborne TV instruction. This is accomplished by having the TV programme or lessons broadcast from a high-flying satellite and beamed downward to cover an area perhaps as large as several countries.
    - The programme can also include the telecasting of suggestions and material for the assistance of teachers whose classes use the TV lessons.
    - Source units describing the objectives and content of each lesson and suggestions for preparatory and follow-up activities can also be made available.

### 3. *Instruction through 'Micro-lessons'* *[Refer to Ch. No. 24]*

### 4. *Instruction through 'Programmed Learning'* *[Refer to Ch. No. 25]*

## EVALUATE YOURSELF

1. Discuss some important considerations with respect to the means of effective instruction.
2. Which are the four fundamental problems of instruction of mathematics? Explain out of them the 'instruction for assimilating understanding.'
3. How far pre-view helps in instructing mathematics for understanding? Explain fully.
4. What should the teacher keep in his mind while teaching new material?
5. What is meant by Heuristic method of teaching and by the Genetic method? What advantages have these method or the lecture method in teaching secondary school mathematics?
6. What is meant by developmental teaching? What suggestions are made with reference to this phase of instruction in mathematics?
7. Contrast the main functions of the developmental phase and the assimilative phase of mathematical instruction. Show that they are complementary parts of the whole learning process and that both are necessary for effective learning of mathematics.
8. As a teacher what will you do to make directed study more effective?
9. Explain — 'Instruction for performance.'
10. What do you understand by 'maintenance programme'? What are the advantages of such a programme?
11. Contrast the specific functions of drill and review.
12. What is 'Instruction for Transfer'? Discuss fully the objects of transfer.
13. How will you secure transfer of training?
14. Enlist some non-traditional patterns of mathematics instruction. Discuss one of them in detail.
15. Write short notes on:

    (1) Film and Film strips (2) Instruction by TV.

> 'Mathematics is a type of thought which seems ingrained in the human mind, which manifests itself to some extent with even the primitive races and which is developed to a high degree with the growth of civilization........... A type of thought, a body of results, so essentially characteristic of the human mind, so little influenced by environment, so uniformally present in every civilisation is one of which no well informed mind today can be ignorant.'
>
> — ***Report of Commission of Mathematics***

# AUDIO-VISUAL AIDS IN TEACHING OF MATHEMATICS

## 13.1 Introduction

- Any teacher has an inherent desire that his teaching should be as effective as possible.
  - What he teaches should be clearly understood, grasped, assimilated and permanentl fixed in the minds of his pupils.
  - If a teacher wants to realise his set objectives, he should make use of different type of aid materials like models, charts, concrete objects, apparatuses, instruments and othe resources.
  - All such material and resources which help the teacher of mathematics in his realisatio of his pre-determined objectives of effective teaching may be termed as *aids* in teachin mathematics.
  - These aids are also termed as AV aids in the sense that they call upon the auditory an visual senses of pupils.
  - The aids like radio, tape-recorder which help the individual to learn through listenin are called 'audio aids'.
  - The aids like filmstrip, projector, epidiascope, newspapers, magic lantern and blackboar which help in learning through watching are called 'visual aids.'
  - Some aids like cinema, TV, where one learns through listening as well as watching ar known as AV aids.
- Education of a child starts with the learning of 3R, *i.e.*, reading, writing and arithmetic.
  - For the development of these three skills, it is essential to use certain TA (teachin aids). For example,
  - To teach alphabets, the teacher has to use a particular picture for a particular letter, *viz.* picture of an apple for A, that of a boy for B, that of a cat for C, etc.

- When the picture of an apple is shown to the child with the letter A and he is told to recite 'A for apple', it becomes easy for him to read and recognise the letter A.

  The law of association works here.
- Similarly to teach the numbers 1, 2, 3, ..., 9 teachers generally use some objects like small balls, marbles, leaves, or fingers. When the child is told to pronounce 'one (1)' he is shown one object, to pronounce 'two (2)', two objects are shown and so on.
- Thus, the presentation of certain number of objects makes the learning of numbers easier and effective.
- This indicates that TA make the teaching and learning more easy and effective.

- Every type of teaching has always involved the communication of ideas through the senses, either orally through the medium of speech or visually by the use of any real object or some printed or written material.
  - The knowledge acquired through the use of more than one sense organ is more useful and retentive.
- According to psychologists and educationists everything cannot be taught and learnt orally or visually.
  - A child learns many things in a better way by visualising, experiencing, handling, touching, doing and interacting with his environment.
  - So, during teaching, the teacher should provide the opportunities to the child to perceive, to experience, to touch, to handle, to act, etc., so that a desired change may occur in his cognitive, affective and psychomotor behaviour.
  - This can be done using TA.
- AV aids, AV material, AV media, communication techniques, Educational/Instructional media, learning resourcing, multi-sensory aids — all these terms, broadly speaking, mean the same thing.
  - Earlier the term used was 'AV aids in education.'
  - With the advancement in the means of communication and that of technology, educator coined new terms.
  - More specifically, 'media' refers to films, film-strips, recording, etc.
  - The use of newer terms 'Educational Techniques or Instructional Techniques' is primarily due to the dynamic expansion of programmed learning, computer assisted instruction and educational TV.
  - This revolution in the field of AV education is the outcome of the development in electronics involving radio, tape-recorder and computer.

## 13.2 Concept and Meaning

Burton — 'AV aids are those sensory objects or images which initiate or stimulate and reinforce learning.'

Carter V. Good — 'AV aids are those aids which help in completing the triangular process of learning, *i.e.,* motivation, classification and stimulation.'

Edgar Dale — 'AV aids are those devices by the use of which communication of ideas between persons and groups in various teaching and training situations is helped.'

Kinder S. James — 'AV aids are any device which can be used to make the learning experiences more concrete, more realistic and more dynamic.'

McKown & Roberts — 'AV aids are supplementary devices by which the teacher, through the utilisation of more than one sensory channels is able to clarify, establish and correlate concepts, interpretations and appreciations.'

## 13.3 Significance

- AV aids are the stimuli for learning 'why', 'how', 'when' and 'where' of education.
- The 'hard to understand principles' are usually made clear by the intelligent use of skillfully designed instructional aids.
- AV aids/learning devices/technological media are added devices that help the teacher to clarify, establish, correlate and co-ordinate accurate concepts, interpretations and appreciations.
  - They enable the teacher to make learning more concrete, effective, interesting, meaningful, vivid and inspirational.
- The aim of teaching with technological media is 'clearing the channel between the learner and the things that are worth learning.'
  - The basic assumption underlying AV aids is — 'Learning (clear understanding) stems from sense experience.'
  - The teacher must 'show' as well as 'tell.'
- AV aids provide significant gains in informational learning, in retention and recall, in thinking and reasoning, in activity, in interest, in imagination, in better assimilation and in personal growth and development.
- Gandhiji — 'True education of the intellect can only come through a proper exercise and training of bodily organs — hands, feet, eyes, ears and nose.'

  Kothari Commission (1964-66) observed — 'The use of AV aids should indeed bring about an educational revolution in the country... The supply of TA to every school is essential for the improvement of the quality of teaching.'

  The National Policy of Education (1986 and modified in 1992) has laid a great stress on the use of TA, especially improvised TA, to make teaching and learning more effective and realistic.

  Edgar Dale — 'Because AV materials supply concrete basis for conceptual thinking, they give rise to meaningful concepts enriched by meaningful association. Hence, they offer the best antidot for the diseases of verbatism.'
- The place of AV aids in education has been recognised long ago.
  - The problem now is that of extending the benefits of AV aids to all teachers and all pupils.
  - The future can be bright if there is proper planning on the part of the government and co-ordination between producers, teachers and pupils.

- Useful and effective aids can be produced after getting the reaction of the audience and doing research work in the field.
- A great deal is done already but a lot more still remains to be done.

## 13.4 Need/Importance/Values of AV aids in teaching Mathematics

- The text books, blackboard, writing materials and geometrical instruments have been used as indispensable equipments for teaching mathematics since long.
  - Now, all these are considered as sensory aids.
  - In mathematics *doing* is more valuable than reading. Therefore, use of certain equipments is essential even at the beginning stage of teaching mathematics.
  - Mathematics is also considered as a dry subject. So, the creation of interest in the learning of mathematics has been a constant problem for the teachers.
  - To cope with the problem, the resourceful institutions and teachers have been using models, charts, geometrical instruments, drawings and other devices since long to stimulate interest and facilitate learning.
- In mathematics, there are so many abstract things to be taught. The abstract ideas are difficult to be followed by the pupils. The use of TA makes them easier to be followed.
  - TA make the teaching-learning process simple, effective and interesting.
  - They are useful in understanding the difficult concepts and abstract ideas.
  - They promote 'learning by doing' and thus pupils participation is ascertained.
  - They help in the development of concentration which is an essential aspect of teaching mathematics.
  - They provide recreation to the pupils which develops interest in mathematics.
  - The use of TA is helpful in minimising the habit of cramming. The concepts and abstract ideas clarified using TA cannot be easily forgotten.
  - They promote self-learning and constructiveness in the pupils.
  - Since most of the learning in children takes place at the sensory level, the TA are helpful to speed up this process because they influence the minds of the learners through their senses.
- The following are the main points due to which a teacher needs TA:
  1. To make the mathematical concepts clear and simple.
  2. To make the teaching meaningful.
  3. To make the lesson interesting and effective.
  4. To make the pupils more active in the class.
  5. To make the learning long lasting since the knowledge acquired through more than one sense organ, is more permanent.
  6. To make the pupils curious, attentive and motivated.
  7. To motivate the pupils towards mathematics individually as well as collectively in the class.

8. To communicate the complex ideas in a simple way.
9. To develop (1) the power of observation of the pupils,
   (2) understanding in the pupils about the applicability of the subject.

### (1) *Antidot to the disease of Verbal Instruction*

- TA help to reduce a verbalism.
- They help in giving clear concepts and thus help to bring accuracy in learning.
- Raymond Wyman (1957) — 'Teachers tell students and teachers provide them with written material so much of the time. Words are wonderful. They are easily produced, reproduced, stored and transported. But the overuse/excessive use of words can result in serious problem, mainly, the problem of verbalism (generally meangingless) and forgetting.'

### (2) *Clear Images*

- AV aids help in clarifying the various abstract concepts of mathematics instead of struggling hard only with the theoretical talks.
- This makes the subject meaningful.
- Clear images are formed when we see, hear, touch, test and smell as our experiences are direct, concrete and more or less permanent. Learning through the senses becomes the most natural and consequently the easiest. *e.g.*, $4 + 3 = 7$ can only be taught effectively if the pupils are given opportunity to count four and three concrete objects separately and then in combination.

### (3) *Best Motivation*

- AV aids are the best motivators. The pupils work with more interest and zeal. They are more attentive.

### (4) *Make Subject Interesting*

- AV aids help in creating and maintaining interest in the learning of mathematics. The subject no longer remains boring, dull and unreal one.

### (5) *Vicarious Experience*

- It is beyond doubt that the first hand experience is the best type of educative experience. But it is neither practicable nor desirable to provide such experience to pupils.
- Substituted experiences may be provided under such conditions.
- There are many inaccessible objects and phenomena, *e.g.*, it is not possible for the pupils living in India to see the pygmies or Eskimose. Similarly, it is not possible for a layman to climb the Mt. Everest or to see the beauty of nature at Switzerland.
- There are innumerable such things to which it is not possible to have direct access. In all such cases, these aids help us.

### (6) *Based on Maxims of Teaching*

- The use of AV aids make the teacher able to follow the important maxims of teaching like 'simple to complex', 'concrete to abstract', 'known to unknown' and to follow the principles such as 'learning by doing,' etc.

### (7) *Variety*

- Mere 'chalk and talk' do not help teaching-learning process. AV aids give variety and provide different tools and techniques in the hands of the teacher.
- They also bring variety in the methods and strategies of teaching mathematics.

### (8) *Freedom*

- Generally, while learning, the pupils like to move about, talk, laugh and comment upon. They want freedom of speech, movement and action.
- Under such atmosphere of freedom, the pupil work wholeheartedly, enthusiastically and co-operatively.

### (9) *Psychological Value*

- Pupils always like to manipulate or observe new things. If they are attracted towards an object or activity, they immediately become more attentive and can concentrate their mind upon the object or activity.
- AV aids make it possible for the pupils to concentrate upon learning new topics or concepts.
- Ultimately, it leads to grasping and assimilating learning and remembering for a longer period.

### (10) *Vividness*

- AV aids give vividness to the learning situation. A film on Mahavira or Buddha provides a vivid picture of his life and teachings. Vividness fixes the learning in the minds of the pupils.

### (11) *Retentivity*

- Use of AV aids increases retentivity as they stimulate response of the whole organism to the learning situation.

### (12) *Development of higher faculties*

- Verbalism promotes memorisation.
- Use of AV aids stirs imagination, thinking process and reasoning power of the pupils and calls for pupils' creativity, initiativeness and other higher mental activities.
- Thus the use of AV aids help the pupils in developing higher faculties.

### (13) *Reinforcement*

- Use of AV aids prove effective reinforcement by increasing the probability of re-occurrence of the response associated with them.
- Thus, it renders valuable help in the teaching-learning process.

### (14) *Fixing up the Knowledge*

- Fixing up the knowledge gained is a must. Otherwise gaining knowledge has no meaning at all. It needs permanent impression in pupils' minds. This can be easily engraved through AV aids; as they provide several activities, experiences and stimuli to the learner.

### (15) *Use of Maximum Senses*

- Senses are the gateways of knowledge. AV aids utilise maximum sense organs. This will certainly facilitate gaining of knowledge.

### (16) *Realism*

- A touch of reality to the learning situation is provided by AV aids.
- By seeing a film show exhibiting the life style of the people of Tundra region, pupils learn it more effectively in a short time of 2 hours than by spending weeks through reading.

### (17) *Saving Time and Energy*

- Use of AV aids saves time and energy of the teachers as well as students.
- Most of the abstract concepts and phenomena may be quite easily clarified, understood, grasped and fixed in pupils' minds through the use of AV aids.

### (18) *Opportunity to handle and manipulate*

- Handling and manipulating is one of the gateways of knowledge.
- Use of AV aids offers opportunity to pupils to handle and manipulate things. Pupils get enjoyment in it.
- This leads to better learning.

### (19) *Making subject interesting*

- AV aids help in creating and maintaining interest in learning mathematics. The subject no longer remains boring, dull and unreal one.
- Interest leads to attention, attention leads to concentration which ultimately leads to fixing up the knowledge permanently.

### (20) *Meeting individual differences*

- No two learners are alike. There exists wide individual differences among them.
- Some are eye-oriented. They like to see. Some are ear-oriented. They like to hear. Some like to learn by doing.
- The use of variety of AV aids helps in meeting the needs of different types of pupils.

### (21) *Healthy Classroom interaction*

- AV aids through their wide variety of stimuli, provision of active participation and vicarious experiences, encourage healthy classroom interaction for the effective realisation of teaching-learning objectives.

- Teaching-learning process becomes quite stimulating and active through AV aids. Their use helps in converting the passive environment of the classroom into a living one.

### (22) *Mass scale education*

- Radio and TV help in providing opportunity for education to people living in remote areas.
- They also help in promoting 'Adult Education.'

### (23) *Promoting Scientific attitude*

- In place of listening to facts, pupils observe demonstration/phenomena through film-strip. Thus, they cultivate scientific temper.
- With the help of AV aids, pupils ultimately adopt the habit of generalisation through actual observations and experiments.

### (24) *Positive transfer*

- Use of AV aids helps the learning of concepts, principles, solving the real problems of life by making possible the appropriate positive transfer of learning and training received in the classroom.

### (25) *Positive environment*

- A balanced, rational and scientific use of AV aids
  (1) develops motivation,
  (2) attracts the attention and interest of the pupils,
  (3) provides a variety of creative outlets for utilising pupils' tremendous energy and thus keeps them busy in the classroom.
  (4) The overall classroom environment becomes conductive to creative discipline.

### (26) *Utility*

- Still pictures, films, film-strips, resource persons, stimulations, mockups, TV and the like provide vicarious experiences, iin addition to reading.
- The more concrete and realistic the vicarious experiences, the more nearly it approaches the learning effectiveness of the first level.
  - Of course, unless the learner realises that he is dealing with a substitute, his learning may not be comparable to that of real life learning.
- It has long been recognised that the various senses condition the reception of messages in the communication act.
- Research by Cobun (1968) indicated that — of what is learnt

  83% is from the sense of *sight.*

  11% is from the sense of *hearing.*

  3.5% is from the sense of *smell.*

  1.5% is from the sense of *touch.*

  1% is from the sense of *'taste'.*

- Cobun also pointed out that people generally remember —

  90% of what they *say as they do a thing.*

  70% of what they *say.*

  50% of what they *see and hear.*

  30% of what they *see.*

  20% of what they *hear.*

  10% of what they *read.*

- The pupils should remember the popular saying —

  'I hear I forget, I see I remember, I do I understand.'

### Characteristics of AV aids

AV aids should be:

(1) meaningful and purposeful
(2) accurate in every respect
(3) cheap, simple and up-to-date
(4) improvised, as far as possible
(5) easily portable
(6) according to pupils' mental level
(7) motivators for learners
(8) large enough to be seen distinctly.

## 13.5 Basic Principles of AV aids

### 1. Principle of Selection

- AV aids are effective only when they suit —
  (*i*) the teaching objective,
  (*ii*) the unique characteristics of the special group of learners,
  (*iii*) the age-level, grade-level, and other characteristics of the learners,
- Again they should have specific educational value such as interesting, meaningful, stimulating, motivating.
- They should be the true representative of the real things.
- They should help the realisation of pre-determined desired leaning objectives.

### 2. Principle of Preparation

- As far as possible, locally available material should be used in preparing the TA.
- The teachers should receive some training in preparing aids.
- The teachers should themselves prepare some aids.
- Students should be associated in their preparation.

### 3. Principle of Physical Control

- Arrange the TA such that they are kept safe and they facilitate the teacher for use at the right time and place.

## 4. Principle of Proper Presentation

1. Teachers should clearly visualise the use of TA before their actual presentation.
2. They should completely acquaint with the use and manipulation of the aids to be used while teaching in the classroom.
3. Take care to handle an aid so that it remain undamaged while using it.
4. Display them in such a way that all the pupils can see them distinctly and derive maximum benefit out of them.
5. Eliminate all kinds of distraction as far as possible, so that full attention may be paid to the aid by the pupils.

## 5. Principle of Response

- AV aids work as the powerful stimuli. The teacher should guide the pupils to respond actively to the AV stimuli so that they derive the maximum benefit in their learning.

## 6. Principle of Evaluation

- This principle stipulates that there should be continuous evaluation of not only the AV material but of the accompanying techniques also, in the light of the achievement of the set objectives.

## 13.6 Various Problems related to AV aids

- Day by day, AV aids are becoming more and more popular. So, their appropriate use is a must. Yet, there are some problems to be faced and solved by the teachers and the students. They are:

### *1. Apathy of Teachers*

Lack of interest and enthusiasm on the part of the teachers is a great problem in using AV aids. Teachers, in general, are yet to be convinced that teaching or learning with words alone is very tedious, boring, wasteful, meaningless and ineffective.

### *2. Indifference of Pupils*

Unconcern of the pupils toward the use of AV aids is also a problem. When used without a definite purpose, the aids lose their significance and importance. The judicious use of them definitely arouses interest towards not only the subject but the methodology also.

### *3. Ineffectiveness of Aids*

- The AV aids do not prove their usefulness and ultimately prove ineffective due to —
  (1) the absence of proper planning,
  (2) the lethargy of the teacher,
  (3) improper preparation of the teacher,
  (4) his incorrect presentation, application and discussion,
  (5) absence of essential follow-up work.

- A film like a good lesson has various steps:

  (1) Preparation (2) Presentation (3) Application and (4) Discussion

### 4. *Financial Hurdles*

- India is not one of the developed countries, but is a developing one.
- The Central and State governments have set up Board of AV Education. They have chalked out interesting programmes for making TA popular.
- But the lack of finance makes them unable to do their best.

### 5. *Shortage of Electricity*

- Most of the projectors, radio and TV cannot work without the electric current which is mostly not available in a larger number of rural schools.

### 6. *Lack of Facilities for Training*

- Colleges of education or specialised agencies should specially provide the teacher trainees and workers the training in using the aids like projectors. If they are used wrongly they become out of function.

### 7. *Centre-State Co-ordination*

- Good film libraries, museums and AV provision are required to train teachers and workers for using TA. This can be done very easily if there is co-ordination between Centre and State.

### 8. *Difficulty of Language*

- Most education films are in English. We should have educational films in Hindi and in other important languages of India.

### 9. *Improper Selection of Films*

- If films are not selected according to the needs of the pupils, their as well as their teacher's time and energy are wasted to a great extent.

### 10. *No Catering to Local Needs*

- In selecting AV aids, little attention is paid to the local sociological, psychological and pedagogical factors. This is quite improper.

### 11. *Large Number of Students*

- According to educational norms, there should be only 30 to 45 pupils in a class.
  - But due to heavy enrolment, sometimes the number goes beyond 80.
  - It creates a great problem for the teacher to control and teach such a large class.
  - In a large class all the pupils cannot see properly the charts, graphs, figures or any other TA presented by the teacher.
  - The aids which are to be used individually may not be available in sufficient number for providing each and every pupil.
  - Thus, effective results cannot be achieved.

*12. Lack of Appropriate TA & Equipment*

- Sometimes appropriate TA for a particular topic/lesson is not available and teacher is helpless to get it.
  - In such cases, the teacher is unable to present the topic effectively.
  - There should be a provision for sufficient budget for purchasing the required equipment by the teacher.
  - Some institutions do not have proper arrangement of light, water and electricity.
  - In the lack of these facilities, teacher is unable to use different types of TA.

*13. Lack of Time*

- In school time-table, mathematics is given same treatment as the other subjects. Generally a period of 35-40 min is allotted to each subject including mathematics.
  - In such a short time it is not possible for the teacher to use TA for each and every topic.
  - He has to cover the prescribed syllabus within the specified time.
  - Thus, even if he intends to use TA, he cannot do so due to lack of time.

*14. Lack of Space*

- Lack of proper space for display of the aids is an accute problem for the teacher.
- Mathematics is generally considered as a non-practical subject and so a full time separate room is not allotted for it.
  - Therefore, the TA such as charts, graphs, figures, photos of great mathematicians, projectors, etc., available with the teacher cannot be displayed at proper place in a room.

## 13.7 Classification of TA

- All the below mentioned TA are useful in the teaching and learning of mathematics, according to the need of content/topic/lesson to be taught. They advance the pupils experiences.

### Edgar Dale's classification

1. Words (Least effective device)
2. Non-projective TA (More effective than words):
   chalk board (white, coloured), charts, display board, models (static, sectional, working)
3. Projective TA (More effective than non-projective aids):
   Epidiascope, over-head projector, slide projector (black-white, coloured), motion picture (silent, black-white, colour-sound), coloured films.
4. TA giving direct experience (Most effective):
   CCTV (demonstration), Experiments (demonstration), Experiments (self doing), projects.

### Classification-II

*Projective aids:* Films, film-strips, opaque projector, over-head projector, slides.

*Graphic aids:* Cartoons, charts, comics, diagrams, flash cards, graphs, maps, photographs, pictures, posters.

*Display boards:* Blackboard, bulletin board, flannel board, magnetic board, peg board.

*3-D Aids:* Models, diagrams, mockups, puppets, objects, specimens.

*Audio Aids:* Radio, recordings, TV

*Activity Aids:* Computer added instruments, dramatics, demonstrations, experimentation, field strips, programmed instruction; teaching machines.

### Classification III

*Audio-materials:* Language laboratories, Radio, sound distribution system sets, tape and disc-recordings.

*Visual-materials:* Bulletin boards, chalk boards, charts, drawings, etc., exhibits, film strips, flash cards, flannel boards, illustrated boards, magnetic boards, maps, models, pictures, posters, photographs, self-instructional material, slides, silent films, etc.

### Classification IV

*Big Media:* It includes computers, VCR and TV.

*Little Media:* It involves radio, film strips, graphic, audio cassettes and various visuals.

- 3-D aids are the substitutes of real objects.
- All the learning experiences which can be utilised for classroom teaching are shown by Edgar Dale in a pictorial device which he called the 'cone of experience.'
  - If we go up this cone of experience from its base, every aid is found to be arranged in the order of increasing abstractness.
  - In short, the cone of experience classifies the AV aids iin such a way that the aids at the base of the 'cone' are most effective and relatively gradually decreases.
  - The direct purposeful experience is gained through the aids, mentioned at the base of the 'cone'. Indeed, 'an ounce of experience is better than a tonne of theory.'
  - Contrary to this, deliberately created experience is like a working model which is an editing of reality and differs from the original in size or in complexity. *e.g.,* aid such as, globe of the Earth' or 'solar system' or 'the model of an amoeba.'

## 13.8 Types of aids

### 1. Personal Equipments

- The equipment which are required by the pupil of mathematics in order to pursue his own individual study may be termed as 'personal equipment.'
  - Text books, writing equipment, simple measuring and drawing instruments in the form of a geometrical box are personal equipments of the pupils.

- These are essential instruments without which a pupil cannot learn mathematics effectively.
- Therefore, every pupil of mathematics should have a geometrical box containing geometical instruments. A teacher should have wooden instruments for his demonstration work on the black-board.
- A pupil can have only simple and less expensive instruments. He cannot afford for costly instruments.

## 2. Institutional or Lab Equipments

- The equipments which can be used in common and has to be provided by the institution in the mathematics laboratory are termed as 'institutional equipments.'
  - Like other sciences and practical subjects, there should be a mathematics lab in each school.
  - This lab should be equipped with all necessary mathematical instruments.
  - The expenses on such equipment should form as legitimate a part of school budget as expenses on equipments of other practical subjects.
  - For storage of these equipments there should be a well-established lab.
  - Models, charts, blackboard, flannel board, weighing and measuring instruments, balances and weights, graduated cylinders, some special geometrical instruments, projector, film strips, tape measures, etc., lie in the category of this type of equipments.
  - Teacher should try to take help of such instruments for gaining practical knowledge of the mathematical facts. They also help much in learning mathematical facts and skills.
  - Use of these instruments is a must specially in Geometry and mensuration.

## 3. Real Objects

- Real objects are vivid, impressive, useful and most effective means of providing direct experience to the pupils.
  - They provide true and real impression of the things on pupils' minds.
  - Use of real objects helps in comprehending abstract concepts.
  - Real objects are indispensable in mathematics and other subjects.
  - They make a direct appeal to the pupils' senses.
  - It is not possible for a pupil to have a clear picture of a river, a mountain, a factory, a cloud, etc., unless he sees them.
  - The list of such objects may consist of objects like beads, coins, toys, money, seeds, sticks, pebbles, coloured balls, solids, pencils, the material used and produced in various work expense areas, weights, balance, measuring tapes, scale, watch, valleys, lakes, old forts, monuments, etc.
- Various topics and concepts concerning four fundamental rules, average, percentage, fractions, profit and loss may be successfully taught through these objects.
  - In framing multiplication tables, counting of beads and sticks prove to be very useful at the earlier stages.

- The real life situations may also be exploited as an aid in the teaching of mathematics.
  - Classroom may work as a real object for teaching *areas* of the four walls.
  - Similarly, blackboard, classroom tables, playgrounds and gardening plots, etc., may prove very helpful in teaching area/volumes and other facts of mensuration.

## 4. Models

- Models are the 3D representation of the real objects.
  - When for some reason or the other it is not possible or advisable to use the real objectives, their models prove very useful and effective means of educating the pupils.
- As far as possible, a model should be least expensive and be made by the pupils themselves.
- For teaching topics like area of four walls of a room, cross roads and other squares, rectangular or circular figures, models may be made out of thick paper and card board.
- Some important models generally used in Geometry are: triangles, squares, parallelogram — all three by using umbrella rods, cylinder, cone, sphere, pyramid, prism, etc. — all these may be wooden or paper-made.
  - While teaching the topics such as area of a sphere/cylinder/cone, the models of sphere, cylinder and cone may be made out of cardboard or chart paper can be easily used.
  - To explain the concept of congruency of triangles, models of two congruent triangles made out of joining rods may be used and congruency may be proved by explaining 1-1 correspondence.
- A model should be a replica/substitute of the original object.
  - Models can be prepared with several kinds of material like cardboard, plastic, plaster of paris, clay, thermocol, wood, etc.
  - Some models are static while some are working.
  - Working model will secure pupils' attention immediately and serve as motivation to learn.
  - It is essential to create interest in creative activity in pupils.
  - Preparation of models could form a topic for project work.
  - Models should be nearest to the reality so that it can draw the real map of things.
  - Being 3D, models evoke great interest and simplify matters.
  - Models are most useful especially in the teaching of Geometry.
- Models are generally of three types: solid, cross-sectional and working
  - Models are concrete objects, some of them are considerably larger or considerably smaller than the real objects.
  - In some cases, working models of the original are used where the specific function of the original is duplicated and could be explained easily.
  - Puppetry is one of the old and popular arts in India, using models of human beings.

## Functions of Model

1. Models simplify reality.
2. They concretise abstract concepts.
3. They enable us to reduce or enlarge objects to an observable size.
4. They provide the correct concept of an industrial unit or a bridge or a dam etc.
5. A working model explains the various processes of machines and machine-like objects.
6. After seeing and handling with models, pupils get self-encouragement to prepare certain models themselves.
7. Models may also serve the best purpose in teaching various concepts and facts related to geometrical theorems and exercises.
    - *e.g.,* to acquaint the pupils with the fact that 'sum of the measures of the three angles of a triangle is equal to 180°, the following paper model may be prepared:

From a paper cut off a triangular region. Cut off from it 3 regions each containing an angle. Now arrange them on a line. They will be exactly arranged such that sides of the two angles will be in a line. The third angle will be between these two angles.

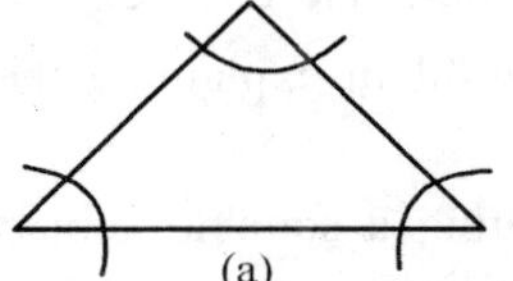
(a)

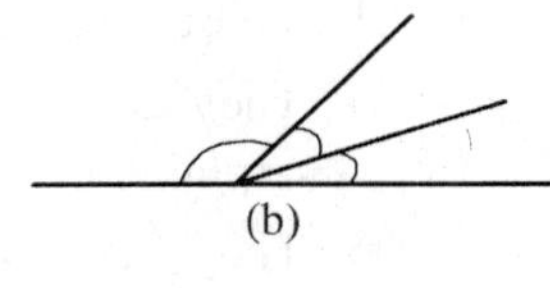
(b)

8. Models can be successfully used to acquaint the pupils with the shape and forms of different numerals and geometrical figures.
    - For this purpose even the square, round or rectangular shape, umbrella rods may serve as models.
    - To give practice in writing numbers, numerals and digits, engraved on the wooden pieces may prove useful models.
9. A model may give the correct perspective of a large industrial unit or even a large machine unit or a minute units of blood.

## 5. Pictures & Charts

- A chart is a combination of pictorial, graphic, numerical or vertical material which presents a clear visual summary.
    - Readymade charts are available for use in teaching in almost all areas in all subjects.
    - But, charts prepared by a teacher himself incorporating his own ideas and lines of approach of the specific topic are more effective, impressive and useful.
- In case, where it is not possible to have an appropriate model or to use real objects, their pictures and charts prove very useful in teaching mathematics. *e.g.,*
    - To teach simple, compound or decimal fractions, circular or rectangle fractional parts may be drawn on the charts.
    - In teaching profit and loss, unitary method, percentage, interest, work and time, the help of charts may be taken to work out principles and formulae.

- Pictures may also be used to make the pupils understand the basic things about the problems.
- In the problems related to area, volume and mensuration, charts may be used for analysing the problems.

- In Geometry, the use of charts may be made in showing figures concerning the proof of the theorem/proposition and helping the pupils in the construction of various geometrical figures and diagrams.
- In Algebra, the charts may be effectively used in teaching directed numbers, four fundamental rules and problems based on equations.
  - The general formulae may also be demonstrated through charts.
- The pictures and charts prove a helping hand to the teachers as they save their time and energy otherwise wasted in drawing figures and diagrams on the blackboard.
  - They may prove constant source of inspiration and means of imparting self-education to the pupils.
- The charts are very simple and cheaper TA.
  - They are very helpful in explaining the point which otherwise would be difficult to explain.
  - They help in creating a suitable subject atmosphere in the classroom and clarifying various difficult things.
- In mathematics, charts can cover a vast range of topics.
- Pupils may be encouraged to prepare charts on various topics.
  - Some commercially prepared charts are also available in the market such as 'International metric system chart', 'Chart of numerals', 'A time chart', 'Linear measure chart', 'chart related to change of currencies of different nations', etc.
- The following type of charts and pictures may be hung in the classroom —

(1) Charts concerning geometrical figures and shapes.

(2) Chart of different geometrical figures, their definitions and properties.

(3) Chart depicting different principles and formulae.

(4) Charts concerning units of weights, measures and coins.

(5) Charts of arithmetical terminology such as fraction, average, area, ratio, interest, profit and loss.

(6) Charts related to proofs of some important propositions.

(7) Charts related to some important informations of schools such as enrolment, results, and other activities being conducted otherwise.

(8) Pictures of great mathematicians of the world.

(9) Pictures related to history of mathematics.

(10) Pictures and charts showing use of mathematics in day to day life.

## Purposes of Charts

Charts serve the following purposes:

1. For showing —
   (*i*) relationship by means of facts, figures and statistics;
   (*ii*) continuity in process;
   (*iii*) development of structure.
2. For presenting —
   (*i*) materials symbolically;
   (*ii*) abstract ideas in visual form.
3. For summarising information.
4. For creating problems and stimulated thinking.
5. For motivating the pupils.
6. For encouraging utilisation of other media of communication.

## Suggestions for Effective use of Charts

1. Charts should be multi-coloured, artistic and attractive.
   - The beauty and colourfulness makes them more appealing.
2. There should not be too many facts/things demonstrated through a simple chart. It should not contain too much written material.
   - It should concentrate on a single definite purpose.
3. A chart should have a proper size, so that it can clearly be seen by each pupil in the class.
   - It should neither be too big nor too small.
   - The drawing and writing must be very distinctive and clear.
   - Irrelevant thing/theme, not connected with the topic, should not be demonstrated through a chart.
4. As far as possible the charts and pictures should be got prepared by the pupils.
   - Chart competitions should also be organised.
   - Teacher-made charts should be preferred to.
5. The spelling of words and numerical data given in the chart should be correct and to the point.
6. Some important and useful charts should remain hanging on the walls of the classroom.
7. The chart or the portion of the chart be depicted only for a short duration whenever it is needed.
8. Teacher should use the pointer to indicate or point out specific part/point of the chart.
9. There should be a collection of charts in enough number on various topics.
   - Charts should be carefully stored and preserved for use in future.

10. Straight pins, staples, peg board lips, gummed hangers, paper clips, folded making tapes may all be used for fastening charts without damaging them.

## Basic Types of Charts

The following is the list of basic types of charts in terms of arrangements and the kinds of ideas which they may express:

### 1. *The Narrative Chart*

- This chart is an extended left-to-right arrangement of facts and ideas for expressing —
  (1) the events in a process such as shoe-making, oil-caking, etc.
  (2) the events in the development of a significant issue to its point of resolution or to present status. *e.g.,* the events to the separation of India and Pakistan.
  (3) technical improvement over a period of years such as improvement in transportation, communication, manufacturing, etc.

### 2. *The Tabulation Chart*

- This chart is a left-to-right, top-to-bottom arrangement of facts and ideas for expressing —
  (1) numerical data for making comparison.
  (2) products, mountains, rivers or the like in selected area, etc.

### 3. *The Cause-and-Effect Chart*

- It is usually a limited left-to-right arrangement of facts and ideas for expressing —
  (1) relationship between the diameter of a circle and its radius/circumference.
  (2) relationship between volume of a cylinder and volume of a cone having the same radius, etc.

### 4. *The Chain Charts*

- It is a circular or semi-circular arrangement of facts and ideas for expressing —
  (1) Cycles, *e.g.* water cycle, $CO_2$ cycle, $N_2$ cycle, etc.
  (2) transition *e.g.,* transition from raw material to useful finished products.

### 5. *The Evolution Chart*

- It is a left-to-right arrangement of facts and ideas for expressing —
  (1) the natural number system and its subsequent development,
  (2) the numerals and its development.

### 6. *Diagrams*

- Diagrams are very helpful in supplementing illustrations in teaching.
- Difficult operations may be explained with the help of diagrams.
- The area and volume etc. in mathematics can be illustrated through diagrams.
- A teacher is expected to possess the skill of drawing diagrams easily, neatly, rapidly, readily and accurately on the blackboard.

## 7. *Blackboard*

- It is the most universally used TA.
  - Writing on clay and sand was the ancient form of blackboard writing.
  - It helps in summarising, reviewing and crystallising the main points.
  - It is can be used for drawing diagrams, sketches, figures, etc.
  - It proves a good helping hand in all the tasks like —
    (*i*) drawing of diagrams and figures
    (*ii*) giving definitions, principles and formulae
    (*iii*) drawing generalisations
    (*iv*) writing the language of the problems and their solutions
    (*v*) having practice and drill work
    (*vi*) assigning home-task.
  - The blackboard with graph lines may be successfully used for –
    (*i*) drawing all types of geometrical figures
    (*ii*) plotting graphs
    (*iii*) solving simultaneous equations graphically
    (*iv*) solving problems on areas and volumes
    (*v*) presenting statistical data.
- Blackboard may be considered as the first and foremost of all items of mathematical equipment.
- As an aid in teaching of mathematics, blackboard is so much effective that it is popularly termed as 'the right hand' of a mathematics teacher and 'a never-failing friend' of a mathematics teacher.
  - The secret of the popularity of the blackboard lies in the fact that one can write and remove what has been written on it at his own will without involving any significant expenditure.
- The teacher writes and explains his writing while writing on the blackboard. In this way, pupils get both the benefits of observing and listening at a time.
- The use of blackboard is indispensable and irreplacable for all the branches and topics of mathematics.
  - This is because, inspite of new devices and techniques in teaching, it still proves a simple and unique device.
  - It begins with the first lesson of mathematics and then goes up to the highest learning in the subject.
  - In mathematics, most aspects can be clarified only through writing.
  - Blackboard and a piece of chalk prove very helpful in illustrating concepts and ideas to the pupils.

- It is the most faithful and oldest, best friend of the mathematics teacher.
- A teacher of mathematics says everything by means of it.
- The blackboard may be called the second tongue of the mathematics teacher.
- It is the minimum equipment for mathematics teaching.
- Teaching of mathematics and blackboard are so closely connected that their separation cannot be imagined.

- In a real sense, without the use of blackboard the teaching of mathematics is a dishonesty.
  - That is why some people does not consider it as a TA of mathematics. They assume it as an integral part of mathematics classroom.
  - Blackboard continues to be the *sine quo non* of our educational system.
- Blackboard is the mirror through which pupils visualise all about the teacher's mind regarding the lesson in hand, his way of explaining, illustrating and teaching as a whole.
- In short, what a teacher wants to communicate to his pupils may be successfully done through this readily available aid and it helps in quick understanding as well as fixing up of the knowledge of the subject.

## Purpose/use of Blackboard

In mathematics, the blackboard is mostly used for the following purposes:

1. To write (*a*) the statement of problems and their solutions
   (*b*) some important points, terms, definitions, symbols and formulae.
2. To draw the diagrams, figures, graphs, graphics, sketches, maps, statistics, etc. and thus stimulate pupils' interest.
3. To present important statistical data and other relevant informations.
4. To do exercises and to provide problems for assignments.
5. To invite (or focus) attention of the pupils to certain important points of the topic.
6. To clarify abstract statements in the exposition stage and to give a summary containing the salient features at the revision (recapitulatory) stage.
7. To note and/or tabulate certain results.
8. To list questions and problems on the blackboard.
9. To provide a lot of scope for creative and decorative work.
10. To erase writing and drawings and start afresh.
11. To take heed of varying capacities and rates of grasp of the pupils.
12. To review the whole lesson for the benefit of the class using blackboard.

## Types of Blackboard

There are five main types of blackboard as under:

1. *Fixed blackboard:* It is fixed in the wall facing the class and normally made of wood or concrete cement.

2. *Blackboard on Easel:* It is portable, and adjustable and put on a wooden easel. It can be taken out of the classroom while taking classes in the open.
3. *Roller Blackboard:* It is made of thick canvas wrapped on a roller. It is mostly used for teaching by teacher-trainees.
4. *Graphic board:* It has graphic lines. It is generally used for teaching mathematics, science and statistics.
5. *Magnet Board:* It is a board which enables teachers to make 3D demonstrations with objects on a vertical surface. Small magnets are used to hold suitable objects fixed on a vertical surface.

## Effective Use of Blackboard

Some suggestions are given below for the effective use of blackboard:

1. The teacher —
   (1) should not speak while writing on the blackboard, as it divides pupils' attention.
   (2) should always be cautious to avoid writing of incorrect and inappropriate things on the blackboard.
   (3) should develop the entire blackboard work with the active co-operation and participation of pupils.
   (4) should develop the ability to draw freely on the blackboard.
      - The map/chart/diagram drawn before the very eyes of the pupils is much more impressive, valuable and useful than a well-finished map/chart/diagram.
      - Occasionally pupils may be asked to write or draw diagram figure, outline, etc. on the blackboard to provide them encouragement and motivation.
   (5) should have sufficient practice for writing, sketching and drawing legibly on the blackboard.
   (6) should always make use of the standard terminology and symbols on the blackboard so that the pupils may not get confused.
   (7) should learn how to face the blackboard while writing on it.
      - He should have a watchful eye over the pupils while keeping himself busy on the blackboard so that they may remain attentive.
2. Writing on the blackboard should be —
   (1) legible (2) neat and clean (3) in straight and horizontal rows
   (4) started from the top left corner (5) visible to all the pupils in the class.
3. It should be ensured that —
   (1) blackboard is well lighted by natural or artificial means
   (2) the class is attentive while teacher writes on the blackboard
   (3) the blackboard is periodically serviced
   (4) the blackboard is smooth, well-polished and painted from time to time.

4. Chalks of different colours may be used —
   (1) to make the writing and drawing attractive, meaningful, clear and effective
   (2) for emphasising particular facts.
5. Letters and drawing should be large enough to be seen from all parts of the classroom.
   - Chalk should be properly pressed while writing.
6. Blackboard should be properly cleaned before making its use.
   - Duster and not hand or handkerchief should be used in cleaning the blackboard.
   - The written matter should not be removed at once. Pupils should be given time to visualise and copying, if required.
   - At the end of the class the written matter on the blackboard should be completely removed off.
7. The problem solved or the work done on the blackboard should follow a logical as well as psychological sequence.
8. A proper margin should be kept on both sides of the blackboard
   - Extreme lower corners of the blackboard should not be made use of as writing there cannot be seen easily.
   - Only salient features/points of the subject matter should be written on the blackboard.
   - Written matter on the blackboard should not be covered by standing.
9. Diagrammatic visual presentation involving many processes should be pre-prepared before the beginning of the lesson.
   - Besides classroom blackboard, teacher may also use roller blackboard to present certain things written or drawn priorly.
10. Everything needed for the blackboard work should be kept together before the class begins. *i.e.,* collection of various colour chalks, T-square, compass, projector, etc.
11. The blackboard should not be used in the manner that the teacher goes on writing and the pupils go on copying.

## 8. *Projective Aids*

- In this type of teaching aids, different diagrams, figures, mathematical formulae, propositions and their proofs, graphs, pictures, etc., made on papers/strips/slides can be seen in enlarged form by projecting it through some projecting aids.
- Projective aids are very useful in teaching as they attract the pupils due to their novelty, visibility and colourfulness.
- With these aids different ideas of mathematics can be presented effectively, impressively and easily.
  - The most advantage of these aids is that they do not create burden on the minds of the pupils and the matter can be shown again and again.
- The following projecting devices are generally used as TA in mathematics:

## 1. Film strip projection

- A film strip is 35 mm wide, a hand operated device and contains a series of still/motionless pictures about 24 to 48 frames arranged in a sequence so that they develop a theme.
  - A film strip can be prepared by taking a series of photographs using a 35 mm camera and then by taking a positive print of the negative film on another 35 mm film.
  - These film strips are then projected on the screen through a projector.
- The teacher may demonstrate the pictures of any period of time irrespective of speed as well as situation demands.
- Various film strips can be used to give altogether new colour and attraction to different ideas of mathematics.
  - These film strips can be easily obtained from the market.
- The mathematics teacher may also seek the co-operation of science teacher in using this aid.
- In mathematics, some useful film strips are available. They are:

  (1) *What is fraction?* (The basic concept of a fraction as an equal parts of an object is explained and presented in an effective and meaningful way).

  (2) *Multiplication of fractions:* (visual examples of multiplying a fraction by another fraction(s) are shown *e.g.* $\frac{1}{2}\times\frac{1}{2}, \frac{1}{2}\times\frac{1}{3}, \frac{1}{2}\times\frac{1}{4}$, etc. several practice exercises are also included)

  (3) *Per cent in everyday life* (Problems related to social application of *per cent* are given, *e.g.,* examples on commission, discount, interest, taxes, etc.)

  (4) *Measurement* (It emphasises the place of measurement in our life and society. *e.g.,* measurement of length, mass, capacity, area, volume, time, temperature).

  (5) *Use of graphs*

  (6) *Transactions in a bank*

  (7) *What is business?*

  (8) *Property Taxation*

- These film strips are very useful TA because the objects and situations presented by them cannot be created in the classroom.
  - Their presentation is very interesting, effective and meaningful.
  - A teacher should know the details presented by a film strip before using them for the pupils.

## 2. Motion Picture (Cinema)

- Motion pictures are very useful for developing certain mathematical concepts and their applications.
  - The real life situations can be interestingly presented through motion pictures.

- This entertainment device can be successfully used for teaching of various facts, definitions, principles, etc. of mathematics.
- The life history of mathematicians, their discoveries and inventions, historical landmarks of the development of mathematics can be successfully demonstrated through cinema films.
- For teaching demonstrative geometry, cinemas may be successfully used.
- The pupils may learn how to use various geometrical instruments while drawing different types of figures and diagrams, how to survey and measure the different dimensions, how to find areas and volumes of differ plane/solid figures, how to use graphs, etc.

- Through films, pupils know how mathematics can be used in solving day-to-day life problems faced in different occupations and fields of action.
  - Thus, the use of cinema films may prove quite effective, impressive, stimulating, motivating and useful for the teaching and learning of mathematics.
- Cinema is such an aid that calls on both the visual and auditory senses.
  - The pupils listen as well as observe the facts at the same time. This provides them a greater stimulating and motivating value for learning something new.
  - Teachers make the students acquaint with the growing knowledge and methods of teaching mathematics.
  - The film may be borrowed from State/Central Education Departments and libraries.

## 3. Over-Head Projector (OHP)

- OHP is a device that can project a chart, a diagram, a figure, a table, and anything written on transparent plates, upon a screen or the white wall before pupils in a class.
  - This make teaching illuminative, illustrative and impressive.
  - It saves a lot of teacher's time used in drawing or writing on the blackboard.
  - These transparencies can also be preserved for future display while taking up the same topic.
  - For preparing transparencies, the teacher has to draw or write upon transparent plates with any dark ink with a fibre tipped pen.
  - It can also be typed on such transparencies any material meant for display, using a good carbon paper.
  - In case, transparencies are to be washed out, washable water colour can be used for writing on the transparencies.

## 4. Slide Projector

- Photographic slides can be projected with a slide projector on the screen or white wall in front of the class.
- First, photographs of relevant matter meant for teaching mathematics can be developed on celluloid slides. They can be displayed using slide projector.

- A teacher-trainee's (or a teacher's) lesson can also be recorded on an audio cassette and played with a tape recorder suitably causing to operate at the same time and rate, with the slides of manipulating a remote control switch.
  - Such an arrangement is called a 'tape-slide sequence.'
- In case, there are several slides to be shown in quick succession, 'the tape-slide sequence' can bring very interesting effect on the viewers like a film.
- An ordinary slide projector has a frame containing two slits into which slides are put for focusing. They are manually and continuously replaced by other slides one after another.
- An improved type of slide projector consists of a circular disc with more slits where even a 100 or more slides can be inserted in a sequential order which can be projected on the screen using a remote control switch to be suitably manipulated by the teacher as he delivers his lesson.

## 5. Magic Lantern

- Magic lantern is the earliest invention in the history of AV aids, used for projecting pictures, diagrams, illustrations, etc. in magnified form, from a slide on a screen or wall.
  - When a figure or diagram or picture is very small and it is to be shown to the entire class, a transparent slide of a small figure is prepared.
  - Then, this slide is placed into the slide carrier part of the magic lantern.
  - This magic lantern device projects it on the screen by enlarging its dimensions and making the vision more clear and sharp.
- While projecting the slides, teacher explains the important aspects of the picture visible on the wall-screen.
  - This instrument of science has proved very useful for teaching mathematics.
- Magic lantern helps the teacher to demonstrate different types of figures, diagrams, pictures related to various topics of mathematics through the slides.
- For getting better results the teacher may also explain the things demonstrated through magic lantern.
  - The demonstration may further be followed by discussion to clarify the various issues on the topic.

## 6. Epidiascope

- The epidiascope is an instrument which can project images or printed matter or small opaque/transparent objects on a screen. It can also project images of 4″ × 4″ slide.
- Using epidiascope any chart, diagram, map, photograph and picture can be projected on the screen, without tearing off from the book.
  - No slide is needed for this purpose.
- Epidiascope works on the principle of 'horizontal line projection with a lamp, plane mirror and projection lens.'
  - Strong light from the lamp falls on the opaque object.

- A plane mirror placed at an angle of 45° over the project, reflects the light so that it passes through the projection lens forming a magnified image on the screen.

- An epidiascope serves two purposes. It works as epidiascope when it is used:
  (*a*) to project an opaque object.
  (*b*) to project slides (by operating a lever).
- It is used for enlarging and then demonstrating the contents, figures and diagrams of the printed or handwritten pages.
- It has shown its value in teaching of mathematics too, specially at the time when the teacher feels difficulty in drawing or giving things on the blackboard.
  - It is quite useful for depicting complicated figures.

## 9. Radio & TV (Non-projective aids)

- At present, radio and TV are not only recreational means but these are used as educational techniques for teaching various subjects including mathematics.
  - Some topics and lessons of mathematics, talks of subject experts on some specific topics — are presented at a specific time by radio and TV.
  - Thus, these devices can effectively be used as TA.
- Radio and TV both have established their due place in the field of education.
  - Almost all the important centres of AIR broadcast different types of educational programmes.
  - For the programmes on mathematics education the regular classes on topics of mathematics are being held regularly. The important discussions and speeches concerning principles and laws of mathematics, life history and contributions of great mathematicians, historical development of the knowledge of mathematics, the applications of mathematics is our day-to-day life — are broadcast.
  - Highly experienced teachers, teacher educators, mathematicians and research scholars take part in such programmes.
  - Radio as a means of communication take their voices to the millions of pupils and teachers listening their programmes with interest and curiosity.
  - TV has far greater advantages as it conveys the voices and the pictures and actual scenes.
  - The pupils sitting far away from the TV broadcasting stations may get advantage through the telecasting programmes almost in the same way as it is happening just in front of their eyes.
- A mathematics teacher should take advantage of such learning opportunities by making himself and his pupils fully conversant with such programmes.

## 10. (Earth) Globe

- Knowledge of map is unreal without that of globe, the true map.
- Globe is the true representative of Earth's physical personality.

- Four types of globe may be kept in every school:
  - (1) Political globe
  - (2) Physical globe
  - (3) Washable projection globe
  - (4) Celestial globe.
- A globe gives a true idea of the total environment at a glance in a classroom situation.
- It is through globe only that a child can understand to concepts of time, space, day and night, seasons, wind's planetary relations and proportion. Hence every school should have globes.

## 11. Visits & Excursions

- Visits and excursions play are effective role in learning mathematics by providing knowledge and direct experiences.
- The pupils get opportunity of learning mathematics in the way it is used in practical life.
- If the teacher wants to develop interest and understanding in mathematics, the visits and excursions prove very helpful.
- The places such as shops and business centres, workshops, industries, mills, power stations, station, markets, banks, post-office, telegraph-office, railways booking-office, agriculture fields, forest, some picnic spots, historical places, etc. should be visited by every pupil of mathematics to get the first-hand/direct understanding of application of mathematics in different aspects of life.
- During these visits and excursions the pupils may face so many problems requiring the knowledge of mathematics for their solutions.
  - The teacher may utilise such situations for giving the essential knowledge of mathematics. Sometimes the pupils may get opportunity for applying the already gained knowledge.

## 12. Newspapers

- Newspapers is also used as an effective aid for teaching and learning of mathematics.
  - They help in correlating teaching of mathematics with day-to-day happenings of life.
- The statistics given in the newspaper in the form of weather-chart, the current prices of various commodities, budgets of State and Central government, interest rates of various private and government agencies, stock and shares, foreign exchange, etc. — all provide good means for making the teaching of mathematics interesting, useful and purposeful.
- The cuttings of the newspapers may be employed to help the pupils in learning the practical application of mathematics in our daily life.

## 13. Running School-Co-operative Store

- A co-operative store running in a school may also be utilised for mathematics education.
- Through such store, the pupils learn the various principles and facts of mathematics regarding profit and loss, profit per cent and loss per cent, four fundamental rules, unitary method,

percentage, weighing and measuring, etc., by becoming shopkeepers or customers in such a store.

### 14. Collections

- The data and materials of mathematical interest collected earlier are also helpful in teaching and learning of mathematics.
- Pupils should be encouraged to collect various types of mathematical data from different sources such as magazines, journals, periodicals, newspapers, etc.
- Pupils may also collect data while on visits and excursions.

### 15. Pictures

- Children like pictures very much, especially of lower classes.
- Pictures provide environment of reality.

### 16. Text Books

- The text books of mathematics is the second most important TA, the first being the blackboard.
- They are the standardised collection of the subject matter. They are useful to both — teachers as well as pupils.
- They play an important role in facilitating the teaching of new concepts and skills in mathematics.
  - They are helpful in self-study. Illustrations help pupil in self-study.
  - Exercises given in the text books encourage the pupils and sometimes challenge them, too.
  - They are the means of preserving and transmitting the knowledge.
  - Therefore, the value of text books of mathematics is beyond measure.

### 17. Mathematical Games & Riddles

- They have their recreational role. Over and above, they may be effectively utilised for learning, practising and using various principles and facts of mathematics.
  - There are so many games which may be successfully utilised for mathematics education.
  - In such games and riddles, competitions can be usually organised by grouping pupils. This provides learning opportunities while playing.
- This device makes the pupils more active and develops a sense of healthy competition.

## 13.9 Developing Low Cost Improvised TA

- In fact, Nature itself is a big source and a treasure of aid material for learning the facts and principles of mathematics.
  - The pupils may gain valuable direct and indirect experiences for the learning of mathematics from their local environmental surroundings.

- In their local set up consisting of their homes, community, physical and social environment they may get a lot of opportunities to practise and learn so many valuable concepts regarding the teaching and learning of mathematics.
- There is a lot of cheap and sometimes waste material available in pupils' local environment that can be successfully utilised for the improvisation of valuable aid material for teaching of mathematics.
- The type of aid material that can be easily improvised for the teaching and learning of mathematics, is given below:

### 1. *Concrete Material and Objects*

- A wide variety of collection of different types of concrete material like beads, seeds, balls, sticks, matches, match boxes, pebbles, different types of corns, etc., may be made with the help of pupils.

All these material may prove quite helpful in the learning of counting, four fundamental rules/operations, multiplication tables, etc.

### 2. *Improvising an Abacus*

An abacus containing a number of beads — wooden, metal or even thermocol — in several metallic wires can be easily improvised for teaching the pupils the facts of counting or four fundamental rules, place-value system, etc.

### 3. *Place-value Pockets*

This may also be improvised. The required boxes for this purpose can be made with using thermocol, thick paper or from wood, etc., and the system be made so operated as help in the learning of the concepts of place-value.

### 4. *Preparation of Models*

- By using the easily available low cost or waste material, various types of models may be improvised.
  - Such models represent the shape of various geometrical figures like rectangle, square, parallelogram, trapesium, triangle, circle, ellipse, cylinder, cone, sphere, pyramid, prism, etc.
  - We can have models made of clay, match sticks, thermocol, wood, wax, etc.
  - Area of cross-roads, area of four walls of a room, area of the circle, area of a quadrilateral, area of a triangle and so many other things related to the learning of mensuration may be easily taught through the use of models made of the locally available low cost material.
  - The waste paper, card boards, thick papers, wooden boxes, etc., available in the packages of the household goods purchased from market can be effectively used for making models with a simple use of pins, nails, scissors, hammers, threads, rubber bands, ropes, etc., easily available in the houses and school workshop.

- Teacher may even utilise the real surroundings as an aid to his teaching. *e.g.*, while teaching about the area of four walls of a room, he can have the classroom as a living concrete model.
    - In teaching the concept of mensuration, teacher may utilise the sport-ground, school garden and neighbouring plots as a living models for necessary surveying and measurement.

5. *Preparation of Charts & Pictures*

- Using the chart paper and drawing material, easily available in the market, the low cost visual aid material may be easily prepared for the teaching and learning of almost all concepts related to all the branches of mathematics.
    - The scrap book prepared from the newspaper cuttings of the data of mathematical interest may also be used as a teaching aid.
- Teacher of mathematics should exploit his resourcefulness, creativity and ingenuity for making the task of teaching and learning interesting and purposeful by using low cost improvised TA.

## 13.10 Suggestions for effective use of TA

For the effective use of TA, following suggestions should be kept in mind:

1. The purpose of using the aid should be clear. It should not be used just for the sake of using it.
2. The aid should be —
    (1) helpful in making the teaching effective,
    (2) presented and used at the right moment and place.
    - Its use at wrong time does not make teaching effective and sometimes it may prove harmful.

    (3) kept before the pupils as long as it serves its purpose.
    (4) removed when it has already served its purpose.
    - If any aid is kept before the pupils throughout the period, they mostly observed it whole the time eagerly or aimlessly.
3. In the selection of TA, the main consideration should be its purpose.
    - The interest and abilities of pupils should be kept in mind.
4. The size of the aid should be appropriate so that it should be visible to all the pupils. It should be neither too large nor too small in size.
5. In mathematics, accuracy is very important. So, the concepts depicted through the aid must be accurate.
6. If more than one aid are to be used, they should be displayed in a systematic sequential manner. Every aid should be presented and used at the proper time.
    - The presentation and use of aid should be fixed in the lesson plan prior to teaching.
    - Before teaching the essential aids should be kept at proper place.

7. The teacher should —
   (1) always keep in mind that the TA are only means and not an end.
   (2) have a good practice of using the aid before its use in the class.
   (3) seek the co-operation of pupils while using the aid in the class.
   (4) seek the co-operation of Head of the institution in the collection, preservation and presentation of TA.
8. To eradicate the 'lack of time' factor, teacher may arrange extra-period so that aids can be used properly and the lesson can be explained clearly.

## EVALUATE YOURSELF

1. What do you understand by teaching aids? What teaching aids would you use in teaching 'Congruency' to the pupils of Std. IX?
2. Discuss the need and importance of AV aids in teaching mathematics.
3. Blackboard is considered as a visual aid. What precautions should be taken during the use of blackboard in teaching mathematics?
4. How far the teaching aids help in teaching and learning mathematics?
5. What are the main teaching aids in mathematics? Discuss the use of models and charts in mathematics.
6. Discuss the importance of blackboard as a teaching aid in mathematics. How can it be used effectively?
7. What are projective aids? Discuss some projective aids useful in the teaching of mathematics.
8. Write short notes on:
   (1) Types of TA in mathematics
   (2) Need of TA for a teacher
   (3) Selection of TA by a mathematics teacher.
   (4) Effective use of TA.
   (5) Difficulties in the use of TA.
   (6) Classification of AV aids.
   (7) Use of Radio and Cinema as a TA.
   (8) Projected and non-projected TA.
   (9) Chart, model, film strips and epidiascope.
9. Explain the use and importance of any two of the following TA in teaching of mathematics.
   (*a*) Models (*b*) Projective aids (*c*) Radio (*d*) TV (*e*) Photos and pictures
10. Give your views regarding the development of low cost improvised TA in mathematics.
11. Give the concept and meaning of AV aids. Also bring out their significance.
12. Why should a teacher use AV aids while teaching mathematics?
13. Discuss the basic principles of AV aids.
14. Explain the various problems faced by a teacher of mathematics in relation to AV aids.
15. Classify TA in four different ways.

16. Explain in detail any two of the following types of TA:
    (1) Models; (2) Real objects; (3) Charts; (4) Blackboard; (5) Over-head projector; (6) Slide projector; (7) Magic lantern; (8) Text Books
17. Give your suggestions for effective use of TA.
18. Prepare TA to teach the following topics in mathematics:
    (1) Area of a circle (Std. VIII)
    (2) Pythagoras Theorem (Std. X)
    (3) Area of a cylinder (Std IX)
    (4) $(a + b)^2 = a^2 + 2ab + b^2$
    (5) $(a + b + c)^2 = a^2 + b^2 + c^2 + 2ab + 2bc + 2ca$.
19. What principles would you keep in mind while using TA in mathematics? Explain.

> 'Algebra is the intellectual instrument for rendering clear the quantitative aspects of the world.'
>
> — ***A.N. Whitehead***

# METHODS OF TEACHING MATHEMATICS

## 14.1 How to teach?

'What to teach?' The curriculum answers it. 'How to teach?' The methods of teaching mathematics are the probable solutions for this very important and pointed question. 'How to teach?' is really a difficult problem for most of the mathematics teachers.

To realise the set aims and objectives to its fullest extent the teacher should know 'in which way?' the content (subject matter or topics) be introduced to the pupils so that they get the expected learning experiences.

Educational thinkers and various schools of thoughts have proposed various methods of teaching mathematics. It is the teacher who adopts some specific ways or devices for imparting the desired theoretical and practical experiences to his pupils. These ways and devices are known as *methods of teaching mathematics.*

No one single method is fully suitable or appropriate for each topic of mathematics. Why? It is due to the following reasons:

(1) The pupils of different levels — primary, secondary and higher — have different age, maturity, mental abilities and interests, mental development, mathematical understanding and capacities, etc.

This means one method cannot be applied to teach mathematics to all the classes.

(2) Besides this, with the use of one method, all the students of the same class cannot be equipped with equal amount of knowledge due to individual differences among them.

Individual difference is an important and remarkable psychological phenomenon which affects teaching and its outcome to a great extent.

(3) According to Thorndike — "There is a much difference between lower and higher categories of pupils of the same class."

So, a teacher has to apply different methods to teach the same topic to same class so that every pupil can understand, grasp and assimilate the given content.

The success in teaching mathematics depends upon —

(1) the mastery over mathematical content

(2) the skill in teaching mathematics.

## 14.2 Various Methods of Teaching Mathematics

Following are the main methods generally used for teaching mathematics:

1. Inductive Method
2. Deductive Method
3. Analytic Method
4. Synthetic Method
5. Lecture Method
6. Demonstration Method
7. Laboratory Method
8. Heuristic Method
9. Project Method
10. Problem-solving Method
11. Dogmatic Method

### 1. Inductive Method

This method of teaching and learning mathematics is based on Induction. Induction means proving a universal truth or theorem showing that if it is true in any particular case, it will be true in the most cases in the same serial order. This is the method of induction.

Induction method takes into account the process of induction.

### Steps of Procedure

Mainly following steps are used:

1. *Presentation of specific examples:* At this step, a sufficient number of similar examples of a particular type are presented to the learners.
2. *Observation:* At this step, pupils observe the various presented examples minutely and try to see relationship among them and seek some general or common elements of findings.
3. *Generalisation:* On the bases of common elements of findings of different similar examples, learner arrives at a general conclusion which leads him towards establishing a general rule or formula.

   Thus, learner arrives at a generalisation or derive a formula through a convincing process of reasoning. The learner has to find out rules or establish a general formula.
4. *Testing and Verifications:* At the last step of this method, learner himself can verify the truthfulness of the general rule or formula by using it to solve another similar problems.

Thus inductive method is a method of constructing or deriving a formula or a rule with the help of adequate number of concrete examples.

This is the method of development in which the learner is made or led to discover truth on its own. While adopting this method, pupils are required not to accept the already discovered formula or rule without knowing how it has been established. He is helped in its discovery by adopting inductive reasoning.

In inductive reasoning teacher proceeds 'from particular to general', 'from concrete facts (examples) to abstract rules' and 'from specific examples to the general formula.' Here, the results are always generalised by studying particular concrete cases and examples.

If one rule applies a particular case and is equally applicable to different similar cases, it is accepted as a generalised rule or formula.

In this method, the rules and formulae are established after extensive study of experiences, experiments and examples.

## *Merits of Inductive Method*

1. It is motivating and stimulating method of teaching mathematics.
2. It is a scientific method as:
   (1) the knowledge attained by this method is based on real facts,
   (2) it introduces heurism in pupils, they act as researchers,
   (3) it encourages self study,
   (4) it stimulates intellectual powers of the pupils, and
   (5) it helps to develop scientific attitude in the pupils.
3. This method is more useful in lessons where principles, rules, definitions, generalisations and casual relation between facts are to be established.
4. This method develops –
   (1) critical observation and logical powers of the pupils,
   (2) curiosity and interest in the pupils to learn mathematics.
5. It is a psychological method as (1) it keeps child's nature in the forefront, (2) it is understanding-centred and (3) many important principles of psychology are used in this method.
6. This method develops self-confidence and self-reliance as the method guides the pupil to do the work himself and the pupils are trained to depend on their own observation and judgement so that the knowledge is assimilated.
7. The pupils get the knowledge of the process of deciding and generalising laws, formulae, etc. by active participation.
8. It is a method of genralisation as its aim is to enable the pupil for general preparation for future life.
9. It leads to discovery and research. Child acts as a discoverer.
10. Knowledge gained by the use of this method is more durable as the pupils attain it by experimentation, examples, observation and testing.
11. This method reduces the tendency of cramming, as there is less possibility of forgetting the process once learnt. No stress is laid on memorisation. Even if the pupil forgets the formula, he can discover it.
12. This method helps to ascertain or establish many laws, formulae, relations and new principles of mathematics. Particular cases or examples are dealt with and from findings of these cases the general law or formula is inferred.

13. This method is very useful and most suitable for lower classes, *i.e.*, for beginners as it provides opportunities for direct and concrete experiences. All teaching in mathematics is inductive in the beginning.
14. The pupils do not get bored or fatigue. They remain active to gain new knowledge.
15. It encourages active participation of the pupils in the teaching-learning process. So, it is a source of pleasure for pupils and make the task of teacher easier.
16. It provides opportunities for better pupil-teacher relationship.
17. Any doubt regarding *how* and *why* of a formula are clarified in the beginning.
18. It is based on actual observation, thinking and experimentation. Therefore, the pupils acquire not only facts and information but also the mode of acquisition or *the line of attack* which proves useful in their later life.
19. In this method, knowledge is self-acquired and is soon transformed into wisdom.
20. A safe method. The general rule is acquired step-by-step. Its meaning is well grasped and applied with success.
21. It is a student-centred method. Both the pupils and teachers are active.
22. It emphasises original and creative work.
23. The teaching-learning process becomes interesting.
24. It is the best method of teaching. Most of the knowledge have been acquired by the human race in this manner. So, it is a natural and psychological method. And it is the most suitable method for the study of mathematics.
25. It promotes mental development as it exercises the mind to develop.
26. In this method, there is upward movement of thought leading to definitions, principles, rules, etc.

### *Demerits of Inductive Method*

1. This is a very slow method. It demands a lot of time and labour from the teachers as well as pupils to learn the process of solving the problems and to reach on an inference. All knowledge is to be acquired first-hand by the pupils. So, gaining knowledge by this method costs more time and labour.
2. Teacher has to do more labour to search the relevant examples. It is neither easy for teachers nor for pupils to present/select real examples for generalisation.
3. This method is not very useful and suitable for advanced stage as the syllabus is very wide in higher classes, so, it is not possible to cover the whole syllabus by using this method.
4. It needs sharp mind, proper planning and enough labour. So, for pupils of all levels it is not easy to attain knowledge by this method.
5. Only an able and experienced teacher can successfully use this method.
6. The ability and capacity of problem-solving cannot be developed by the use of this method.
7. Results drawn by using this method is not always true if they are drawn from less number of examples. Their truthfulness and reliability depends upon a number of examples on

which they are based because the truthfulness or reliability of any result goes on increasing if it is drawn from more and more number of specific examples.

8. Inductive method helps the pupils to generalise or formulate a rule on the basis of a few concrete examples but '*what nexts*?' remains unanswered.

   Thus only the discovery of a formula does not complete the study of the topic but it requires a lot of supplementary work and practice to fix the topic in the minds of learners. Thus, the method is limited in range.

9. This method sometimes leads us to erroneous conclusions and wild generalisations specially if the learner jumps the hasty conclusions.

   For example, after studying the lines in a plane, Ravi concludes... "Two non-parallel lines always intersect.' His conclusion is hasty and therefore erroneous. Two non-parallel lines may not intersect at all if they are in different planes.

10. This method should not be confined only to understanding the rules at the early stage of learning. After establishing a formula/rule, time should not be wasted in rediscovering it for every subsequent problem.

### Inductive Reasoning in our daily life — Application of Inductive Method

*[Please, see the deductive method]*

## 2. Deductive Method

Deductive method is exactly opposite to inductive method. This method is based on deduction. Deductive reasoning (*i.e.*, logic) is used or followed in this method.

It is a process by which a particular fact is derived from some general unknown truth. Thus, in this method of teaching, learner proceeds 'from general to particular', 'from abstract to concrete' and 'from formula to examples.'

It is mainly used in Algebra, Geometry and Trigonometry because different relations, laws and formulae are used in those subject-branches of mathematics.

According to Joseph Landon — 'Deductive teaching secures first the learning of definitions or laws or rules, then carefully explains its meaning and lastly illustrates it fully by applying to facts.'

### Steps of Procedure

Mainly following steps are used:

#### 1. *Presentation of rule/formula*

Just after presenting the problem to be studied, the teacher provides readymade and relevant pre-illustrated rule/formula/principle/law to the learners. They learn them by heart. Teacher explains the formula and its use.

#### 2. *Application of the formula*

The teacher solves few problems on the blackboard to explain the application of formula to problems. Thus, learners learn how the formula can be applied to solve the related problems.

Then the teacher asks them to solve some related problems by using that formula. The learners apply that formula to the problems and solve them according to the procedure explained by the teacher.

The learner has to perform only calculation or to simplify the substituted known values in the given formula to get the solution of the problem.

### 3. *Inference*

After getting proper solutions of the problems with the help of the given formula, the learners come to understand that the formula is the key to solve this type of problems.

### 4. *Verification*

On reaching to the conclusion, the learner needs the verification of the conclusion/inference. So, he applies the formula to solve many other similar problems and thus he rechecks/verifies the validity of the conclusion.

## Inductive and Deductive Reasoning in our Daily Life

[IR means Inductive Reasoning, DR means Deductive Reasoning]

1. (IR) Dhyani observes that a bullock-cart has wheels, a horse-cart has wheels, a scooter has wheels, a motor car has wheels, a train has wheels. These all are vehicles on land. She concludes that all the vehicles on land have wheels.

   (DR) Vismay is taught that all the vehicles on land have wheels. Then he observes bullock-carts, horse-carts, scooters, motor cars, trains, buses, cycles, rickshaws and verify the conclusion.

2. (IR) Kshitij observes the formation of day and night in turn. He also observes that a day follows a night and a night follows a day. He also observes sunrise and sunset. He concludes that with sunrise day starts and with sunset night starts.

   (DR) Krupa is told that day follows night and night follows day. She is also told that with sunrise day starts and with sunset night starts. She observes this phenomena for days together and verifies its truthfulness.

3. (IR) Ravi comes across the death of his grandfather, his grand mother, his neighbours, his friends and other people in his surrounding. He concludes that 'man is mortal.'

   (DR) Kavya is taught that 'man is mortal', one day or other, everybody has to die and leave this world. She verifies the generalisation by carefully observing some cases of death surrounding her.

4. (IR) Shreyas tastes green unripe mangoes and yellowish ripe mangoes for days together. He concludes that unripe mangoes are sour while ripe mangoes are sweet.

   (DR) Dhyani is told not to eat unripe green mangoes as it is sour in taste but eat ripe mangoes as it is sweet in taste. Dhyani verifies the fact as and when the occasion permits.

5. (IR) A scientist weigh various types of matter at the bottom of a mountain and at the top of the mountain so many times. He concludes that the weight of a particular object is less at the top of a mountain than that at its bottom.

(DR) Students are taught that the weight of a particular object is less at the top of a mountain than that at its bottom. They verify the conclusion by comparing weights of so many different objects at the bottom and at the top of mountains.

## Applications of Inductive and Deductive Methods while teaching Mathematics:

**Topic:** To derive the formula: Area of a rectangle = $l \times b$

**(Inductively)** The teacher asks each pupil to draw a rectangle of any size in full centimetres. Then he asks them to divide the enclosed region (*i.e.,* area) of each rectangle in unit squares. Then students count the number of unit squares of each rectangle. Then he tabulates their observations on the blackboard as below:

| *Sr. No.* | *Length l (in cm)* | *Breadth b (in cm)* | $l \times b$ | *(Area) No. of unit squares* |
|---|---|---|---|---|
| 1. | | | | |
| 2. | | | | |
| 3. | | | | |
| 4. | | | | |

From the last two columns, the pupils will conclude,

Area of a rectangle = $l \times b$.

**(Deductively)**

**Topic** : To find the area of a given rectangle.

**Application** : Find the area of a rectangle having length 5 cm and breadth 3 cm.

**Teacher gives the formula** : Area of a rectangle = $l \times b$

**Teacher substitutes** : = 5 cm × 3 cm

**Teacher calculates** : = 15 sq cm. (Ans.)

Using the formula he solves two or three more examples.

Now he asks pupils to solve many similar problems.

**2. Topic:** To find the sum of measures of the angles of a convex quadrilateral.

**(Inductively):** Teacher asks each pupil to draw a convex quadrilateral ABCD of any size and shape. The teacher asks them to measure all the four angles of the quadrilateral. He tabulates their results on the blackboard as below:

| *Sr. No.* | $m\angle A$ | $m\angle B$ | $m\angle C$ | $m\angle D$ | $m\angle A + m\angle B + m\angle C + m\angle D$ |
|---|---|---|---|---|---|
| 1. | | | | | |
| 2. | | | | | |
| 3. | | | | | |

From the last column the pupils will conclude — 'The sum of the measures of the angles of a convex quadrilateral is 360°.'

**(Deductively):** Teacher first points out that the sum of the measures of the angles of a quadrilateral is 360°. Then he asks each pupil to verify the established fact by actually drawing a quadrilateral and measuring its angles and then finding the sum.

**3. Topic:** To find out the factors of $a^2 - b^2$

**Inductively:** Teacher asks pupils to expand $(x + y)(x - y)$, $(a + 12)(a - 12)$, $(m + 5)(m - 5)$, $(11 + 6)(11 - 6)$, $(a + b)(a - b)$

| | | |
|---|---|---|
| Pupils expand | : $(x+y)(x-y)$ | |
| They use distributive property | : $= x(x-y) + y(x-y)$ | |
| They simplify | : $= x^2 - xy + xy - y^2$ | |
| They further simplify | : $= x^2 - y^2$ | |
| Similarly they expand | $(a + 12)(a - 12)$ | $= a^2 - 144$ |
| | $(m + 5)(m - 5)$ | $= m^2 - 25$ |
| | $(11 + 6)(11 - 6)$ | $= (11)^2 - (6)^2$ |
| | $(a + b)(a - b)$ | $= a^2 - b^2$ |

Teacher have already explained them that expansion is opposite of factorisation. This means, if $x^2 - y^2$ is the expansion of $(x + y)(x - y)$, then $(x + y)(x - y)$ are the two factors of $x^2 - y^2$.

Now the students generalise that the factors of $x^2 - y^2$ are $(x + y)(x - y)$. *i.e.*, (First term)$^2$ – (Second Term)$^2$ = (ft + st) (ft – st)

**Deductively:** Factorise : $a^2 - 64$

Teacher gives the formula : $a^2 - b^2 = (a + b)(a - b)$

Learners substitute : $(a)^2 - (8)^2 = (a + 8)(a - 8)$

The learner works out similar examples.

## *Merits of Deductive Method*

1. Deductive method needs little labour and time to solve the problems. Thus, it is economical method in terms of labour and time.
2. It enhances speed, skill and efficiency to problem solving. The speed of gaining knowledge increases as pupils directly use the formula for solving problems.
3. Teacher's work is much simplified by giving a rule with an example and asking the pupils to verify it by application to other concrete and similar examples. Therefore, teachers and authors like to adopt this method preferably.
4. A quick method. The pupil awaits opportunities of getting finished knowledged acquired by others (*i.e.,* of intellectual heritage).
5. This method is simple and practical for the pupils as they get a readymade key to unlock/ solve the relevant problems.
6. By using this method mathematical work becomes very easy and comfortable. Both the teacher and the pupil do not find any difficulty in using this method. Pupils can do the exercise quickly and easily.

7. More knowledge can be obtained in less time. It can be used when there is shortage of time.
8. It is most suitable and useful in higher classes *i.e.,* at the advanced stage.
9. It increases the tendency of cramming. Cramming power of pupils increases. It develops the habit of memorisation because pupils have to memorise a considerable number of formulae to solve different types of problems.
10. It is most suitable at the application stage. The finished form of mathematics is deductive.
11. Very useful for teaching theorems and axioms of Geometry and tables in Arithmetic.
12. Laws, principles and formulae can easily be checked. General rule/formula is first inunciated. Then, it is applied to solve particular problems.
13. It is a method of specialisation. So, here, pupil acquires some special knowledge to be useful for some specific purpose.
14. It emphasises on problem-solving.
15. If properly practised and revised, this method is adequate and advantageous.
16. Mathematically, if inductive method is 'much training + little information', then deductive method is 'much information + little training.'
17. It promotes mental growth as it feeds the mind to grow.

### Demerits of Deductive Method

1. This method is not in accordance with psychological principles. It is memory-oriented and unnatural, too. Since the beginner has no ability to understand nor aptitude to appreciate abstract knowledge without having first gone through concrete examples.
2. It is not suitable and useful for beginners (lower classes) as they are unable to understand the abstract formula and its application without understanding of the terms, concepts, etc., used in it.
3. Here, the stress is laid on cramming/memorisation than understanding or discovering. It requires a formula for every specific type of problems. So, its extensive use demands the memorisation of a large umber of formulae which ultimately reduces the educative process to memorisation of facts.

   If he forgets the formula, he will not be able to solve examples. Without comprehending, the memorised facts are soon forgotten and knowledge is rendered useless. Here, memory is more important than understanding and intelligence. So, the learner remains educationally unsound.
4. In this method, pupils work like machines without knowing the purpose of proceeding in that particular way.
5. Knowledge gained, here, is unclear, unstable as it is not gained by their own efforts.
6. This method is unpsychological because this is the method of presentation. No originality and creativity is developed.

   Again, pupils have every doubt about the formulae. Why should they take formula for granted? Most of the time, pupils learn without understanding.

7. This is not a scientific method. It does not develop scientific attitude.
8. In this method, there is no scope of developing powers like reasoning, logical thinking, investigating.
9. No opportunity to gain new knowledge. It depends upon induction for new knowledge. It does not provide education, it provides instruction.
10. Teachers are more active and pupils are passive listeners. So, it is a teacher-centred method. Pupils are passive recipients of knowledge. Pupil gets formulae, rules and definitions readymade. They verify them by applying on solving the relevant problems. Thus, it is a method of verification.
11. The pupil cannot become an active learner as it gives no opportunity to the pupil to do things ownself and thus he is deprived of the pleasure of self-activity and self-effort.
12. It does not help the child to assimilate and turn the knowledge to his own use, so, the knowledge does not become the wisdom. Thus, this method seems contrary to the important empirical saying — 'General truths in order to be learnt should be earned.'
13. This method encourages dependence on others and so the knowledge acquired may be soon forgotten.
14. This is not a safe method. The general rule may be imperfectly grasped and this may lead to faulty application.
15. Laws/formulae are already told to the pupil. He is not able to derive them on his own.
16. The process become uninteresting and dull.
17. In this method, there is a downward movement of thought leading to non-comprehension of the principles, rules or formulae.
18. This is not the best method of learning.
19. Practically it is impossible to verify each law and formula.
20. This method is useful only if it is combined with inductive method. In this method help is taken from assumptions, postulates and axioms of mathematics.

## Conclusion

Both the methods have their advantages and disadvantages. The best way is to combine both the methods in such a way as to derive maximum advantages. Deductive method is supplementary to inductive method, so, its inadequacies and incompleteness can be removed.

To start with inductive method should be used. Later on deductive method, Inductive method is a forerunner/predecessor of deductive method. The deductive method is more faithful as a follow up.

Mathematics is understood inductively and applied deductively. Induction leaves a learner at a point where he cannot stop. The after work has to be completed by deduction.

Thus, the combination of these two methods termed as 'Inducto-Deductive Method' is most appropriate, desirable and useful.

## 3. Analytic Method

The original meaning of the word 'analysis' is 'to separate things that are together.' Analysis is a process of breaking/disintegrating a thing into its simple and smaller parts.

Thus, separation of different parts of a problem is known as 'analysis'.

Analysis is a process of thinking. It is an explanatory process. By analysing a problem we mean to break the problem into simpler elements or to unfold its hidden aspects in such a way that its solution may appear quite obvious. By using it, the difficult part of any problem can be analysed to find out the solution of the given problem.

Thorndike has rightly stated — 'All thought, at any rate, all the highest performance of the mind is analysis.'

He also remarked — "The mind's most intellectual act is to connect one thing with the other, but its highest performance is to think a thing a part into its elements."

According to Kuppuswami — 'In Logic and Mathematics we analyse in order to find out how things can be combined together to make up the whole."

Analysis starts with 'what we have to find out (*i.e.*, conclusion, unknown) and traces the connection between it and 'what is given (*i.e.*, data, known)'. Thus, analysis proceeds 'from unknown to known.'

The beginning is made always 'from conclusion (unknown)' and then operating it analytically, the unknown is ultimately linked with the 'data (known hypothesis)'.

This method is used when we have —

(*a*) to prove any theorem

(*b*) to do construction work in Geometry

(*c*) to find out the solution of some problems in Arithmetic.

This method is identified with induction as here inductive reasoning is applied. This method is based on the process of analysis, an operation of breaking a statement or problem into simpler and smaller elements.

This is a general, formative method. It is an informal method.

One starts from what is to be proved and then comes back to what is given. In this method, all steps have full reason and purpose for their own importance alongwith a regular sequence.

This is a method of discovering. Proof/solution of a given theorem/problem is discovered by an organised and systematic thinking. Thus, this is a method for thinkers and discoverers. Here, every step is logical and is explained to understand the learner.

It involves trial and error. So, this method is slow and lengthy.

**Application of Analytic Method:** Please see the application of synthetic method.

### *Merits of Analytic Method*

1. Thought provoking and logical method. Pupils get enough opportunities to present their original thoughts. So, it develops originality and logical abilities.

2. It develops scientific attitude as (1) it leads to the spirit of inquiry and investigation, and (2) it proceeds on heuristic lines.
3. It helps in developing thinking, reasoning, decision-making power and analytic power of the learners, *i.e.*, intellectual powers of the learner.
4. It is based on heuristic approach as it is a discovery method since here learner has to work as a discoverer of the facts.

   Pupils learn to acquire/discover knowledge with their own attempts. So, they become self-confident and self-reliant.
5. This is a psychological method as important psychological principles are taken into consideration.
6. It creates originality, creativity and proper scientific attitude among the pupils.
7. It is a formative method based on inductive reasoning.
8. By this method knowledge gained is more solid and durable. There is a very little scope of forgetting. The pupil can recall and reconstruct easily any step if forgotten.
9. Pupil is always curious for attaining new knowledge, since it answers the questions/doubts arised in the mind of the pupil very satisfactorily.
10. Memory does not play a leading role. Using systematic and organised thinking, what is to be done in the subsequent steps may be properly realised. Each step has its reason and justification and therefore no cramming is required.
11. Teacher carries the whole class with him as there is active participation of the pupils in the teaching-learning process. As a result, there is more contact between the teacher and the taught. Both are active and the solution of the problem is found out with the help of the pupils.
12. It facilitates understanding as the pupils have to go through the whole teaching-learning process themselves.
13. Here, the teacher throughout faces with the questions like 'how can it be proved?', 'how can it be done?', 'what are the possible ways for it?' 'how can it be resolved into simpler elements?'. Thus, it helps the teacher to tackle the problem confidently and intelligently.

## *Demerits of Analytic Method*

1. In this method, facts are not presented in any set pattern. Thus, there is a lack of systematisation. Solution of the problems or proof of a theorem cannot be systematically presented with this method.
2. Uneconomical in terms of time and labour as it is time consuming, lengthy and laborious. Whole syllabus cannot be completed within certain period.
3. Skill, speed and efficiency needed in the computation work cannot be properly acquired.
4. It is not suitable for each and every topic of mathematics.
5. Every teacher cannot use it successfully.
6. Not fruitful for below average pupils.

7. This method is possibly more useful if —
   (*a*) the teacher has the knowledge of known facts and unknown conclusions,
   (*b*) it is used as forerunner of synthetic method.

## 4. Synthetic Method

Synthesis means to place together things that are apart or to join separate parts. In synthesis, the smaller constituents/parts of a thing are combined/put together, so as to give something new. It is a process of putting together known bits of information to reach the point where unknown information becomes obvious and true. So, it leads from known to unknown.

Therefore, we start with the data available and connect it with the conclusion. Thus, here we start from hypothesis (and not with the conclusion as in analytic method) and end with conclusion.

In meaning 'synthetic' is opposite of 'analytic' but in practice, it is the complement of analytic.

This method is identified with deduction. Here, deductive reasoning is applied.

This is the method of presentation of the discovered facts. Pupils are not required to discover something. They have to present the discovered proof/solution in a concise form so as to convince the learner. What is already given (known) is arranged in such a way that the synthesised structure may lead the learner to the desired results (conclusion).

One starts with what is given and ends with what is to be proved. Though every step, in between these two, is correct but for its sequence one has no reason. This method fails to explain why a particular step has been taken.

It is an informative method. It is the method of formation, recording and presenting concisely the discovered solution omitting the trials and errors. No heuristic essence in it.

Synthesis without analysis is dogmatic. Analysis followed by synthesis has a place in the classroom.

Most of the philosophers, logicians and educationists believe that the highest form of man's intellectual activity is *synthesis*.

### *Applications of Analytic – Synthetic Methods*

*1. Problem:* If $\frac{a}{b} = \frac{c}{d}$ prove that $\frac{ac + 3b^2}{bc} = \frac{c^2 + 3bd}{dc}$ $(b, c, d \neq 0)$

### *Analytically*

| | |
|---|---|
| Let us start with what is to be proved | $\frac{ac + 3b^2}{bc} = \frac{c^2 + 3bd}{dc}$ |
| Simplifying by cancelling c in the denominator | $\Rightarrow \frac{ac + 3b^2}{b} = \frac{c^2 + 3bd}{d}$ |
| Let us cross-multiply | $\Rightarrow acd + 3b^2d = bc^2 + 3b^2d$ |
| Removing $3b^2d$ from both the sides | $\Rightarrow acd = bc^2$ |

Dividing both sides by c ($c \neq 0$) $\Rightarrow ad = bc$

Putting the equation in the given form $\Rightarrow \frac{a}{b} = \frac{c}{d}$

As this is given, we can say that $\frac{ac + 3b^2}{bc} = \frac{c^2 + 3bd}{dc}$

*Synthetically*

We are given $\frac{a}{b} = \frac{c}{d}$

Adding $\frac{3b}{c}$ to both sides (why? we do not know) $\therefore \frac{a}{b} + \frac{3b}{c} = \frac{c}{d} + \frac{3b}{c}$

Simplifying $\therefore \frac{ac + 3b^2}{bc} = \frac{c^2 + 3bd}{dc}$ (proved)

2. *Problem:* The length and breadth of a rectangular field are 60 m and 40 m respectively. There is a 5 m wide path around the field enclosing it from outside. Find out the area of the path.

*Analytically*

Draw a rough sketch of the data

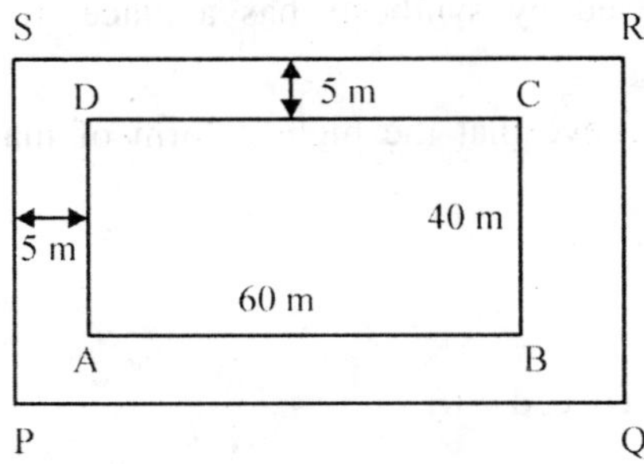


What is given in the problem?

(Length and breadth of the field and width of the path)

What does the figure show?

(PQRS represents the area of the field with path. ABCD represents the area of the field)

What is to be found out in the problem? (Area of the path)

How to find out the area of the path? (PQRS – ABCD)

How to find out PQRS? (By multiplying its length and breadth)

How do we know the length and breadth of rectangle PQRS if we know the *l* and *b* of rectangle ABCD? (By adding the width of the path to those of the field)

What is the length of rectangle PQRS? (60 m + 5 m + 5 m) = 70 m

What is the breadth of rectangle PQRS? (40 m + 5 m + 5 m) = 50 m

Then, what is PQRS? PQRS = $l \times b$ = 70 m × 50 m = 3500 sq.m

what is ABCD? ABCD = $l \times b$ = 60 m × 40 m = 2400 sq.m.

Now, what is the area of the path?

Area of the path = PQRS – ABCD
= 3500 sq.m – 2400 sq.m
= 1100 sq.m *(Ans.)*

## Synthetically

Length of the rectangle PQRS = (60+5+5) m = 70 m

Breadth of the rectangle PQRS = (40 + 5 + 5) m = 50 m

Then PQRS = 70 m × 50 m = 3500 sq.m

ABCD = 60 m × 40 m = 2400 sq.m

∴ Area of the path = PQRS – ABCD = 3500 sq.m – 2400 sq.m
= 1100 sq.m *(Ans.)*

3. *Problem:* Construct ΔABC such that base BC = 7 cm, AB – AC = 2 cm and m$\underline{|B}$ = 50°.

## Analytically

Draw a rough sketch of the data in which AB > AC by 2 cm. What does this mean? AB – AC = 2 cm.

This figure represents what is given. Which triangle can be drawn right away? (ΔDBC)

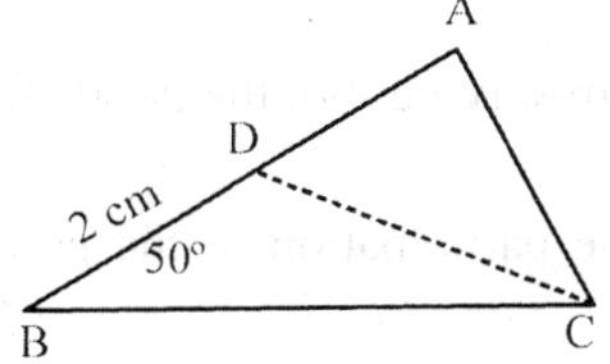


Draw it.

What can be said regarding AD and AC? (equal, ∵ $\overline{AD} \cong \overline{AC}$ )

If AD = AC, then how is the distance of A from D and C? (equal)

How can we get the point A equidistant from two points D and C?

(By drawing a ⊥ bisector of $\overline{CD}$)

On which ray is the point A? (on $\overrightarrow{BD}$)

Let us draw $\overrightarrow{BD}$. Why? (∵ it contains point A)

And ⊥ bisector of $\overline{CD}$ also contains point A.

Now, draw $\overline{AC}$.

ΔABC is the required triangle.

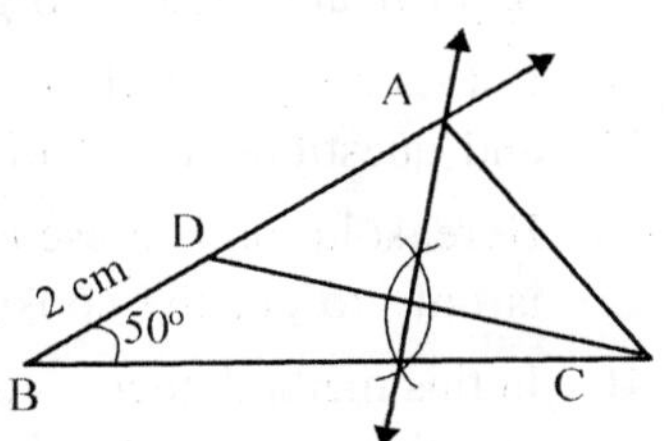


## Synthetically

Draw ΔDBC first in which BC = 7 cm, m$\underline{|B}$ = 50° and BD = 2 cm. Draw $\overrightarrow{BD}$ and a ⊥ bisector of $\overline{CD}$. Where they intersect, is the point A. Now draw $\overline{AC}$. ΔABC is the required triangle.

## Merits of Synthetic Method

1. Economical in terms of time and labour as it is short, quick (time saving) and concise method as it does not involve trial and error.
2. It glorifies the memory of the pupils. It helps to develop only the power of memory.
3. Solution of the problem or proofs of a theorem can be properly presented with this method.
4. Skills, speed and efficiency needed in the computation work can be properly acquired.
5. It is suitable for the majority of the learners.
6. It can be applied to teach most of the topics of mathematics.
7. It is more useful if it is used as the follow up of analytic method.

## Demerits of Synthetic Method

1. It tends to rote memory. Memory plays a leading role. It does not provide full understanding. All the steps are crammed. Once forgotten it is not easy to recall them. This is the method for crammers.
2. It does not provide opportunity for the development of metal powers like thinking, reasoning, imagination and many other mental abilities. The pupils work by mere imitation. There is no scope for discovery.
3. Logical method. It does not care for the psychological principles.
4. It proves an obstacle for the development of scientific attitude, originality and creativity among the pupils, as there is no heuristic approach in it.
5. It provides no opportunity for independent discovery or problem solving. So, the pupils lack in self-confidence and self-reliance.
6. Teacher is unable to carry class with him as there is no active participation of the pupils. This method makes the pupils passive listeners.
7. Steps of this process are obtained by special device and these are not well-explained to understand the teacher. Recall and reconstruction of each step cannot be possible for every pupil if any step is forgotten.
8. It does not give full satisfaction to the pupils because this method does not satisfy the doubts and questions arised in the minds of the pupils.
9. Here, solution is presented by the teacher. No help is needed from the pupils and their work is only to get the cooked solution.
10. In this method, there is no scope for originality because it only repeats the thoughts presented by others. So, it develops only memory.
11. Homework assigned by the teacher may likely to be more difficult for the pupils.

## Conclusion

Both these methods have merits and demerits. No one can advise one method, completely discarding the other. In logic and mathematics, these two methods always go together.

It seems that analytic method is superior to synthetic method. But in actual practice they both are complementary and inter-dependent. One method is incomplete without the other.

Analysis is the forerunner of synthesis. Synthesis is follower of analysis. So, analytic method is useful in the beginning for discovering the solution or proof. But at the practice stage, it is not proved much useful. What is discovered by analysis can be properly mastered and applied through synthesis. At the practical/application stage synthesis is more suitable and useful.

It can be justified by quoting the statement of Arthur Schulze — 'Analysis is the method of discovery, synthesis is the method of concise and elegant presentation.'

The need is to synthesise both these methods. In the beginning analytic method and for presentation synthetic method. Analysis leads to synthesis and synthesis makes clear and complete the purpose of analysis.

We cannot synthesise without analysing and analyse without synthesising. Analysis is useless if not followed by synthesis just as induction without deduction or deduction without induction.

Both analysis and synthesis are required in induction and deduction. 'Analytico-Synthetic Method' is the complete method.

## 5. Lecture Method

'Lecture' means the methodical preparation of an idea through oral word-picture *i.e.,* through speech. Here, verbal explanation is given for facts. The teacher plays the role of a speaker and pupils are listeners.

It is mostly used by a competent and experienced teacher and also misused by incompetent and unexperienced teacher.

### *When to use Lecture Method?*

Lecture method is to be used —

(1) for initiating a discussion.

(2) for explaining abstract concepts.

(3) for introducing a new lesson or topic.

(4) for giving necessary instruction regarding new and recent mathematical knowledge.

(5) for correlating the new knowledge with the previous knowledge or mathematics with other subjects.

(6) for giving mathematical information at random.

(7) for summing up and review certain concepts or solution of a problem.

(8) for summarising the lesson or content which has been taught.

(9) for giving demonstration, instruction and clarification.

(10) for giving illustrative, interesting and motivational talk.

(11) for fulfilling queries and information.

(12) for giving information not easily available.

(13) for making critical appraisal.

(14) for preparing the child mentally to study new lessons or topics.

(15) for presenting interesting personal experiences.

(16) for teaching a large number of pupils at the same time.

(17) for presenting a new approach.

(18) for giving information regarding historical development of mathematics and contribution of the great mathematicians.

### *Steps in the process of Lecture Method*

1. Selection of a specific topic by the teacher
2. Planning by the teacher
3. Presentation by the teacher
4. Receiving the information by the learners.

It is clear from above that there is no place of pupils' activities.

### *Merits of the Lecture Method*

1. More suitable and useful at higher level classes and adult learners.
2. In a well-planned lecture there is a sequence of ideas which makes the topic easily understandable and effective.
3. It is useful in relating some of the historical and mathematical incidents.
4. Easy, quick, brief, attractive and most convenient method for teachers. It simplifies the work of the teachers.
5. More information or content can be given in a short period. Thus, economical with respect to time and labour.
6. A single teacher can teach a large group of pupils at a time.
7. A word-picture of ideas and experiences can be well-presented.
8. It is useful for introducing new knowledge. Introductory talk/lecture is most impressive and useful.
9. It is inspiring and motivating method. Effective in providing information and facts.
10. It is helpful in maintaining the discipline. If a lecture is delivered impressively, pupils listen attentively with pin-drop silence.
11. It gives a sense of satisfaction to both — the teacher and the listener. Teacher feels satisfied that he has finished a certain part of syllabus successfully and pupils feel that they have learnt something.
12. The flow of teacher's thoughts is maintained undisturbed.

### *Demerits of Lecture Method*

1. This method ignores basic principle of 'learning by doing'.
2. As it is oral and verbal method, not useful for lower level of education.
3. There is no possibility of inter-personal contact between the teacher and the pupils. No teacher-taught relationship is built.
4. Teacher cannot know the difficulties as well as potentialities of the pupils. So, there is no scope for individual attention and guidance. As a result, the needs of pupils are not fulfilled.

5. The sense of satisfaction felt from this method is false, illusive and finishes sharply. So, it is dangerous and harmful.
6. Teacher-centred method and not a child-centred method. This is against the psychological principles, because —
   (*a*) only teacher is an active participant and pupils are passive listeners.
   (*b*) the teacher speaks/delivers a lecture on a particular topic and the pupils simply listen. They may become inattentive.
7. It is a one-way traffic and 'one man show' method. It is only from who communicates. There is no scope to argue. So, the lecturer may deliver false and any type of irrelevant information.
8. The method does not provide opportunity to develop various mental abilities like reasoning, logical thinking, mathematical training, etc.
9. In this method there is no provision for practical and creative work.
10. Lectures imparted through this method are not durable. They can be easily forgotten by the pupils.
11. Except the sense of hearing, no other senses are used. So there is no scope for multi-sensory experiences.
12. Experimentation is totally neglected. So, it does not develop scientific attitude and skills.
13. There is a very quick and hurried flow of ideas in a lecture. So, it is not easy for pupils to comprehend every point properly. During a lecture, if attention of listener is diverted and something of an idea is missed, he cannot understand the rest of the topic at all.
14. It is often used to teach lower classes due to convenience of teachers.
15. It is difficult to know the extent to which the pupils have been able to learn.
16. The feedback channel is extremely poor in lecture method.

### *How to make Lecture Effective and Interesting?*

1. Property analyse the topic/content and present in a systematic and logical manner. Give the importance to the previous knowledge of the pupils while preparing lecture.
2. Present appropriate examples to make teaching-learning process more effective and interesting.
3. Use blackboard as and when you think fit. Write on the blackboard teaching points, definitions and other important information.
4. Use proper audio-visual aids to make the lecture effective and more interesting.
5. Keep the students active by putting questions from time to time.
6. Use simple, clear and appropriate language. Have clear and effective voice. Have speed of delivering lecture slow.
7. At the end of the lecture, present summary which should be taken down by the pupils.
8. Use, as and when you think fit, information that recreates the listeners' minds.

### *Conclusion*

This method is not suitable and useful for teaching and learning of mathematics, specially in lower classes.

## 6. Demonstration Method

The teacher makes the theoretical investigation and proves it in the classroom. He performs the experiment and the pupils acquire knowledge with careful observation of the experiment.

Demonstration can be performed by a single teacher or a group of teachers.

### *Criteria of a Good Demonstration*

A good demonstration requires that the teacher (demonstrator) should —

(1) state the purpose of demonstration clearly before the pupils.

(2) be well-versed in handling the apparatus and equipments.

(3) arrange the demonstration table such that all pupils are able to see the demonstration clearly. For that, he should keep the demonstration table on a higher level than pupils' desks.

(4) perform all experiment in front of pupils.

(5) keep the equipments required for the demonstration ready at hand and in the order of requirement on the demonstration table.

(6) take pupils' help while performing experiments.

(7) clear the doubts of the pupils simultaneously.

(8) discuss the observations and results of the demonstration immediately after the completion of the demonstration.

(9) use easy and simple language.

(10) involve students so that they actively participate the demonstration.

(11) supplement demonstration with other audio-visual aids to make it more interesting and effective.

(12) maintain interest and discipline in the class during demonstration.

(13) emphasise major points in the demonstration and preferably write them on the blackboard.

(14) ask some reflective type of questions to stimulate the power of reasoning and interest of pupils in the classroom.

### *Application*

(1) To derive the formula of distance between two points on a Cartezian Plane.

(2) To find out the total area of a hemisphere.

(3) To find the solution of two simultaneous equations, graphically.

### *Merits of Demonstration Method*

1. In this method, both — the teacher and the pupils — are active.
2. This method is appropriate for lower classes.
3. The pupils can understand the principles, laws, formulae clearly.

4. Teaching becomes effective even if the number of applications is less.
5. The pupils develop the power of observation, reasoning and thinking.
6. They learn by seeing, observing and hearing. So, the sight and hearing sense of pupils are more active.
7. It is useful where the experiment involves some difficult and complex operations.

### *Demerits of Demonstration Method*

1. Not an appropriate method from the psychological point of view as it is not based on the principle 'learning by doing', but is based on the principle of 'see, hear and understand.'
2. Pupils only observe what the teacher does. Some pupils may not observe properly.
3. Pupils do not get the chance to perform experiments. Therefore, first hand experience is not possible. They do not get the direct experience.

## Lecture-cum-Demonstration Method

This is the combination of lecture method and demonstration method. Thus, it includes the merits of both the methods and it removes the demerits of both the methods to a great extent.

Lecture-cum-Demonstration method can be proved one of the best methods if the demonstrations are well-planned, well-arranged and effective.

It is also economical with repeat to time and labour.

This method is based on the maxims of teaching, 'from concrete to abstract' and 'from simple to complex.'

### *Procedure*

The teacher explains the theoretical portion with the help of lecture method using diagrams, figures, statements, etc. and perform the experiment in the class to make the learning experiences of the pupils more effective and clear.

It involves an active participation of pupils. No one-way communication like lecture method. The pupils watch the instruments and operations and help the teacher in his demonstration. During demonstration the teacher keeps asking questions and gets responses from them.

Thus, pupils observe the demonstration critically.

### *Merits*

It helps in developing observation, reasoning and logical powers.

## 7. Laboratory Method

Laboratory method of teaching mathematics is that method in which the pupils learn mathematics by doing experiments and laboratory work in the Mathematics Laboratory on the same line as they learn sciences by performing experiments in the science laboratory.

Laboratory method stimulates activity and discovery on the part of the pupils and avoid the disadvantages of the lecture method. The proponents of this method maintain that pupils attain better mastery of mathematical concepts and principles by deriving them in this way from concrete experience.

This method involves the fundamental principles of teaching like: (1) Principle of activity, (2) Principle of interest, (3) Principle of definite aim, (4) Principle of learning by doing, (5) Principle of observation and the maxims of teaching like (*i*) from concrete to abstract (*ii*) from known to unknown. So, the pupils take interest in their work.

It provides the practical base to inductive reasoning.

Criticism is levelled against the present day teaching of mathematics that it provides only theoretical knowledge, acquired only by reading and writing, without any practical ground. Laboratory method is quite competent to check this evil.

Of course, this method needs a laboratory in which equipments and other useful teaching aids related to mathematics are available. *e.g.*, geometrical instruments, mathematical models and charts, graph papers, equipments related to mensuration, etc.

At the same time, it also needs a laboratory-conscious skilled mathematics teacher.

Practical work demands individual attention from the teacher. He has to keep watch on the working of pupils and to render adequate and proper guidance at the appropriate time.

Through this method, pupils acquire mathematical knowledge using equipments, material aids and experiments in mathematics laboratory. His method assumes that mathematical knowledge and skills cannot be acquired by only reading and writing.

Practically the laboratory method is the experimental version of inducive method with heuristic approach.

J.W.A. Young rightly states — 'The laboratory method aims to arouse teachers to a belief, not only theoretical but practical and effective as well, that mathematical dishes must be made appetizing and palatable. They are to be accepted with pleasure and digested with ease.'

## Procedure

1. The pupils after analysing the problem, tries to solve it through experimentation. He himself find the solution by viewing, observing and calculating. He carries out experiments himself in the laboratory and gets knowledge through direct experiences.
2. He establishes and narrates a law or principle in his own words.
3. By active participation and after necessary verification, he arrives at a definite conclusion. In this way pupils develop creative and heuristic attitude amongst them.
4. The teacher observes the pupils' working from time to time and render his appropriate guidance by giving instructions whenever needed. Thus, the teacher also has to be active with the pupils.
5. New facts are explored through this method. Discovered facts are further testified in similar other practical situations.

The success and effectiveness of experiments in laboratory depends upon the ability, capacity and intelligence of both — the teacher and the pupils.

## Applications of Laboratory Method

*1. Topic:* To find the relation of the measures of the angles of a triangle with the lengths of the opposite sides of the same triangle.

Teacher asks each pupil to draw a triangle ABC of any size and shape. Then teacher asks pupil to measure the angles and sides of the triangle ABC. Now teacher summarises the data on the blackboard as below:

| *Sr. No.* | *Angle having greatest measure* | *Side having greatest length* | *Angle having least measure* | *Side having least length* |
|---|---|---|---|---|
| 1. | | | | |
| 2. | | | | |
| 3. | | | | |

The pupils generalise: 'In a triangle, the side opposite the angle having greatest measure, is the longest and vice versa. In a triangle the side opposite the angle having the least measure is the shortest and vice-versa.'

2. *Topic:* To find the relationship of opposite angles of a cyclic quadrilateral.

Teacher asks each pupil to draw a circle of any suitable radius. In the circle, draw a cyclic quadrilateral ABCD of any size and shape.

Then teacher asks them to measure all the four angles of the cyclic quadrilateral ABCD.

The teacher summarises the data in the tabular form as below:

| *Sr. No.* | $m\angle A$ | $m\angle B$ | $m\angle C$ | $m\angle D$ | $m\angle A + m\angle C$ | $m\angle B + m\angle D$ |
|---|---|---|---|---|---|---|
| 1. | | | | | | |
| 2. | | | | | | |
| 3. | | | | | | |
| : | | | | | | |

The pupils genenralise: 'The sum of the measures of the opposite angles of a cyclic quadrilateral is 180°' *i.e.*, 'opposite angles of a cyclic quadrilateral are supplementary.'

## Merits of Laboratory Method

1. This method makes learning easy, lasting and enduring. The knowledge learnt and acquired by practical method is durable, meaningful, permanent and cannot be forgotten.
2. This method presents mathematics as a practical subject.
3. The method helps in getting practical and useful information rather than bookish one. Here, the pupil learns through doing and hence finds himself quite capable of using the acquired knowledge in his life.
4. This method always keeps the pupil busy in doing practical work in the observation of phenomena or outcome of the results. So, the problem of indiscipline is automatically solved.
5. It is a scientific method which helps to develop in the pupils —
   (*a*) observation power and logical thinking
   (*b*) scientific attitude towards mathematics
   (*c*) problem-solving ability

(*d*) genuine interest in mathematics

(*e*) positive attitude towards mathematics

(*f*) to work systematically and in an organised manner.

6. It has a psychological base. It is a child-centred method in which the basic interest and natural instinct of the child are given due weightage.
7. It is helpful to develop in pupils the attitude of discovery and habit of self-study since they arrive at the solution of a problem by means of experiments.
8. Senses are the gateway of knowledge. Here, the pupil gets the opportunity of receiving knowledge through his senses — eyes, ears and hands, knowledge is acquired through the combined use of different sense-organs and motor-organs. So, the acquired knowledge is real and permanent.
9. Here, the learner discovers and find facts with his own efforts. Thus, he acquires a clear understanding of the subject.
10. It provides opportunity for independent work and thinking which helps to develop self-confidence and self-reliance.
11. This is a child-centred method. Every activity is performed by him. So, it is helpful to develop creative attitude in the child.
12. It provides pleasure to the learner since a successful experiment is a source of joy and encouragement. A pupil likes to do something with his own hands. That is why the pupil takes interest in experimenting.
13. Pupils get opportunity of working in a group. So, the group-spirit and we-feeling are inculcated. They develop a social outlook and learn to work and get along with others. It also inculcates the spirit of co-operation and exchange of ideas where laboratory work is performed in groups. Again it helps to establish good relationship between teacher and taught since the teacher is required to supervise the works of pupils and they remain in contact with teacher for a long time while doing laboratory work.
14. Pupils get the opportunity to acquaint themselves with the facts through direct first hand experiences individually. Pupils themselves verify the facts and laws of mathematics with the help of experiments.
15. This method is more useful and scientific as compared to other methods.
16. It makes the teaching of mathematics interesting and meaningful.
17. It helps in learning mathematics in the way it is used in our day-to-day life. Here, pupils learn to apply the mathematical principles in practical life. So, the knowledge of mathematics becomes functional and meaningful to them.
18. It helps to develop very good qualities in the pupils like honesty, concentration, observation, innovative thought, hard-working, etc.
19. It improves the efficiency of pupils through handling of instruments and material aids.
20. Some topics of mathematics are best understood through this method.
21. The theory and practice may proceed side by side in this method and hence it makes the processes as interesting, useful, meaningful and lively as possible.

22. The pupils learn the use of different equipment which are used in the laboratory.
23. The pupils get the opportunity of doing creative and practical work.
24. The problems of Algebra and Geometry can be solved easily by using this method.
25. Day-to-day experimental and practical work in laboratory method —
    (*a*) teaches pupils dignity of labour,
    (*b*) inculcates love for truth and honesty,
    (*c*) provides sufficient freedom to work according to one's capacity and abilities. Gifted, average and below average pupils can work at their own pace,
    (*d*) helps in smoothening the teaching-learning process as the teacher and the taught come closer and closer.

### *Demerits of Laboratory Method*

1. This method has a partial applicability. Only those topics of mathematics which can be experimented upon can be taught through this method. This method is not practicable in higher classes where abstract ideas and concepts are to be developed.
2. This method is not suitable and useful for large classes and lower class pupils as it requires independent efforts and working.
3. It is not suitable for all pupils as they are not equally efficient in handling the practical tasks. Student of lower classes cannot perform the experiments in the laboratory.
4. The method is too expensive. Maintenance of a laboratory equipped with a lot of apparatus and the need of more staff involves huge expenditure. All schools are not able to adopt this method.
5. It is too expensive in terms of time also. The process of planning experiments, drawing conclusions and verifying the analysed results — all will go very slow. Vast syllabus cannot be completed within the time limit.
6. This method can be used for a small class only. Individual attention cannot be paid with large classes.
7. The appropriate text book written on the lines of laboratory method is hardly available, say, practically non-available.
8. This is a laborious method. It needs individual attention to be paid to every pupil. Whereas an excessive amount of help defeats the very purpose of this method, the lack of attention and guidance make the pupils discouraged and disappointed. This is why, here, the task of the teacher becomes too difficult.
9. All mathematics teachers cannot use this method effectively.
10. All topics of mathematics cannot exclusively be taught by this method.
11. Sometimes pupils take practical work as an end and thus they remain at the concrete stage only and do not reach upto abstract stage which is the ultimate goal of mathematics.

### *How Teacher should make Laboratory Method Successful?*

To make this method successful, a teacher can do the following:

1. Decide well in advance the objectives of topic of Arithmetic, Algebra, Geometry and Trigonometry.
2. Give theoretical knowledge related to the topic and the objectives before experimenting.
3. Divide pupils into groups if there is a large number of pupils in the class.
4. Make clear the steps and procedure of the experiment so that the pupils do not face any problem while experimenting.
5. Make available the equipments and other necessary things related to the experiment well in advance.
6. Observe the work of pupils and guide them properly while they experiment in the laboratory.
7. Encourage and help the pupils to make the experiment successful so that pupils can get the best possible practical knowledge.

### *Conclusion*

For teaching of mathematics, laboratory method should be used only as a complementary method to develop interest and love in the learning of certain mathematical concepts.

For teaching of certain topics, this method should be a must if essential equipments and facilities are easily available.

### *Comparison*

| *Demonstration Method* | *Laboratory Method* |
|---|---|
| 1. Pupils see different equipments, experiments and processes in the classroom only. | 1. Pupils themselves use different types of experiments and do different activities in the laboratory. |
| 2. Fast method. It takes less time. | 2. Slow method. It takes more time. |
| 3. Teacher is more active than pupils. | 3. Pupils are more active than teacher. |
| 4. Not expensive in terms of money. | 4. Expensive in terms of money. |
| 5. Pupils do not get direct experience as the teacher himself demonstrate. | 5. Pupils get direct experience by experimenting individually in the laboratory. |
| 6. Less opportunity for developing scientific attitude. | 6. Scientific attitude can be developed. |
| 7. Not appropriate for psychological point of view, as it is based upon the principle of 'see, hear and understand'. | 7. Psychological method as it is based upon the principle of 'learning by doing'. |
| 8. Pupils do not get the opportunity to develop creative and investigative powers. | 8. Creative and searching habits can be developed. |

## 8. Heuristic Method

### Meaning

The word 'heuristic' is originated from Latin word 'Heurisco' which means 'I myself have found.' Prof. Henry Edward Armstrong propounded this method.

Prof. H.E. Armstrong — 'This is the method of teaching which places the pupils as far as possible in the attitude of a discoverer.'

Westaway — 'The heruristic method is intended to a training in method. Knowledge is a secondary consideration all together.'

Herbert Spencer — 'Students should be told minimum and as much as possible they should be encouraged to discover.'

N. Kuppuswami Aiyangar — 'The heuristic method is intended to change the passive recipient of knowledge into an active independent inquirer or discoverer of knowledge.'

All these definitions can be summarised as follows:

- In heuristic method pupil work like a researcher and solve the problem.
- The main aim of this method is to make the pupil a researcher/discoverer.
- In this method more emphasis is given on 'How the knowledge can be obtained' rather than the teaching of facts, principles, etc.
- Heuristic method is not a specific or separate method in itself. In a true sense, it aims to develop an attitude called 'heuristic attitude' among the pupils.
- As a general rule — Give the minimum amount of help. Do not tell anything which the pupil can find out for himself. Avoid leading questions. Let the questions be such as require real thinking on the part of the pupil to find solution for. Too much help is, of course, against the spirit of this method.
- The maxims 'practice makes a man perfect' and 'learning by doing' are applicable to not only to physical activities but to intellectual activities also.
- Heurism is the essence of all the methods. Any method of teaching mathematics that develops in the pupils the attitude of doing, thinking and discovering by themselves is heuristic.
- Here the teacher puts such thought-provoking questions that may lead the pupils to independent thinking, reasoning and striving for the discovery of the solution of the problem and to find truth for himself.
- Contrary to lecture method, it demands complete self-activity and self-education on the part of the pupil.
- Here, pupil has not to remain a passive listener but has to take an active part in the process of achieving knowledge as an independent inquirer and discoverer.
- H. Spencer believed that the school should develop thinking power of the child and for this the latter must be given an opportunity to think.
- Here, primary consideration is the development of thinking power, self-confidence, self-reliance, originality and self-judgement in the child to make him on ever successful citizen of India rather than an information monger.
- In contrast to the lecture method, there are certain other ways of presenting new material which aim to avoid the shortcomings of the lecture method.
  - The heuristic method of teaching is the antithesis of the lecture method.
- It is the method which aims to lead the pupils, by well-chosen questions to discover facts and information, relationships and principles for himself rather than having them handed out to him in the manner of direct information by the teacher.

- To use this method effectively the teacher must be very skillful in the art of questioning and must be adapt at sensing precise key points of difficulty which perhaps are not definitely recognised even by the pupil himself.

## Place of a Teacher in Heuristic Method

If every child is to be made a discoverer or an inventor, then the teacher should remain aside and in the background as an onlooker. Let the child select his own way to proceed onwards to arrive at the solution of the problem. Teacher should be passive observer and child learns in his own manner and at his own pace.

But child is after all a child. He is unexperienced and ignorant of many new things and is unable to discover facts all alone by himself. At times, he needs guidance and help of the teacher at various stages.

If the pupils are to be helped in discovering things for themselves, the questions must not be allowed to degenerate into a mere TF type in which the nature of the answer is so evidently implied that the element of discovery is largely removed from the situation, leaving little to the imagination of the pupil.

Therefore, the teacher occupies an important place in heuristic method though his role is confined to certain conditions as given below:

- He is to act as a guide only.
- He should give as necessary and little amount of help as possible.
- He should never give pupils the finished product of his own thinking and reasoning.
- He should help the child only when he has totally failed to overcome his difficulties by his own efforts.
- He should carefully select the material and offer his aid in the form of questions, suggestions and minimise direct telling.
- He should make constant effort to skillfully develop the heuristic skill and attitude in the pupils.

## Procedure

In this method there is no definite steps to be followed.

(1) Some sort of problem is given to pupils and a learning situation is created by the teacher.

(2) The pupils try to solve the problem with their own individual efforts independently.

(3) By careful questioning the teacher may arouse curiosity in the pupils to keep up their heuristic attitude.

## Application

**Topic:** (1) Draw a tangent from a point outside a circle using the centre of the circle.

(2) Using Pythagoras Theorem, derive the Distance Formula.

## Merits of Heuristic Method

1. It removes the drawbacks of lecture method.
2. It is the method of discovery. It encourages independent learning. The pupils learn all what he wants to learn through his own efforts. No spoon-feeding.
3. It imparts a sound training in self-education.
4. It develops among the pupils self-confidence, self-reliance, heurism attitude, power of thinking and logical reasoning, critical attitude, creativity, habit of weighing evidences, making accurate statements, etc.
5. It helps pupils to be original and creative in their outlook and thinking. Thus, spirit of inquiry is also developed among them.
6. Psychologically sound method as it is based on —
   (*a*) psychological facts that child's own experience is the basis of real learning.
   (*b*) psychological principles (*e.g.,* Learning by doing).
   (*c*) the needs, interests and motives of the pupils.
   (*d*) principle of activity. It demands quite alertness and presence of mind on the part of the pupils for responding to the heuristic questions by the teacher.
   (*e*) increased contemplation and awakening in the pupils.
   (*f*) the promotion of self-discipline in the pupils as they feel self-responsible to their work.
   (*g*) training the pupils to think.
7. It does not emphasise on the bookish, readymade and teach-made arguments.
8. It gives enough opportunity for developing teacher-pupil intimacy. Teacher has to remain in living touch with the pupils for giving suggestions and necessary guidance at the proper time. Teacher has to study every pupil carefully and know his interests, abilities, aptitudes and limitations.
9. Knowledge obtained by this method is more stable. It is assimilated, remembered and applied to a new situation. Thus, acquired knowledge is real and significant.
10. Pupils learn by doing. So the learnt concepts and facts cannot be forgotten.
11. This method makes pupil exact and brings them closer to truth.
12. It inculcates in the pupils the willingness to work hard.
13. The pupils are entrusted with the great responsibility of self-learning and discovering the solution of the problem. They have no empty mind for making mischief. So, discipline in the class is maintained.
14. Pupils acquire a real understanding and clear notion of the subject. Thus, they have a good command of the subject matter learnt.
15. This method leaves no extra scope for assigning homework. The pupils and the teacher get a sort of relief as there is no burden of homework.
16. After discovering something by his own efforts and independent thinking, pupils feel pleasure and pride for his achievement. It gives him satisfaction and enough encouragement for further achievement.

17. It makes the pupil an active participant in the learning process.
18. It provides a spur to quicken his interest since it places him in the role of at least a quasi investigator rather than a mere passive recipient of information.
19. The fact that the discoveries which he makes have been made previously by someone else neither alters nor distracts from the fact that to his mind they are new and largely original.
20. That he has been guided toward his discoveries by the helpful and stimulating questioning of the teacher should not distract from his justifiable pride in his achievement.
21. The pupil's part as an active participant in the unfolding of a problem of the mathematical scroll seldom fails to add zest to his work and to give him a more complete and enduring mastery of what he has learnt.

## *Demerits of Heuristic Method*

1. This method expects too much from the pupils. It demands the discovery of truth with their own independent efforts. To discover/explore a new field needs a lot of hard work, patience, habit of deep concentration, sound logical reasoning, sound thinking power and creative abilities, intelligence, etc.

   All students do not have these qualities. So, it is not suitable for lower classes and for average pupils, because they are not mentally matured for independent thinking and working.

   It is not proper to assume that every pupil is a discoverer.

2. This method also expects too much from the teachers. They have to coin proper heuristic questions for stimulating thinking in pupils. Also, teachers should provide them individual guidance and aid at the proper time. For this they should know every pupil's basic potentialities and interest.

   Again, it needs extraordinary labour and special preparation from the teacher. Every teacher may not be hardworking and enthusiastic and having a scientific attitude. So, every teacher may be unable to use it successfully.

   A thorough checking and rectification of errors by the teacher is essential. Sometimes teacher is unable to make good and imaginative questions to provoke real thinking in the pupils. This fails the purpose of this method.

   Sometimes teacher are unable to distinguish between true and false heuristic questions. *e.g.*,

   *False heuristic question:* Do you know that a prime number has 2 factors?

   *True heuristic question:* How many factors are there of a prime number?

3. It is in fact a slow and time-consuming method, as most of the investigations take much time.
4. Formational method rather than informational.
5. It is an expensive method. The successful use of heuristic method requires adequate laboratory textbooks and library facilities. There is lack of such facilities in our schools. Lack of such facilities create potential difficulties in the use of this method. To discover a new thing requires a lot of money.

6. It presupposes a very small class which is impossible in Indian conditions.
7. Due to lack of experience and proper abilities, the pupils often draw misleading erroneous conclusions or inferences out of their observations and independent work. This may prove very harmful to the pupils.
8. This method requires that the pupil should discover or rediscover the facts. Thus, much of the time is wasted in discovering the already discovered facts. This actually creates obstacles in pupils' progress.
9. Being slow and time-consuming method, it creates difficulties in covering the lengthy prescribed syllabus in time.
10. In mathematics there are so many things that have to be accepted as such. So, it is not desirable to discover everything.
11. It will be effective only in the hands of a teacher who has great patience, together with a high degree of insight into the workings of the pupil's mind and of skill in the use of questions for the purpose of accomplishing certain desired results.

### *How to make Heuristic Method successful?*

- It should not be applied frequently for younger pupils, as they are unable to discover facts.
- The fact to be discovered should be in accordance with the level and abilities of pupils.
- The teacher must —
  (*a*) have heuristic and scientific spirit and that also be inculcated in pupils.
  (*b*) provide only the necessary and that too minimum guidance.
  (*c*) be well-versed in framing true heuristic questions.
- This method should be —
  (*a*) applied if there are less number of pupils in a class.
  (*b*) supplemented by other methods of teaching.

### *Conclusion*

The spirit behind this method is quite constructive, meaningful and useful. Hence, it should be preserved. The pupils should not be told everything rightaway. They should be encouraged for independent thinking and make conscious efforts for self-learning.

## 9. Project Method

This method is based on pragmatic philosophy propagated by Sir John Dewey. His disciple, Sir William Kilpatric, an American educationist, advocated this method. But as a perfect method of teaching, it was presented by Dr. J.A. Stevenson.

### What is a Project?

Kilpatrick — 'A project is a wholehearted purposeful activity proceeding in a social environment'.

Stevenson— 'A project is a problematic act carried to completion in its most natural setting.'

Ballard — 'A project is a bit of real life that has been imparted into school.'

These definitions clearly reveal the following characteristics of a project:

A project is — (*i*) a purposeful and problematic activity.
(*ii*) an act related to actual life activities.
(*iii*) an act which is most interesting and absorbing.
(*iv*) achieved in natural, real and social environment.

## What is Project Method?

- The central idea — 'What is to be taught should have a direct relationship with the actual happenings in life' — forms the basis of project method.
- The project method is based on the following basic principles:
  (1) Principle of correlation (2) Principle of activity
  (3) Principle of experience (4) Principle of reality
  (5) Principle of freedom (6) Principle of utility
- Through this method the principle of correlation is given a very practical shape, as this tries to impart education of all the subjects in an integrated way by correlating them with the real life activities.
- Here, the children set to themselves a problem or task and carry out that task through their own planning and activities.
- This method consists chiefly of building a comprehensive unit round an activity which may be carried in or outside the school. It involves a variety of activities. Hence, all the pupils work co-operatively.
- This method aims to make learning effective and to give children the real training of life.
- It emphasises not only 'learning by doing' but also 'learning by living.'

### *Types of Projects*.

- Generally projects are of two types:
  (1) Individual projects (2) Group projects
- Kilpatrick categorised projects into four types:
  (1) Creative/Constructive projects (2) Artistic projects
  (3) Problematic projects (4) Drill projects.

## Steps involved while working on a project

Generally the following six steps are involved while working on a project:

## 1. Creating and Providing a Situation

- At first stage of project method, the teacher is expected to know interests, attitudes and aptitudes of the pupils.
- Then the teacher creates problematic situation in front of pupils when they study in the classroom or while they go on excursion or participating a co-curricular activity or while holding conversation on various topics or discussion on pictures, buildings, cities, stories, lives of mathematicians, etc.

- While creating a situation, due importance should be given to pupils' interest and abilities.
- Then situation is provided to pupils for studying the different problems from different angles. The pupils see the desirability of solving any specific problem for themselves.
- Generally, social problems are preferred to, as they provide a genuine satisfaction and training.

## 2. Proposing and choosing the Project

- While proposing a problem the teacher stimulates discussions by making relevant suggestions.
- The aims and objectives of the proposed project is properly discussed through group participation.
- The purpose of the project should be well-defined and understood by the pupils.
- The proposed project should be according to the real need of the pupils.
- Teacher must guide them tactfully in proposing and choosing the topic of the project.
- If the pupils feel that the choice is their own, it will be better for them to plan and carry out their project.

## 3. Planning the Project

Planning of project is of ultra-importance for the success of the project. A good planning must have following considerations:

(1) Material and equipments essential for the project.

(2) Resources available.

(3) Time limit and estimated cost.

(4) Division of work and duties to be assigned according to their interest.

(5) Probable difficulties and alternative ways to eradicate them.

(6) Possibilities of outside help, if need be.

## 4. Executing the Project

- This step involves various kinds of activities such as collecting information, discussions, reading and writing, visiting different places and people, consulting reference books, drawing maps and charts, inquiring rates, calculating prices, etc.
- Every pupil should contribute actively in the execution of the project in the natural way. They play their role according to their abilities and capacities with a true social and co-operative spirit *e.g.*, A pupil interested in reading should be assigned the task of referring reference-books and literature. One interested in calculation should be given the work of keeping accounts and so on.
- The teacher should guide and observe the progress of the project.

## 5. Evaluation of the Project

- The teacher and the pupils should jointly evaluate the project. They should discuss whether the aims and objectives of the project are achieved or not.

- Pupils find out their mistakes and see whether they have proceeded according to the plan or not. This imparts training of self-criticism.
- The line of action and mode of execution may be rectified and modified on the results of such evaluation.

## 6. Keeping Records of the Project

- The pupils should maintain a complete and convincing record of the project work, *e.g.,*
  (1) How the project was proposed, chosen, planned and executed.
  (2) What duties were assigned and to which group?
  (3) What difficulties were faced and how they were solved.
  (4) How the project was evaluated from time to time.
  (5) To what extent the aims and objectives realised.
  (6) What their experiences were.

### *Illustration*

**Project:** To make a garden on a small plot.

The following different aspects may have to be dealt with for the accomplishment of the selected project:

- To find out the total area of the plot.
- To calculate the quantity of seeds and saplings to be brought.
- To prepare a list of materials and equipments for cultivating the area as well as for rearing the plants.
- To explore the alternative ways for collecting materials and equipments.
- To manage the fund for the purchase of essential materials and equipments from different sources.
- To ascertain the availability of the different requirements.
- To estimate the total cost to be involved for the completion of the project.
- To list the names of pupil-volunteers.
- To assign the various duties and works to the volunteers.
- To estimate and fix the time for looking after the garden.
- To prepare a written plan for every aspect of the project.
- To execute the work according to the plan.
- To evaluate the completed work from different points of view and remove the drawbacks, if any.
- To return the unused material and equipments, if any.
- To prepare the account of total expenditure on the project.
- To prepare a list of purchased material and equipments which can be used in future and can be preserved in the school store.
- To prepare a complete report of the project.

## Some suitable projects for the pupils of mathematics

1. Establishment of Mathematics club/Mathematics laboratory/Mathematics library.
2. Running a school bank/co-operative store.
3. Contribution of Indian/foreign mathematicians in the field of mathematics.

### *Merits of Project Method*

1. This method suits the modern theories of learning. It is based on the principles of activity, reality, effect, learning by doing and keeps an eye on individual differences. Pupils are motivated to learn and act.
2. Here, students work in an atmosphere of freedom and so they acquire knowledge without stress and strain.

   Liberty, equality and fraternity are the cardinal principles which form the basis of project method. Sufficient freedom of thinking and decision-making are sufficiently provided.
3. This method presents an ideal picture of correlated teaching and learning. It brings about correlation of activities and subjects as well as concentration of studies.

   Here, the knowledge is imparted as a united whole.
4. It is psychological and scientific method. It is based on psychological laws and principles.

   The innate tendency, interests and aptitudes of the pupils are best utilised in this method. The instinct of curiosity, creativeness and hoarding also gets satisfaction in project method.

   It arouses interest, encourages intuitiveness and provide satisfaction to the pupils on successful completion of the work.
5. It upholds the dignity of labour. Pupils learn value of the work. A little lethargy on their part may bring disappointment to them.

   Pupils develop respect and taste for all kinds of work.
6. It promotes co-operative activity and group interaction. So, it introduces democracy in education. All the pupils co-operate in a common project to their taste, temperament, abilities and capacities. Thus, they learn the lesson of democratic and scientific way of living together.
7. The problem of indiscipline is also automatically solved as the pupils are completely absorbed in their tasks. The pupils remain active throughout the execution of the project.
8. It emphasises on problem solving rather than cramming. It develops in pupils critical thinking, proper planning, habit of hard working, discovery attitude for successful completion of the problem/project.
9. It challenges the abilities and capacities of pupils and put them on the tract to think and act.
10. Through project method, so many virtues essential for good and true citizenship like self-confidence, self-reliance, self-respect, self-dependence, self-discipline, initiativeness, group interaction, tolerance, patience, sense of responsibility, duty-boundness, foresight, resourcefulness, mutual love and co-operation, power of judgement and decision-making, freedom of thought and actions, etc., are inculcated.

11. It provides incidental way of teaching.
12. Here, physical and social environment become real platform for the spread of knowledge.
13. Authorities have not to make an arrangement of big classrooms, furniture and other costly material.
14. Knowledge gained by this method becomes solid and durable.
15. Here, no question of giving home tasks arise. So, neither the teacher nor the students have to worry.

## *Demerits of Project Method*

1. **Expensive method:** It requires a lot of material not easily available. This is uneconomical method in the sense that time, labour and expenditure are quite larger than the return received.

   Pupils, irrespective of the guidance, waste so much time, energy and money due to their lack of experience and immaturity.

   In India, our schools can neither afford sufficient money nor provide appropriate personnel for teaching with project method.

   Suitable text books and written learning material befitting teaching through this method is also not available.
2. The teacher cannot complete lengthy prescribed school syllabus easily within the specified period. Through projects hardly a part of the syllabus can be covered. So, it does not suit the present day classroom teaching.
3. The backbone of mathematics is drill and practice work which cannot be done properly through teaching by this method. It does not provide necessary collective and individual drill work essential to acquire skills and efficiency in different fields of mathematics.
4. In India, schools are overcrowded and educational structure is examination-oriented. In our examination system no provision has been made for the project method.

   Not suitable for crowded classes as the teacher cannot guide and supervise so many projects properly.
5. Every teacher is not equipped with enthusiasm, abilities and leadership required for this method.

   The teacher is expected to be a walking encyclopaedia having an all round knowledge of every subject with its practical applications in the day-to-day life.

   This method produces many challenges to the teachers right from the beginning to the end of the project.
6. In this method teaching and learning become deorganised, irregular and discontinuous.
7. Certain practical difficulties like lack of resources, wide curriculum, limited time, crowded classes, non-availability of reference books, lack of library facilities, lack of trained, efficient and experienced teachers for guiding the project may come in the way of this method.

8. It provides incidental teaching. Organised and systematic teaching is not possible.

   Mathematics cannot be taught purely by this method because incidental teaching cannot suffice without supplementary and planned teaching.

9. There are so many branches, topics and aspects of mathematics that may be hardly covered through projects.

10. Learning by this method is not uniform as the pupils have to carry out different work for completing the project.

11. It is not a method of learning new facts and principles, but it is a method of utilising the application of already discovered facts.

### *Conclusion*

Irrespective of having good many points to its credit side, this method suffers a lot of handicaps and limitations.

Only the spirit of this method can be occasionally used by the mathematics teacher. Teachers should select certain projects which can be undertaken in schools without upsetting regular time.

## 10. Problem Solving Method

### *Introduction*

- Whenever there is obstruction in the teaching-learning situation, we say there is some problem.
- Pupils studying mathematics have to make constant efforts for finding the solution of the given problem.
- Human life is full of problems. A successful man in life is he who is fully equipped with adequate sufficient knowledge and reasoning power to tackle these problems.
- A child has to meet and solve various problems which present themselves in his physical, intellectual, emotional and social life. These problems grow in number and complexity as he grows older and older. These problems are to be solved by the combined efforts of the teacher and the taught.
- The teaching and learning of mathematics involve innumerable problems to be solved, since mathematics itself is a subject of problems.

### *Meaning of 'problem'*

The term 'problem' is used to describe a situation when one is faced with something unknown and is asked to find about its identity. Problem means a sort of obstruction which has to be overcome to reach the goal.

### *Nature/Characteristics of a problem*

- A problem should be —

  (*a*) well-defined, meaningful, practical and interesting,

  (*b*) related with the previous knowledge of the pupil, and with the daily life of the pupil, (*c*) challenging, so that the power of thinking and reasoning can be developed,

(*d*) according to the mental and physical level of the pupil.

- A problem should have —

  (*a*) some educational value,

  (*b*) correlation with other study-subjects also.

- A problem should develop imagination, critical powers, mental skills and scientific attitude amongst pupils.

### *What is Problem Solving?*

- The process in which the pupil is bound to be engaged for finding out the answer/solution of the problem is named as 'problem solving.'
- Thus, what one does when one does not know what needs to be done and yet by trial and error, one finds out what needs to be done, is known as 'problem solving.'
- Gagne — 'Problem solving is a set of events in which human being tries to achieve some goals.'

  Risk — 'A process of raising a problem in the minds of the students in such a way as to stimulate purposeful reflecting thinking in arriving at a rational solution.'

  Ausubel — 'Problem solving involves concept formation and discovery learning.'
- Problem solving is an essential skill which needs to be learnt by everyone for his adequate adjustment to his environment and for leading his life smoothly.
- It would be better if this skill could be learnt during the school days. Mathematics gives full of opportunity for learning this skill through different types of various problems.

### *What is Problem Solving Method?*

- It is a method which provides opportunity to the individual pupil for analysing and solving a problem faced by him using his pre-knowledge and following some systematic and scientific steps.
- This method aims at presenting the knowledge to be learnt in the form of a problem. The problems are set to the learners in a natural way.
- Thus, it begins with a problematic situation and consists of continuous and well-integrated activity leading to a meaningful solution.
- The efficiency and ability in solving problems is the basis of success in learning mathematics.
- This method proceeds in a scientific way involving the inductive-deductive procedure of learning.
- It is a method of experience-based learning.

## Procedure (Steps) in Problem Solving Method

### 1. *Recognising/Sensing the Problem*

- In this stage, pupils are made to face a problematic situation. This problem may occur spontaneously or is created deliberately by the teacher.

In teaching-learning process of mathematics, there is no scarcity of such a situation. Enough problems in the form of exercises and assignments are already there in the prescribed text books or practice books.

- Spontaneous problems: (1) Why is $5 \times 3 = 15$ only and not 20?
  (2) What is the cost of labour for painting four walls of a classroom having 10 m length, 8 m breadth and 5 m height at the rate of ₹ 25 per sq. m.?

## 2. *Proper Understanding of the Problem*

- In this stage, defining, interpreting and delimiting the problem take place.
- Problem is well-analysed and understood before attempting for its solution.
- One can think about the probable solution of the given problem only when he is fully aware about the nature, magnitude and direction of the problem.

## 3. *Formation of Hypotheses*

- It means preparation of a list of probable reasons of the occurrence of the problem.
- It develops thinking and reasoning powers of the pupils.
- Formulated hypothesis must be testable.

## 4. *Search for probable solution of the problem*

- On the basis of pre-knowledge, skills and experiences, pupils try to solve the problem. If the problem is new then the alternate attempts should be made. It may require —
  (*a*) study in the library.
  (*b*) practical work in the laboratory and workshop.
  (*c*) surveying, weighing, measuring or any such useful activity.
- Pupils may take help and guidance from the subject teacher and experts, reference books and literature. Thus, multidimensional efforts are required to find the probable solution of the given problem.
- Pupils should be stimulated to collect relevant data and information in a systematic order.
- Then, various techniques are used to analyse and organise the data.
- Formulated hypotheses are to be tested and evaluated.

## 5. *Finding the correct solution*

- Out of the probable tentative solutions the best and correct one is searched. The best solution should be discussed and weighed in terms of its validity and practicability.
- The solution should be in tune with the pre-established laws, principles and facts. Now, by reasoning, one should arrive at a correct solution.

## 6. *Application/Utilisation of the accepted solution*

- No solution should be accepted without having properly verified.
- One must have to be very critical while testing solution/conclusion.

- The correctness of the solution is proved by applying it in new and different situation.
- While verifying, if the solution is found not in tune with the pre-established principles or facts, then further attempts are to be made for searching again some reliable and valid solution.

*Illustrations:* (1) To find the solution of a quadratic equation by perfect square method.

(2) To derive the formula: $\sin^2\theta + \cos^2\theta = 1$

## Merits of Problem Solving Method

1. This method is psychological, scientific and systematic in nature as it is child-centred and problem-oriented.
2. This method helps the pupils —
   (*a*) to develop good study habits, such as habit of self-study, doing the work independently,
   (*b*) to develop power of expression,
   (*c*) to develop group feeling while working together,
   (*d*) to develop ability to arrive at correct conclusion,
   (*e*) to develop power of synthetising, analysing, criticising, reasoning, systematising and generalising,
   (*f*) to develop mental and cognitive abilities,
   (*g*) to improve and apply knowledge and experiences,
   (*h*) to maintain discipline in the class,
   (*i*) to verify an opinion and satisfy curiosity,
   (*j*) to get rid of many teaching-learning problems like indiscipline, assigning the homework, etc.,
   (*k*) to develop valuable social qualities like patience, co-operation, self-confidence, etc.
3. It makes pupils self-reliant in solving any type of problems related to curricular or co-curricular areas as it is the method of self-efforts.
4. It develops the power of initiation in the pupils as they have to face the problematic situation themselves.
5. It involves reflective thinking. So, it stimulates thinking, reasoning, imagination and critical decisions in pupils.
6. This method develops harmonious relationship between the teacher and the taught. For breaking the crux of a problem, pupils need individual guidance from the teacher. So, there is a possibility of close contact between the teacher and the taught. Teacher becomes familiar with his pupils.
7. Here, learning becomes more interesting and is easily grasped and assimilated as it is the result of purposeful activities.
8. The pupils learn to utilise the acquired facts and procedure for solving their day-to-day problems. This method trains pupils to face and solve problems in their actual life. It enforces the pupils to recognise and face the problems properly.

9. Thus, it motivates them to think and act to overcome the problematic situation in their life. It proves a good source of internal motivation to the pupils.
10. It is quite suitable for teaching of mathematics which is full of problems.
11. The acquired knowledge and information is retained for a long time as the pupils learn by doing and by self-effort.

## Demerits of Problem Solving Method

1. This method faces so many practical limitations with respect to teaching and learning conditions:
   (*a*) Large crowded classes.
   (*b*) Lack of adequate library and laboratory facilities.
   (*c*) Heavy syllabus to be completed within a limited number of working hours.
   (*d*) Scarcity of trained and experienced teachers.
   (*e*) Making examination results as a sole criteria of evaluating teachers effectiveness.
   (*f*) Lack of suitable text books and reference books.
2. This method demands from the pupils to be trained in the specific procedure, specific thinking and in problem solving. Every pupil may not possess such abilities.
3. The task of thinking and formulating hypotheses is a quite challenging one. The pupils are more often tempted to pick up wrong hypotheses and follow the wrong path of solving problems.

   Thus, they may waste their time and energy in useless and irrelevant attempts.
4. This method has a partial applicability in dealing with mathematics content, as there lies so many things in the prescribed syllabus of mathematics apart from the teaching of how to solve the problems.
5. This method is time-consuming. Progress in learning is slow.
6. Not suitable for: (*a*) the pupils of lower classes,
   (*b*) all topics of mathematics.
7. Here, mental activity dominates, physical and practical experience are ignored.
8. This method is suitable only for highly intelligent and creative pupils and they are few in number.
9. An average teacher may find this method difficult to adopt as it requires a lot of study and efforts and preparation.
10. Text books and reference books written in traditional style do not help the pupils in this method.

## Conclusion

As and when possible teacher should make use of this method as it has many merits, too. This method should be given due weightage, in every scheme of mathematics, as it is similar to other progressive methods like inductive method, heuristic method, project method, etc.

## 11. Dogmatic Method

- Dogmatic method is an outcome influenced from classical method of teaching. The followers (*i.e.,* dogmatists) of this method claims that —
  - (*a*) Mathematics is an exact science.
  - (*b*) The mathematics pupils must be trained in exactness so that they can learn by heart its knowledge in exact form and can present it exactly in the same way.
  - (*c*) Any departure from high standard of exactness will certainly fail the very purpose of teaching mathematics.
  - (*d*) Therefore, mathematics must be taught rigorously by the teachers and it should be practised rigorously by the learners.
- Thus, in this method rigour is extremely emphasised which means the strict enforcement of rules. So, in this method, the pupils are enforced to memorise the mathematical definitions, rules, principles and to cram up the formulae and method of getting solutions of some typical problems.

### *Procedure*

1. Teacher gives some rules and formulae to the pupil with the expectation that they cram them exactly.
2. Then a problem is presented which is to be solved using the rule or formulae already given.
3. Teacher suggests — what to do, what to observe, how to attempt and how to conclude.
4. Generally, solution of the problem is presented by the teacher on the blackboard in cooked form. Pupils are asked to copy it in their notebooks.
5. Of course, in the whole process pupils have to follow the teacher and his presentation strictly verbatim.
6. Thus, the pupils cram up the presented matter as they are.
7. The pupils are asked to follow the same pattern while solving other similar problems.

### *Merits of Dogmatic Method*

1. It emphases on (*a*) rigour which is helpful to develop mathematical aptitude in the pupils.
   (*b*) memorising and cramming up of formulae and rules, which is useful at the application and revision stage.
2. It enhances memory which promotes speed and efficiency in arriving at the solution of the problem. Again, there is no unnecessary thinking, so it saves time and energy of both the teacher and the taught.

### *Demerits of Dogmatic Method*

1. Unpsychological and unscientific method as —
   - (*a*) it ignores the abilities and capacities of learners except the memory.
   - (*b*) it stresses on rigour and mechanical cramming of formulae and rules in exact form rather than comprehending them.

(*c*) it provides only information which is not appropriate approach for teaching of mathematics.

(*d*) it involves mechanical process which makes the teaching dull and uninteresting.

2. No emphasis on development of original and independent thinking and on power to acquire and apply knowledge. So, the real aim of teaching mathematics is ignored.
3. Rules and formulae are given readymade in the beginning while they should be at the end of knowledge.
4. Pupils with good cramming capacity is considered successful even if he lacks real mathematical ability.
5. It makes the students the slave of pattern and ideas given by others and they cannot initiate themselves.
6. It puts more stress on subject matter and not on learner which is unpsychological. Thus, it is subject-centred and not child-centred.

*Conclusion*

This method is unsuitable for the learners as well as for the subject itself. It may be used only at the revision and application stage. It is not desirable for the teachers to use this method in the usual teaching of mathematics.

## 14.3 What is a suitable method of Teaching Mathematics?

- The teacher should study and analyse these methods and then make his own decision about the most suitable method for teaching a particular topic of mathematics.
- The most suitable methods for teaching of mathematics are inducto-deductive, analytico-synthetic, heuristic, laboratory, project, problem solving. Of course, not a single method can be proved the best one for teaching all the topics of mathematics. He needs not stick to the same method.
- Teacher should always keep in mind the good qualities as well as the limitations of all the methods of teaching mathematics.
- He should have up-to-date knowledge of all the methods and should exploit their advantages to the maximum.
- The best method for a teacher is his own individualised and personalised method which is the outcome of his varied experiences in teaching mathematics.
- Always remember that the method should be pupil-dominated, to a certain extent topic-dominated rather than teacher-dominated.
- Teacher should select such methods wherein pupils get maximum opportunities of participation in the teaching-learning process.
- The twin combination of inductive-deductive methods and analytic-synthetic methods may be preferred for almost every topic as day-to-day teaching of it.

The inductive-deductive combination is more suitable for teaching of Arithmetic and Algebra, while analytic-synthetic combination can be more suitably applied for the teaching of Geometry and Trigonometry.

- By using heuristic method, heurism should be inculcated in the pupils.
- Occasionally the teacher should use project method and laboratory method to remove monotony created by theoretical methods and to make the teaching more interesting. At least for some specific topics these methods are best suited. Using these methods, some good habits can also be inculcated in the pupils.
- To introduce a new topic of mathematics or the contributions of the great mathematicians of the world, lecture method is also a reasonably suitable approach.
- To solve the problems of actual life, problem solving method will be a suitable one.
- Dogmatic method seems to be appropriate when a number of things have to be remembered thoroughly and accurately and also when the teacher wants to keep the subject matter in the forefront.

## EVALUATE YOURSELF

1. What is Inductive method? Illustrate its application in teaching Arithmetic, Algebra and Geometry by providing examples.
2. Describe steps of procedure, merits and demerits of Inductive method of teaching mathematics.
3. What is Deductive method? Illustrate its application in our daily life.
4. Describe merits and demerits of Deductive method.
5. What is Analytic method? Illustrate its application in teaching mathematics by providing examples.
6. Describe merits and demerits of any one method of the following:
   (1) Analytic Method; (2) Synthetic Method; (3) Lecture Method; (4) Demonstration Method; (5) Laboratory Method; (6) Heuristic Method.
7. Illustrate application of Analytic and Synthetic method in teaching mathematics.
8. What is Lecture method? When should the teacher use this method?
9. Give some suggestions to make lecture effective and interesting?
10. What are the criteria of a good demonstration?
11. Write short note on:
    (1) Application of Laboratory method (2) Place of teacher in Heuristic method.
12. How should a teacher of mathematics make Laboratory method successful?
13. Compare Demonstration method with Laboratory method.
14. What do you mean by Heuristic method? How will you introduce Heurism while teaching mathematics?
15. Discuss at length the steps involved while working on a project.
16. Write merits and demerits of Project method.
17. Explain project method of teaching mathematics with suitable examples.
18. How far can Project method be successfully employed in teaching mathematics in our Secondary Schools?
19. What is a problem? Describe the nature or characteristic of a problem. Also explain what problem-solving is.

20. What is a problem-solving method? Discuss steps involved in problem-solving method.
21. Describe merits and demerits of problem-solving method.
22. Which method of teaching mathematics will you use in teaching of —
    (1) Problems of percentage and profit and loss.
    (2) Properties of quadrilaterals.
    (3) Distant formula in co-ordinate geometry.
    (4) Sum of the measures of the angles of a triangle.
    (5) Irrational numbers.

    Support your answer with arguments.
23. How will you make use of Inducto-Deductive method in the teaching of one of the following topics:
    (1) Area of a triangle = $l \times b$.
    (2) Sum of measures of the angles of a convex quadrilateral is 360°.
    (3) $a^2 - b^2 = (a + b)(a - b)$
24. What is Dogmatic method? Describe its merits and demerits.
25. How will you decide the suitability of the method of teaching mathematics?
26. 'No induction is complete without deduction' — Justify the statement.
27. What is problem solving method? What is its scope in the teaching of mathematics? How can it be used in routine teaching?
28. Which is the best method of teaching mathematics? Support your preference with arguments.
29. 'A practical teacher of mathematics cannot be a slave of any single method of teaching. He evolves his own method comprising good points of all the methods.' — Discuss.

'Behind the artisan is the chemist, behind the chemist is the physicist, behind the physicist is the Mathematician.'

***— White***

'Mathematics in earnest should be fun, mathematics in fun may be earnest.'

***— N.A. Court***

# TECHNIQUES OF TEACHING MATHEMATICS

## 15.1 Methods, Techniques and Strategies

- 'Method' is a wider term. It includes techniques and strategies of teaching. Methods are directly linked with teaching objectives.
- 'Techniques' are not directly linked with teaching objectives, but they are linked with teaching methods.

  Teaching techniques are such aids which are used —

  (*a*) to make the lesson interesting,

  (*b*) to explain the content, and

  (*c*) to remember the content by heart during teaching-learning process.
- The term 'teaching strategy' owes its origin to military science, whereas 'method' is a term of pedagogy.

  Different strategies may be adopted in following a method. Teaching strategies are a purposefully conceived and determined plan of action.
- Thus, teaching or instructional strategies refer to a pattern of teaching acts that serve to attain outcomes and to guard against others.

  Teaching strategies may include different techniques of teaching. Various techniques may be used within the same strategy and method.
- A teaching strategy assumes that teaching is a science while teaching method assumes that teaching is an art. Hence, teaching strategies and techniques are used in order to make the teaching effective, interesting and successful.

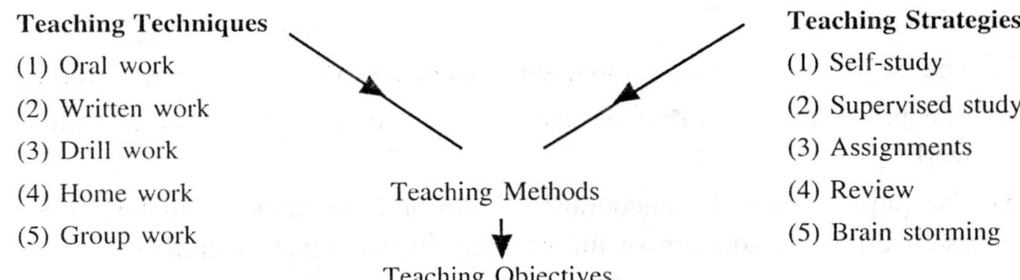


## 15.2 Teaching Techniques

### 1. Oral Work in Mathematics

- (Def) When all processes and calculations regarding the solution of the problem are carried out orally, without using paper and pencil, the work is called 'mental work or oral work'.
- In oral work there is either a mental visualisation of the process of calculations alone in writing or there is some kind of direct application of the results and formulae learnt by heart.
- Though, major part of mathematics has to be covered in written form, its application lies in oral form.
- In carrying out oral work, pupils may be asked questions or problems in the oral or written form. They have to solve them mentally and then to answer in written or oral form.
- The solution of problems in mathematics require an oral as well as written work. Thus, oral work occupies a special place in life and in mathematics.
- Dr. Salamatullah — 'Mental arithmetic should be regarded as an essential part of education for citizenship and effective living.'
- An appeal to the eye and ear is more effective than written work alone. It is the physical and psychological reality that children love to listen to talk and talk themselves. Hence their education should essentially be started through oral work.
- All new processes and methods should be introduced initially in the pupil's mind orally.
- The lesson can be introduced through short, easy and appropriate oral questions. They make the lesson easily comprehensible and clear the process of learning. They can be graded according to difficulty in a better manner.
- Oral (mental) work is the backbone of not only written work but also overall works in mathematics. It demands power of careful listening, visualisation, quick thinking and quick decision-making.
- In primary classes —
  (1) most of the time should be devoted to oral work.
  (2) the children should be taught so many things and facts of mathematics orally using concrete things and real situations.

- In higher classes —
  (1) The beginning of a new topic should always be made through oral work.
  (2) The principles and formulae should be fixed through oral questioning and oral drill work.
  (3) The pupils should be encouraged to do oral calculations, making oral estimates and discovering the solution of the problem in mathematics orally.

## *Importance/Merits of Oral Work*

It can be summarised in the following points:

1. Oral work helps —
   (*a*) in developing the habit of exactness and precision.
   (*b*) in training the auditory senses.
   (*c*) in developing quick hearing and power of mental visualisation.
   (*d*) in fixing the learning of new principles and formulae.
   (*e*) in mental calculations.
   (*f*) in diagnosing the difficulties and doubts of individual pupils.
2. Most of the mathematics used in our practical life is oral. *e.g.*
   (*i*) day-to-day sale and purchase of commodities.
   (*ii*) the small transaction of money or exchange of things.
   (*iii*) the estimate of income and expenditure.
   (*iv*) calculations in purchasing tickets from the railway window, from the conductor of a bus.
   (*v*) making purchases from a busy shop.

These all are made through oral mathematics. Often one feels handicapped without the knowledge and practice of oral mathematics.

3. Pupils become more attentive in the class, as at any moment any pupil can be asked oral-question. The process of quick questioning makes the pupil mentally alert.
4. Oral work in mathematics gives enough practice for independent thinking an analysis of the problem. Thus, it provides good mental exercises, alertness and readyness of the mind *i.e.,* quick thinking.
5. Oral work encourages healthy competition among the pupils. It also motivates them to achieve higher rank in the class.
6. Oral work proves a very economical device for saving time and energy. It develops speed in solving problems.
7. It is helpful in imparting education. *e.g.*
   (*a*) It helps —
   (*i*) in testing the pre-knowledge of the pupils. New knowledge can be imparted based on the pre-knowledge.
   (*ii*) the teacher in introducing the lesson and announcing the aim of the lesson.

(*b*) Oral questions help the presentation of the new subject matter.

(*c*) They help much in carrying out recapitulation and revision work through proper practice or drill and testing their understanding.

(*d*) Oral questions put time to time help the teacher in judging whether the pupils are following the subject matter or not.

(*e*) Teacher may easily pay individual attention by distributing oral questions all over the class which help to catch hold of individual attention.

(*f*) Oral work proves one of the best attention-catching device and it makes the pupils concentrate.

8. With this technique, memory of the child can be tested.
9. In the process of learning, confidence, thinking, understanding and imagination power can be developed.
10. This technique can be used for teaching a good number of topics in mathematics.
11. It quickens the wit and sharpens intelligence.
12. In mathematics, oral work is interesting as well as effective especially in the initial stages. It gives quick and easy start to process of learning.
13. Through oral work in mathematics it is very easy to discover the weaknesses of the pupil and his mistakes can be rectified.
14. Oral questions help in creating, maintaining and stimulating interest of pupils in the study of mathematics. It also breaks monotonous routine of the classroom.
15. Oral questions help in making a lesson easily comprehensible and clear.
16. It saves a lot of time and cuts short the process that we have to be done unnecessarily in written form.
17. Oral work builds strong foundation for latter written work in mathematics.
18. It removes shyness and hesitation of children and provide motivation for oral expression.
20. The same thing can be expressed orally in a number of ways.
21. The learning of various new concepts requires sufficient oral drill.
22. Oral repetition of multiplication tables in mathematics, is often a source of enjoyment to pupils. Later on, it takes the form of oral recitation.

## *Limitations of Oral Work*

1. Record of the learnt material cannot be kept for reference and matter cannot be retained for a longer time.
2. It is very quick device and is not suitable for all the pupils and for all the topics of mathematics.
3. It develops a hasty attitude in the pupils. They may jump at the wrong conclusion in haste.
4. In written mathematics, work has to be done very systematically step-by-step but in oral mathematics no such thing is required.

5. It oral work is not conducted properly —
   (*a*) there is likelihood to develop unsystematic and haphazard outlook in the pupils.
   (*b*) there is likelihood of inaccuracy. Mistakes may be caused because of the speed and haste. Lack of any systematic work may happen.

   Hence, it will be waste of time and energy.
6. All the problems cannot be worked out verbally.
7. Expression and writing power of the pupils cannot be checked properly.

### *Precautions to be observed*

1. To yield proper results, oral work should be based on the pre-knowledge of the pupils.
2. Oral work should be used as a means of revision and testing the knowledge imparted.
3. Oral work should be properly graded. It should start from simple to complex. While doing gradation the psycho-physical needs of the pupils must be kept in mind.
4. The mathematics teacher, while using oral mathematics, should try to create an atmosphere that is conducive for sharp mental working. The atmosphere should not be dull and melancholy.
5. The teacher should not reach to any conclusion about pupils on the basis of the oral mathematics. He should give enough practice of oral mathematics everybody in the class.

### *Questions to be used in Oral Mathematics*

1. The oral questions should help —
   (*a*) recall of the past knowledge.
   (*b*) in classification and definition of figures and other subject material.
   (*c*) in proof and plan of the subject matter.
   (*d*) in analysis and synthesis of problems (subject matter).
   (*e*) in comparison of the present with some other aspects of knowledge.
   (*f*) in evaluation of certain things or in illustration of certain points.
2. Questions should explain the cause and effect relationship.
3. Questions should show contrast with certain other things.

## 2. Written Work in Mathematics

- When calculation work in a problem becomes more complicated, lengthy and tiresome and moreover mind cannot carry out these calculations orally, then one has to resort to writing.
- If one has an unusual memory and developed thinking and reasoning ability — he is free to use oral mathematics in solving complicated problems and written work is not at all essential in solving them.

  Thus, written work is just an extension of oral work.
- In written work the help of writing material is necessarily taken.
- In order to attain precision and accuracy, written work is a helping hand in mathematics.

## *Importance/Values/Purpose/Merits of Written Work*

The importance/values/purpose/merits of written work in mathematics can be summarised as under:

1. It is an admitted fact that 'reading makes a full man, conference a ready man and writing an exact and perfect man'.
2. Written work is of permanent nature, so the performance of pupils can be judged in a better way. Again, record of the learnt material can be kept for the purpose of reference. We can use it for the future life.
3. Expression and writing power of the pupils can be checked properly. In written mathematics, errors if any could be caught easily. Thus, it diminishes the chances of making mistakes.
4. In conducting the large classes of mathematics, it is very helpful to teacher to solve the problem on the blackboard in written form. The pupils can easily take it down in their notebooks.
5. In written work teacher can make the pupils work in accordance with proper rules, principles and processes.
6. Written work is quite helpful —
   (*a*) in solving lengthy problems and complicated operations which are a bit difficult to be solved orally.
   (*b*) in clearing thoughts and in making proper reasoning.
   (*c*) in mental development of the pupils.
   (*d*) in enabling the teachers to know the pupils comprehension and amount of work done by them.
   (*e*) in improving the speed of writing.
   (*f*) in developing the confidence in the process of learning.
7. Learning by written work is retainable for a longer time.
8. Through written work memory of the pupils can be tested.
9. It leads to neat and systematic working and ensures exactitude, precision and accuracy.
10. Verbalism can be reduced in the process of teaching and learning of mathematics.
11. If need be, suggestions to improve handwriting can be given.
12. Practice of the learnt material can be easily carried out. It also helps in testing the knowledge imparted orally.

## *Demerits of Written Work*

1. Time consuming and laborious device.
2. Not suitable for —
   (*a*) beginners because learning of tables and counting can be done more effectively by proper drill work.
   (*b*) physically handicapped children.
3. Written work is totally dependent upon oral work.

## *Relative Importance of Oral work and written work*

- Written work and oral work both combine to make the process of instruction complete.
- Written work should always be regarded as an extension of oral work because it is the written work which is to be aimed at.

  Oral work gives the start, written work follows it. Oral work preceeds written work.
- Oral work can never be isolated from the written work. Thus, both are necessary for the teaching and learning of mathematics.
- Only the beginning should be made through oral work. The rest of the responsibility lies with the written work.
- The mental images and impressions carried through oral work do not last long, and therefore, what has been done orally should always be fixed through written work.
- Written work gives accuracy and exactness to the progress and products of oral work. On the other hand, oral work gives precision and speed to written work.

## *Precautions and Suggestions regarding written work*

The following precautions and suggestions should be adopted to make written work more useful, meaningful and effective:

1. The teacher should give proper instructions to the pupils about the written work and its procedure.
2. The work to be done by the students should be very clear and definite *i.e.,* to the point.
3. The written work should not be beyond the capacity and needs of the pupils.
4. The work should be such that the entire class is kept busy.
5. The written work must be verified by the teacher to ensure its correctness.
6. The pupils must be encouraged to get their work examined and properly corrected by the teacher.

## 3. Drill Work in Mathematics

- Saxena and Oberoi — 'The meaning of drill work is to apply the learnt task or skills or reading material in novel situations.'
- Drill work is based on the psychological principles like 'learning by doing' and 'law of exercise.'
- Drill is not mere repetition of an act. It is the serious work activity leading to perfection of the skill.

  'Practice' may be the right synonym of 'drill'.
- Teacher has to ascertain whether the knowledge given to the pupils has been fixed in their minds properly or not. If not, sufficient follow-up work has to be carried out for making the knowledge gained a permanent, useful and practicable asset.

For these purposes (*i*) Drill work, (*ii*) Review, (*iii*) Questioning, and (*iv*) Considering outstanding unsolved problems, are generally used.

Out of these four devices, drill work is considered the most effective and widely used device for fixing the knowledge of mathematics and the impression of the material learnt in the mental make-up of education.

- Never forget that understanding precedes the drill, otherwise the practice becomes an exercise in academic futility and none benefits.
- Careful questioning by the teacher is usually needed in drill work.
- One cannot achieve speed and accuracy in solving mathematical problems without a good practice (drill) of using the fundamental operations.
- The basic facts and tables of mathematics have to be memorised through ample practice.

  But the practice should be done with understanding and with a clear idea of the goals and objectives and there should not be a mere mechanical cramming.
- It is an admitted fact that 'practice makes a man perfect'.
- Drill work is a means to strengthen the knowledge already acquired.
- This technique is widely used by teachers to revise a lesson already taught.
- It is not the testing of results but the strengthening of learning.
- It leads to good habit formation.

## Functions/Role of Drill work

Drill and exercise have an important role to play in the learning process.

1. Various operations, rules, facts, formulae, etc., are to be fixed as mental habits in the children. Drill work does it perfectly.
2. It is an erroneous view that drill work has no place in progressive education as it brings drudgery and boredom.

   However, after teaching self-directed study-assignments, etc., the learning on the part of the pupils needs further strengthening. The learning of mathematics requires more practice and exercise. It can be fulfilled only by means of drill.
3. The place of drill in mathematics has been a much discussed issue in recent years.
   (A) The old pedagogy undoubtedly laid too much emphasis upon memorisation and mechanical learning and to a considerable extent neglected meaningful learning with understanding.

   (B) Eventually, however, a strong reaction set in, with the extremists taking the position that meanings alone have value. But the development of new concepts and understanding is *all* that matters and drill in its restricted sense has no place at all in the educational process.

   This point of view overlooks the important element of fixation, without which it would be impossible to organise and relate concepts or to carry on any process at a reasonable level of efficiency.
4. An enlightened present day view of mathematical instruction must reject both of the above mentioned untenable extreme positions.

(1) Both are necessary and neither alone is sufficient.

(2) Drill is extremely necessary for cementing the knowledge and skills in the minds of pupils. Similarly, strong emphasis upon concepts and meanings must be regarded as essential for understanding.

(3) Very useful operations of mathematics must be performed correctly and with considerable speed.

Some of them need to be actually automatised through systematic and repeated practice *i.e.,* through drill.

(4) If instruction is to be valuable, understanding and drill must go hand in hand.

5. Children should first understand and should drill the mathematical concepts. If drill lacks both significance and motive, it becomes simply drudgery.

The functions of drill work may be summarised as under:

(1) To fix the material learnt in the minds of the children.

(2) To develop —

(*i*) speed and accuracy in the learning of mathematics.

(*ii*) communicational skills for the learning of mathematics.

(*iii*) confidence and a sense of achievement in the pupils.

(3) To provide opportunity to the students to develop a habit of independent working with speed and accuracy.

(4) To motivate average and below average pupils to learn by tried and error.

(5) To involve the pupils in the learning of details of the content minutely.

(6) To revise the knowledge already learnt.

## *Principles of Drill Work in Mathematics/How to make Drill work effective?*

Educational psychology, in recent years, has tried much to provide teachers with well-established principles to make drill work interesting and effective.

Authors and publishers have combined to make available materials specially designed to facilitate the application of these principles.

1. Drill, to be most effective, must be well-motivated.

    - If the material contains no intrinsic interest, and if the pupils do not see any value in it, their work will be without interest.
    - If pupils consider the work important and interesting in itself, they will definitely work with zest and with concentrated attention. Ultimately, their work will be correspondingly more effective.
    - Drill should be a interesting affair and not become unpleasant or boring.

2. Drill exercises should be conducted in such a manner that pupils can work at different rates and at different levels according to their abilities.

    - The certainty of individual difference within a group makes it clear that the individuals, even if they all may need drill on the same topic, will not be able to do it at the same rate or at the same rate of difficulty.

- Drill exercises should contain enough material to keep all the pupils profitably occupied throughout the drill period.
- Drill should have sufficiently diversified material to provide worthwhile and stimulating practice for pupils of different attainments and capacities.
- Drill should consist of several distinct activities involving different strategies of learning.
- Variety of problems will make the drill interesting.
- Individual difference should be given due consideration while engaging the class in drill work.
- Much drill work should be individualised.
- It is uneconomical for above average pupils to continue drilling on tasks which no longer challenge them. It is equally wasteful to have them do nothing while waiting for others to catch up.

3. Drill periods should generally be short.
   - The attention span of children is very small. Long periods of continuous drill become tiresome and ineffective.
   - No drill period should extent for more than 20 minutes. If need be, periods should be distributed in relatively small amount at recurring intervals which should become more widely spaced as time goes on. Thus, drill periods should be brief and distributed over a period of time.
   - The principle of 'spaced learning is very important and is widely recognised in the organisation of text books and instructional material. The idea of complete immediate mastery on the content is not in vogue now-a-days.
   - Drill work should be in appropriate quantity.
4. Drill must be specific in order to be most effective.
   - It should be concentrated upon particular skills or on particular details of operation.
   - The objective of all drills is that of fixation of the particular detail/skill. For the moment, that detail/skill should be dissociated from its setting and context and drilled upon in itself.
5. When drill is begun on any process/skill, correctness should be insisted upon as the prime consideration and for the time being, speed should be regarded as of secondary importance.
   - In drill work every effort should be made to detect mistakes of pupils' work immediately and eliminate them at the outset. Failure to do so will inevitably have unfortunate consequences because a wrong habit is fixed as readily as a right one. Then it becomes much harder to eliminate it, and to replace it by a correct one.
   - It is of ultra-importance to supervise closely the initial work of the pupils on any new process/skill.
   - For the emphasis on right practice from the start, teacher should use his discretion. Teachers should not overlook this important principle. They should not give any drill work on the contents which have not been previously mastered in the classroom.

- A small amount of careful supervised drill will certainly avoid making such mistake.
- In drill work, accuracy should be given more consideration than the speed, at least in the beginning.
- After proper identification, the mistakes committed by pupils should be immediately pointed out and rectified.

The practice of a mistake may be proved very costly for the future progress.

6. It is advisable and desirable to have pupils apply mathematical checks to ascertain the correctness of their own work.
   - The checking of work in this manner is a real educational exercise as fully valuable as the original work itself.
   - This method of applying mathematical checks can be conveniently used in drill work just as it can with problem work.
7. For the drill work in the classroom, answers should be provided for selected problems of exercises.
   - If this is not done, specific and efficient checking — techniques should have been developed previously. Pupils should be required to check all results carefully.
   - Really speaking, it will prove a definite stimulus to the pupils to know *immediately* whether his responses are correct or not.
   - If this results are correct, he gets immediate satisfaction. If not, he is challenged to correct his work.
   - Providing answers actually affords a real training in honesty and self-responsibility. Moreover, it will add zest to the work itself.
   - Pupils should be taught to test the validity of the solutions of the problems. This will certainly a good reinforcement agent to the pupils for doing more and more drill work.
8. If and when possible, drill material should be provided with some means whereby the student can *store* his own work and compare his performance with that of the classmates and with established standards and also with his own performance on previous occasions.
   - Generally the pupils are very much interested in noting their own progress. This device of scoring his own work is the best incentive.
9. Make the pupils aware that drill work is only a part of their mathematical training but without it they would be handicapped in their attaining of understanding, appreciations and generalisations.
   - Pupils would be handicapped without correctness and speed in their fundamental mathematical skills.
   - In the absence of these skills, they cannot give full attention to interpretation and analysis of mathematical problems/theorems/processes.
10. Finally, drill must be well-oriented and related to an instructional programme designed to emphasise understandings, appreciations and generalisations.
    - The tendency to overemphasise the proficiency in mechanical skills should be avoided.

- No doubt, accuracy and speed in the fundamental skills are very much desirable goals of mathematical instruction. But the teacher should never forget to emphasise the careful study of interrelationships, the intelligent comprehension of underlying truths and the thoughtful generalisation of principles and processes.

## Principles of Drill work by Sueltz

Some of the principles of drill by Sueltz (1953) are summarised as under for convenient reference.

1. The learner should understand what he is practising and also appreciate its significance to him as an individual.
2. The learner should have enough experience so that the *newness* in what he is practising does not create a mental block for him.
3. The learner should be an active participant in setting his goals as well as in the thinking for making great efforts of learning. He should not merely repeat 'parrot fashion' from a teacher or a textbook.
4. Drill should follow the developmental and discovery stages of learning and be used to reinforce and extend basic learning.
5. Drill should be varied to avoid monotony. Drill work should involve 'principle of change and variety.' It should not become a routine work. It should be given in various forms like oral, written, practical or play-activities.
6. Drill should be spaced so that —
   (*a*) time is not wasted in excessive over-learning in initial stages, and
   (*b*) previous learnings are kept fresh and useful.
7. Drill should be an integral part of various phases of learning but should not be used to hasten the achievement of results at the sacrifice of meaning and understanding.
8. Drill policy should recognise different rates and modes of learning with different pupils and not try to fit all into a common mould.
9. In general, it is better to provide for drill upon whole processes rather than parts thereof, unless some particular part such as subtraction in a long division exercise, causes trouble and needs teaching and practice for reinforcing.
10. Drill should be done with correct processes lest a child practices errors which need to be remedied later.
11. Drill should be based upon or involve thinking and insight so that it never becomes a mere mechanical repetition.
12. Drill should be used as and when needed. It should not be used as a punishment. Things already well learnt be not assigned for more practice.
13. There should be some organisation of drill so that —
    (*a*) pupils see the sense and relationships of what they are doing, and
    (*b*) important elements are not overlooked.
14. It seems that pupils of lower mental abilities require more drill than the more able, but this may be due to other related factors such as attention, insight and other such causes.

### Some More Points to make Drill Work effective

1. After the pupils have done some practice, teacher should try to elicit a summary of what has been learnt in the classroom.
   - The summary can also be developed by asking relevant questions related to the concept developed.
2. Introduction of playway spirit and use of the proper aids in drill work may serve very well the desired purpose of making drill work interesting and stimulating.
   - The element of play, competition and group work should be introduced in drill work.
   - Drill work should never be conducted in a routine, half-hearted and stiff and unnatural fashion.
3. Drill work must be relevant. The work and problems should be related to the current topic or topics being taught in the class.
   - Drill work should be meaningful and useful.
4. Proper environment for engaging pupils in an independent pursuit of self-study through drill work should be provided.
5. Drill work must have some purpose. It is to be intelligently planned so that it accomplishes its purpose. Otherwise, it may be a sheer waste of time and energy of teacher and the pupils.
6. Moderate initial practice and systematic review are superior to overlearning.
7. Teacher should be resourceful to elicit efficient and continuous reactions.
8. Drill assignments should not be made tasks. Student should enable to take pleasure in them.
9. The goal and objectives of learning should be clarified so that the learner appreciates his efforts to achieve the goal.
10. The number-games, flash cards, self-direction material and application of ideas in various situations may be used.

### Importance/Merits of Drill Work

1. It is an economical device of teaching and learning.
   - It is a less time-consuming technique.
   - It increases speed and accuracy in solving mathematical problems.
   - The speed and accuracy in mathematics cannot be possible without drill work.
2. Importance of drill is felt and realised in learning of every branch of mathematics.
   - In Arithmetic, there are numerous processes and operations which are to be made automatic by drill.
   - The four fundamental rules should be concentratedly repeated until the pupils get a fair degree of accuracy and speed.
   - The rewriting of multiplication tables and charts makes the knowledge perfect in lower classes.
3. Drill work plays a dominant role in learning and applying the facts, theorems, propositions in Geometry, and principles and formulae in Algebra.

4. It keeps the pupils awake and they work regularly.
5. Drill leads to habit formation.
   - Mental, physical and emotional outcomes of school activities are always the results of habit formation and it is dependent on drill.
   - Pupils self-confidence is increased. Later on this habit makes them courageous and bold to face hardships of life.
   - Habit of self-study, independent work and self-development is inculcated through drill work.
6. Drill work affords a convenient and efficient medium for the rapid memorisation of details and the automisation of processes.
   - Drill work easily checks the memory of the pupils.
7. Drill provides opportunities of self-learning, self-improvement and of independent work. They try themselves to analyse and solve the problems.
8. The ability to apply knowledge comes through practice.
   - The application of any principle/formula in any branch of mathematics becomes easy and simple through drill work.
9. The concepts, facts and so many fundamentals of mathematics become quite clear by continuous revising and practising them through drill work.
10. Drill work gives ample opportunities to realise the basic aims and objectives of teaching mathematics.
11. It stimulates and develops pupils' mental powers.
12. It helps in the learning of skills like computational and geometrical skills.
13. Learnt material can be retained for a longer time and gets consolidated.
14. For beginners it is a good technique of learning.
15. Immediate reinforcement through practice and application is desirable.

### *Demerits of Drill Work*

1. Not applicable for all topics of mathematics.
2. Without good and clear voice, it may not be effective.
3. It may create disturbance in other classes.

## 4. Home Work in Mathematics

- Mathematics is such a specific subject that needs quite a lot practice (drill).
- At present, the curriculum in secondary schools is so vast that school time is not sufficient to give due consideration to everything provided in the curriculum.

The school hours are limited. The mathematics teacher has to teach two-three subjects in two-three classes. Under the circumstances, the teacher does not find sufficient time to review, revision and practice all the facts and principles of mathematics.

So, if the teacher wants to do justice with the curriculum, he has to counterpart with homework.

- Homework plays a vital role as the teachers get very short time to cover the vast and heavy load of curriculum.
- By giving homework means creating a study environment for pupils at home.
- Home work should be assessed as a part of internal assessment and proper weightage should be given.
- Homework in mathematics may consist of —
  (*a*) learning some definitions, principles and facts by heart,
  (*b*) drawing graphs, charts, tables, etc.,
  (*c*) solving some problems based on facts taught in the classroom,
  (*d*) constructing or inventing something new or constructive on the basis of knowledge and skills learnt,
  (*e*) observing some phenomena in nature or social world relevant to the knowledge or skills taught in the classroom.

### *Should Homework be Assigned or Not? Ill effects/Evils of HW*

Some educationists are of the opinion that children should not be assigned any HW because —

(*i*) It creates school mania.

(*ii*) The school time is quite sufficient to make pupils learnt all the essential things.

(*iii*) In assigning HW we commit a sort of cruelty and injustice to the pupils by snatching away their leisure time pleasure.

(*iv*) Doing HW at odd hours may adversely affect pupils' health.

(*v*) 'All work and no play' cannot make Jack a good boy.

(*vi*) Over-emphasis on HW and the fear of punishment may create distaste for the subject which may result into distaste for the teacher and the school.

- The fear of punishment for not doing HW gives birth to so many undesirable complications like the habit of copying, telling lies, truency which ultimately may result into emotional tensions.

(*vii*) Home may not provide adequate conditions for doing HW.

(*viii*) Some pupils may unnecessarily involve their parents or others to complete their HW.

(*ix*) Heavy load of HW in one subject may affect the achievements in other subjects.

### *How should HW be assigned?*

- HW in itself is not evil. The way in which it is assigned needs to be blamed.
- Some teachers assign —
  (*a*) too much HW not considering the knowledge and abilities of their pupils.
  (*b*) difficult and much HW to boast their hard-working nature and unusual enthusiasm.
  (*c*) HW to save their own labour and to evade their duties.
- Never give HW in the form of punishment.

- HW should be —
  - (*a*) given regularly.
  - (*b*) based on the teaching work done in the classroom.
  - (*c*) assigned keeping in view the HW assigned in other branches and subjects.
  - (*d*) carefully planned and wisely assigned. It should neither be too heavy nor too light/ simple.
  - (*e*) suitably graded according to the individual needs and abilities to suit all types of pupils in the class. Gradation of HW is very necessary.
  - (*f*) given in brief, so that the pupils will be more willing to try to complete it.
  - (*g*) checked and corrected regularly and intensively.
- 'The principle of individual difference' should always be kept in mind while assigning HW.
- 'The principle of change and variety' should be followed in assigning HW.
  - It should take the form of oral, written, practical work and field activities or hobbies.
- The nature and amount of HW should be kept in mind. HW should be according to the abilities and capacities of the pupils.
- Problems on the newly developed topic of the day should not be given in HW.
- HW time-table must be prepared by every subject teacher.

## *Objectives of giving HW*

The pupil (1) utilises the leisure time properly and beneficially.

(2) cultivates the habit of regularity and hard work.

(3) snaps opportunity of independent work and for application and practice of the gained knowledge and skills.

(4) gets supplements of classroom teaching.

(5) develops environment of school feeling at home.

(6) plays a role as a link between parents and teachers.

## *Merits of Assigning HW*

1. Most of the knowledge gained in mathematics becomes useful only when one applies it and uses it in day-to-day life activities. Assigning HW meets all such requirements.
2. If HW is assigned with great care and in a proper amount, it is sure to bring healthy results. *e.g.*,
   - (*a*) It can provide a good means for utilising the leisure time of the pupils.
   - (*b*) It can cultivate the habit of hard work and independent self-study.
   - (*c*) It brings regularity and punctuality in the study-habits.
   - (*d*) Through HW parents may be acquainted with the progress of their children.
   - (*e*) Regularity of HW may prove a helping hand in covering the lengthy syllabus and an effective device for fixing the knowledge and skill acquired in school.

3. HW brings the closer relationship among the parents and the school.
4. It develops a sense of responsibility, self-confidence and self-reliance among the pupils.

### *Correction of HW*

- The correction of HW in mathematics is very necessary and important. It is absolutely essential and is a must.

  If it remains unchecked it does not fulfil its purposes and consequently many mistakes or faulty processes may become fixed in the minds of pupils.
- Regular checking of HW is not an easy task, as it will not be possible for a teacher to spend much of his time and energy as required by this work.

  The help of some brilliant pupils proves necessary in this task.
- The teacher may write the correct answers and solution on blackboard, and ask the pupils to check the correctness of their HW.
- The teacher may also introduce surprise checking or cross checking or mutual checking by exchanging notebooks or sample checking day. This will save his time and energy a lot.
- While checking HW in mathematics the following points should be kept in view:

  (1) Stressing neat and clean work.

  (2) Transcription should be reduced to a minimum.

  (3) Remarks should be written and suggestions should be given.

  (4) Mistakes should be pointed out by suitable remarks.

  (5) Common errors be ticked and discussed in the class.

  (6) No omission of any step. Move step-by-step.

## 5. Group Work in Mathematics

- Group work is also known as 'collective work' or 'Group study'.
- The pupils engaged in a group receive group instruction, do drill or practical work in cooperation, complete group assignments and discuss or plan common projects. Such type of work or study in a group is termed as 'group work (group study)'.
- To make a group, the pupils of a class are divided into ceratin homogeneous groups, keeping in view their common interest, aptitude, abilities and capacities.
- The number of students in a group is kept in such a way that smooth functioning of the group as an organised unit within the capacity of the resources available, is possible.
- In mathematics, there is an ample scope of group work. In it, the teacher teaches by activities, projects, assignments or by practical work.
- The techniques of oral work and drill work are conducted generally in groups. The recitation of multiplication tables, preparation of mathematical models, charts, etc. are also generally done in groups.

  Students may voluntarily engage in group for completing their HW and assignments, their project work, practical work and many other such activities in mathematics.

- For a teacher, individual method of work is almost impossible because —
  (1) of crowded classes in the school.
  (2) a teacher cannot give full attention to individual pupil.

So, some via media have to be sought so that the purpose of modern education can be fulfilled. Group work is that via media.

## *Characteristics of Group Work*

1. The principles lie under group work are: (*a*) Principle of active participation, (*b*) Principle of freedom for work (*c*) Principle of equal opportunity.
2. Group work is a via media between class teacher and the individual self-study.
3. It aims at securing the advantages of individual instruction and at the same time retaining the economic and socially advantageous way of class teaching.
4. In this technique, the unit being smaller, greater attention can be paid to individual student.
5. These small groups are generally homogeneous. In smaller homogeneous groups, pupils work under group-feeling (we-feeling) with more co-operation and healthy competitive attitude than in the larger heterogeneous classes.
6. In group work, pupils pool their resources and thus complete the assigned work jointly which none of them might be capable to finish single-handed.
7. The group for the group work is homogeneous in the matter of age-level, abilities and capacities, attitude and aptitude, intelligence and level of achievement.

## *The Need of Group Work*

The group is required —

(1) to consider, examine and investigate the various aspects of a question or a problem or a topic.
(2) to work for completing HW.
(3) to consider thoughtfully the relationship in topic or problem under group study.
(4) to analyse, compare, evaluate and conclude the relationship in the problem.
(5) to collect mathematical data from the field.
(6) to prepare mathematical models, charts and other material.
(7) to exchange the idea, opinions, suggestions and experiences of the pupils.

## *How to Organise Group Work?*

1. First, the teacher should collect all the relevant information about the interests, abilities, attitude, aptitude and capacities of all the pupils in the class.
2. Then the teacher should make adequate number of homogeneous groups.
3. All the members of the group should be actively involved in the selection and then planning of the group work. They should frame general details of the group work.
4. Pupils should be helped in distribution of duties by mutual discussion and prepare a plan of the minute details of their work.

5. Teacher should provide all necessary guidance and facilities to various groups in a proper amount at the proper time.
6. Teacher should carefully supervise their work so that no member of the group shirk his assigned duty.
7. Teacher should see that every group works as a cohesive unit. The differences of opinions in the group should be settled by mutual discussion. Also the spirit of mutual trust, love and team-feeling should be created among the members of the group.
8. As a precautionary measure, teacher should not leave matters entirely on the groups. For the success of group work or study programmes, he should render appropriate guidance and help at the proper moment.

### *Merits of Group Work*

1. Group work provides opportunities to the pupils for the development of —
   (*a*) their interest in mathematics.
   (*b*) social qualities and virtues such as co-operation, we-feeling, mutual love and respect, tolerance and collective responsibility.
2. Working in a group usually provides very pleasant experiences.
3. Group work in mathematics stimulate and attract the pupils towards the study of mathematics.
4. Group work breaks the monotony of the routine classroom teaching.
5. It reduces the problems of wide individual differences.
   (*a*) It helps in paying individual attention.
   (*b*) The group being homogeneous, teacher can attend it properly and carefully.
   (*c*) Normally the classroom teaching suits the average learner. The needs of gifted and below average pupils can hardly be met through classroom teaching. The small homogeneous group provides solution of the problems of individual differences.
   (*d*) in such groups the pupils progress according to their own pace and none has to suffer on account of others.
6. Group Study helps the process of learning.
   (*a*) Mathematics being a practical subject needs the help of practical methods like laboratory method, project method, etc.
   (*b*) Group work provides proper platform for implementing these progressive methods and thus helps the process of learning.
7. Utilisation of experience and learning from one another is possible.

### *Limitations of Group Work*

1. Group work may encourage shirkers. They get opportunity to escape work. They may conveniently bank upon the labour of the other sincere and hardworking members of the group.
2. It does not provide the information about the individual progress, which may be neglected.

3. In group work, pupils may acquire limited and partial knowledge. Members of the group are assigned various duties according to their interest and abilities. So, members are able to learn only the piece of knowledge. They do not get opportunity for learning the *whole task* or acquiring complete knowledge of the topic.
4. There is a possibility of disharmony in the group. No group in a strictly real sense is perfectly homogeneous. So, in a group work there is possibility of disagreement and differences. As a result, the group work may suffer seriously collapsing the very basis of the group participation.
5. The pupils may not realise the importance of collective responsibility in group work. So, group work may not remain anybody's work and thus may result in a sheer wastage of all types of resources.

## How to make Group Work effective?

1. No group should be too large or too small. A group of 3 to 7 students is considered suitable for the group work.
2. For exchange of ideas and opinions at least two groups are better than one.
3. The purpose of group work should be made adequately clear to every member of the group to ensure equal efforts and equal responsibility.
4. Every member of the group must get due share of activity and nobody, even the leader, should be allowed to dominate others.
5. The allotment of pupils to different groups should not be rigid but flexible.
6. Teacher should encourage healthy group competition. At the same time, he should guard against mutual jealousy and differences.
7. This technique should be adopted as when and where it suits.
8. The best age-level at which this technique be most profitable is 8-12 years of age.
9. It is not a suitable technique for higher classes and for all the topics of mathematics.
10. In a group, every member should respect the ideas and opinions of other members. Instead of showing disagreement, they should mutually discuss and convince the other members.

## EVALUATE YOURSELF

1. Discuss the scope of oral work in Mathematics. How will you make it more effective?
2. Enumerate the merits and demerits of oral work in mathematics.
3. Explain the importance and use of oral work for the teaching of mathematics.
4. What do you mean by Methods, Techniques and Strategies of mathematics teaching? What are various techniques for the teaching of mathematics?
5. Write short notes on —
   (*a*) Suggestion for written work
   (*b*) HW in mathematics
   (*c*) Drill work
   (*d*) Oral work.

6. What precautions will you observe while giving oral work? Discuss the characteristics of questions to be used in oral mathematics.
7. Discuss the merits and demerits of written work in mathematics.
8. Bring out the relative importance of oral work and written work.
9. What do you mean by drill work in mathematics? Bring out the functions of drill work.
10. Discuss at length the Principles of Drill work in mathematics.
11. Throw light on the principles of Drill work by Sueltz.
12. How will you make drill work more effective?
13. Discuss the merits and demerits of drill work in mathematics.
14. Opine whether HW be assigned or not. How should HW be assigned?
15. Mention the objective of giving HW. What are the merits of assigning HW?
16. How will you correct the HW?
17. Point out characteristics of Group Work. Also mention its need.
18. How will you organise Group Work?
19. Discuss the merits and demerits of Group Work.
20. How will you make Group work more effective?
21. 'Home work is indispensable in the teaching of mathematics' — Comment on it.
22. Discuss the place of oral work and drill work in mathematics.

'What science can there be more noble, more excellent, more useful for men, more admirable, high and demonstrative than that of Mathematics.'

— ***Benjamin Franklin***

# STRATEGIES OF TEACHING MATHEMATICS

## 16.1 Strategies of Teaching Mathematics

There are mainly five strategies used in the teaching of mathematics. They are —

(1) Self study

(2) Supervised study

(3) Assignment work

(4) Review

(5) Brain storming

## 1. Self Study in Mathematics

### Meaning

- Through self study, the pupils are able to solve problems, acquire knowledge and skills, and learn new concepts of mathematics with their own independent efforts.
- (Definition) Self study is a way of independent learning which results in developing the habit of acquiring knowledge and skills in a pupil through his own independent efforts.
- Here, the pupil is his own helper and guide. He has to proceed on his own.
- Self study means individual pupil's own independent study. It is the habit of independent learning. The individual studies and learns himself. The individual attempts and solves the problems himself without any outside help.
- In this strategy, the pupil learns to make use of his knowledge and experiences in tackling various problems.
- It is in everyone's interest to depend upon self-study. Ultimately every pupil whether brilliant or otherwise, has to prepare for his examination by self study.
- At the stage of preparation and comprehension, it is the most suitable strategy of learning.

- Self study is the golden rule for self-education. It need not remain confined to school education. It should be the habit of learner throughout his education.
- Preparation of projects, debates, discussions, seminars and other competitions require self study.

## Need/Importance of Self Study

The importance of self study in mathematics may be summarised as under:

1. Self study develops in the pupil —
   (*a*) problem-solving attitude.
   (*b*) genuine interest of the pupils in the learning of mathematics.
   (*c*) initiative and independent thinking.
   (*d*) heuristic and problem-solving attitude.
   (*e*) self-reliance and self-dependence in the process of learning.
   (*f*) ability to properly utilise leisure time in the best way.
   (*g*) intellectual capacities and how to use them judiciously for acquiring knowledge.
   (*h*) the sense of responsibility and regularity.
   (*i*) the habit of practice (drill).
2. In the study of mathematics, the pupil has to do a major part of exercise work on his own efforts. Therefore, self study is most useful.
3. It builds up self-confidence in the pupils in —
   (*a*) their independent learning and problem-solving ability
   (*b*) tackling the problems of mathematics.
4. Self study enables the pupils to make use of their knowledge learnt in the class in solving various problems.
5. It prepares pupils for real life so that they could do their work independently, without seeking the help of others.
6. It stimulates the pupils in knowing more and more about mathematics and encourages them in solving new problems independently.
7. The experience of constructing figures, proving the theorems or propositions, solving the riddles and riders in geometry, has to be achieved largely by pupils' own thinking and reasoning. Self study helps them to do so.
8. Usually classroom teaching aims at the coverage of the syllabus. Self study makes possible intensive deep study of mathematical facts.
9. Self study in mathematics widen the mental horizon of the pupils. It takes them higher and higher on the staircase of mathematical knowledge.
10. It makes the pupil —
    (*a*) research minded. In true sense the habit of self study is responsible for discovering new facts in the field of mathematics.
    (*b*) able to practise the learnt mathematical facts and principles, in their day-to-day life.

11. Self study in mathematics gives opportunity for solving different types of various problems and in doing independent practice and drill work which is most needed in mathematics.
12. It makes it possible for some gifted pupils to try to study the topics before hand. This helps them to understand properly the facts concerning that topic during classroom teaching.
13. Self study is required preparation for competitions such as debates, discussions, seminars, workshops, examinations, etc.
14. It is essential —
    (*a*) for the regular progress of the pupil.
    (*b*) for completing other assignments in mathematics.
15. In mathematics one problem solved by self efforts is worth than solving ten or more problems solved by borrowing help from others.
16. Self study inspires the learner to engage in the independent research work.
17. It discourages habit of cramming or rote memory.
18. It helps them significantly at the decisive, critical or crucial juncture of any examination/ test.
19. It is the best way to supplement the class work and practise various things.
20. In self study the pupil is his own guide and supervisor.

## *Making Self Study More Effective and Meaningful*

*(How to encourage self study in mathematics?)*

The problems arise: How to make self study more effective and meaningful? How to encourage self study in mathematics? In response to these problems, some suggestions are made as under:

1. The pupil should be —
    (*a*) convinced about the fact that mathematics is learnt best by self-efforts.
    (*b*) made to understand that self study is most rewarding and it is the only strategy which will pay in long run.
    (*c*) advised to read a topic in advance before the teacher takes it up in the class.
2. Self study can be made more systematic by giving regular HW or assignment in proper amount.
3. Some interesting problems should always be presented to the pupils which may encourage them earnestly to study and get the solution on their own.
4. In case a pupil fails to show any output in self study, the teacher should find out its causes and remove them properly.
5. The teacher should inform his pupils about the topic to be taught on the following day. Teacher should give major outlines concerning this topic alongwith the relevant references. Thus, pupils should be encouraged for preparing any new topic or learning beforehand through self study.
6. The co-operation of parents should also be sought to ensure regular progress of the pupil in self study.

7. The work accomplished by the pupil in self study should be checked, corrected and evaluated by the teacher.
8. The habit of self study should be developed as early as possible.
9. The teacher should encourage the child —
   (*a*) to work independently in the classroom as well as at home.
   (*b*) to make proper and full use of library books. There should be properly organised mathematics library. He can suggest them specific reference books and text books.
10. The pupils who study independently should be praised, recognised and rewarded in the classroom or school.
11. The pupils should be guided to develop the habit of making notes of their self study and also that of difficulties faced.
12. Periodical assignment and regular HW should be given in a proper way. Pupils should not get any opportunity of copying the solution from the notes, or guide and keys or from the notebooks of their classmates.

    The problem/work assigned thus should be stimulating and should meet the individual needs, interests and capacities.
13. The stimulating literature concerning history of mathematics, life history of mathematicians and recreational aspect of mathematics to contribute and encourage significantly in forming the habit of self study.
14. There is a need to develop proper learning habits, heuristic attitude and problem-solving attitude amongst the pupils.
15. Pupils should be encouraged to discover the facts or solve the problems with their own attempts. Spoon-feeding and rote learning are the major obstacles in the path of self study.

    This will lead them to independent thinking, reasoning and self-learning.
16. Organisation of healthy competitions involving mathematical skills and knowledge provide sufficient motivation and stimulation for self study.

## 2. Supervised Study in Mathematics

### *Meaning*

- To study under supervision is called 'supervised study.' Supervised study is the study/ execution of assigned work, by the pupils in the presence and under the direct supervision of the teacher.
- This study may individual or collective.
- In this strategy pupils solve problems or do some practical work in the school hours.
- The teacher's presence makes the atmosphere more disciplined and congenial for hard work.
- In this strategy, the needy pupils get on-the-spot help and guidance at once.
- Their mistakes and difficulties can be removed on-the-spot, then and there only.

- The teacher provides proper guidance and direction to the pupils in solving the problems or performing the work assigned to them.
- Here, every student has to devote the prescribed time compulsorily for completing the assigned work.
- Supervised study attempts to combine the main advantages of individual instruction for those who need it, with the economy of time and other advantages of group instruction.
- If the pupils are to acquire the ability to do effective independent study, they need specific instruction in methods and habits of study.
- Under the recitation and HW plan of teaching mathematics, the pupils are often compelled to do their studying under conditions both — physically and psychologically unfavourable to effect work adversely.

For example, many homes are not in a position to provide suitable desks in quiet rooms where pupils can study advantageously.

Atmosphere of such homes is strongly suggestive of other things and distracting elements are the rule rather than the exception.

Most school maintain some form of study-halls during school hours. As a rule, these provide conditions which are more favourable for study than those which pupils find at home.

These study-halls are normally quiet. As they are made use of during school hours, they eliminate certain physical obstacles to effective study which are likely to operate outside of school hours.

## Forms of Supervised Study in Mathematics

- Pupils study general literature related to mathematics in the form of individual or group assignments.
- Pupils discover the principles or facts through their own independent efforts while learning mathematics through laboratory method or heuristic method.
- Drill work (practice work) in mathematics may be conducted through supervised study. They apply the learnt facts or principles in solving new problems.
- The practical application of mathematical knowledge and skills may be made a subject for the supervised study.

  For this purpose pupils may take so many individual or group projects.

## Importance/Merits of Supervised Study

1. Supervised study helps —

   (*a*) in creating a suitable atmosphere for the self study with an exception of getting the help from the teachers to remove their difficulties during the work.

   (*b*) in controlling the problems of indiscipline.

   (*c*) in exercising proper control over the shirkers and irresponsible pupils.

   (*d*) in inculcating the habit of regularity, punctuality and systematic work.

   (*e*) the teacher in knowing the difficulties of the pupils and errors or mistakes committed by them in their work.

(*f*) the teacher in having a continuous appraisal of the progress of his pupils.

(*g*) in building the self-confidence of the pupils for the solutions of the problems independently.

2. It provides —

   (*a*) a well organised supervision of the work of the pupils.

   (*b*) enough scope for mutual consultation amongst the pupils and also between individual pupil and teacher whenever the need arises.

3. It is very helpful to those students who cannot do their HW at home due to unfavourable atmosphere to study. It diminishes the burden of HW on the pupils.
4. It creates a formal and studious atmosphere for the self study of pupils because the pupils are free to work independently in consultation with their teacher.
5. In supervised study pupils are bound to complete work given to them.
6. It is the best way to keep the pupils busy in the learning process.
7. It encourages pupils for self-learning.
8. It saves time and energy of pupils as they get proper suggestions and guidance at the proper time and help from the teacher at once.
9. It leads a living contact between the teacher and the taught and thus helps in developing cordial and intimate relations.
10. Pupils while remaining under supervision develop proper learning habits and behavioural habits.
11. Under such study pupils do a lot of work without wasting their time.
12. It reduces the chance of wastage and stagnation.

## *Demerits of Supervised Study*

Supervised study alongwith its plus points does also suffer from some limitations and defects. These negative points are not so much alarming. Too much depends upon devotion and will power of teacher.

A well-organised supervised study in mathematics has no match. With little care and experience the teacher may learn the art of good supervision. The teacher may drive his pupils towards self-learning, self-discipline and self-supervision requiring minimum help and guidance from the teacher for their independent self study or group study.

Demerits of supervised study are as under:

1. In supervised study, the teacher is required to supervise and guide each student individually. In large classes such as in India, such a supervision is not possible. The present day crowded classes hardly leave any scope for such study.

   Paying individual attention to every pupil of the class may be only possible with a limited number of pupils.

2. Supervised study in mathematics demands too much work from the teacher. It overburdens the teacher.

Teacher has to plan, supervise, guide and evaluate the work of all pupils. The regular heavy schedule of the present day mathematics teacher hardly allows him to devote so much time, attention and energy for such special work.

3. It needs a lot of supervision. It is practically impossible to supervise the individual or group work of the pupils from the beginning till the end.

   Therefore, in supervised study the possibility of wasting time and energy by the pupils can never be ruled out.

4. In supervised study, guidance is to be rendered in the proper amount and at the proper time. Too much guidance spoils the habit of pupils by making them dependent on teacher.

   Non-availability of the guidance at the proper time may discourage the pupil to the extent that he may develop distaste and apathy towards the subject, subject-teacher and even the school.

5. Sometimes, teacher is very strict and rigid. The pupils afraid to consult him. So, the purpose of supervised study fails.
6. Over-guidance may be an interference in the free-thinking and working of the pupils.
7. In supervised study, the teacher should know the exact purpose and the significance of his supervision. The supervision done merely for the sake of fault-finding, accusing, alarming and penalising the pupils does not bring any fruitful results.

   Rather, it destroys the very purpose and foundations of the supervised study.

8. This strategy becomes ineffective, purposeless and meaningless if it is only a show and used merely to keep the pupils busy or to penalise them.

### *Making Supervised Study More Effective*

A well-organised supervised study is quite helpful in learning mathematics. Its ultimate goal is self-learning.

To make supervised study more effective, the following hints and suggestions may be kept in view:

1. Be sure that the assignment of the work to be done is made clear to all the pupils so that each one will know precisely what is expected from him.
2. Be sure that each pupil has the equipment which he will need for his work. The practice of borrowing breeds carelessness, wastes time and causes disturbance to others also.

   Teacher should keep on hand a limited amount of equipments with which to provide against emergencies.

   If it becomes absolutely necessary for a pupil to borrow any equipment, it is better for him to borrow from the teacher than from a fellow pupil.

3. Soon after the supervised study period has begun, make a rapid inspection of the worth of all the pupils, noting which pupils seem to be most in need of help. The purpose of the survey is —

   (1) to ascertain whether there is a need for immediate reteaching of any part of the work, and

(2) to see what pupils, if any, seem unable to get started with their work.

4. If such reteaching is needed, it should be done immediately with the class as a whole. The supervised study period can then be resumed.
5. If the survey shows that no general reteaching is needed, the teacher may then properly pay attention to the difficulties of individual pupil.

   As in the general developmental work, it should aim to enlist the pupils' fullest participation in the intellectual task — to guide his thinking rather than to give him readymade procedures.

   In most cases the heuristic method should be used. This is a method which fosters self reliance and independent thinking.
6. Spend no more time than is necessary with the pupils. Do not allow yourself to be rushed through a conference with one pupil by the persistent or pressing request of others.
7. Supervise the pupils work actively instead of sitting passively in a corner.
8. Establish with your pupils the understanding that in general, you would determine who needs help and when.
9. At all times and above all other considerations, maintain an atmosphere conducive to study in the room.
10. Give sufficient freedom and facility to the pupils for (*i*) mutual exchange and collaboration and (*ii*) working in their own way.
11. Provide to the point and minute guidance when pupils feel the need of it.
12. Do not keep the session of supervised study too long.
13. If need arises, take the help of other mathematics teachers for the supervision work of different groups.
14. Let the school provide some extra time for supervised study so that the burden of HW can be minimised.

## *Precautions to be taken for Supervised Study*

1. Many teachers make the mistake of rushing to assist pupils at the first sign of difficulty and almost doing their work for them. This is a bad practice for the following reasons:

(1) It does the pupil little or no good.

- Mastery can come only through individual efforts.
- If supervised study programme is to be effective, the teacher must be able to detect the pupil who relies to the teacher's excessive assistance.
- He should refuse to extend them assistance unless he is convinced that they are seriously in need of it.

(2) If the teacher allows pupils to impose unduly upon his willingness to help them, he will soon find himself so swamped with their demands that he will be unable to take care of them in a satisfactory manner.

- The pressure and stress will almost certainly leave him physically tired, mentally and emotionally disorganised and generally unfitted for effective work.

- It is a fine art to determine —
  - (*i*) just who really needs help.
  - (*ii*) just what and how much assistance is needed, and
  - (*iii*) in what manner it should be given.
- This can be done successfully only by a teacher —
  - (*i*) who has a sympathetic understanding of the attitudes and abilities of his students,
  - (*ii*) who has a good knowledge of the difficulties to be expected and the errors commonly made in the work underway,
  - (*iii*) who possesses a trained insight which will enable him to get directly at the root/key of the pupils's difficulties.

2. Pupils often employ wasteful and inefficient procedures in studying mathematics. Sometimes they do not know how to begin their work and they fail to form the habit of depending upon themselves.

(1) They aimlessly trying one thing after another.

(2) They are unsystematic.

(3) They allow their attention to be distracted and their work interrupted by trivial things.

(4) They are careless in their reading, in their listening and in their written work.

(5) They become impatient and do not take time for deliberate analysis and planning before starting their work.

3. Pupils must be helped to become more natured and form stable characteristics.

### Conclusion

Supervised study is the most illuminating and valuable experience for the teacher. It keeps him in touch with the work of all pupils. It often reveals unsuspected omission or inadequacies in his teaching.

It is one of the most effective means of keeping his viewpoint adjusted to that of the less matured pupils.

For the pupils also, it is one of the best strategies to be employed in their teaching-learning process of mathematics.

## 3. Assignment Work in Mathematics

### Meaning

- Assignment work aims at providing to the pupils some work to do.
  - An assignment may be a revision of the lesson learnt or a sort of preparation for the lessons to be learnt.
  - Assignment may be of the following varieties —
    - (*i*) solving a few mathematical problems,
    - (*ii*) solving riders based on propositions,
    - (*iii*) undertaking a proposition and trying to verify it,

(*iv*) collecting mathematical data,

(*v*) finding out applications of mathematical knowledge,

(*vi*) carrying out a mathematical project, and so on.

- Pupils may do his assignment at school or at home as desired by the teacher.
- Pupils take upon the responsibility of carrying out the work assigned.
- Like HW, assignment is also a supplement to classroom teaching.
- It provides the teacher with an opportunity to direct the learning activity and developing habits of more study.
- Long, vague, indefinite and irrelevant assignment do not achieve the desired results.

### *Problems of Assignment*

Assignment in mathematics includes two different kinds of problems:

(1) Repetitive problems (2) Review problems

(1) Repetitive problems are based on new work.

- The repetitive problems serve to emphasise some aspects of what has been newly learnt in the classroom that day.
- By assigning problems on several different topics, the teacher provides the pupil with variety in his assignment.
- Thus, the teacher provides the pupils an opportunity to see if he has really got mastery on what was taught.

(2) Review problems are those which spiral back over the skills and concepts learnt in the previous topics. Hence, they are also called 'spiral assignments.'

- Spiral assignment contains both repetitive and review problems.
- Review problems do not allow the child to forget topics in mathematics which he has learnt previously.
- So, these problems should be selected very carefully.

### *Purposes of Assignment*

1. To solve (*a*) mathematical problems, and (*b*) riders based on a proposition.
2. To develop (*a*) the skill of problem solving, and (*b*) the habit of practice (drill).
3. To prepare illustrations for a topic.
4. To collect mathematical data.
5. To understand a proposition or a group of propositions.
6. To create interest in mathematics.
7. To trace out the background of a mathematical topic or concept.
8. To carry out some mathematical projects.
9. To formulate problems on a topic or concept.
10. To apply the mathematical knowledge in solving problems.

11. To correlate the experiences and previous knowledge of the pupil.
12. To motivate students, clears up misunderstandings and develop insight.

## General Characteristics of Assignment

A good assignment possesses the following characteristics:

1. It should — (1) correlate experiences with the previous knowledge of the pupils.
   (2) recognise the individual differences.
   (3) remove the difficulties of comprehension on the part of the pupils
   (4) give proper reinforcement to the pupils.
2. It should be (1) stimulating and directing the learning activities of the pupils.
   (2) motivating and interesting.
3. There should be (1) clarity and definiteness in assignment.
   (2) emphasis on essentials.

## Steps for preparing Assignment

Assignment is generally prepared in written form. The subject matter and length of assignment are adjusted according to the age and grade level of the pupils.

In preparing the assignment the following steps should be followed:

1. Reference to previous knowledge or learning.
2. Discussion leading to new learning and activity.
3. Acceptance of activity.
4. Anticipating and removal of difficulties.
5. Planning for the material to be used.
6. Details of the task to be done.
7. Carrying out the assignment.
8. Overseeing and checking the work.

## Making Assignment Effective

The success of effectiveness of assignment depends on the amount of work done independently by the pupils.

The following suggestions may be quite useful to make an assignment effective, meaningful, interesting and useful:

1. Better if the assignment be given in the form of a cyclostyled or typed or printed sheet.
2. It should cater to the need of additional work to be done by the pupils.
3. A good assignment requires a judicious choice of material such as text books, reference books, maps, charts and other illustrative material.

   Such material is always useful in stimulating and directing the independent study of the pupils.

4. Teacher must familiarise himself with all the available pedagogical material relevant to the assignment. They should direct the students accordingly.

   He should encourage the pupils to consult good text books, related reference books and encyclopaedia in the school library.

5. An assignment work done by the students should be —
   (1) well-prepared with a proper planning quite in advance.
   (2) a co-operative activity wherein the teacher and the pupils both participate actively.
   (3) insightful, motivative, clear of doubts and misunderstandings.
   (4) properly checked, mistakes, if any, be pointed out.
   (5) activity-centred, need-based and interest-based.
6. An assignment should not be a mere dictation of questions. Proper guidelines and hints should be given to the pupils —
   (1) for its successful completion.
   (2) for regarding the consultation of required material.
7. The purpose of assignment should be definite and it should be clear to the teacher as well as to the pupils.
8. The subject and material should be according to the need, interests and level of pupils.
9. While giving assignment, individual differences must be considered.
10. Interaction between pupils and teacher is a must in an assignment.
11. It should be brief so that the pupils will be more willing to try to do it.
12. The teacher should be aware of any usual difficulties.
13. The task of assignment should be pin-pointed because vague and lengthy assignment is of no use to achieve better results.
14. While making the assignments, the teacher must be familiarised himself with the teaching-learning material relevant to the assignment.
15. If an assignment is worth giving then it should be worth checking too.
16. The comments by the teacher for improvement may also be helpful. Good comments stimulate the pupils for better learning.
17. Assignment on complex problems, learning of new skills and knowledge should be carried on under the supervision of teacher otherwise they may frustrate the pupils.

## 4. Review

### *Meanings and Characteristics*

- Review means to view again.

  'The mental process of *going over* material already learnt is ordinarily term as *review*.'
- Review aims at recalling the past experiences to produce better retention.
- Review comes after initial learning. It involves not only reviewing but also rethinking, regrouping, reunderstanding and reconstructing.

- It takes place under the active supervision and guidance of teacher.
- In review, the learning activities are alike the original but it is retracing of steps.
- When facts and information accumulate and there is only partial understanding, there is need of the mind to reorganise and revise different relationships.
- Review usually concerns with more or less comprehensive units of mathematics.
- Review is to promote the development of grasp and understanding.

**COMPARISON WITH DRILL WORK**

| *Drill* | *Review* |
|---|---|
| 1. It is the repetition of facts or skills in their original form. | 1. It introduces new elements and reorganisation of thought. |
| 2. It is the rehearsal of facts and skills already learnt. | 2. It involves new relationships and reorganisation of old material. |
| 3. It aims mainly at automatisation of relatively detailed processes and reactions. | 3. It aims at the fixation and retention of details as well as at the thoughtful organisation of the important things in a unit into a coherent whole. |
| 4. It is less broader and less inclusive. | 4. It is more broader and more inclusive. |
| 5. It is the activity involved in repeating the data. | 5. It is the reworking of the material learnt. |
| 6. It emphasises habit formation. | 6. It emphasises thought and meaning. |

### *Similarities*

Review is sometimes identified with drill because —

(1) they both are characterised by repetition, and

(2) they both aim at the fixation of reactions, concepts or relationships.

## Types of Review

### 1. *Incidental Review*

- Review work may be incidental in the sense that it may be integrated with the other work of the course.
  - It is especially valuable for the gradual building up and clarification of concepts through repeated reference and through continual reapplication in those situations in which they play component parts.
  - One of the strong arguments for a continuous programme of integrated mathematics is that this sort of incidental (or integrated) review would not necessarily run systematically throughout the entire programme giving strength and coherence to the entire structure through continual inter-association of the components.

### 2. *Specialised Review*

- Review work may be specialised in the sense that it may be specialised by making it the primary feature and objective of particular assignment.

The functions of the specialised review are —

(1) to help the pupil to organise more or less comprehensive bodies of material with respect to their logical relationships,

(2) to assist him in classifying their important ideas, and

(3) to give him a sense of the unity of the whole, which might otherwise be lacking.

- The review lesson which is planned with this idea dominant, will generally follow the assimilative study of a unit.

*In short*

(1) Both of these types of review are necessary to the most effective teaching.

(2) There is need of specialised review work to supplement the incidental review.

## Purposes of Review

1. To fix the knowledge.
2. To have better understanding.
3. To develop new interest in old materials.
4. To prepare background for new learning.
5. To introduce new elements.
6. To recognise thoughts.
7. To discover relationships between various topics and subjects.

## Place of Review in Mathematics

- In mathematics, the review strategy is helpful in recalling the facts and maintaining the sequence of material learnt.
- It is very useful to consolidate the learnt material in the mind.
- One of the functions of review is to make recall more certain and more effective. But, it aims to achieve this through the deliberate processes of organising, systematising and relating elements to each other through giving a *re-view* of a new look at the unit which has been studied.
- When data are organised in tabular forms, graphs, charts, statistical tables, etc., there takes place a good deal of reflective thinking.
- During the learning process of mathematics, certain facts, formulae, principles, propositions and characteristics of geometrical figures are to be retained.

  In order to minimise forgetting of the acquired knowledge, a systematic review is often needed.

## How to Conduct Review?

- Teacher should be very careful in conducting reviews. It should not be used as an escape when the teacher is unprepared with his lesson of the day.
- It is not for the sake of keeping the pupils busy.

- In preparing for a review-lesson, the pupils summarises the outstanding ideas considered in the unit and they also make an outline from which he can give a brief, coherent and systematic discussion of the material in the unit.
- It should be used to introduce new and interesting experiences in a varying manner.
- In continuation of the original work done by the pupils, they may be required to review it by preparing a summary, an outline of the work done or a pictorial presentation.

  This will make it necessary for the pupils to review the unit in the fullest sense of the term.
- Through making the necessary association of the ideas in the unit, he will be aided in remembering them and in appreciating their inter-relations.
- The task of helping pupils in planning their review work is a responsibility which every teacher should take seriously.

## Making the Review Effective

1. Never forget that review is different from drill. They are not identical in character.
2. Review is a part of teaching process. It requires teaching of the highest quality.
3. It is to be considered as learning exercises leading to better retention and reorganisation.
4. Pictorial, symbolic, graphical and tabular presentation may be used as reviewing strategy.
5. Review should involve new learning. It should not be for the purpose of repeating the material learnt.
6. Review should provide a new organisation to the previous knowledge. It should bring about unity, coherence and continuity in the various units and topics.
7. Questions and exercises given at the end of the chapters of the text books may be used as reviewing strategy.
8. Review should be directed at the weak points or doubts of the pupils.
9. Review should focus on main points rather than on the details.
10. It is to be valuable experience adding new insight, fixing facts and perfecting skills.

## 5. Brain Storming

What is brain storming?

- Brain storming means a spontaneous group discussion to produce ideas and ways of solving problems.
- It is democratic and problem-centred strategy.
- It is based on —

  (*a*) modern theory of generalisation of task.

  (*b*) the assumption that a pupil can learn better in a group rather than in individual study.

  (*c*) the principle that the pupils can be provided with more and more knowledge through interaction.

So, here, such ways and means are used which create movement in the minds of the pupils of the class for mutual consultation, logic, reasoning and discussion in order to solve some mathematical problem.

- In this strategy the topic/the problem is largely determined by the pupils.
- It creates situations for the teacher and the learners interaction wherein both remain active in solving he problem.
- It encourages the creativity and originality among the pupils.

Some qualities like reasoning, self-confidence, self-reliance, we-feeling etc. may also be developed in the minds of the pupils.

- The higher order or cognitive and affective objectives can be realised through brain storming.

## *How to Conduct Brain Storming?*

(1) To start with, in this strategy the teacher assigns a problem to the group of students.

(2) Pupils think over the problem independently.

(3) Then, pupils discuss by arranging a debate.

- The pupils are asked to express their views and ideas which came to their minds frankly.
- It is not necessary that whether the ideas and viewpoints are meaningful or not.

(4) The teacher writes pupils' ideas and views on the blackboard.

(5) In this way, the problem is solved through brain storming.

## *Importance of Brain Storming*

1. It is a problem-oriented strategy of teaching-learning process.
2. It is a democratic strategy of teaching and learning.
3. It provides more ideas and views to the pupils.
   - The pupils select ideas most likely to lead the solution. As a result, the habit of decision-making is developed in their minds.
4. It has both psychological and educational importance. Because —

   (1) it increases the pupils' knowledge,

   (2) it promotes creativity and originality of ideas among the pupils,

   (3) it creates the situation for more independent study, thinking and reasoning,

   (4) it makes classroom interaction more impressive and effective,

   (5) it develops problem-solving ability,

   (6) it helps to achieve higher order to cognitive and affective objectives.

# EVALUATE YOURSELF

1. What do you mean by self study in Mathematics? Discuss in detail.
2. What is the need or importance of self study in mathematics?
3. Suggest measures to be taken to make self study more effective and meaningful.
4. What is supervised study in mathematics? Explain various forms of supervised study in mathematics.
5. Discuss the importance/merits and demerits of supervised study.
6. As a good teacher what steps will you take to make supervised study in mathematics more effective and meaningful.
7. Explain precautions to be taken for supervised study.
8. Discuss the meaning and purpose of Assignment work in mathematics.
9. What are the general characteristics of Assignment? What steps will you take for prepariing assignments?
10. Write short notes on:
    (*a*) Problems of Assignment
    (*b*) Review in Mathematics
    (*c*) Types of Review
    (*d*) Purposes of Review
    (*e*) Importance of Bank storming
    (*f*) Assignment.
11. How will you make Assignment more effective?
12. Explain the meaning and characteristics of Review.
13. Compare Drill work with Review.
14. Make the place of review in Mathematics clear.
15. How will you conduct review?
16. Suggest for making Review effective.
17. What is Brain Storming? How to conduct Brain Storming?
18. What do you mean by strategies of teaching? What are various strategies for the teaching of mathematics?
19. What is the difference between self study and supervised study? How will you employ these strategies in teaching of mathematics?
20. How do you distinguish between home work and assignment? What should be done to make the best of both in the teaching of mathematics?

# 17 USING INFORMATION & COMMUNICATION TECHNOLOGY (ICT)

## 17.1 Introduction

- A new teacher, interested in the possibilities offered by emerging technology, made no headway until he had a computer of his own at home.
- He was later loaned a graphic calculator but it sat in the cupboard until he attended an inspiring workshop. The workshop gave him a vision of possibilities and enabled him to overcome the initial deliberate harassment of starting with a portable, but less friendly, piece of technology.
- Personal access is a major advantage in allowing teachers, the time and space to make good progress in the use of technology.
  - As well as access, you need inspiration to see possibilities for yourself and your class before you can start to make progress along what can at times be a frustrating road.
  - Happily, these days access is relatively easy and there are inspirational leaders and resources to help you along the way.
- We are going to consider the role of new technologies in the mathematics curriculum.
  - Important resources, whose role one considers include —

    calculators, graphic calculators, graph plotters, spreadsheets, dynamic geometry, small programmes (like SMILE) and programming languages (like LOGO).
  - Some research evidences will also be presented in order to support the development of critical thinking in pupils.
- Some important general features of working mathematically with computers are —
  - learning from feedback;
  - observing patterns;
  - seeing connections;
  - working with dynamic images;
  - exploring data;
  - teaching the computer.

- Teacher will consider different organisational structures for working with ICT in the classroom, such as whole-class, small-group or individual ways of working, whether structured or exploratory.
- The teacher will be asked to compare and contrast different kinds of software use, some appropriate and some inappropriate, in relation to his/her pedagogic goals.
- ICT (including calculators and computers) can make to learn and teach mathematics.
- An appropriate environment (including tasks) enables pupils to learn from feedback, observe patterns, see connections, work with dynamic images, explore data and *teach* the computer.
- Knowledge of particular software enhances mathematics teaching, including getting access to available resources and support for using ICT in the mathematics classroom.
- ICT is changing rapidly. Although there is much potential for improved learning, there is also the possibility of wasting a great deal of time and resources.
- When using ICT in the classroom it is worth remembering that —
  (1) some pupils will know more than the teacher,
  (2) among the pupils there may be wide ranges of fluency and comfort with ICT and access to machines.

## 17.2 Background Matters

- where the teacher thinks fit, he should give pupils opportunities to develop and apply their IT (Information Technology) capability in their study of mathematics.
- There are six major ways in which IT can provide opportunities for pupils learning mathematics.

### *(1) Learning from Feedback*

- The computer often provides fast and reliable feedback which is non-judgemental and impartial.
  - This can encourage students to make their own conjectures and to test out and modify their ideas.

### *(2) Observing Patterns*

- The speed of computers and calculators enables pupils to produce many examples when exploring mathematical problems.
  - This supports their observation of patterns and the making and justifying of generalisations.

### *(3) Seeing Connections*

- The computer enables formulae, tables of numbers and graphs to be linked readily.
  - Changing one representation and seeing changes in the others, helps pupils to understand the connection between them.

### (4) *Working with Dynamic Images*

- Pupils can use computers to manipulate diagrams dynamically.
  - This encourages pupils to visualise the geometry as they generate their own mental images.

### (5) *Exploring Data*

- Computers enable pupils to work with real data which can be represented in a variety of ways.
  - This supports interpretation and analysis.

### (6) *Teaching the Computer*

- When pupils design an algorithm (a set of instruction) to make a computer achieve a particular result, they are compelled to express their commands unambiguously and in the correct order, they make their thinking explicit as they refine their ideas.

## 17.3 Calculating Devices

- Throughout history various invented devices (such as mathematical tables, abaci, slide rules and mechanical/electronic calculators) have been devised to assist with the performing of calculations.
  - With each one, there are practices and conventions to be learnt, concerned with how to *use* the device to implement an algorithm (such as when and how to move beads or change rows, or how to read off from the cursor, or which buttons to press and in which order).
  - With each device there are questions about what service they may be in *learning* mathematics directly, (rather than merely helping it to be done).

### 1. *On the Slide Rule*

- We start with neither an account of the abacus nor the electronic calculator, but with a brief look at the slide rule.
  - Costel Harnasz (1993) has produced a clear and illuminating account of educational history of slide rule and relates his discussion to current concerns about the use of electronic calculators in schools.
  - The issue is practice over understanding. Teachers should be able to say that a pupil has understood only when they exhibit successful practice.

### 2. *On the Abacus*

- Historically, abacuses were, widely used (in Russia and Japan still are used) as counting boards.
  - These historical counting devices and their associated practices provide a mental image of a computation.

- On the Japanese abacus Catherine Hoare (1990) remarks on how, after gaining remarkable facility with the abacus in performing computations, the Japanese school-children (aged 8 to 11) were given mental arithmetic six-light additions and subtractions. She saw:

  > 'The pupils set with their eyes shut or half-closed, running their fingers an inch above the desk-top as if the abacus were still there! At the end of each question just under half of the pupils had the correct answer, but all had attempted questions which would have been unthinkable within our conception of mental arithmetic. Their method consists of mentally visualising an abacus and working through the problem using standard techniques.'

  - This account raises many questions. *e.g.*
    (1) What range of images do pupils have when carrying out mental computations?
    (2) What support do these images offer?
- Hoare adds: 'Through mechanisation of operations, the Japanese abacus becomes as automatic to the Japanese as the calculator has to the younger generation of English.'
  - Yet, as with the differences between numeration systems, the structural differences of these two devices are relevant to mathematics education.
- With the Japanese abacus the algorithm is accessible to view, implemented by the user, and can be internalised through repetition of hand movements.

### 3. *On the Calculator*

- Modern electronic calculator are nowhere near as 'transparent' with regard to their functioning and therefore do not offer much imagistic support.
- Numbers are entered from right to left, as when written down, which acts to *move* the digit across each *place*.
  - It is an interesting and open question whether this relative absence of associated imagery with a calculator is a potential weakness or a potential strength w.r.t using such devices to help to gain either numerical fluency or understanding.
- With most calculators, there is no difference between any of the four arithmetic operations and taking powers or square roots.
  - All are carried out by pressing a single operation key.
  - With the calculator, everything is inaccessible, invisible.
- The calculator has single buttons that perform an increasing variety of mathematical functions.
  - But with a calculator, you lose the sense of algorithm for these operations, as there is no evidence of intermediate steps.
  - Such single buttons become *primitive* in the sense that no further interrogation of how the calculations are being carried out is possible — they become inaccessible.
  - What is the difference between a set of square-root tables and the square-root button on a calculator?
  - Written tables may not provide much clue as to their genesis, but each table is a single object open to inspection and analysis, complete with interpolation rules.

- Cresswell and Gubb (1987) claimed to show that numeracy has declined since the first study in 1967. This coincided with a general availability of relatively cheap calculators. However, the classroom teacher in the study claimed that they were not allowing the use of calculators.
- Ann Kitchen (1998) has shown that in nearly every country, children aged 9 who were encouraged to use calculators in their mathematics lesson performed better than those who were not.
- It is possible to draw the conclusion that the reduction in numeracy is due to the general reduction in the use of number skills. *e.g.*
  - Most shops use electronic tills (a cash register) and other developments in new technology have reduced the level of mental arithmetic skills required to function in everyday life.
  - For much of the past 20 years, the attention of teachers has been drawn away from the very important question of how calculators can be used to best effect in the teaching of mathematics.
  - The burning question was: Should pupils be allowed to use calculators?
- In the 16th century, Johannes Kepler was rebuked for using the latest new idea to facilitate his calculations, he used logarithms.
  - The question remains, why are schools still not teaching pupils how to use calculators?
  - There is a general perception that calculators damage children's mathematics.
  - Calculators have a role as a tool in the teaching and learning of mathematics.
  - It would have been better practice to encourage *estimation*, both as a way of checking the answer and a way of reinforcing a sense of number.
- Calculators offer the possibility to produce rapid, accurate feedback for the pupils. Pupils can try many different strategies in a relatively short-time, without having their progress impeded by their own difficulties with performing algorithms quickly and accurately.
- It is very important to be aware of the danger of inadvertently reducing pupils' mental arithmetic practice by allowing them, particularly slower pupils to use the calculator as a crutch.
- Teachers need consciously and explicitly to acknowledge the role of estimation and mental arithmetic when using a calculator with pupils.

### 4. *Spreadsheets*

- In number work, pupils should be given opportunities to use calculators and computer software, *e.g.,* spreadsheets.
- Although much of the power of a spreadsheet derives from using the algebraic potential of linking values in one column to those of another by means of formulae, it is, on the surface, a tool for operating on tables of numbers.
- Thinking of a spreadsheet as an animated table might help you to conceive of this superficially simple but mathematically sophisticated tool in a more accessible way.
- Spreadsheet enables teachers and pupils to leave access on disc to large data sets such as world record data for track and field events.

- A spreadsheet is also a powerful tool for modelling, widely used in industry and commerce. So, once you have access to this powerful resource, it is worth discovering what else it can be used for in the mathematics curriculum.
- Spreadsheet activities can be thought of as two distinct kinds:
  (1) Sometimes it is appropriate to give the pupils a spreadsheet document that has already been created and to invite them to work with this.
  (2) At other times, it may be better for the pupils to create their own spreadsheet documents from scratch.
- The use of logical functions in a spreadsheet can provide a simple introduction to programming.

## 5. *Graphic Devices*

- Graphic calculators are a relatively new feature of mathematics classrooms.
- The most accessible tool, in physical terms, is the graphic calculator.
  - They can be seen as the point where computers and calculators converge, an interim technology.
  - Their most striking feature is their accessibility — owning one means that powerful technology is available as and when it is needed.
  - They represent a major force for change in mathematics teaching and learning.
  - This force is generally outside the control of the educational establishment in the sense that, although there is some contact between educators and manufacturers, their development is very much market-led.
  - So, pupils can buy machines with the power to do much of the routine work that forms the basis for advanced level courses.
  - There is, therefore, a very real need for educators to think carefully about what really needs to be learnt in mathematics.
  - Whilst this need may seem most obvious at advanced level, there is an equivalent challenge to be met in the education of younger pupils.
- If teachers have access to graphic calculators in their lessons, then they tend to ask more high-level questions than they would otherwise do.
- Teachers should know how to use the basic facilities of a graphic calculator to explore graphs and to find solutions of equations graphically.
- In order to optimise the use of graphic calculator, teacher needs to learn how to produce a table of values of a function on her calculator.
  - Then teacher can begin to use in her teaching the three different representations of a function the graphic calculator offers: graphic, algebraic and numeric.
- New developments in calculator technology are appearing every year, so, the teacher needs to keep an eye on the mathematics education press for news.
- Already, calculators are available that can be connected by a cable to a computer and can receive data downloaded from the internet.

- Remote data capture devices can collect data about motion or light or temperature, etc. and this can be loaded immediately into a calculator.
  - Devices such as this make it possible to use a calculator to control a simple robot.

## 17.4 Dynamic Geometry

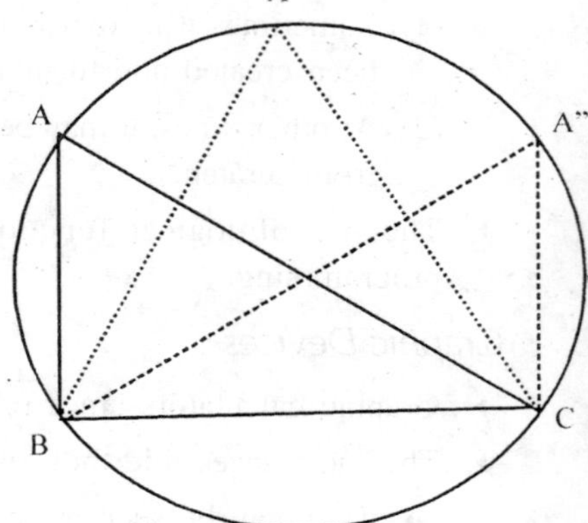


- Imagine you are trying to convince a pupil that the measure of the angle subtended by the chord BC, remains the same even if the point A moves round the major arc of the circle. You trace round the circle with your finger as you speak. The diagram would move.
- There are several implementations of the idea of a dynamic diagram using Dynamic Geometry software.

  *e.g.* (1) Determine the locus of the points equidistant from the two arms of an angle.

  (2) Determine the locus of the points equidistant from the end-points of a line-segment.

## Mathematics and the Internet

- The internet is a rapidly growing resource. The main problem is that it can absorb a lot of time as you search from one list of sites to another.

### EVALUATE YOURSELF

1. What is ICT?
2. Enumerate the major ways in which IT can provide opportunities for pupils to learn mathematics. Explain each way.
3. Name some calculating devices. Explain Abacus in detail.
4. What are calculators? How will you use them in the teaching of mathematics?
5. What are spreadsheets? How will you use them?
6. State what graphic devices are. Write their importance in the teaching of mathematics.
7. Explain 'Dynamic Geometry' with an illustration.

# COMMUNICATING MATHEMATICALLY: SUPPORT TECHNIQUE

- Most of the activities concerned in the teaching and learning of mathematics involve some form of communication between (*i*) teachers and pupil(s), (*ii*) pupils and pupils, (*iii*) pupils and text, (iv) pupil and computer.
  - There is oral communication (speaking and listening) and written communication (reading and writing).
  - There are special features of mathematics classroom and mathematical language that make communication a significant issue for mathematics teachers.
  - As a mathematics teacher you have a particular responsibility to help pupils to learn to speak and write *mathematically*.
  - The teacher cannot assume that when he tells a pupil something, however clearly, he will necessarily hear and understand what the teacher intended to communicate.
  - It is useful to bear in mind that a child may not find easy to communicate their state of mathematical understanding to you.
  - Learning mathematics is sometimes compared with learning a foreign language.

## 18.1 The Nature of Mathematical Language

- Mathematics has special forms. and ways of using language that make it possible to communicate specifically mathematical ideas.
- Mathematics has developed through history, mathematicians have developed new words (or new meanings for old words), new notations and conventional style of argument with which to think about and communicate new mathematical ideas and ways of thinking.
- Learning to understand and to use this mathematical language is an essential past of learning mathematics.

## 18.2 Mathematical English

- One of the most obvious places to start is with the *vocabulary* of mathematics.
  - The teacher distinguishes between words that are unlikely to be encountered outside the mathematics class-room. (*e.g.*, quadrilateral, parallelogram, hypotenuse, diagonal) and those that have been *borrowed* from everyday English (*e.g.*, face, power, product, rational).
  - Unfamilar words may cause difficulties for learners simply because of their unfamiliarity and they are often long, multi-syllabic and difficult to pronounce and spell.
  - Borrowed words can bring with them their own problems simply because their mathematical meanings are subtly different from their everyday meanings.
  - In some cases, pupils' ability to come to terms with specialist mathematical uses of language may be further complicated by the emotional charges associated with words such as *odd, vulgar, improper, irrational.*
  - The negative connotations of such terms can prevent a pupil from attending to that 'pure' mathematical meanings alone.
  - A particular area of potential difficulty is in the precise ways in which mathematical logic uses words like *and, or, some, all* or *any.*

    For example, when faced with a problem like — 'show that the sum of any two odd numbers is an even number', some pupils will believe that they have answered satisfactorily if they give an example such as 3 + 7 = 10.

    This may indicate that the pupil giving such an answer believes that a single example is enough to prove a general statement.

    On the other hand, it may be that they have understood the problem to be asking them to provide *any* example that confirms the statement.

    In mathematical discourse, the convention is that *any* is used to indicate more arbitrariness (*e.g.*, 'any old one will do').
- While evaluating pupils' work, it is important for you to consider how they may have understood the question. In this case, you cannot know, without further investigation, whether the problem lies in the pupil's understanding of the nature of mathematical proof or in their understanding of the conventions of mathematical language.

## 18.3 Non-verbal forms of Written Communication

- Much written mathematical communication is characterised by its use of symbolism and graphic components such as diagrams and graphs.
  - While such forms of communication are very powerful for expressing mathematical ideas, they can also be confusing for learners who are not familiar with the conventions of the system.

## [A] Algebraic Symbolism

1. Reading text that includes mathematical symbols involves different skills from those needed for ordinary verbal texts.

   ⏩ whereas ordinary English texts can be read, in order, from left to right, some arrangements of symbols require the reader to attend to the components in a non-linear way. For example.

$$\left(\frac{3}{5}-4\right)^2 \text{ or } \frac{5x+4}{8x^2-7} \text{ or } \sqrt[3]{\left(\frac{a}{b}\right)^2}$$

2. Some learners will find it difficult to cope with symbols if they do not have any way of articulating them – reading them aloud to themselves or to others. For example,

   The introduction of Greek letters like $\alpha$, $\theta$, $\Sigma$ should not be seen as a simple extension of pupils' existing familiarity with algebraic symbolism.

3. The commonly used 'metaphor' that algebraic symbols are 'shorthand' (*e.g.,* a for apples, b for banana) does not provide a sound conceptual base for the idea of letters as *variables* and may contribute to some of the common difficulties the pupils have with algebra.

## [B] Graphs & Diagrams

- In most cases, graphical elements are used to supplement or illustrate information contained in verbal form elsewhere in the text.
- In Mathematics, graphs, tables and diagrams are often used independently to communicate information that may not be available in any other form.
  - ⏩ We cannot assume that pupils will naturally pick up the skills needed to make sense of such diagrammatic forms.
  - ⏩ There is considerable evidence that many secondary pupils do not read graphs in the conventional mathematical way.

    *e.g.,* Pupils may read distance — time graphs as if they were pictures of a journey. The graph shown in the figure may be described by the pupil as 'climbing a mountain' or 'going up, going down, then up again'.

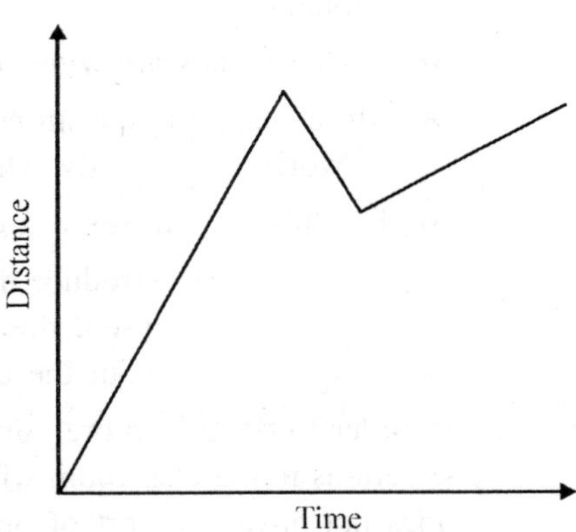


  - ⏩ As well as learning to read and interpret the values of separate points on a graph, pupils also need to learn how to interpret its overall shape.

## 18.4 Talking Math

- A lot of talking goes on in many mathematics lessons, as in lessons of other subjects.
  - ⏩ It is important to ask how much of this talking is likely to be productive for pupils' learning of mathematics and of mathematical language.

- Much of the talking is done by the teachers.
- There are many areas in which it is possible for teachers' talk to be misunderstood. So, we should look at —
  (1) how teachers may try to ensure that pupils do understand and improve their knowledge of spoken mathematical language.
  (2) how pupils may themselves be involved actively in speaking mathematically, through conversation or discussion with the teacher or other pupils.
- This may be done through the use of questioning or teacher-pupils discussion. The discussions can play an important role in the mathematics classroom.
- The ability to 'say what you mean and mean what you say' should be one of the outcomes of good mathematics teaching. This ability develops as a result of opportunities to talk about mathematics, to explain and discuss results that have been obtained and to test hypotheses.
- Discussion between pupils or between pupils and teacher can be a good way of exploring and developing pupils' concepts and their awareness of relationships between different areas of mathematics.
- A good mathematics teacher involves pupils in higher-level thinking or to encourage them to use and develop other aspects of the language needed to express more complex mathematical ideas and reasoning.

- For such purposes the questioning teacher needs to create opportunities for pupils to think and to formulate contributions in their own words.
  - This means asking more searching questions that demand higher-level thinking rather than straight forward recall (*i.e.,* questions that ask for observation, comparisons, explanations).
  - It also means allowing pupils time to think about their answers.
  - More searching questions need to be thought about before an answer is given, in order to work out not only what needs to be said but also the words with which to say it.
  - For this (1) develop a culture in your classroom that values thinking before talking.
    (2) introduce the idea of a 'hands-down think' after such a question had been posed, the pupils knew that they were then expected to think seriously about the question and that their contributions would be valued.
- In order to develop more complete verbal communication skills, it can be helpful to create situations in the classroom where the pupil is trying to communicate with another pupil who does not have this sort of prior knowledge of what is being communicated. *e.g.,*

  When working with 3D shapes, one pupil may be asked to construct a 3D object like a prism or pyramid or cone and then describe it to a partner who must construct the same object from the verbal description.

  This task includes its own automatic feedback, the partner will ask for further clarification if necessary and the match or mismatch, between the two objects will reveal whether or not the communication has been successful.

## 18.5 Writing Mathematically

- Until relatively recently, very limited writing took place in secondary school mathematics.
  - Most secondary pupils are now expected to produce quite lengthy pieces of writing, reporting on their work on mathematical tasks.
  - Many find this a difficult task, even some of those who are otherwise very successful in mathematics may have difficulty in constructing effective reports of their mathematical activity.
- Writing explanations and justifications is particularly challenging for many pupils.
  - Few pupils respond adequately to the questions that demand written description or explanation and many leave these sections out completely.
- While explanation and justification may be difficult in themselves, the requirement to write about them seems to make the task even harder, *e.g.*

  (1) 'The mean is the most useful measure of central tendency' — Discuss.

  (2) Explain — 'Why the sum of three consecutive integers is always divisible by three.'

  (3) Factorise: $7x^2 - 62x + 48$. Explain how you did this. Describe your general strategies for factoring quadratic expressions efficiently.
- The forms of language needed to construct a concise and precise mathematical definition or a rigorous justification are different from those required in everyday or literary writing or in other subject discipline.
- It is not possible to judge the complete effectiveness of a written definition or justification without the sort of mathematical content knowledge that belongs to the mathematics teacher's expertise. *e.g.,* See the definition of a circle:

  (1) 'The set of all points equidistant from a single point.' Is this true? Then, what is the definition of a sphere?

  (2) 'Circle is something whose area is equal to $\pi r^2$.' Is this the definition of a circle or its formula to find its area?

  (3) 'A closed continuous rounded line.' This is illogical.
  - The students should know the difference between a definition and a list of property for a geometrical concept.
  - There must be an agreed revised definition that is acceptable to all the learners of mathematics.
- Talking together with other pupils and/or with a teacher and drafting and redrafting in a group can be provided much needed support and feedback and increase awareness of the requirements of effective communication.

## 18.6 Communicating Using Algebraic Notation

- The introduction of algebraic notation early in the school is felt to have been the turning point at which an otherwise academically successful student started to fail in mathematics.

- To many pupils, symbols appear to have little meaning and attempting to work with them may be a frustrating and anxiety – including activity.
- At the same time algebraic symbolism is enormously important in mathematics as a means of —

  (1) expressing generalisation, and

  (2) thinking about and manipulating problems that might otherwise prove intractable.

  - It is, therefore, important to help pupils to develop meaning for symbols and to see them as useful means of communicating mathematical ideas.
- One way of demystifying symbolism is to introduce it as a natural development of pupils own attempts to record their generalisations of patterns.

## 18.7 Communication as a Key to Assessment

- One very important type of communication goes on in classrooms is that involved in assessing pupils' understanding.
- Most of a teacher's knowledge about pupils' achievement is gathered through listening to their talk and reading their written work.
- The use of short 'writing prompts' getting pupils to write briefly about a specified topic, can (1) encourage the pupils to reflect on and hence reinforce what they have learnt, and (2) provide the teacher with valuable insight into what pupils have learnt and where they may still have difficulties. For example, you might ask pupils:

  (1) to explain *how* to add fractions and *how* to factorise an algebraic expression ...

  (2) to write *what* they know about a topic (triangles, equations, ...)

  (3) to explain *why* $3 \div 42$ is not the same as $42 \div 3$, why a quick way of multiplying a decimal number by 100 is to move the decimal point two steps to the right, ...
- The teacher must be cautious about relying too much on written forms of communication in order to assess pupils' understanding.

  - Children's written work may not always fully represent what they can do because —

    (1) they lack full familiarity with the necessary forms of language,

    (2) they may be unsure of what aspects of their work and their thinking need to be recorded.
- It is useful for the teacher —

  (1) to plan deliberately to talk with *small* groups of pupils about their on-going work, and

  (2) to provide them with some help in making better decisions about what should be recorded in writing.

## EVALUATE YOURSELF

1. Write short notes on:
   (1) Nature of mathematical language
   (2) Mathematical English
   (3) Algebraic Symbolism
   (4) Graphs and Diagrams
   (5) Writing mathematically.
2. Explain the non-verbal forms of written communication.
3. 'The ability to say what you mean and mean what you say.' — Comment.
4. What is 'communicating using algebraic notation'?
5. Explain fully 'the communication as a key to assessment.'

> Everything has its proper place and proper value, for mathematical proportion is a fundamental principle in the cosmos.
>
> — ***Pythagoras***

# 19 CORRELATION IN TEACHING OF MATHEMATICS

## 19.1 What is Correlation?

- Nature is a primary source of human knowledge.
  - As a result of different forms of increasing needs of human being, the various branches of knowledge have been developed.
  - Obviously, there should be some form of correlation among these branches of knowledge.
- Correlation of Mathematics is a technique with the help of which one can bring Mathematics close to our actual life activities on one hand and integrates its knowledge with the study of other subjects on the other hand.
- The major aim of education is the all-around and harmonies development of the child.
  - This aim can be gained through a comprehensive education, *i.e.,* the unification of knowledge existing in various branches of learning.
  - To achieve such a unification, a conscious effort has to be made by the teachers who teach various subjects.
  - A teacher can do so by correlating the knowledge of a subject with that of the other subjects and its application in other branches of knowledge or different situations of human life.
- (Definition) Ferguson — 'Correlation is concerned with describing the degree of relation between two variables.'

  (Definition) Lathrop — 'Correlation indicates a joint relationship between two variables.'
- According to Webster's new dictionary of English language, correlation means —
  - 'mutual relation of two or more things/parts.'
  - 'whenever two variables x and y are so related that a change in one is accompanied by change in the other, then the variables are said to be correlated.'

- ⏩ If x and y vary in the same direction, the correlation is said to be positive, if they vary in opposite direction, the correlation is said to be negative.
- The child cannot learn the various subjects of curriculum in isolation because he is interested to learn things which are related to his experience and pre-knowledge.
- According to the principle of correlation, knowledge cannot be achieved in piece meals.
  - So, the knowledge of various study-subjects must be integrated and provided to the pupil in the form of whole/unit.
  - And then only the knowledge of mathematics may be more interesting and realistic.
- Mathematics is not only related to all the subjects but it contributes a great deal in the advancement and progress of most of the subjects. That is why mathematics is called 'the science of all sciences' or 'the queen of all the sciences.'
- The reliability and validity of various theories and laws, which every branch of knowledge consists, depend upon their possibility of presentation in a mathematical form.
  - The numerical form of a fact is always reliable and valid.
- The concept of correlation should be considered in context of curriculum.
- Correlation is the process of putting together the related content of various fields having concerned with human experiences.

## 19.2 Need and Importance of Correlation

1. Primary source of every field of human knowledge emerges from the nature. So, naturally, they should be interrelated. Therefore, no subject can be taught in isolation.
2. It was assumed that the human mind consists of so many mental faculties like faculty of thinking and reasoning, faculty of imagination, faculty of memorisation, etc.
   (*i*) Each faculty was supposed to be developed through the study of a specific subject. Thus, each subject had its own independent function. This theory is now discarded by educationists.
   (*ii*) It is now proved that mind functions as a whole and it receives knowledge as a whole.
   (*iii*) The learning of a subject does not develop a particular mental faculty by excluding the other subjects.
   (*iv*) All the subjects and activities of the school curriculum aim to develop the intellectual power of the pupils as a whole. So, there is every justification in correlating the study of a subject with others.
3. Since every piece of knowledge is gained through one and the same mind, so what we have learnt in past and will teach tomorrow should be properly linked with what we are going to teach at present.
4. Mind is not the only means of receiving knowledge. In the acquisition of knowledge, 3H – Head, Heart, Hands) play an important role.
   (*i*) An all round development of child's personality is possible only if he makes use of his whole personality for gaining knowledge and experience.

(*ii*) So, teacher must set the child to gain knowledge as a whole by integrating activities related to head (mind, knowing) heart (feelings) and hands (labour, doing).

5. The pupils understand and grasp the content of any subject very easily if it is correlated with the context of other subjects.
6. Education has to serve many purposes. Parents wish to educate their child when he is taught the different subjects as a whole.
   (*i*) All subjects of the school curriculum aim towards certain common goals. There is no conflict and contradiction among them as they all are meant for the welfare of the child.
   (*ii*) Subjects have been divided and separated into such different pieces of knowledge for smoothening the teaching-learning process.
   (*iii*) For the child this separation has no meaning. He always picks up knowledge as a whole. So, he is entitled to get the knowledge as a whole.
7. Knowledge is useful only when it can be applied in our practical life and in our practical life knowledge is always used as a whole.
   (*i*) In solving a problem related to our day-to-day life, we employ what we have in our knowledge as a whole.
   (*ii*) For example, if we wish to purchase a piece of cloth for our shirt we have to utilise the knowledge of Geography and Mathematics, our aesthetic taste, knowledge of trends of current fashion, texture and science of the material, etc.
8. For effective teaching, the teacher has to take full advantage of various correlation among different subjects.
9. Mathematics has high correlation with most of the school subjects and with human experiences. So, it is essential for a mathematics teacher to have a good knowledge of correlation of mathematics with other subjects to make the teaching-learning process effective and interesting.
10. Now-a-days a conscious effort is made to integrate various branches of mathematics and to treat the subject as a synthetic whole.
11. The correlation of mathematics with other subjects works as a stimulus to the learners of mathematics.
12. The knowledge of correlation helps —
   (*i*) in developing and maintaining the interest of learner in mathematics,
   (*ii*) in presenting the various subjects in an integrated form at various levels of education,
   (*iii*) in removing the isolation of traditional teaching of mathematics,
   (*iv*) in understanding and explaining the complex phenomena,
   (*v*) in providing opportunity for applying the operations of mathematics in the study of other subjects,
   (*vi*) in providing opportunity to establish perfect co-ordination between 3H, *i.e.*, between knowing, feeling and doing.

13. Correlation makes the teaching-learning process economical in view of time, energy and money.
14. It motivates the pupils for learning of mathematics.
15. The project method, team teaching method and problem-solving methods can be made practical and effective by correlating mathematics with other subjects.

### *Dimensions of Correlation*

- There are two dimensions of correlation in mathematics:

  (1) Incidental correlation (2) Systematic correlation
- In incidental correlation, the correlation of different subjects is not pre-decided.
  - To establish this type of correlation, a teacher must have versatile knowledge of basic elements of different subjects. Without having such a knowledge a teacher cannot establish incidental correlation in mathematics.
  - To establish systematic correlation is the responsibility of the curriculum framers.
  - The content of different subjects is arranged in a particular sequence.
  - Here, attention is paid towards the application of the principles, facts and laws of mathematics to other subject areas.
  - Thus, knowledge becomes more meaningful, interesting, realistic and natural.

## 19.4 Types of Correlation

There are mainly four types of correlation related to mathematics:

Correlation of Mathematics with —

1. aspects of life.
2. different branches of mathematics
3. different topics in the same branch
4. other study-subjects.

### *1. Correlation of Math with Life*

- We use mathematics in some way or the other in our day-to-day life.
  - Whatever may be our profession, mode of living of daily routine, we cannot live without mathematics.
- Mathematics is utilised by everybody — right from an ordinary man to the big landlords and businessmen, from a small child to the mature adult and from an ordinary housewife to the manager of a big industrial concern.
  - Some knowledge of mathematics is absolutely essential to everyone whether he or she is a labourer, farmer, housewife, artisan, shopkeeper, vendor, salesman, clerk, accountant, driver, cleaner, tailor, washerman, and so on.
  - Thus, every sphere of life is related with mathematics.
  - In this universe, we can hardly search anyone who is beyond the use of mathematics in his day-to-day life.

- Mathematics is not confined to classroom or school only. Its utility is very comprehensive and wide.

- Actually, it is difficult to lead a happy life without any knowledge of mathematics.
  - So, mathematics should be taught in the way as it is utilised in our life.
  - The present day teaching of mathematics does not fulfill this requirement.
  - The teachers teach it in an isolated way by completely divorcing it from the actual necessities of life.
  - In each and every sphere of our life, mathematics provides us its help and patronage without which we cannot do anything.
  - The knowledge of mathematics is very versatile and required in all the fronts of our day-to-day life activities beginning from awakening to sleep at night.
  - In our daily life mathematics is as mixed as oxygen in the air.
- Every dealing of our life begins and ends with the mathematical thinking and reasoning, *e.g.*, daily household problems, food, clothing, idea of quantity and quality, daily accounts of income and expenditure, allocation of funds, home budget, etc.
- Young JWA — 'whenever we turn in these days of iron, steam, and electricity, we find that mathematics has been the pioneer. Were its backbone removed our material civilisation would inevitably collapse.'

  Hubsch — 'Mathematics is like a wheatstone and by its study one learns to think distinctly, consequently and carefully.'
- To highlight the importance of mathematics in various fields of life, the teacher should always make an effort to explain to the pupils the practical application of the mathematical knowledge.
  - He may point out big industries, dams, bridges, prominent buildings, electrical installations, etc., and explain the pupils that all these has been made possible with the help of mathematics.
- The need of mathematics is felt by human beings right from his existence on this earth.
  - It is but natural to imagine that to know the number of members of his group or the quality of things in use, mathematical concepts and processes might have been introduced.
  - When man first wanted to get the solution of questions, like how many? how much? how big? etc., he must have invented a form of mathematics called Arithmetic.
- Without the proper knowledge of mathematics, literate as well as illiterate people cannot solve their daily life problems.
- The pupils should be explained the utilitarian and cultural values of mathematics in practical life.
- Modern society is an achieving and progressing society. Here, human beings always think and work for profitable and better returns.
  - For this, a good planning based on mathematical approach is necessary.
  - The modern business system is entirely based on mathematics.

- - The price rates, production, distribution, inflation, rebates, interests, discounts, commissions, shortages, taxes, etc. are the important issues which cannot be tackled without the knowledge of mathematics.
- The modern civilisation is also based on mathematics.
  - The modern age is the age of science and technology. The scientific inventions and technical progress is basically depended on mathematics.
  - Now-a-days computer has become a widely used and essential technique of our daily life.
  - Mathematics also plays an important role in the development of knowledge of all other subjects and extention of their scope.
- Evaluation is also an important aspect of human life.
  - Man needs not only day-to-day work and things to be evaluated, but self-evaluation also.
  - The self-evaluation and overall life-evaluation provides him are assessment, judgement, guidance and direction for the future.
  - Undoubtedly this evaluation must involve mathematical approach as it should be objective.
- The development of mathematics is also the result of our needs of life.
  - Algebra was developed to simplify arithmetical computations.
  - To study the form and measurement, geometry was invented.
  - For the study of heights of peaks of mountains, width of a river, position of stars, trigonometry was introduced.
  - Similarly, other branches of mathematics were developed as a result of our growing needs.
- If we analyse the teaching of mathematics, we will come to know that we teach so many things to our pupils which are never used in their life, *e.g.,*

  (1) Multiplication and division of four or five-digit numbers such as,

  $79638 \times 57964$, $876543 \div 5792$, etc.

  (2) Meaningless fractions like $\frac{41}{47}$ m, ₹ $\frac{53}{119}$, etc.

  (3) Surds and indices

  (4) Complex identities

  (5) $\log \frac{257}{4673}$
- The main task of education is to prepare the child for his future life. If the teaching of a subject does not fulfill this requirement, it is futile to teach it.
- The purpose of the study of mathematics is to link it with our actual needs of life.

- We must put only those real problems before the pupils which are related to their actual life happenings.
  - The problems giving wrong notions of the reality pose false and unreal portrait of our life. *e.g.,*

    rate of cycling 60 km/h, rate of flying an aeroplane 12 km/h, rate of walking 16 km/h, height of a tree 800 m, purchasing a commodity on each instalment of ₹ 195.79, etc.
- In some text books of mathematics the problem on mixture or profit and loss are selected so carelessly that they teach the pupils the profit of mixing low priced items with pure ones or the value of weighing less than the actual weight.
  - Here, we teach and encourage dishonesty and corruption among our pupils.
- We must teach only those topics and problems which have practical utility in our day-to-day life.

## 2. *Correlation of Math with its Branches*

- In our school, the branches of mathematics — Arithmetic, Algebra, Geometry, Trigonometry, Statistics, etc. — should not be taught as closed water-tight compartments.
- The pupils should be able to use the knowledge of one branch in understanding and solving the problems of the other branches.
  - The unrelated study of various branches of mathematics cannot be helpful in the proper learning of mathematics.
  - It is simply the waste of time and energy in repeating the learning of the same thing in different branches.
- There are many problems in Arithmetic which can be easily solved, using algebraic formulae and equations.
  - As the History of Mathematics reveals, Algebra has been invented only to discover simple ways to solve the problems of Arithmetic and Geometry. *e.g.,*

(1) Multiply: $496 \times 504$

(2) Solve (*a*) $8888 \times 8888 - 1112 \times 1112$

(*b*) $6666 \times 6666 - 3334 \times 3334$

(3) Solve: $\dfrac{0.1296 - 2(0.36)(0.25) + 0.0625}{(0.36)^2 - (0.25)^2}$

(4) Solve: $(37)^2 - (37)(97) + (97)^2 - \dfrac{(37)^3 + (97)^3}{37 + 97}$

(5) Divide 128 into four parts such that if we add 7 to the first part, subtract 7 from the second, multiply the third by 7 and divide the fourth by 7, the result is the same in all cases. *(Ans: 7, 21, 2, 98)*

- In solving a problem our aim is to get accurate solution with greater ease. So, we should make use of knowledge, irrespective of to which branch of mathematics it belongs, for the solution of any problem.
  - The notion that the branches like Arithmetic, Algebra, Geometry, etc. are different subjects must be removed.
  - Those branches need a perfect correlation among themselves. *e.g.*, if we are teaching identity like $(a + b)(a - b) = a^2 - b^2$ in Algebra, we should deal with it geometrically, arithmetically and graphically and to teach it in all aspects with all possible ways.
- The problems of Arithmetic related with the topics like profit and loss, simple and compound interest, partnership, area, mensuration, work and time, etc. should be allowed to be solved by algebraic methods as it is easier to solve them by such methods.
- Problems in Geometry should also involve arithmetical treatment like extraction of the square root of 2, distance formula in co-ordinate Geometry, etc.
- Mathematics highly concerns with the phenomenon of correlation between its various branches, *e.g.*,

  (*i*) Without having elementary knowledge of Algebra, Arithmetic and Geometry, one cannot solve the problems of Statistics, and that of Trigonometry.

  (*ii*) One cannot change the operation of addition into subtraction and vice versa, multiplication into division and vice versa, without the knowledge of integers.

  (*iii*) HCF, LCM, squares, fractions, etc. in Algebra are based upon the rules of Arithmetic.

  (*iv*) The four fundamental operations of Arithmetic are widely used in all branches of mathematics.

  (*v*) Each and every branch of mathematics are interdependent to each other. So, all the branches of mathematics must be integrated by correlating one another.

  (*vi*) The modern mathematics, applied mathematics and pure higher mathematics have a lot of bearing upon the elementary rules and regulations of Arithmetic, Algebra and Geometry.

  (*vii*) Apart from the main branches of mathematics — Arithmetic, Algebra, Geometry, Trigonometry, Statistics, there is modern mathematics, applied mathematics and higher/pure mathematics, which include astronomy, hydro-dynamics, mechanics, computing, etc.
- There is a very high correlation of mathematics with its different branches. So, the teacher should make it clear to the pupils that the knowledge of correlation will be helpful in their future study.

## 3. *Correlation of Math with its different Topics in the Same branch*

- In mathematics, the study of one topic depends upon the learning of other topics.
- There must be a logical sequence or continuity in the different topics of same branches of mathematics.
  - The different topics/units must be so correlated as to bring out clearly the objectives of teaching the whole subject matter.

- This also helps the pupils in comprehending the subject.
- It is necessary that there must be an orderly treatment of mathematics showing the relationship of one topic with another.
- Study in any branch of mathematics should be so planned that the different topics have links with each other and so, learning of one topic may stimulate and make necessary the need of studying other topics.
- The teacher should make the pupils realise the importance of studying different topics in a specific sequence. *e.g.,*

(1) LCM is useful in adding and subtracting fractions.

(2) Percentage is useful in calculating profit/loss per cent and in banking.

(3) Linear and simultaneous equations can be very easily correlated.

(4) Expansion and factorisation can be correlated.

(5) In Algebra, teaching of factorisation, formulae and equations must be made the centre of learning.

(6) The knowledge of factorising (specially of trinomials) is essential before solving quadratic equations.

### 4. *Correlation of Math with other Subjects*

- Mathematics has a high correlation with most of the subjects.
  - This correlation is of two types — direct and indirect.
  - Mathematics has a direct bearing on subjects of pure sciences like Physics, Chemistry, Zoology, Botany.
  - Mathematics has an indirect bearing on subjects of social sciences such as History, Geography, Sociology, Economics, etc.
- All subjects of school curriculum contribute towards the realisation of the aims of education.
  - Study of one subject helps the study of the other subjects and vice versa. Study of mathematics helps the learning of other subjects and the learning in other subjects also helps the learning of mathematics.

## 1. Correlation of Math with Physical & Biological Sciences

- Mathematics is the pivot of all the sciences and all the arts.
  - Mathematics is an efficient and necessary tools for the progress and development of any type of science or technology or Art.
  - It, sometimes, may be a backstage performer but is a very effective and powerful one.
  - Without its use, the existence and advancement of any science or art is not possible.
- Compte — 'All scientific education which does not commence with mathematics is necessarily defective at its foundation.'

  Kant — 'A mathematical science is a science only in so far as it is mathematical.'

  Berthelot — 'Mathematics is the indispensable instrument of all physical researches.'

Roger Bacon — 'Mathematics is the gate and key of the sciences ... Neglect of mathematics works injury to all knowledge, as who is ignorant of it cannot know other sciences or the things of the world. And, what is worst, men who are thus ignorant are unable to perceive their own ignorance and so do not seek a remedy.

- It has placed a very important role in building up modern civilisation by perfecting all the sciences. It is rightly said that mathematics is the science of all sciences and art of all arts.

## 2. Correlation of Math with Physics

- Mathematics and physics are closely related and have a very high coefficient of correlation. Perhaps, no other science is so close to mathematics as physics is.
- Almost all rules and principles in physics take mathematical form and mathematics gives final shape to the rules, laws and principles of physics.

  All the laws, rules, etc. of physics are expressed in mathematics language and equation.

  *e.g.*

  (1) Laws of motion, Laws of floatation, Law of momentum, etc., are dependent on mathematics.

  (2) The coefficient of linear expansion of different metals, cubical expansion of liquids, Charle's law of expansion of gases — are all based on mathematical knowledge.

  (3) Various types of measurements, laws of levers, the law of gravitation, numerical problems related to mechanics, light, heat, sound, electricity, magnetism show that these two subjects are closed related.

  (4) Working of a machine — simple or complex — involve the mathematical computation to find out their mechanical advantage.

  (5) Calculation of specific heat, humidity, latent heat, etc. require the knowledge of mathematics.

- The study of physics needs mathematical calculations at every step.
- For advanced study in physics, a good knowledge of mathematics is a must. It is also required to solve numerical problems in physics.
- For cent per cent accuracy and exactness of results, physics depends upon mathematics. *e.g.*,Launching of satellite requires —

  (*i*) right amount of thrust in rockets,

  (*ii*) accuracy in time and speed,

  (*iii*) angle of launching,

  (*iv*) provision of minimum friction, and so many other calculations.

- Working of a machine is possible only when there is high degree of adjustment of its component parts.
- It is the experience of college students that many times they completely forget whether they are attending the lecture on Physics or Mathematics? So closely these two subjects are related!

## 3. Correlation of Math with Chemistry

- Chemistry is closely related with Mathematics.
- All chemical combination and their balanced equations are governed and controlled by certain mathematical laws.
- All chemical compounds have their constituent elements in a definite ratio. *e.g.,* formation of water is possible when exactly 2 atoms of hydrogen combine with one atom of oxygen. *i.e.,* $H_2O$.
  - Chemical equations are balanced by counting the number of atoms of a certain element on either side of the equation . The number be the same.

    *e.g.,* $2H_2 + O_2 \longrightarrow 2H_2O$
- For estimation of elements in organic compounds, the use of percentage, and ratio-proportion, etc., has to be made.
- J.W. Mellor — 'It is almost impossible to follow the later development of physical/general chemistry without a working knowledge of higher mathematics.'
- The atomic weight and molecular weight of organic/inorganic compounds are calculated mathematically. Valencies of elements and radicles have a mathematical base. The sensitivity of chemical balance depends upon the use of mathematical principles. These are some examples of correlation between Mathematics and Chemistry.
- In a structure of an atom or of an isotopes, there are some relations concerning electrons ($e^-$), protons (p+) and neutrons (n).

## 4. Correlation of Math with Biology

- Formerly there was misconception that Biology has nothing to do with mathematics. Biology was considered as totally uninfluenced by mathematics.
- But now, in the development of Biology the role of mathematics is very clear.
- Mathematics has direct relation on biology and its related sciences like zoology, botany, physiology, anthropology, etc.
- New research techniques have now proved that the application of mathematical rules and principles is unavoidable in the advancement of biological sciences.
  - The advanced studies in biology depends largely on Bio-physics and Bio-chemistry and they depend on mathematics.
  - Role of mathematics in the study of biological sciences has become so wide that Bio-mathematics and Bio-statistics are also growing as the important fields of study.
- Mathematical laws and principles have a lot of applications in observing and interpreting biological phenomena.
  - Biological phenomena are described, classified and compared for generalising and deriving a biological law.
- Mathematics helps a lot at every stage of the process of investigation in biological researches.
- Life process are the most intricate of all natural phenomena, *e.g.,*

(*i*) composition of animal cell and plant cell.

(*ii*) osmosis in plants.

(*iii*) photosynthesis, etc. are studied and expressed clearly and concisely in a simple intelligible language of mathematics.

- A biologist must have sufficient knowledge of mathematics to understand Bio-physics and Bio-chemistry. *e.g.*,

  (*i*) The caloric and nutritive values of foot items are based on mathematics.

  (*ii*) the role of respiration, transpiration, supply of water, etc., in connection to all living bodies are related to mathematics.

  (*iii*) Number of bones, organs and the whole structure of a living body is mathematical.

  (*iv*) Study of living cells — animal cells and plant cells, composition of blood, category and age of plants/animals is possible through mathematical knowledge.

  (*v*) Mathematical processes and calculations are applied to advanced studies in heredity, nutrition, growth, maturation, etc.

- Compte — 'In mathematics, we find primitive source of rationality and the biologist must resort to mathematics for means to carry on their researches.'
- Various experiments in Biology also need analysis. For many a complex problems, the solution can be found only by using statistical methods.
- Gestalt used statistical method for measurement of inheritance of stature of children and stature of their parents. He found the coefficient of correlation to be 0.67.

## 5. Correlation of Math with Social Sciences

- Almost all the disciplines under social sciences are now claiming themselves as a science.
  - It is so because of increasing tendency to apply scientific method in their studies. In scientific method, statistical decision-making is highly involved.
- In social studies, statistical processes of classification, tabulation, testing, estimation, analysing of the data, etc. are commonly used. All these processes are the contribution of Mathematics.
- Though the correlation of mathematics with all the disciplines of social studies is not very high, yet it is quite good.
  - Some disciplines such as economics, psychology, education, sociology, etc., have a correlation with mathematics. In other disciplines such as political science, history, geography, etc., we use graphs, charts, curves, etc., in which mathematics is involved.
- This clearly indicates the relationship of mathematics with social sciences.

## 6. Correlation of Math with History

- Mathematics and History reciprocate their contribution to each other.
- Mathematics helps History in calculating days, time, dates of various historical events and in having their records in a scientific manner, while History helps it in providing information about the origin, growth and development of mathematics.

- History also provides the knowledge about the great mathematicians and their contributions to mathematics.

- This shows the relationship between mathematics and history.

## 7. Correlation of Math with Geography

- The study of Geography requires the knowledge of mathematics.
- There is a great application of mathematics in Geography.
  - It helps in drawing and understanding of maps, charts and graphs.
  - The knowledge of longitudes and latitudes, rotation and revolution of Earth leading to the formation of days and nights and various seasons, calculation of time at various places, falling of rains, causes of winds, zones of Earth, different paths of satellites, shape and size of Earth, heights of mountains at various places, etc., — all depend upon mathematical calculations.
- The human geography, economic geography, demography are some specific branches of Geography. The study of all these branches requires a good knowledge of mathematics.
- Mathematics plays an important role in studying rivers, canals, mountains, climate, depth of seas, population, density of population, per capita income, drawing of graphs and figures — in all these, mathematics plays a prominent role.
- Hence, all the Geological and Geographical studies are not possible without the proper application of mathematics.

## 8. Correlation of Math with Economics

- In explaining, describing and interpreting any economic phenomena, mathematical laws, principles, methods and language are often used.
- J.B. Say — 'Economics is the science which treats wealth.'

  Marshall — 'The direct application of mathematical reasoning to the discovery of economic truths has recently rendered great services in the hands of mathematics.'
- In economics, mathematical knowledge is applied —
  - (*i*) in collecting, analysing, calculating, interpreting and presenting data regarding population, investment, demand and supply of commodities, income, expenditure, banking, production, wastage or side product, business, etc.
  - (*ii*) to economic forecasts regarding trade cycles, trends of export and import, employment, volume of trade, industrial trends, population trends, share market, etc.
- For the businessman, who is considered an important pillar of economic system, the knowledge of mathematics is of utmost importance.
- Almost all economic magazines, newspapers, periodicals, etc., are full of figures and graphs regarding population, investment, employment, industrial growth and development, crops, estimation of production, marketing, etc.
  - All these employ various numerical and statistical procedures.
- In most of the universities a course in advanced mathematics and statistics is introduced as a part of degree course in economics.

## 9. Correlation of Math with Psychology

- Psychology is now-a-days considered as a science.
  - It is a science of mind, *i.e.,* of mental processes.
  - It has become possible by applying scientific methods to a great extent in its studies.
- The experimental psychology utilises scientific principles at every stage.
  - It has become highly mathematical due to the use of higher statistical techniques in drawing inferences.
  - The calculation of measures of Central Tendency (CT), measures of dispersion, coefficient of correlation, probable errors of measurement and testing, the significance of difference between means and other statistics — are very common in the study of experimental psychology.
  - IQ (Intelligence Quotient) is very popular phenomenon in psychology.

$$IQ = \frac{\text{Mental Age}}{\text{Chronological Age}} \times 100 = \frac{MA}{CA} \times 100$$

The MA is determined by using an intelligence test.

- Psychology deals with the study of behaviours of living organisms.
  - The living organism cannot be easily isolated and experimented upon.
  - No single individual can be representative of the whole species.
  - So, psychological experiment are generally performed on large groups taken at random.
  - For interpretation of results, statistical analysis is necessary.
  - Thus, statistical analysis is the only reliable method for understanding the psychological phenomena.
- Herbert — 'It is not only possible but necessary also that mathematics be applied to psychology.'
- While learning mathematics, to make the learning child-centred, psychological laws, principles, theorems and concepts are applied.
- Some psychological principles like — learning by doing, learning through experience, learning by problem solving, law of readiness, law of exercise, teaching by introducing heurism, team teaching, etc. — all are very useful to understand mathematics.
  - Similarly, various mathematical and statistical techniques are used to collect, analyse and interpret psychological data.

## 10. Correlation of Math with Philosophy

- In bygone days, all the subjects, including even mathematics, were considered as the part of philosophy.
  - Mathematics was also taught as the part of philosophy.
  - Most of ancient scientists and mathematicians were philosophers.

- Mathematics was the first subject which separated itself from philosophy due to its methodology of teaching and learning.
  - Mathematics is an exact science and its inferences are definite. Philosophy tries to find the solution of indefinite questions such as — Who am I? From where did I come to this Earth? What is the purpose of my life? To where will I go after my death? Is there anything like rebirth?, etc.
  - Phislosophy deals with abstract ideas while mathematics tries to draw attention on the ideas that are practicable and worthwhile.
  - Therefore, for a common man, it appears that there cannot be any relationship between these two disciplines.
  - But the fact is otherwise.
  - Mathematics helps the philosophers in reaching the truth from falsehood.
- A.N. Whitehead — 'Philosophers, when they have possessed a thorough knowledge of mathematics, have been among those who have enriched the science with some of its best ideas.'

  I.S. Mill — 'Mathematics will ever remain the most perfect type of deductive method in general, and the applications of mathematics to the simpler branches of physics, furnish the only school in which philosophers can effectively learn the most difficult and important portion of their art, the employment of laws of simpler phenomena of explaining and predicting those of more complex.'

The great educationist Herbert has categorically put the functions of mathematics in the development of philosophical thought in these words —

> 'The real finisher of our education is philosophy, but it is the office of mathematics to ward off the dangers of philosophy.'

- In mathematics, the philosophers find orderly and systematic achievement of unambiguous truths.
  - The philosophers can rely on mathematics. The great philosopher Plato and other thinkers came under the influence of mathematics in search of distinction between fact and fiction.'
- Mathematics occupies a central place between natural philosophy and mental philosophy.

## 11. Correlation of Math with Logic

- Mathematics is the science of logical reasoning.
  - In mathematics, the logical reasoning/laws are applied and results can be verified by the method of logical reasoning.
- W.C.D. Whelhem — 'Mathematics is but the higher development of symbolic logic.'

  C.J. Keyser — 'Symbolic logic is mathematics, mathematics is symbolic logic.'

Pascal — 'Logic has borrowed the rules of Geometry. The method of avoiding error is sought by everyone. The logicians profess to lead the way, the geometers alone reach it and aside from their science there is no true demonstration.'

- D'Alombert — 'Geometry is a practical logic because in it, rules of reasoning are applied in the most simple and sensible manner. Geometry is the true demonstration of Logic.'
- On the other hand, the symbols and methods used in the investigations of the foundation of mathematics can be transferred to the study of logic. They help in the development and formulation of logical laws.
- The aims of mathematicians and those of the logicians are practically the same. So, these two subjects are interrelated.
  - Logic is the only branch of knowledge in which logical reasoning and laws are applied.
  - The results can be varied with the help of logical reasoning.
  - Logic is the scientific study of condition of accurate thinking and valid inferences.

## 12. Correlation of math with Languages

- Language is a necessary element of teaching. No subject can be taught without using language. This is applicable to mathematics also.
  - The principles and methods of mathematics are expressed through the medium of language.
- The symbols, notations and formulae used in mathematics are the short methods of expressing the statements of language. That is why it is called mathematical language. So, it is language that helps mathematics and its teaching.
- The correctness of language is also an important factor in the effective teaching of mathematics.
  - The incorrect language cannot convey the exact and correct idea of mathematics. But it may put a wrong impression on the minds of pupils.
- Mathematics also helps the language in correct writing and expressing.
- Mathematics develops an attitude of exactness in the teacher and pupils which helps in maintaining the correct us of language. *e.g.*,

  (1) 'Circle is a set of points equidistant from a given point.' This is not an exact definition as the condition 'in the same plane' is missing.

  (2) 'Triangle is the union of three segments determined by three non-collinear points, in the same plane.' Here, the condition 'in the same plane' is not necessary. Because three non-collinear points always determine one and only one plane.
- Mathematics contributes a lot to poetry and grammar of the language. 'Metres' of a poetry require the knowledge of mathematics.

## 13. Correlation of Math with Fine Arts

- The great mathematician pythogoras — 'Where there is harmony, there are numbers.'
- Geometrical drawing is an important branch of drawing. In geometrical drawing, various principles of Geometry are frequently used.
  - The knowledge of Geometry also helps in the study of other branches of drawing such as memory drawing, figure drawing, letter drawing, design, etc.
  - Good drawing is needed to draw good geometrical figures.
  - In the study of mathematics, the pupil has to draw and construct various shapes, figures, graphs, etc. All these activities require the knowledge of drawing and arts.
- Keats — 'Truth is beauty.'

  Bertrand Russel — 'Mathematics rightly viewed possesses not only truth but supreme beauty, too — a beauty cold and austere, like that of sculpture, without appeal to any part of our weaker nature, without the gorgeons trappings of painting or music, yet sublimely pure, and capable of a stern perfection such as only the greatest art can show.'

  W.F. White — 'Mathematics too has the triumphs of the creative imagination, its beautiful theorems, its proofs and processes whose perfection of forms has made them classic. He must be a '*practical*' man who can see no poetry in mathematics.'
- In Fine Arts, the mathematical knowledge is applied in many ways, *e.g.*,
  (1) Drawing and painting with symmetry.
  (2) Ratio and proportion in Drawing, Painting, Sketching, etc.
  (3) Almost all musical notes and systems work on mathematical principles.
  (4) Exactness of a figure, shape, etc., can be measured using mathematics.
  (5) Similarity of triangles, a human being and his photograph, a thing and its virtual image, etc.
- The basic elements of fine arts are rhythm, harmony, proportion, balance and symmetry.
  (1) The proper expression of these elements form the beauty of a piece of art.
  (2) The above characteristics belong to mathematics to a great extent.
  (3) Thus, mathematics provides a basis and background for aesthetic appreciation.
  (4) That is why, only mathematical mind can fully appreciate a beautiful piece of art, painting, architecture and music.
- Mathematics is considered as the science of reality and truthfulness.
- Leibnitz — 'Music is a modern hidden exercise in Arithmetic of a mind unconscious of dealing with numbers.'
  - It is very true that something like mathematics exists in music. Similarly, something like music exists in doing the exercises of mathematics.

- One will certainly agree that the recitation of multiplication tables is like reciting a poem, is like a music in mathematics.

## 14. Correlation of Math with Commerce

- The knowledge of mathematics helps to understand various concepts and branches of commerce.
    - The basis of Banking, Business and Accountancy is mathematics.
    - It is considered that without having good knowledge and practice of mathematics one cannot become a good accountant.
- In commerce, calculation of profit and loss, interest, purchase and selling of shares, debentures, mutual funds, accounting, sales tax, etc. requires the application of mathematical knowledge.
- Many statistical techniques are also used to solve the problems of different branches of commerce.

## 15. Correlation of Math with Engineering

- Mathematics is the foundation of Engineering.
    - Engineering is defined as 'The art of directing the great sources of power in nature, for the use and convenience of man.'
- For admission to any engineering course requires mathematics and physics which are having very high coefficient of correlation, at the qualifying class.
    - In all the branches of engineering such as civil, mechanical, electrical, information technology, aeronautical, architectural, etc. mathematical principles are directly applied.
    - The development of space technology, genetic engineering is possible by using mathematical and scientific principles in researches of these fields.
- In engineering, scientific principles and laws are applied to a task.
    - Engineering deals with surveying, levelling, designing, estimating, constructing, etc., and for all these the knowledge of mathematics is essential.
    - By the application of geometric principles to design and construction, the durability of product can be increased.
- Mathematical knowledge also helps in the verification of results in Engineering.
    - Thus, it is clear that mathematics and engineering are highly correlated.
    - The existence of engineering cannot be imagined without mathematics.

## 16. Correlation of Math with Agriculture

- The advanced study of agriculture as a science is highly dependent on Mathematics.
    - Agricultural statistics have been developed as a field of study. It helps in agricultural studies and researches.
    - Now-a-days the use of modern techniques in agriculture has made it more dependent on mathematics.

- The traditional agriculture was also based on mathematics.
  - The farmers used a certain quality of a particular seed for sowing in a certain area to get more production of crop.
  - Time and season for sowing the seeds, watering the plants at fixed intervals, etc., requires mathematical knowledge.
- Various aspects of agricultural science require direct application of mathematics such as measurement of land and area, assessment of production per unit area, cost of labour, time and work, average return, rate of seed, manure, artificial fetilizers, insecticides, profit and loss, etc.
  - An agriculturist can attain desirable target only if he has a calculative attitude.
  - It is the need of the time that a common agriculturist should be so calculative as to be able to compare the amount of return he is likely to get with the input — time, labour and money.
  - Progress of production can be judged with the help of graph and other statistical techniques.

## 17. Correlation of Math with Work Experience

- Under work experience the pupils learn —

(1) to grow flowers, vegetables, etc.,

(2) to preserve food and fruits,

(3) to learn to do wood-work, sewing, embroidery, paper-work, book-binding, printing, screen-printing, cycle-repairing, stove-repairing, cake/chocolate making, etc.,

(4) to make baskets, ropes, inks, soaps, etc.,

(5) to prepare toys like micky-mouse, etc.

  - The study of mathematics may be well correlated with the different activities of these work-areas.

For example, take growing flowers/vegetables:

We can locate a lot of opportunities of learning mathematics while gathering work-experiences in these areas, *e.g.*,

(1) surveying and measuring the piece of land,

(2) borrowing/collecting money,

(3) keeping the accounts of expenditure incurred in purchasing seeds, saplings, plants, manure, etc.,

(4) ploughing and watering,

(5) calculation of profit/loss after the sale of products, etc.

- Teachers should provide practical opportunities for teaching so many concepts of Arithmetic, Algebra and Practical Geometry.

- In doing wood-work or metal-work one has to take help from mathematics in —
  (1) estimating and purchasing the raw material,
  (2) designing, finishing and selling of the finished products,
  (3) calculating profit.
- Work-experience activities provide sufficient opportunities for realising the need of mathematics. While teaching, it the problems should be related to work-experience, making the study of mathematics more purposeful and interesting.

## EVALUATE YOURSELF

1. Explain the term: Correlation.
2. What are the need and importance of correlation?
3. Write short notes on:
   (1) Dimension of correlation (2) Types of correlation.
4. Correlate mathematics with any one of the following:
   (1) Life (2) Different branches of mathematics
   (3) Other subjects (4) Different topics in the same branch
   (5) Social Sciences
5. How will you correlate Mathematics with Physical and Biological Sciences?
6. Correlate mathematics with any one of the following:
   (1) Physics (2) Chemistry (3) Biology
   (4) Logic (5) History (6) Geography
   (7) Economics (8) Languages (9) Psychology
   (10) Philosophy (11) Fine Arts (12) Commerce
   (13) Engineering (14) Agriculture (15) Work Experience
7. 'Mathematics is a science of all sciences and an art of all arts.' — Justify.

# 20 ENRICHMENT & RECREATIONAL PROGRAMME FOR GIFTED

## 20.1 Selecting enrichment & recreational material

- All good teachers recognise the importance of gearing the mathematical programme to the intelligence and abilities of the pupils.
  - If the material is too difficult, the pupils lose interest and develop a dislike for and even fear of mathematics.
  - If the material is too easy, the class as a whole, does not make sufficient progress and the bright pupils who are not challenged sufficiently may get bored and develop poor study habits and a careless attitude towards their work.
- The mathematical concepts included in a series of text books and the amount of practice provided to ensure sufficient skill in computation are selected carefully so that a foundation is laid at each grade level for further mathematical education.
  - Pupils' text books usually provide both —
    (1) additional enrichment material for gifted pupils; and
    (2) additional review material for those who need more practice in *fixing* basic skills.
- These provisions are helpful but usually are not sufficient to take care of the problems created by the wide range of individual differences found among the pupils in a class.
- The teacher still is confronted with the problems of either —
  (1) grouping the more able pupils and moving them ahead of the class at an accelerated rate, or
  (2) of providing them with additional interesting mathematical activities while they proceed with the regular programme at the rate of the others.
- The problem of how best to accelerate the more able pupils always has been a difficult one in all areas of the school curriculum.

- It is suggested that the elementary school should be made *ungraded.* In this type of organisation, the pupils are advanced through various *levels* of achievement throughout each school-year without regard to any particular grade level.
    - Here, the level of achievement is given more importance than the grade.
- We should find out a type of curriculum organisation which permits the more able achievers to proceed more rapidly than the slower ones.
- 'Enrichment' as a technical term is used for enriching the already available opportunities of education.
    - Basically it consists in the selection and organisation of the learning experiences and activities appropriate to the pupils' adequate development.
    - Thus, the 'enrichment of curriculum' should be considered a need of all students.
    - The term 'enrichment' here refers to mental activities provided for the more able pupils in addition to the activities required of pupils in the regular programme.
    - This enrichment includes material often referred to as 'recreational material', however, it should be in no sense be restricted to this type of material.
    - Children who are gifted mathematically are stimulated by being introduced to new strands of mathematical concepts and also by more sophisticated interpretations of the materials they studied formerly.
    - For these children, material in addition to the regular programme should be designed to lay a foundation systematically for a much wider programme than that pursued by average achievers.
- Recreational material has an important place in the programme for bright children, just as it has an important place as part of the regular programme for all children.
- One of the characteristics of an outstanding teacher is his ability to stimulate the interest of his pupils in the material they are studying.
    - Pupils are motivated in various ways to expend the effort necessary for their success.
- The use of recreational mathematics is one way for the teacher to increase the enjoyment of pupils in mathematics.
- The material suitable for recreational mathematics can be separated roughly into —

  (1) the type suitable for the class to work on as a whole, as a class activity, and

  (2) the type that lends itself to individual efforts.

    - When the class works as a whole, this group activity often takes on some of the characteristics of a game in which the class is challenged to find the answer to a problem.
    - In this environment the enthusiasm of some of the pupils influences the rest of the class and a relaxed informal atmosphere should contribute to the enjoyment of all, including the teacher.
    - The recreational material suitable for individual effort provides one of the answers to the problem of keeping the fast workers in the elementary school classroom profitably occupied while the slower workers are finishing an assignment.

- The common characteristic of good recreational material is that it encourages pupils to solve problems and to discover mathematical concepts through their own initiative.
  - As a pupil's skill increases, he will develop more and more interest in mathematics and he will be willing to accept material that provides greater challenges.
  - Some bright pupils may become interested in the history of mathematics. They should be encouraged to give reports to the class on various topics.
- Behind every invention or discovery in the field of literature, art or sciences, there have always been a genius or gifted brain.
  - The need and importance of nurturing gifted children, becomes more pronounced in mathematics on account of its key role in the modern world of science and technology.

## 20.2 Identification of Gifted Children in Math

- The nurturing of gifted children in mathematics, first of all, requires their identification.
  - These gifted children try to show their unique characteristics right from the very beginning. The earlier they are recognised, the better it is for the teacher, and the society.
  - The criteria to identify gifted children are as under:

(1) The Intelligence Quotient (IQ): $120^{+}$

(2) The academic achievement in the previous class as well as at the present. The achievement test and aptitude test may be administered.

(3) The opinion of the teachers of previous as well as present class.

(4) The report of the interest inventories and aptitude test in mathematics.

(5) The report of the previously planned interview with the child.

(6) The opinion of the teacher himself based on day-to-day observations of the child's behaviour.

- In this connection generally the following type of behaviour shows the sign of giftedness:

(1) He learns rapidly and easily by responding quickly and correctly.

(2) He grasps, digests and assimilates the subject matter quite easily.

(3) He shows originality, novelty, creativity, a great deal of common sense and practical knowledge.

(4) He remains aware, alert and keenly observant in the teaching-learning process of mathematics.

(5) He can put intelligent, thought-provoking and pointed questions demanding to know more and minute details about the subject.

(6) He solves complicated problems and understands the things more advanced to his age and grade.

(7) He provides clear evidences of his fine imagination, remarkable memory and fully developed reasoning and logical thinking.

(8) He can generalise the things and draw appropriate correct conclusions.

(9) He has the power to associate and correlate the various pieces of knowledge concerning different topics and branches of mathematics.

## 20.3 What Teacher can do for Gifted

1. The gifted children have tremendous energy with a lot of curiosity and determination to progress.
   - This energy should not go waste and create serious problems for the individual and for the society.
   - As the number of gifted children in a particular class is too less, the idea of giving special attention to them by framing 'model classes' is quite impracticable.
   - Again, this breeds segregation and so, becomes highly undemocratic.
   - The other option is to arrange 'enrichment programmes' for gifted children without disturbing much the existing framework of a school.
   - But in the case of gifted children, it will certainly imply an urgent need of providing them a great variety of experiences or tasks at a more advanced level.
   - Thus, enrichment programme in mathematics aims to provide additional learning opportunities to gifted children in mathematics.

- Through enrichment programmes the gifted children must find something new and challenging to their abilities.
   - In providing additional learning opportunities under the enrichment programmes, for the pupils of mathematics the following two channels are suggested:
      (1) Provision of different curriculums for gifted children.
      (2) Enrichment for gifted children within the existing curriculum.
   - Under the first channel, gifted children may be provided with different curriculum which consists of more advanced topics, generally at the college level. It may include more analytic and heuristic approach to the subject. It may have additional topics selected with other areas of experience and applied nature. In India, this seems to be impracticable.
   - Under the second channel, no separate curriculum is recommended to the gifted children. Instead of that, attempts are made to provide additional educational opportunities to them for the learning of mathematics within the existing curriculum. This provision may include the following suggestions:

1. To ask the gifted children —
   (*a*) for solving more difficult and complicated problems.
   (*b*) for making deep and intensive study of the topics.
   (*c*) for working on some useful projects independently or in a group.
   (*d*) for constructing mathematical models, aid material and improvised apparatus.
   (*e*) for arranging and contributing to mathematical or science fairs and exhibitions.

(*f*) for participating in panel discussion, seminar, symposium, conference or contest concerning mathematics and to prepare and produce its report.

(*g*) for participating and organising activities concerning Mathematic Club.

(*h*) for criticising in favour and against of any reference book on mathematics.

(*i*) for writing articles in educational journals, magazines, etc.

2. To encourage the gifted children, the teacher should —

(*a*) ask them questions that satisfy their curiosity and thirst for knowledge.

(*b*) bring novelty and originality in his approach while teaching.

(*c*) make them active independent inquirers and discoverers of the knowledge.

(*d*) associate and establish correlation within topics, branches and different subjects of the school curriculum.

(*e*) carry the learning of mathematics to their daily life activities.

(*f*) ask them to write essays and articles on the topics of mathematics.

(*g*) encourage them to do independent 'action research' — in the field of mathematics and allied subjects.

(*h*) suggest them to help the weak students in their studies.

(*i*) invite them to teach a particular topic of their interest to the whole class.

3. The teacher should hand over some special assignments to them.

- The above list for enriched learning experiences to the gifted children should not be taken as complete in itself.
  - The mathematics teacher may plan some or the other learning experiences for the benefit of gifted children depending upon the available resources and circumstances.
- Enrichment of the learning experiences or programmes provided within the existing framework of the curriculum is the most suitable plan for the education of the gifted children.
  - It helps in evolving a school programme that is beneficial to all — below average, average, above average and the gifted.
  - All of them can develop according to their own interests, abilities and capacities without interfering the development of others.
  - It provides —

    (1) facilities for the full development of special mathematical abilities and potentialities of the child.

    (2) care for the development of his total personality.
  - Therefore, a mathematics teacher should strive hard for the enrichment of learning experiences according to the needs of the gifted children.

## EVALUATE YOURSELF

1. 'Enrichment of the learning experiences within the existing framework of the curriculum is the most suitable plan for educating gifted children.' — Comment.
2. How will you select enrichment and recreational material for gifted children?
3. How are gifted children in mathematics identified?
4. As a teacher what can you do for gifted children?
5. Write short notes on: What is enrichment?
6. Suggest a suitable enrichment programme for gifted children.

Children learn more from what we are than from what we say. It is neither desirable nor necessary that the basis of habit should be reasoned into before the habits are formed.

— ***H.H. Horne***

# 21 BACKWARDNESS IN MATH: DIAGNOSTIC TESTING & REMEDIAL TEACHING

- Sometimes a pupil is seriously lagging behind in knowledge and experience in comparison with the other pupils of his own class.
  - If he is lagging behind in all the subjects, his backwardness is termed as 'general backwardness.'
  - If his performance shows satisfactory progress in all other subjects but is repeatedly failed in a particular subject, his backwardness is termed as 'specific backwardness.'
- It is necessary for a mathematics teacher to know the causes of backwardedness in mathematics alongwith remedial tasks.

## 21.1 Causes of backwardness in Math followed by Remedial tasks

### 1. *Physically handicap*

- Pupils who suffer from some defects in their physical body may turn educationally backward.
  - Poor vision, hard of hearing, pains in stomach or in head, disabled in leg or foot, very thin and very fat body, deformity or loss of some parts of body, leprosy, etc. — emerge into the feeling of inferiority.
  - All these may result into acute social and emotional maladjustment.
  - This affects their development and progress in learning which results into backwardness in learning mathematics.
- These children should get proper individual attention and careful handling by the teachers.
  - The co-operation of parents and school authorities is a must. They should give possible sympathetic and normal treatment.
  - These pupils should be given appropriate and timely guidance in their studies to remove their inferiority complex.

### 2. *Mentally Handicap*

- Mentally handicapped pupils lag behind in their studies of mathematics due to some mental abnormalities or diseases, lower IQ, lack of concentration power, poor memory or inadequacy in other mental abilities and capacities.
- The symptoms of mental diseases/abnormalities should be immediately brought to the notice of their parents.
  - Such pupils should be helped to get proper treatment psychologically and clinically, too.
  - Individual attention should be given to such pupils. Extra coaching may be provided to them.
  - They should be helped in developing —
    (*i*) proper reading and learning habits,
    (*ii*) power of concentration, memorisation and self-confidence.

### 3. *Emotional Maladjustment*

- In some cases, educational backwardness is caused due to emotional maladjustment among the pupils.
  - Such pupils are too much sensitive and sentimental.
  - They cannot control over their emotions. They are intolerant and impatient. They are restless and usually commit mistakes in computation work and they give up their self-confidence.
  - It results in the failure and makes them backward in mathematics.
- Teacher should help them in gaining emotional stability and self-confidence in solving problems in mathematics.
  - They need most sympathetic dealing and careful handling.

### 4. *Lack of Interest in Mathematics*

- Interest is the mother (a basic factor) in learning If some pupils have no interest in learning mathematics, it may be due to —
  (*a*) improper method of teaching, (*b*) wrong attitude towards mathematics,
  (*c*) faulty method of learning, (*d*) faulty framing of curriculum.
- Pupils should be given proper stimulation and motivation to learning mathematics.
  - Mathematics should be correlated with their natural interest and basic needs.
  - Care should be taken to develop positive attitude towards mathematics.
  - Curriculum framers should present the syllabus in psychological and logical manner.

### 5. *Lack of Individual Attention*

- In the process of teaching and learning, individual difference plays an important role. All the pupils in a class are not alike.
  - What the gifted pupils understand things with no or very little efforts, average and below average pupils need concrete illustrations, slow explanation and sufficient fixation work.

- Sufficient individual attention is not paid by teachers or by the parents. This results in making the below average pupils lagging behind in their studies and making them backward in mathematics.

- Teacher should pay proper individual attention at the proper time. An individual should be helped in solving he problems independently. His HW should be regularly supervised and the difficulties be timely solved.

## 6. *Lack of Proper Educational Guidance*

- Pupils possess wide individual differences in terms of their interest, aptitudes, attitudes, abilities and capacities. Lack of proper educational guidance at the right moment turn any pupil into a backward pupil.
  - Parents should not fulfill their unfulfilled ambition through their children by compelling them to persue a course without taking care of their potentialities, interests, aptitudes and talent.
- Careful educational guidance is a must not only for the pupils but their parents, too.
  - Administer Intelligence test, Aptitude test, Attitude test, Interest inventory, etc., twice or thrice during the year and let the parents know the results.
  - Let the parents, thereby, know the strengths and weaknesses of their children.
  - Pupils should be given educational guidance through the properly arranged guidance services at the school.
  - This will prevent the child from turning into a backward child.

## 7. *Improper Method of Teaching*

- An inefficient teacher may bring disaster to the youngsters in his charge.
  - By his improper method of teaching he can create distaste, disinterest, apathy and scornful attitude towards mathematics.
  - He may furnish wrong information, build wrong concepts and teach wrong skills to the pupils.
- Only efficient, capable and duty bound teachers should be appointed to teach mathematics.
  - They should use adequate and proper methods of teaching.
  - They should be fully conversant with the knowledge of mathematics.

## 8. *Irregular Attendance*

- Irregularity in attendance causes backwardness in mathematics, because this subject is a sequence subject. If the link is broken between the topics, pupil will surely be unable to understand and grasped the later topic. He will lag behind and if this is repeated he will become backward in mathematics.
- Teacher should keep healthy atmosphere in the class, so that no student tries to remain absent. If the absence is unavoidable, the teacher and parents should help the pupil to fill up the gap.

### 9. *Problem of Transfer*

- Migration of pupils from one school to another for any reason, causes difficulty to the pupil to pick up the thread of learning in the new school.
  - The pupil may experience social or emotional maladjustment. He may lose self-confidence and he begins to lag behind in his study.
- Uniformity of the standard and common syllabi throughout the State, and if possible, throughout the country, may solve this problem to a great extent.
  - Teachers should realise their responsibility towards migrated pupils and help them in their study and adjustment.

### 10. *Unsuitable Environment at Home*

- The unsuitable environment at home pushes the pupil to backwardness in his studies.
  - Unpleasant relationship between the parents or among other members of family, loss of one of the parents or both, too much indulgence of the parents, engagement of the pupil in home affairs and family occupation, poverty, cultural or social deprivation of the family, indifference of the parents toward their child's studies, quarrelsome nature of the neighbours, etc., make the environment unsuitable for study.
- The teacher can play an effective role in removing this unsuitable environment at home.
  - He should gain and maintain confidence of parents and should become their friend, philosopher and guide. He should frequently visit such homes and do the needful in the matter.
  - Such pupils should be given sympathetic treatment which may protect them from the danger of insecurity and help them to gain confidence in their studies.

### 11. *Improper Behaviour of the Teacher*

- Behaviour of the teacher plays an important role to a great extent in developing positive or negative attitude towards mathematics.
  - Teacher with his improper behaviour may do a great harm to his pupils.
  - He should bear in his mind the individual differences among pupils.
  - His indecent remarks make the pupils feel inferior or worthless.
- Teacher should try to come close to the pupils and try to know their problems.
  - He should never lose his patience. He should be optimistic and never discourage or curse or scold the youngsters.
  - He should change his fault-finding nature and at times, if a backward pupil does a little good, should praise him in the class and build self-confidence in the backward pupil.

### 12. *Defective Handwriting and Drawing*

- Defective and unreadable handwriting, lack of expression power and poor in drawing skill, ultimately lead the pupil towards backwardness in mathematics.
  - Mathematics has its own language. If the pupil is unable to read and understand it, he will be a handicap in learning mathematics.

- From the beginning, every effort should be made to improve handwriting, skill of drawing and expression power, which is a must in learning mathematics.

### 13. *No Pre-school Experience*

- No or very little pre-school experience at the time of entering the school may turn a child backward in his future learning.

  *e.g.*, (1) Without having number-sense, there will be difficulty in understanding fundamentals of Arithmetic.

  (2) If a pre-school child has no knowledge of shape and size, it will be extremely difficult for him to understand the concepts of congruency and similarity in Geometry.

- The parent should give ample opportunities to their child to gain adequate pre-school experience before sending him to a school.
  - Teacher should convince the parents to send their child to Kinder Garten or Nursery schools.

## 21.2 Diagnostic Testing & Remedial Teaching

- An evaluation programme be carried out by a mathematics teacher for diagnosing the nature and extent of the learning difficulties and behavioural problems of pupils.
- Probably one of the most significant steps toward improved instruction is that of incorporating into the instructional programme, plans for discovering learning difficulties and detecting needs for remedial teaching.
  - Once the weaknesses and difficulties regarding the learning of a particular concept, knowledge and skill etc. are identified, efforts are then made to list out the probable causes responsible for these weaknesses and difficulties.
  - The listing of such probable causes then is made a base for building a remedial programme.
- Diagnosting programme call for the intelligent use of inventory and diagnostic tests alongwith personal interviews to discover and analyse pupils' difficulties with a view to setting up specific remedial measures to correct errors and remove difficulties.
- Diagnostic programme should be keyed to bring to light distinct weaknesses in learning which call for specifically planned remedial action.
- An important by-product of any diagnostic programme which is carefully constructed will be the discovery of latent interests and abilities which need to be challenged.
  - A second important by-product of the diagnostic programme can be the evaluation of instructional procedures.
- The intelligent use of such a programme of diagnosis is an important aspect of effective teaching.
  - Its real value definitely will be dependent upon a carefully planned follow-up remedial programme and a careful check on attained results and their interpretation.

## 21.3 Diagnostic Evaluation

- To know the weaknesses of the pupils in learning and the reasons for these weaknesses is called 'diagnosis'. For it, diagnostic tests are used.
- These tests are very useful for the subjects in which pupils are generally weak.
  - In the teaching of mathematics, diagnosis has an important place.
  - So, diagnostic type of evaluation is an important function of evaluation in mathematics.
- Diagnostic evaluation, if performed prior to teaching may help the teacher to plan his instructional programme suiting the needs, interests and abilities of the pupils.
  - Strategies used for such evaluation may be both —

    (*i*) informal (like observations, discussions, etc.)

    (*ii*) formal (like pre-test, inquiry, questionnaire, etc.)
  - Diagnostic evaluation can be used during pre-stage (beginning of the instruction) and also during the unit of teaching for diagnosing his pupils' understanding and interest.
- The main objective of diagnostic evaluation in mathematics is to find out the nature and causes of the persistent learning problems and to formulate a plan for seeking suitable remedial actions.

## 21.4 Characteristics of an Efficient Programme of Diagnosis

1. Diagnosis must be —

   (*a*) made in connection with worthy objectives of a good evaluation programme.

   (*b*) objective, reliable and valid.

   (*c*) as specific as desired outcomes permit.
2. It should yield results that would be comparable over a period of time and between groups of pupils.
3. It should be —

   (*a*) sufficiently precise to note progress during small units of time.

   (*b*) comprehensive.

   (*c*) appropriate to the educational programme.
4. The person making the diagnosis must understand the educational programme and be familiar with the fundamental problems of pupils.

### To be most effective, the remedial material should be —

(1) selected to bring about certain definite ends.

(2) correlated with instructional material being used.

(3) provided with answers.

(4) on component elementary skills.

(5) of such a nature that it could be administered to a class/an individual.

(6) largely capable of self-administration by the pupil.

## 21.5 Self-Diagnosis by Pupils

- One of the most important functions of tests, as an aid to the improvement of instruction, is pupils' use of tests to secure evidences concerning individual development.
  - Such tests, called 'practice tests' may be oral or written.
  - They can play a very important role in the assimilative period of instruction.
  - They can aid the pupil in self-diagnosis but they should never be used by the teacher in any other capacity than to help the pupil discover for himself, information concerning his status of achievement in intelligent understanding of subject matter, speed and accuracy with which he can perform the prescribed operations and his relative progress as a member of his class group.
  - Such tests must be shaped to reflect individual efficiency in the perspective of group activity.
- *Oral practice tests* may be used with material that calls for responses which can be readily obtained and simply stated.
  - They may be administered through pointed questions casually, yet evenly distributed over the entire class or through the medium of team contests.
  - The two principal key notes of successful oral practice are speed and accuracy of response.
- *Written practice tests* may be used for both — the simple response and the difficult response type of practice.
  - As in the case of oral tests, written tests may be shaped to emphasise speed and accuracy.
  - It should be re-emphasised at this point that understanding is a major responsibility of instruction in mathematics and some of the practice tests should be designed to that end.
- Some of the different ways of administering written practice tests are —

  (*a*) all pupils at board,

  (*b*) some at the board and others in their seats,

  (*c*) all pupils in their seats.
  - In any of the above cases all pupils may be working on the same assigned problems or separate groups may be working on separate problems.
  - These problems may be dictated by the teacher or printed or mimeographed or otherwise reproduced.
- Timed tests frequently serve to stimulate interest and attention through competition with other pupils or competition with one's own previous time record or similar material.
- *Precautions* which the teacher must observe are as follows:

  (1) Do not over-emphasise the speed at the expense of accuracy.

  (2) Provide for (*a*) check up and practice of understanding, and

  (*b*) speed and accuracy.

(3) Vary the type of practice material to prevent monotony of effort.

(4) Do not continue practice to the point of fatigue.

## 21.6 Prognosis & Guidance

- The main function of Criterion-Referenced-Evaluation are:

  *(1) Prognosis:* To assess the level of performance of an individual and to take decision about the success or achievement of objectives, in relation to the pre-fixed criterion is the prognostic function of evaluation.

  *(2) Diagnosis:* To know the weakness of the pupil and the reasons of these weaknesses is called diagnosis. For it, diagnostic tests are used.

  *(3) Prediction:* From the analysis of performance results or scores obtained by an individual on a test, his future competencies can be predicted *e.g.,*

  . If the achievement of a pupil in mathematics is excellent, then on this criterion it can be predicted that he should also be good in engineering.

- As an aid to more effective pupil-guidance, tests have been used to analyse present status of mastery and to predict possible future achievement.
  - Such tests should be provided —
    (1) to measure mechanical ability and functional information.
    (2) to make inquiry into pupils' intelligence, aptitudes, work habits and study skills.
- An inventory test is used for 'taking stock' of mathematical information and ability.
  - It should show what a pupil knows about a particular topic.
  - Skillfully used seasonal inventory tests —
    (1) will prevent a good deal of unnecessary repetition of experience on the part of the pupil and waste of effort on the part of teacher.
    (2) will bring to light the pupils' background for the study of new units and this aid in the guidance programme.
- The construction of an inventory test on a unit of instruction is not essentially different from the construction of a final achievement test on the same unit.
  - The use of two such comparable tests, one before and the other after the teaching of the units will serve as a good indicator of the learning that takes place during the unit.
- Prognostic tests can be used to reduce the number of failures either —

  (1) by eliminating those who are unprepared or unable for any cause to proceed further with mathematical study, or

  (2) by providing a basis for the construction of a differential mathematical curriculum.
- Prognostic test should also serve as an aid in the vocational and educational guidance of pupils and in the better classification of pupils.
- The discovery of superior ability and unusual aptitude in mathematics is just as important a function of prognosis as is the discovery of the inferior or average.

- For the construction of efficient prognostic tests in mathematics, the teacher should be familiar with those abilities and interests essential to further progress.
  - Mathematical tests which are to be used as an aid in vocational guidance, should be based on a knowledge of those mathematical skills, concepts and principles incident to success in any chosen vocation.
  - The general characteristics of comprehensiveness, discriminative power, reliability, validity, balance and flexibility must be carefully observed in the framing and organisation of the test-items.

## EVALUATE YOURSELF

1. What is meant by backwardness in mathematics? How will you identify such children in mathematics class?
2. Explain the causes of backwardness in mathematics followed by remedial tasks.
3. What is diagnostic evaluation? Bring out the characteristics of an efficient programme of diagnosis.
4. How should be the remedial programme most effective?
5. Write short notes on:
   (1) Self diagnosis by pupils (2) Prognosis and guidance.
6. Explain the term 'prognosis'. Also, explain the tests used as an aid to more effective pupil-guidance.
7. Suggest the ways employed for removing the backwardness in mathematics.
8. 'Backwardness in Mathematics is not always due to low IQ of a pupil.' — Comment.
9. Suggest diagnosis and remedial measures for the pupils who repeatedly commit the following mistakes:

   (1) $a^5 \times a^3 = a^{15}$ (2) $51^\circ = 51$ (3) $\frac{3}{4}+\frac{1}{5}+\frac{4}{8}=\frac{8}{17}$

   (4) $4-\frac{1}{5}=\frac{3}{5}$ (5) $2a - 5 = \frac{a+5}{2}$ (6) $3m - 4 = 3(m-4)$

* * *

# UNIT PLANNING AND DAILY LESSON PLANNING IN MATH

## 22.1 The Unit

- A unit may be defined as a large subdivision of the subject matter wherein a principle or a topic or a property is at the centre of the well-organised matter.
  - The teacher may combine the different alike topics of the syllabus for the formation of units. *e.g.*,

(1) Area of all types of regular-shaped bodies and geometrical figures.

(2) Volume of all types of regular-shaped bodies and geometrical figures can make a unit.

  - He may formulate the units on the basis of similarity/symmetry observed in the structure, principles and system of mathematics.
  - The following can make a unit:

    (1) Number systems and its expansion.

    (2) Measurement systems (lengths, weight, capacity, coinage, etc.).

    (3) Decimal system and its addition, subtraction, multiplication and division.

    (4) Equations — simple, linear, simultaneous, quadratic.

    (5) Trigonometrical ratios and functions.

    (6) Co-ordinate geometry.

  - While forming units, a mathematics teacher should note the following points:

    (*a*) Total days and working hours available for the teaching of mathematics in a particular grade.

    (*b*) The completeness and meaningfulness of the units formulated in terms of some special purpose or objectives achieved.

(*c*) Suitability in terms of the —

(*i*) age, interest, needs and abilities of the learners.

(*ii*) resources and teaching-learning conditions available for the teaching-learning of units.

(*d*) The proper division of the whole syllabus in view of the total time and resources available.

(*e*) The proper integration and correlation of the content and learning experiences available within the units themselves.

(*f*) The proper correlation, co-ordination and integration among the different units formulated out of the prescribed syllabus for the needed continuity and convenience.

## 22.2 The Unit Planning

- Planning is a must for the successful execution of a task/project.
  - It caters the proper achievement of the aim and purposes of doing that task.
  - It also helps in proper utilisation of the time and energy on the part of human resources as well as material resources.
  - The teachers who plan their work properly prove quite effective in teaching mathematics.
  - A mathematics teacher may have three types of schemes for such planning:
    (*a*) Yearly planning (*b*) Unit planning (*c*) Daily lesson planning.
  - Unit planning stands for the planning for the instructional work of the session by dividing the prescribed syllabus into some well-defined and meaningful units.
  - While planning a unit, the following factors should be kept in mind:
    1. Objectives with specifications (the *why* aspect of the unit);
    2. Content analysis (the *what* aspect of the unit);
    3. Learning activities (the *how* aspect of the unit);
    4. Testing procedure (evidence of achievement).

These four factors are the successive steps in unit planning.

- After organising the subject matter and learning experiences in some complete and meaningful units, the further work of planning is undertaken in the following ways:
  1. Unit should be divided into suitable sub-units. A sub-unit should contain that much of the content and learning experiences which can be covered within a period of 35 or 40 min.
  2. Objectives related to the teaching and learning of the unit should be pre-determined and be expressed into behavioural terms.
  3. Proper discussions should be held about —
     (*a*) the methods and techniques used.
     (*b*) AV aids and other teaching material utilised.
     (*c*) teaching-learning experiences given for the realisation of the set objectives.

(*d*) the type of interactions among the teacher and pupils and the role played by them in performing the various activities during the teaching-learning process.

(*e*) the evaluation of teaching and learning of the unit covered. Desired unit test should be prepared beforehand.

(*f*) the time and resources needed for the administration of unit test should be well-decided.

## Advantages of Unit Planning

1. It helps (*i*) in the proper coverage of the syllabus of mathematics within the available time and duration of the session.
   (*ii*) the proper organisation and systematisation of the teaching-learning process.
   (*iii*) in the proper evaluation of the teaching-learning task.
2. It makes —
   (*i*) the teacher and pupils both clear about their functions and goals.
   (*ii*) the task of teaching-learning quite interesting and absorbing.
3. It leaves no scope for the problems of indiscipline in the class.
4. It provides —
   (*i*) for the diagnosing the learning difficulties of the pupils and subsequent remedial instruction.
   (*ii*) for the review, recapituation, practice and drill work related to the contents and learning experiences relative to the sub-units.
5. The teacher can utilise proper methods, strategies and resource-materials for providing instruction.
6. It paves the way for an appropriate daily-lesson planning.
7. It proves quite advantageous both from the educational and psychological angles of the pupils.

## Limitations of Unit Planning

1. Unit planning makes the teaching-learning as planning-centred and not child-centred.
2. The division of the contents of the syllabus into meaningful and complete units and sub-units is a very difficult task.
3. Overloaded with teaching and other duties, teacher takes too little interest in the proper planning of the units.
4. While organising the syllabus into units, one has to set aside the logical and sequential development of the subject.
5. Unit planning may become an end in itself instead of means for the realisation of the set objectives.
6. It puts restrictions on the freedom of teachers. The set objectives, learning experiences, methods and resources, method of evaluation, etc. have little scope for originality and creativity of the teacher.

7. The teaching-learning process becomes too much time bound. Mathematics is a skilled and applied subject which needs a lot of exercise and activities for the practice and drill work.
8. It makes learning monotonous and stereotyped.

## 22.3 Approaches to Unit Plan

1. Herbartian Approach: Herbart stresses on the contents and information in a unit plan.
2. Dewey & Kilpatrick's Approach: They emphasise on the experiences of learners in a unit plan rather than information.
3. B.F. Skinner: He stresses on the modification of behaviour. He assumes that pupil learns better if the content is presented in small units.

### Daily Lesson Planning in Math

*What is Lesson Planning?*

- A teacher, while trying to perform his duties regarding the classroom teaching, has to pass through the following phases of teaching:
  1. Pre-active phase
  2. Inter-active phase
  3. Post-active phase.
- Planning is essential in teaching as well as in all spheres of life. Pre-planning is essential for quality teaching.
  - Every teacher who intends to teach something meaningfully, successfully and effectively has to plan an outline of his topic in his mind or in written form.
  - At cognitive level, the written form of outline of the topic is known as 'lesson plan' and the process of preparing it is called 'lesson planning.'
- Lesson planning means the planning of daily lesson related with the particular unit of mathematics to be covered in a specific school period for the realisation of some stipulated instructional objectives.
- The origin of lesson plan is from Gestalt psychology.
  - 'Gestalt Theory of Learning' has a great influence on human learning.
  - According to this theory, the learner perceives a thing or a problem or a situation as a whole, *i.e.,* in totality.
  - Thus, the whole is perceived by a part and a part conveys the whole.
  - The meaningful activities are related to one another within a unit. So, lesson plan is a part of unit plan.
- A teacher has to create learning situations and organise them in such a way that the child feels the inner urge to know, to think and to do.
- In planning and administering of the lesson plan, a teacher has to apply the theoretical knowledge of the principles of education, teaching and instruction.

- A lesson is not mere giving of instruction or mere doing out of facts. It becomes an occasion for learning, thinking, understanding as well as judging.

- The lesson plan is a good servant but a bad master. It is a means to an end but not an end by itself.
  - A teacher should be able to discard his lesson plan if a sudden situation demands it.

## Definitions and Meaning

- Lester B. Stands — 'A lesson plan is actually a plan of action. It, therefore, includes the working philosophy of the teacher, his knowledge of philosophy, his information about and his understanding of pupils, his comprehension of the objectives of education, his knowledge of the material to be taught and his ability to utilise effective methods.

  Bining and Bining — 'Lesson planning involves defining the objectives, selecting and arranging the subject matter and determining the method and procedure.'

- Lesson planning is the progamme of the teacher which indicates the objectives, subject matter, learning experiences, AV aids, methods and techniques, etc.
- Before entering the classroom whatever activities are planned and recorded, may be put in the pre-active phase of teaching.
  - So, the lesson planning is the pre-active phase of teaching.

### *Need/Importance of Lesson Planning*

1. Lesson planning helps the teacher —
   (1) in maintaining the sequence of content while presenting it.
   (2) in relating the teaching activities to the learning structure.
   (3) in determining the suitable techniques, strategies, tactics and appropriate use of TA before the actual teaching.
      - It compels teacher to think about the proper use of adequate TA.

   (4) in identifying suitable places of reinforcing and controlling the pupil behaviour during teaching.
   (5) in evaluating his teaching.
2. It provides guidelines to the teacher —
   (1) to proceed systematically in the classroom teaching.
   (2) an immediate impetus to realise the aims and objectives and to perform his activities in the direction to achieve the objectives.
3. It delimits the teacher's field of work and thus enables him to define his aims and objectives more clearly.
4. It seems as a check on the possible wastage of time and energy of teacher's teaching pupils in haphazard manner. Thus, it makes teaching-learning a systematic, orderly and economical process.

- It prevents the teacher to deviate from the topic.

5. It has psychological basis. The apperceptive mass of the learner is developed or encouraged by linking the new knowledge with the previous knowledge of the pupils.
   - It establishes proper correlation between the new and the old knowledge.
6. It guides the teacher about *what* and *how* he must teach.
7. It stimulates the teacher and pupils to think in an organised way.
8. It develops —
   (1) self-confidence in the student-teacher to perform the classroom teaching activities satisfactorily.
   (2) the power of reasoning, decision-making and imagination.
9. The effectiveness of the student-teacher depends upon a good lesson plan.
10. The micro-lessons are helpful in developing specific teaching skills.
11. It inspires the teachers to improve the further lessons.
12. I.K. Davis — 'Lessons must be prepared, for there is nothing so fatal to a teacher's progress as unpreparedness.'

## 22.5 Principles of Lesson Planning

Principles of lesson planning are as under:

1. *Plan should be flexible:*
   - Plan should be concrete and specific but at the same time flexible too.
   - Pupils have individual differences w.r.t. their ability, experiences, interests, needs, attitudes, etc.
   - Necessary extension, revision, reorganisation, modification of plan is a favourable index of the quality of teaching.
2. *Plan should be specific in nature*
   - Plan should provide specific information as to how the teaching-learning process is expected to move ahead.
     - There should be specific provision for anticipated procedures.
3. *Plan should be realistic*
   (1) Planning should be done in the real sense by the mathematics teacher.
   (2) The level of educational development must be taken into account.
   (3) The amount of time anticipated should be carefully examined.
   (4) Teaching resources should be assessed carefully by the teacher.

### *Pre-requisites for Effective Lesson Planning*

The following are important pre-requisites/elements of effective lesson planning:

1. Teacher's mastery on the content to be taught.
2. Teacher's awareness of individual differences among pupils.

3. His ability of content analysis and that of identifying learning objectives in taxonomic categories.
4. His ability and skill for writing objectives in behavioural terms and for writing specifications using action-verbs.
5. His ability to select methodology, strategies, tactics and TA in view of content and objectives to be achieved.
6. Teacher's competency in relating teaching activities to learning experiences using appropriate communicating strategies.
7. His competency in (1) planning and organising the teaching activities, (2) reinforcing pupils activities, and (3) controlling pupils behaviour.
8. His skill for the effective use of blackboard in presenting the content.
9. Teacher's good knowledge and skill in developing pointed questions.
10. His ability in constructing criterion test for evaluating the learning outcomes of pupils.
11. Teacher's impressive and effective personality and sympathetic attitude towards students.

## 22.6 Evaluation of A Good Lesson Plan

A good lesson plan possesses some essential qualities which can be taken as the criteria of its evaluation. Main characteristics of a good lesson plan are as under:

1. A good lesson plan should be flexible, specific in nature and realistic and not too rigid and mechanical.
2. It should be based on the background of the class.
3. The content and TA should be well selected to suit the pupils.
4. A good lesson plan should preferably be written and not oral or mental.
5. The objectives and specifications to be achieved must be clearly stated.
6. The lesson unit must be finished within the specified time.
7. Blackboard summary to be reproduced should be to the point and unambiguous.
8. The teaching techniques and strategies, questions to be asked, illustrations to be given and devices to be applied — all must be incorporated in the plan.
9. The psychological and logical units of planning should be well-sequenced.
10. Application of the concept or definitions learnt should find a suitable place in the plan.

## 22.7 Types of Lesson Plans

On the basis of realising objectives, the lesson plans may be classified into three categories:

### *(1) Knowledge Lessons*

The purpose of such type of lesson is to provide factual information regarding the content.

In mathematics, such type of lesson plans may be prepared for giving factual information, *e.g.*, Life history of great mathematicians, values of learning mathematics, etc.

### (2) *Skill Lessons*

- To achieve the psychomotor learning objectives, the skill lessons are designed. They may vary from learning elementary skills like speaking, reading, writing, minutely observing, etc. to complex skills like dancing, music, gymnastic exercises, marching, rifle shooting, etc.
- Skill is always acquired through the method of trial and error.
- Younger children like to repeat activities and thus they get mastery over the psychomotor skills.
- The psychological 'Law of Effect' has a great bearing on the learning of any skill.

### (3) *Appreciation Lesson*

- It aims to enable the children to appreciate beauty, to discover grace in performing any activity and to enjoy it. Thus, the aim of appreciation lesson is to develop affective behaviour of the pupils.
- Ultimately it results into balanced emotional life.
- The appreciation lessons are prepared for developing attitudes, feelings and values among pupils.
- This type of lessons are used in the teaching and learning of poetry, music, dancing, painting, even some prose pieces, etc.
- This type of lessons are seldom used in the teaching of science and mathematics. *e.g.*, Multiplication tables can be taken as a poetry in mathematics, formation of rainbow, mirage, etc.

- Virtually, each type of lesson includes cognitive, affective and psychomotor objectives. There is no water-tight compartment among them.

## 22.8 Main Forms of Lesson Planning

- There are various forms of lesson plans. The pattern/model of lesson plans differs from country to country and sometimes within a big country like India, too.
- The following three forms of lesson planning are most popular and are commonly used:

  (1) Herbartian Approach

  (2) Bloom's Approach/Evaluation Approach.

  (3) RCEM Approach.

### 1. Herbartion Approach to Lesson Planning

Accordiing to Herbartian School of Pedagogy, the five formal steps are as follows:

| | |
|---|---|
| (1) Preparation | (Introduction, Statement of Aim) |
| (2) Presentation | (Questions-Answers, |
| (3) Association & Comparison | Discussion Explanation, |
| (4) Generalisation | Blackboard Summary) |

(5) Application (& Recapituation) (Knowledge gained is used in new situations, Review Questions)

### Advantages of Herbartian Lesson Planning

1. It is simple and easy approach of lesson planning.
2. It is useful in the teaching and learning of all the school subjects.
3. It is the logical and psychological approach of lesson planning.
4. It includes the principles of learning.
5. It is easier for the students to grasp the new knowledge as it is based on the previous knowledge.
6. It employs the Inducto-deductive and Analytico-synthetic methods of teaching.
7. It is generally useful for realising the cognitive objectives of teaching.

### Disadvantages of Herbartian Lesson Planning

1. This planning emphasises teaching more and learning less.
2. It is highly dominated by the teacher. Pupils are mostly submissive.
3. It is so highly structured that it does not provide the opportunities for learner's creativity and originality.
4. There is no proper stimulation and motivation for learning.
5. It ignores affective and psychomotor objectives.
6. It confines the teaching upto memory level only.
7. Here, mastery of the content is the end and not a means to realise desired behavioural change on the part of the pupils.
8. In this type of lesson planning, there is no mention of objectives and specifications.
9. It is feasible only for knowledge lessons and not for skill and appreciation lessons.
10. Here, 'presentation' is the only main aspect of emphasis.

## 2. Bloom's Approach/Evaluation Approach

- This approach is a new innovation in the field of education, which has revolutionised the teaching, learning and testing process.

### Main features

1. This process stresses that education is a tripolar process.
2. It covers cognitive, affective and psychomotor learning outcomes.
3. The testing is based on teaching. Teaching and testing-both are objective centred.
4. The pupils' performances are measured in terms of learning objectives and not only in the terms of achievement of the content.
5. It includes the total behavioural change of the pupils.
6. It evaluates the teaching-learning objectives, methods and devices of providing learning experiences.

- According to B.S. Bloom, the three steps of teaching-learning process are:
  (1) Formulating educational objectives.
  (2) Creating learning experiences.
  (3) Evaluating the change of behaviour.
- Herbartian approach is now considered as out-of-date. Bloom's approach is in vogue at present in many countries.

## Formate of Bloom's Evaluation Approach of Lesson Plan

| Teaching points | Teaching-learning situations | | Blackboard work | Teaching Method & strategies | Evaluation |
|---|---|---|---|---|---|
| | Teacher's activities | Pupils' activities | | | |
| | | | | | |

### *Merits of Bloom's Approach*

1. It is based on scientific, psychological and logical principles.
2. The objectives are written using non-action verbs and specifications by using action-verbs.
3. The teaching activities result into learning experiences.
4. This type of lesson plan makes the teaching and learning purposeful and meaningful.
5. It has greater scope for the improvement and modification of learning experiences, *i.e.*, teaching activities.

### *Demerits of Bloom's Approach*

1. This approach is highly structured and mechanised. It does not provide sufficient opportunity for originality and creativity of the teacher and the taught.
2. Any teaching activity may confine to more than one domain. They are not exclusive to one another.
3. While writing objectives in behavioural terms, the students' mental abilities are not taken into account.

## 3. RCEM Approach

- This approach is developed by Indian educationists. This approach is suggested by Regional College of Education, Mysore (RCEM).
- In this approach, the design of lesson plan consists of three aspects:
  (*i*) Input (*ii*) Process (*iii*) Output

### *(1) Input*

- It is related to identification of objectives. It is termed as Expected Behavioural Outcomes (EBO).

- These objectives are broadly classified into four categories:

  (1) Knowledge (2) Understanding (3) Application (4) Creativity.
- The entering behaviours of the pupils are also identified.
- The sequence of instructional procedure is fixed using these objectives.

### *(2) Process*

- It is related with presentation of content/topic and learning experiences. Learning situations are created for providing learning experiences to the learners.
- The communication strategy and AV aids are employed for the effective and meaningful presentation of the content.
- The process also includes the techniques of stimulation and motivation, so that the pupils behaviour can be reinforced for the desirable responses. Interaction of teacher and pupils is also implied.

### *(3) Output*

- It is related with the 'Real Learning Outcomes (RLO)'. The change in behaviour is termed as RLO.
- Various measuring devices are employed for evaluating RLO. The measuring tools are developed on the basis of EBO.

## 22.9 Unit Planning vs. Daily Lesson Planning

| *Unit Planning* | *Daily Lesson Planning* |
|---|---|
| 1. It is meant for division, organisation and planning of the prescribed syllabus for a session | 1. It is meant for organising of teaching-learning in terms of a lesson to be delivered during a classroom period. |
| 2. Its scope is much wider comparatively. | 2. Its scope is comparatively less wider. |
| 3. Its duration extends to several days. | 3. Its duration is strictly limited to a fixed duration of a classroom period of 35-40 min. |
| 4. Its teaching-learning objectives have a quite wider coverage. | 4. Its teaching-learning objectives are strictly limited to narrower coverage. |
| 5. It gives birth to a number of daily lesson plan depending upon the number of sub-units. | 5. Daily lesson plan depends upon a single sub-unit. |
| 6. Content is grouped under the heading of terms, concepts, facts, principles, generalisations, etc. | 6. Content is presented in a form of teaching points and is serialised in a psychological and logical sequence. |
| 7. Learning activities are merely mentioned. | 7. Learning activities are shown in detail. |

## EVALUATE YOURSELF

1. What is a Unit? What is the Unit Planning?
2. Bring out the merits and demerits of Unit Planning.
3. Write short notes on:
   (1) Approaches to Unit Plan
   (2) Principles of Lesson Planning.
   (3) Main forms of lesson planning.
   (4) Format of Bloom's approach of lesson plan.
4. What is Lesson Planning?
5. What are the needs/importance of Lesson planning?
6. What are the pre-requisites for effective lesson planning?
7. Suggest the criteria of the evaluation of a good lesson plan.
8. Explain fully the types of lesson plans.
9. Point out the advantages and disadvantages of Herbartian Lesson Planning.
10. Discuss the merits and demerits of Bloom's approach.
11. Explain the three aspects of RCEM approach of Lesson Planning.

Education is a progressive discovery of our own ignorance.

— ***William Durant***

Educationis the manifestation of the perfection already in man.

— ***Swami Vivekanand***

# EVALUATION IN MATH

## 23.1 Concept of Test, Measurement & Evaluation

- The concept of test, measurement and evaluation is very old.
  - The origin of measurement may be considered with the development of human civilisation.
  - In physical sciences, the use of measurement is very old. While in education, the process of evaluation was adopted from very beginning.
- *A test* is simply a measuring instrument consisting of a standard set of questions for being answered by the individual pupil w.r.t. one or the other characteristics of his behaviour.
  - The use of the term *test* is only limited to the use of same or the other specific set of questions.
  - *Testing* is a process of making the pupils answer that set of questions.
- *Measurement* is one step ahead to the process of testing.
  - When the work of testing ends, measurement comes into picture for assigning numerical values to the test results.
  - Measurement is quite a broader concept. It does not necessarily rest on tests and testing.
  - Both testing devices (like achievement test, intelligence test, etc.) and non-testing devices (like observations, rating scales, etc.) may be used in the process of measuring a characteristic, *i.e.,* obtaining information in a quantitative form.
  - The measurement is a quantitative process while evaluation is a qualitative process.
  - In education, cognitive, affective and psychomotor aspects are developed through teaching-learning process. But only cognitive aspect can be measured by means of achievement tests.
  - It is difficult to measure the affective and psychomotor aspects because the measurement of qualitative variable is not possible.
  - So, the process of evaluation is more useful in education.

- Carter V. Good (1959) — 'Measurement is the comparison of a quantity exhibited in a particular case with an appropriate scale for the purpose of determining the numerical value on the scale, corresponds to the quality to be measured.

  Remmers, Gage & Rummel (1960) — 'Measurement refers to observations that can be expressed quantitatively and answers the question 'How much?'

  Mahesh Bhargava (1987) — 'Measurement is the process of assigning numerals to observations, objects or events in some meaningful or consistent manner according to rule.'

  - The measurement is limited to quantitative description (of pupils) expressed in numbers.
  - Out of the responses given by the pupil, the teacher obtains a measure/score, *i.e.,* a numerical value of the characteristic possessed by the pupil in relation to his performance in a subject of intelligence or aptitude, etc.
  - Each of the instrument like achievement tests, aptitude tests, intelligence tests consists of a standard set of questions needed to be answered by the pupil.
  - It does not include qualitative description nor does it imply judgement concerning the worth or value of the obtained results.
  - This can be summarised as — 'measurement is nothing but a process of quantification as precisely and objectively as possible.
- In education, only the measurement of achievement is not sufficient, but the evaluation of appropriateness and suitability of achievement of teaching objectives, the process of teaching, teaching methods and techniques, TA, curriculum, etc. is also essential.
- *Evaluation* is a quite comprehensive and broader term than testing and measurement.
- Carter V. Good (1959) — 'Evaluation is a process of ascertaining/judging the value/amount of something by use of a standard of appraisal.'

  Remmers, Gage & Rummel (1960) — 'Education is not just a testing programme. Tests are but one of the many different techniques such as observation, checklists, questionnaires, interviews, etc., that may contribute to the total evaluation programme.'

  Stufflebeam *et al.* (1971) — 'Evaluation is the process of delineating, obtaining and providing useful information for judging decision alternatives.'

## 23.2 Nature and Purpose of Evaluation

- There are three main steps of formal evaluation process.

  (1) *Fixing up the objectives:* (*a*) Fixing up the general objectives

  (*b*) Fixing up the specific objectives (specifications)

  (2) *Arrangement of learning activities:*

  (*a*) Selection of teaching points

  (*b*) Providing appropriate learning experiences or activities.

(3) *Evaluation*: (*a*) To know the changes in the behaviour of pupil.
(*b*) To evaluate on the basis of evidences obtained.
(*c*) To apply the results as a feedback.

- Evaluation is a comprehensive multi-dimensional and continuous process.
  - It also begins with the beginning of process of education.
  - Teacher evaluates the pupils during the whole year/session with the help of oral questions, tests, assignments, co-curricular activities, etc.
  - Besides such type of informal evaluation, periodical formal tests or examinations — monthly, quarterly, half-yearly, annual — are also given to asses the pupils' performance.
- Mathematically it can be said that —

  Evaluation = Measurement (Quantitative description of pupils' achievements)
  + Assessment (Qualitative description of pupils' abilities)
  + Value judgements about achievements and abilities.
- Evaluation is a comprehensive, multi-dimensional and continuous process.
  - It is a process of collecting evidences of behavioural changes and judging the direction and extents of such changes.
  - An efficient programme of evaluation consists in the continual appraisal of pupils' progress towards the attainment of pre-established aims and objectives.
  - Such a programme should be outlined in terms of significant instructional objectives and used for more efficient pupil-guidance.
- A careful analysis of evaluation programme — the technique used; the aims, objective and functions implied; and the interpretation and use of obtained results — is an accurate barometer of the fundamental philosophy of any curriculum.

## Situations of Evaluation

- The situations of measuring and evaluating the educational achievement and other related abilities of pupils may be as under:

  (1) During the classroom teaching.

  (2) At the end of daily teaching.

  (3) At the end of teaching of a unit.

  (4) Periodicals — monthly, quarterly, half-yearly, yearly.

## Preparation of Evaluation Programme

- In the preparation of an evaluation programme following steps should be followed:

  (1) Determining the objectives or purposes of evaluation programme.

  (2) Selection of suitable measuring tools.

  (3) Administration of measuring tools/tests.

  (4) Scoring.

(5) Analysis of scores and their interpretation.

(6) Application of results obtained.

(7) Retesting to determine the success of the remedial or modified programme.

(8) Making suitable records and reports.

## Teaching-Learning Process and Evaluation

- All teaching is directed towards bringing desirable changes in pupils' behaviour for their adequate progress and development.
  - Setting of proper teaching-learning objectives is required for bringing desirable changes in pupils' behaviour as a result of teaching-learning process.
  - As a result, suitable learning experiences in the form of subject matter and other practical activities are planned and organised with the help of proper teaching-learning methods, techniques, strategies, aids and devices.
- Teacher and pupils both strive hard for the realisation of the teaching-learning objectives by taking proper help from the organised learning experiences and methodology and strategy of teaching and learning.
- To know the desired outcome of their teaching and learning efforts and to what extent the stipulated objectives have been realised, appropriate scheme of evaluation is to be planned out.
- Evaluation helps in passing value judgements —

  (1) over the desirability and worthwhileness of the set objectives;

  (2) over planned and organised leaning experiences;

  (3) over methods, techniques and strategies adopted for teaching and learning.

Each one of them alone or in combination provides the basis for the selection and employment of various evaluation devices.

## Comprehensiveness of Evaluation

- Evaluation is quite comprehensive in terms of the employment of tools for carrying out its task.
  - It is not limited to the use of tests and measuring devices providing quantitative information and results. But it extends its scope for providing valuable qualitative information without using testing and measurement devices.
  - Thus, measures providing quantitative, qualitative or both type of information/results in a formal or informal way may be used in the process of evaluation.
  - Evaluation is more comprehensive because —

    (1) it goes beyond the state of presenting appraisal results in quantitative and qualitative forms by passing value-judgements over their desirability and worthwhileness.

    (2) the planned changes in behaviour of the pupils through a teaching-learning process or educational efforts may be well-adjudged in all the three demands of behaviour, *i.e.,* cognitive, affective and psychomotor.

(3) the value judgements may be passed about the desirability and worthwhileness of all the involved components of a teaching-learning process like suitability of —

(*i*) set teaching-learning objectives,

(*ii*) curriculum, subject matter and organisation of learning experiences,

(*iii*) methods, techniques and strategies of teaching and learning,

(*iv*) teaching-learning environment,

(*v*) efforts of the teacher and the pupil himself.

- Evaluation works as a driving engine and a controlling agency for the proper upkeep of an instructional or educational system by providing proper feedback to the input processes and output of those systems.

## Continuity of Evaluation

- Evaluation is quite a continuous process, because —
  1. during a teaching-learning session, a teacher resorts to evaluation of the performance of his pupils as and when he feels a need to do so.
  2. evaluation is intended to make value judgements over the results of a teaching-learning process.
     - The changes occurring in the cognitive, affective and psychomotor domains of the pupils' behaviour are non-stopping and continuous.
     - A teacher notifies these changes even through a simple observation or interaction between his pupils.
     - A teacher maintains continuity in the use of evaluation devices for keeping the teaching-learning process on a proper track for the proper realisation of the set objectives and also helping the pupils in his progress through feedback, according to their needs, strengths and weaknesses.

## Functions of Evaluation

The following type of purposes and functions may be served through the results derived from the process of evaluation:

1. Motivational Functions
2. Informational or Communication Functions
3. Planning Function
4. Decision-making Function

## Techniques of Evaluation in Math

A mathematics teacher may use so many formal or informal techniques for the measurement and assessment of the teaching-learning outcomes as given below:

### *I. Quantitative Techniques of Evaluation*

(A) Written Tests: (*i*) Essay Type Tests (*ii*) Objective Type Tests

(B) Oral Tests

(C) Practical Tests.

### *II. Qualitative Techniques of Evaluation*

| | |
|---|---|
| (A) Observational Techniques | (Tools: Participation charts, Checklists, Rating scales, Anecdotal Records, Cumulative Records) |
| (B) Sociometric Techniques | (Tools: Guess Who Technique, Nominating Technique, Social Distance Scales) |
| (C) Self-report Techniques | (Tools: Interview, Inventories or Questionnaires, Attitude Scales) |
| (D) Projective Techniques | (Tools: Sentence completion, Perception of ink-blots, Interpretation of pictures, Draw-a-person Test) |

## Selection of Appropriate Evaluation Technique

- The decision about adopting a particular evaluation technique or combination of techniques depends upon so many factors, such as —
  (1) Objectives of teaching and learning.
  (2) Content or the learning experiences provided to the learner.
  (3) Methodologies and strategies for carrying out the teaching-learning process.
  (4) The behavioural domain, in which behavioural changes are to be measured and assessed.
  (5) The purposes like diagnostic, formative or summative, or providing information, feedback, incentive, etc., served by the evaluation.
  (6) Emphasis of mastery learning, required level of performance or reliable comparability and grading, etc.
  (7) The level, memory, understanding, reflective of the organisation of teaching and learning.
  (8) The nature of the evaluation technique(s), suitable for serving some particular or required purposes.

## 23.3 Improving the Evaluation Programme/System

- Effective controlling of teaching-learning demands effective measures of evaluation.
  - The effective measures should be sufficiently reliable, valid, objective, comprehensive, diagnostic, formative, summative and practicable.
  - Some significant measures for improving the evaluation system are suggested below:
    1. Construction of the evaluation techniques in the light of the clearly defined behavioural objectives and the learning experiences provided to the learners.
    2. Measurement and assessment of the total changes in the behaviour of the pupils falling in all the three domains.

3. Giving place to all the three types of questions (essay, objective and short answer) in the setting of the written question paper.
4. Bringing improvement in the —
   (*a*) construction of essay type, short answer type and projective type questions.
   (*b*) scoring and interpretation of the written answers of the examinees.
5. Holding internal periodical examinations and making provisions for internal assessment.
6. Maintaining cumulative records of the achievement and performances of the pupils.
7. Recommending the use of books by the pupils at the time of testing or examination and bringing sufficient modifications in the paper and testing procedure in the light of such concession.
8. Provision of Question-Banks.
9. Adoption of suitable 'Grade System.'

The last two provisions are quite innovative in their utility and application.

## EVALUATE YOURSELF

1. What do you mean by a 'test' and 'testing'?
2. What is 'measurement'? Support your answer by giving some definitions.
3. Describe the nature and purpose of Evaluation
4. Write short notes on:
   (1) Situations of Evaluation
   (2) Preparation of evaluation programme
   (3) Teaching-learning process and evaluation.
5. Discuss the comprehensiveness of evaluation.
6. 'Evaluation is quite a continuous process' — Justify.
7. Enlist: (1) Purposes and Functions of Evaluation.
   (2) Techniques of Evaluation in Math.
8. What will you keep in your mind while selecting appropriate 'Evaluation Technique'?
9. Give your suggestions for improving the 'Evaluation Programme'.

# 24 MICRO-TEACHING (MT)

## 24.1 Need of MT

1. The art of classroom teaching, in colleges of education, is poorly organised, improperly conducted and hopelessly evaluated.
2. In our colleges of education the traditional pattern of such student-teachers' training programme has resulted in producing incompetent and ineffective teachers who have no knowledge of latest educational theories.
   - This has resulted in a general belief that trained teachers are not better than untrained ones.
3. To bring improvement and innovation in the student-teachers' teaching programme, some alternate measures and techniques should be thought about.
   - MT is one of such innovations and improvement in teaching student-teachers in the colleges of education.
   - MT develops the desired teaching skills among student-teachers.

The term MT was first coined by A.W. Dwight Allen of the Stanford University in 1963 for developing teaching behaviour and teaching activities.

## 24.2 Definitions and Meaning

Many educationists have defined Micro-teaching (MT) from different angles. Some of the important definitions are as under:

A.W. Dwight Allen (1963) — MT is a scaled-down teaching encounter in class size and class time.'

Allen & Eve (1968) — 'MT is a system of controlled practice that makes it possible to concentrate on specific teaching behaviour and to practise teaching under controlled conditions.'

R.N. Bush (1968) — 'MT is a teacher education technique which allows teachers to apply well-defined teaching skills to a carefully prepared lessons in a planned series of 5 to 10 minutes, encounters with a small group of real students often with an opportunity to observe the performance on video-tape.'

McAlleese & Unwin (1970) — 'The term MT is most often applied to the use of closed circuit TV to give immediate feedback to a trainee-teacher's performance in a simplified environment.'

Clift & Others (1976) — 'MT is a teachers training procedure which reduces the teaching situation to a simpler and more controlled encounter achieved by limiting the practice teaching to a specific skill and reducing teaching time and class size.'

Passi & Lalita (1976) — 'MT is a training technique which requires student-teachers to teach a single concept using specified teaching skill to a small number of pupils in a short duration of time.'

L.C. Singh (1977) — 'MT is a scaled-down teaching encounter in which a teacher teaches a small unit to a group of 5 pupils for a short period of 5 to 20 minutes. Such a situation offers a helpful setting for an experienced or inexperienced teacher to acquire new teaching skills and to refine old ones.'

N.K. Jangira & Ajit Singh (1982) — 'MT is a training setting for the student-teacher where complexities of the normal classroom teaching are reduced by (1) practising one component skill at a time, (2) limiting the content to a single concept, (3) reducing the class size to 5 to 10 pupils, and (4) reducing the duration of the lesson to 5-10 minutes.'

## 24.3 Nature & Characteristics of MT

The above definitions lead us to summarise the following conclusions about the nature and characteristics of MT:

1. MT is a training technique to prepare effective teachers.
   - It is relatively a new experiment/innovation in the field of teacher-education.
   - It is not a method of classroom teaching like other methods such as inducto-deductive, heuristic and so on.
2. It is micro/miniaturised teaching which scaled-down the complexities of real teaching which provides —
   (*a*) practising one skill at a time,
   (*b*) limiting the subject matter to a single concept,
   (*c*) minimising the class size to 5-10 pupils,
   (*d*) minimising the duration of lesson to 5-10 minutes.

3. It is a technique of training in which a student-teacher experienced or inexperienced, learns the skill of teaching through a scaled-down process of teaching and learning.
4. It is highly individualised training device.
5. It permits grand and impressive undertaking of a high degree of control in practising a specific skill.
6. Here, the plan of teaching is focussed on micro-events.
7. It provides adequate feedback to the teacher-trainees regarding their performance immediately after completion of their lesson.

## 24.4 Procedure/Steps in MT

- According to Clift *et al,* 1976), MT as a training technique involves 3 phases:

1. **Knowledge acquisition phase:** This phase consists of two activities:
   (1) Observation of demonstration skill.
   (2) Analysis and discussion of the demonstration.
2. **Skill Acquisition Phase:** In this phase following activities are performed:
   (1) Micro-lesson planning
   (2) Practising the specific skill
   (3) Evaluating performance.
3. **Transfer Phase:** In this phase, the trainees are provided an opportunity to use the skill achieved, in normal classroom teaching.

In view of these phases, a standard procedure of MT conducted in the Colleges of Education consists of the following steps:

### *(1) Orientation*

- To start with, the pupil-teachers are given essential theoretical background about MT by having a fair and free discussion of following aspects: (1) Concept of MT, (2) Significance of using MT, (3) Procedure of MT, (4) Requirement and setting for adopting MT technique.

### *(2) Discussion of teaching skills*

The student-teacher develops knowledge and understanding by following aspects:

(1) Analysis of teaching into component teaching skills.

(2) The discussion of the rationale and the role of these teaching skills in teaching.

(3) Discussion about the component teaching behaviours comprising various teaching skills.

### *(3) Identification & selection of specific skills*

- A particular skill in terms of teaching behaviour is identified.
- After the identification, it is defined in the form of teaching behaviour for providing knowledge and awareness of teaching skill.
  - A teaching skill is to be practised by taking one skill at a time.
  - So, the pupil-teacher has to select a particular skill for practice.

- For this practice, he is provided processing material, chosen from the literature available with NCERT, Delhi.
- The pupil-teacher may be given a necessary background for the observation of a demonstration lesson given on the selected skill.

### (4) *Presentation of a demonstration lesson*

- A demonstration/model lesson for the use of the selected teaching skill is presented before the trainees by the teacher-educator.
  - It can be given in a number of ways:
    (1) By providing written material such as illustrations, guides, handbooks, etc.
    (2) By exhibiting a film or a video-tape.
    (3) By making the trainee to listen an audio-tape.
    (4) By arranging a demonstration by a teacher-educator or an expert.

### (5) *Observation of Demonstration & Criticism*

- In a demonstration/model lesson given by a teacher-educator/an expert the trainees are expected to note down their observations.
- What is viewed, listened and observed through a model lesson is carefully analysed by the trainees.
- Trainees are trained how to use an observation schedule, designed for the observation of a specific skill.
- On their observation, the relevant criticism takes place. This will provide feedback to the demonstrator.

### (6) *Preparation of Micro-lesson plan*

- Now, the pupil-teacher plans a micro-lesson. For that, he selects proper concept for the practice of a particular skill.
- Micro-lesson planning includes detailed preparation of micro-lesson plan, selection of media, preparation of teaching aids, etc.
- He may, here, seek the help of the teacher-educator or from simple lessons available in NCERT literature or from other books on MT.

### (7) *Creation of MT setting*

- Now, the proper conditions are to be provided to create appropriate facilities for practising the teaching skill. The standard setting for a micro-lesson, as developed by NCERT is as under:

  (*a*) Number of pupils : 5-10
  (*b*) Type of pupils : Preferably peers or real pupils
  (*c*) Type of supervisor : Teacher-educators and peers
  (*d*) Time duration of a micro-lesson : 6 min.

(*e*) Time duration of a MT-cycle : 36 min. This is divided as under:

(*i*) Teaching session 6 min.
(*ii*) Feedback session 6 min.
(*iii*) Re-plan session 12 min.
(*iv*) Re-teach session 6 min.
(*v*) Re-feedback session 6 min. (Total 36 min)

## (i) *Teaching Session*

- The pupil-teacher teaches his prepared micro-lesson for 6-7 min, in a micro-class having 5-10 peers or real pupils and a teacher-educator — all act as supervisors. They all have appropriate observation schedule.
- If need be or if possible, pupil-teacher may have his lesson taped on a video or audio-tape.
- The observations may be recorded on a video-recorder or on a CCTV.

## (ii) *Feedback for Evaluation*

- The greatest advantage of MT lies in providing immediate feedback to the pupil-teacher on his teaching performance demonstrated in his micro-lesson.
- It is possible to play back the recorded teaching.
- The trainee can be shown the AV (audio-visual) tape of his own teaching activities.
- This is followed by discussion so that appropriate feedback can be provided.
- During discussion a constructive criticism is made on different aspects of lesson presented by the pupil-teacher.
- The trainee becomes aware of his own teaching performance. This definitely provide positive reinforcement to the teacher-trainee.
- The mechanical gadgets like CCTV, video-tape, audio-tape, etc., are very useful in the procedure of MT.

## (iii) *Re-planning of Micro-lesson*

Getting feedback and reinforcement from the various sources, the teacher-trainee re-plans his micro-lesson.

## (iv) *Re-teaching session*

The revised lesson is re-taught with improved teaching to the same class for the same duration to practise the same skill.

## (v) *Re-feedback & Re-evaluation*

- On the basis of trainee's performance in the re-taught micro-lesson, the peers and teacher-educator provide re-feedback in the way outlined earlier.
- The recorded teaching is re-played back for evaluation and further criticism.
- Then, it is followed by discussion to provide re-feedback.

## Repetition of MT Cycle

This teach re-teach cycle is followed till the desired level of skill is achieved. This cycle can be shown as under:

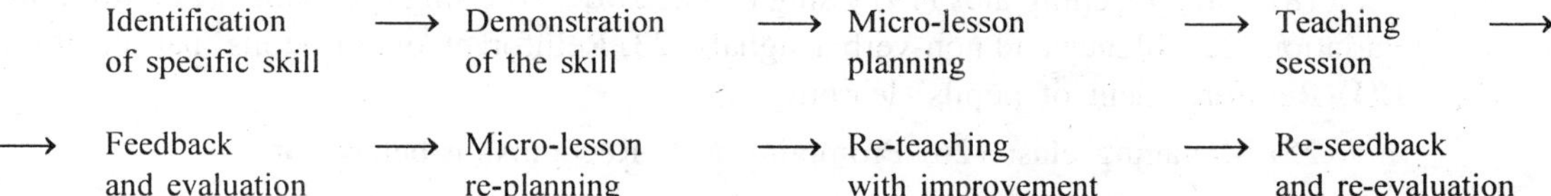


## (8) Integration of Teaching Skills

- The last step involves the task of integrating serious teaching skills individually mastered by a pupil-teacher.
- This helps in bridging a gap between training in isolated teaching skills and the real teaching situation faced by the pupil-teacher.
- Thus, the main purpose of MT is to provide training of teaching skills to pupil-teachers.

# 24.5 Identification of Teaching Skills

- Teaching is a complex skill comprising of various specific teaching skills. This view is considered by the analytical concept of teaching.
- (Definition) 'The teaching skills are a set of inter-related component teaching behaviours for the realisation of specific instructional objectives.'
- The following questions lead us to the identification of teaching skills.
  - What are these specific teaching skills that are associated with the complex task of teaching?
  - In how many components can the task of teaching be analysed?
  - What are those skills known as teaching skills that lead towards efficient and effective teaching?
- The research workers working in various areas have tried to identify several sets of component teaching skills. These areas are:

  (*a*) teacher effectiveness

  (*b*) analysis of teaching

  (*c*) psychology of teaching and learning

  (*d*) observation of teaching and that of pupils' teaching, etc.
- A list of stagewise component teaching skills is given below:
  1. **Planning stage:** (1) Writing instructional objectives (2) Selecting content (3) Organising content (4) Selecting AV aids.
  2. **Introduction stage:** (1) Introducing the lesson
  3. **Presentation stage:** (1) Structuring questions (2) Fluency in questioning (3) Probing questions (4) Using higher order questions (5) Divergent questions (6) Delivering questions (7) Distributing questions (8) Managing response

(9) Pacing the lesson (10) Lecturing (11) Explaining (12) Discussing (13) Experimenting (14) Demonstrating (15) Illustrating examples (16) Communicating (17) Increasing pupils' participation

(18) Using teaching aids (19) Using blackboard (20) Using text books (21) Stimulus variation (22) Silence and non-verbal signals (23) Reinforcement of pupils' participation (24) Reinforcement of pupils' learning.

(25) Managing class (26) Prompting (27) Recognising behaviour

4. **Closing stage:** (1) Achieving closure (2) Planned repetition, (3) Giving assignment (4) Evaluating pupils' progress (5) feedbacking (6) Diagnosing pupils' difficulties (7) Taking remedial measures.

## More about some Teaching Skills

- MT primarily aims at the development of component teaching skills involved in the complicated task of teaching.
- Each skill involves its own component behaviour.
- It is necessary to understand some important skills in detail. *e.g.*,

## I. Skill of Introducing the Lesson

- **Meaning:** Skill of introducing the lesson is — 'proficiency in the use of —
  (*a*) verbal and non-verbal behaviour
  (*b*) teaching aids and adequate devices for making the pupils realise the need of studying the lesson by establishing cognitive and affective rapport with them.'
- This skill involves the following component behaviours:

### *1. Utilisation of Previous Experiences:*

- The new learning is to be based on the previous learning/knowledge/experiences acquired through formal or informal education or direct/indirect experiences.
- A teacher has to obtain the art of utilising such knowledge/experiences. For this purpose he has to consider:
  (1) Ability of creating situations in the class,
  (2) Previous knowledge of the class,
  (3) The general awareness of the pupils with their physical and social environment,
  (4) Techniques, strategies and devices of exploring the previous knowledge.
  (5) Techniques of establishing link between the previous and new knowledge.

### *2. Use of Appropriate Techniques/Devices:*

- The teacher should achieve the ability of using appropriate techniques/devices for introducing a lesson. The following devices may be used:
  (1) Questioning (2) Narration, description, lecturing (3) Story-telling (4) Using AV aids (5) Demonstration/Experimentation (6) Dramatisation/role playing (7) Visits, excursions (8) Use of examples, analogies, similarities and differences, etc.

### 3. *Maintenance of Continuity*

- Proper introduction requires the continuity in the ideas presented to the pupils.
  - There should be a logical sequence between the main parts of the introduction.
  - One learning or statement or activity on the part of the teacher should lead to the other related ones in a chain of continuity creating the need of studying the lesson.

### 4. *Relevancy of Verbal/Non-verbal Behaviour*

- A teacher should try to observe relevancy in his verbal/non-verbal behaviour.
- Whatever the teacher states, asks, demonstrates, dramatises, illustrates or experiments should—
  (1) test the pre-knowledge,
  (2) utilise past experiences,
  (3) establish cognitive and affective rapport with the pupils,
  (4) make the pupil feel the need of studying the lesson,
  (5) pin-point the objectives of the lesson.

### Remember

A teacher educator or fellow trainees supervise the micro-lesson given by a trainee to provide feedback on the teaching performance.

For having better objectivity and reliability in the process of observation, an observation schedule-cum-rating scale for the skill of introducing a lesson, is used. It has two main columns as under:

| *Components* | *Rating (Extremely Poor to Excellent)* | | | | | |
|---|---|---|---|---|---|---|
| 1. Using pre-experience of the pupil | 0 | 1 | 2 | 3 | 4 | 5 |
| 2. Proper use of techniques/devices | 0 | 1 | 2 | 3 | 4 | 5 |
| 3. Maintenance of continuity | 0 | 1 | 2 | 3 | 4 | 5 |
| 4. Relevancy of verbal/non-verbal behaviour | 0 | 1 | 2 | 3 | 4 | 5 |
| 5. Overall impression about introducing a lesson | 0 | 1 | 2 | 3 | 4 | 5 |

## II. Skill of Probing Question

- **Meaning:** Questioning is one of the major devices used in any teaching-learning situation.
- (Definition)— 'Skill of probing questions is the art of response management comprising a set of techniques/behaviours for going deep into pupils' responses with a view to elicit the desired responses.'
- Its success lie in evoking desired response from the pupils.
- A teacher has to learn the art of managing the responses of the pupils using probing questions, for realising the teaching objectives.
- This skill involves the following component behaviours/techniques:

## 1. *Prompting*

- In dramatics, this technique of prompting is used by someone behind the curtain to help the character to speak the correct dialogue and demonstrate the desired behaviour before the audience.
- In teaching-learning process, it refers to the hints provided by the teacher through well-framed questions to the pupils for arriving at the desired response.
- The selection of specific prompts in a particular situation depends upon the factors like —
  (*a*) level of maturity of the pupils,
  (*b*) their previous experiences,
  (*c*) their ability to manipulate the relevant facts/concepts, etc.,
  (*d*) logical consistency of the response,
  (*e*) the desired responses, etc.

## 2. *Seeking further Information*

- Incomplete or partially correct responses require the technique of 'seeking further information.'
- (Definition) It is a technique of acquiring additional information from the pupils to bring his incomplete or partially correct responses to the desired response-level.

  The teacher can put the questions as — What else can you say? How can you make it more clear? Elaborate your response by giving more evidences, etc.

## 3. *Refocussing*

- This technique is used in a correct-response situation to strengthen the response given by pupils.
- Here, the teacher asks the responding pupil to provide a sound reason to relate his correct response in a more complicated situation or with something already studied. He can put the questions such as —

  How is it applicable to the real life situations? How does it differ from ...? How is it similar to ...? How can you prove it?

## 4. *Re-direction*

- This technique is generally applied in a no/incorrect/incomplete-response situation. For eliciting correct response, re-directing the same question to a number of pupils, is required.
- It helps teacher in probing by 'prompting' or 'seek further information' with the help of re-directing several pupils.

## 5. *Increasing Critical Awareness*

- This technique is useful in a correct-response situation to increase critical awareness in the pupils. Teacher can put the questions such as —

  How can you justify it? Why do you think so? How does it happen? Give scientific reason for it. How can one believe it?

**Remember:** Here also rating scale can be used as given in the 'skill of introducing the lesson.'

## III. Skill of Stimulus Variation

- (Definition) 'A set of behaviours for bringing desirable change (*i.e.*, variation) in the stimuli used to achieve and sustain pupils' attention towards the classroom activities.'
- A teacher uses an appropriate stimulus for evoking desired response.
- This skill involves the following component behaviours/techniques:

### 1. *Movements*

- Moving objects can capture more attention than non-moving ones.
- While practising the skill of stimulus variation, the teacher should make well-planned, meaningful and fruitful movements for —
  (1) securing and sustaining pupils' attention, and
  (2) bringing positive results.

### 2. *Gestures*

- Gestures are non-verbal prompts for action provided in the oral message given by the teacher for enhancing the value of his message.
- Gestures are usually made using the movement of eyes, hands, head, body, facial expression, extending the hand in a typical shape to indicate how big or small the object is.

### 3. *Change in Voice*

This attention-capturing behaviour of the teacher involves the art of bringing proper variation in the tone, pitch or speed of his voice.

### 4. *Focussing*

- The behaviours that help in focussing pupils' attention on a particular object/idea/rule/generalisation are known as 'focussing.'
- Such behaviours, generally, take the following forms:
  (*a*) Verbal statements *e.g.,* Look at this model, it is very important to note, it will be very useful to you, etc.
  (*b*) Gestures
  (*c*) Both verbal statements and gesture at the same time.

### 5. *Change in Interaction Styles*

- The communication process going inside the classroom is known as 'interaction.'
- This type of interaction has 3 main styles:
  (1) Teacher-pupils interaction: Here the teacher conveys and gets response from the class (*i.e.,* group as a whole).
  (2) Teacher-pupil interaction: Here, the teacher communicates with an individual pupil.
  (3) Pupil-pupil interaction: Here, the teacher employs many pupils in a dialogue without doing direct discussion.

- To bring effectiveness in his teaching, the teacher should learn the art of bringing variations in interaction styles.

### 6. *Pausing*

- It refers to the behaviour related with introducing silence during his talk.
- A pause of about 3 sec is regarded as quite effective in securing and sustaining pupils' attention.

### 7. *Audio (Aural)-Visual Switching*

- This behaviour refers to the introduction of the change/variation in the use of medium. *e.g.*,

  (1) from aural to visual; (2) from visual to aural, and

  (3) a combination of aural and visual.

### 8. *Physical Involvement of Pupils*

- It involves the introduction of variation in the types, forms and styles of the physical involvement of the pupils in the class.
- Pupils may be engaged sometimes in (*a*) dramatising, (*b*) singing, (*c*) reading, (*d*) writing on the blackboard, (*e*) participating in the demonstration or experimentation or (*f*) handling some aids or instruments or material, etc.

**Remember:** A rating scale may be used as is given in 'skill of introducing a lesson.'

## IV. Skill of Reinforcement

- (Definition) Reinforcement is the art of teaching the judicious and effective use of reinforces by a teacher for influencing the pupils' behaviour in the desired direction, directed towards maximum pupils' participation for realising the better results in the teaching-learning process.
- **Meaning:**
  - Reinforcement is a technique helps in influencing the behaviours of learners.
  - There are two types of enforcement.

    (1) Positive reinforcement, (2) Negative reinforcement.
  - *Positive reinforcement* provides pleasant experiences and contributes towards strengthening the desirable behaviours/responses.
  - *Negative reinforcement* provides unpleasants experiences and contributes towards weakening or eliminating the desirable behaviours.
  - This skill involves the following component behaviours/techniques:

    The first 3 are desirable behaviours and the last 3 are undesirable ones.

### 1. *Use of 'Positive Verbal Reinforcers'*

- They refer to those verbal behaviours of the teacher that bring positive reinforcement, *i.e.*, they increases the chances for the pupils to respond correctly.

- They may be divided in the categories such as —
  (*a*) The use of praise words like 'yes', 'good', 'very good', 'excellent', 'fine', 'right', 'well-done', etc.
  (*b*) The use of statements accepting pupils feeling, like 'yes, you have solved/judged correctly', 'now explain it in detail', etc.
  (*c*) Repeating and re-phrasing or re-summarising pupils responses.

2. *Use of 'Positive Non-verbal Reinforcers'*

- They refer to all those non-verbal (without using words) behaviours of the teacher which bring positive reinforcement.
- They may be divided in the categories such as —
  (*a*) Writing the response on the blackboard.
  (*b*) Using gestures and all other non-verbal actions conveying pleasant feeling or approval of pupils responses like, 'nodding the head', 'smiling' 'clapping', 'keeping eyes towards the responding pupil', 'turning ears' or 'moving' towards the responding pupil.

3. *Use of 'Extra-verbal Reinforcers'*

- This type of reinforcers fall midway between positive verbal and negative verbal reinforcers.
- They consist of such remark as 'hm-hm', 'oof', 'Aaah', etc.

4. *Use of 'Negative Verbal Reinforcers'*

- Negative verbal reinforcers refer to those verbal behaviours of the teacher that bring about negative reinforcement, *i.e.,* decreasing the chances for the pupils to participate in the classroom or to respond correctly.
- These reinforcers may be categorised as below:
  (*a*) Using discouraging words like, 'no', 'wrong', 'absurd', 'stop it', 'non-sense', 'totally incorrect', etc.
  (*b*) Using discouraging cues or voice toned in a sarcastic voice.
  (*c*) Using statements like, 'I disgust at what you are doing', 'I am fed-up', 'do something else', 'It is bad', etc.

5. *Use of 'Negative Non-verbal Reinforcers'*

- Negative non-verbal reinforcers are those non-verbal behaviours of the teacher that bring about negative reinforcement.
- The examples of such behaviours are frowning, raising the eye brows, raising the hand, disapproving stares, tapping foot impatiently, impatient walking, etc.

6. *Inappropriate use of Reinforcement*

- Only proper and right use of possible reinforcers bring encouraging results.
- The following type of reinforcers should be completely avoided by the teacher:
  (*a*) Using reinforcer when not needed.
  (*b*) Not using reinforcer when needed.

(*c*) Using reinforcers in a less or excess amount than required.

(*d*) Encouraging/Reinforcing only a few responding pupils.

***Note:*** An observation schedule-cum-rating scale for the skill of reinforcement can be prepared and used as given in the 'skill of introducing the lesson.'

## V. Skill of Promoting Pupil Participation

### *Meaning of Pupil Participation*

- A teacher has to play a leading role in an act of teaching.
- He has —

  (*a*) to provide information

  (*b*) to demonstrate relevant experiments for helping pupils to attain new knowledge

  (*c*) to build theories and principles

  (*d*) to learn practical applications of theories and principles.
- However, the role of learners is no less important. Actually it is the learner who has to learn and for whose learning, the task of teaching is performed.
- For the better and fruitful results, pupils' proper involvement in the teaching-learning process is quite necessary.
- This involvement/participation cannot be confined to merely observing and listening. It is the active participation on their part which is the most effective.
- (Definition). The skill of promoting pupil participation is an art and technique of managing teaching-learning situations including the behaviour of the participants in such a way as to maximise pupil participation.
- This type of observable behaviour involves the following types of pupils behaviour:

  (1) Pupil responds to what the teacher asks for.

  (2) Pupil contributes his own ideas related to the topic being taught by the teacher.

  (3) Pupil reacts overtly to other's ideas in the classroom.

  (4) Pupil helps in the process of demonstration.

  (5) Pupil tries to draw conclusions/generalisations.
- This skill involves the following components behaviours/techniques.

### *1. Creating set/mental readiness*

- The pupil should be made mentally prepared or motivated for learning the task in hand. This can be done in the following ways:

  (*a*) Telling pupils beforehand the topic to be discussed alongwith its main points and references.

  (*b*) Introducing the topic by utilizing their pre-knowledge.

  (*c*) Posing a problem/situation.
- When an unit or a part of it is over, the need of creating mental readiness for the learner of another part/unit may be felt. A teacher should always do it for the success of his mission.

### 2. *Questioning*

- Questioning is an effective technique for getting maximum pupil participation.
- For it, verbal or non-verbal questioning behaviour of the teacher is to be so arranged as to maximise pupil participation and minimise teacher's dominance/participation.
- The following type of questions are generally found to elicit greater pupils participation.
  (1) The questions that require longer responses.
  (2) The divergent questions which require more than one response.
  (3) Re-directed questions.
  (4) Questions requiring further information.
  (5) Questions for re-focussing/increasing critical awareness.

### 3. *Pausing & non-verbal cues*

- Pausing refers to a kind of deliberate silence, used by teacher while teaching.
- Pausing proves more effective for eliciting mere participation if it is accomplished by non-verbal cues (*i.e.,* behaviour that convey meaning without the use of words) like, facial expression, body/hands/head movements, etc.
- The use of this component behaviour may be found quite suitable in some of the following situations:
  (1) Re-directing a question to many pupils.
  (2) Maximising attending behaviour for seeking pupil participation.
  (3) Discouraging dominant pupils and encouraging the slow learners to participate.

### 4. *Encouraging Pupil Participation*

- For initiating and continuing pupil participation, it is necessary for a teacher to make use of the verbal and non-verbal behaviours for providing due encouragement to the pupils.

  Encouraging words/statements/gestures/non-verbal cues help in this direction.

*Note:* Observation schedule-cum-rating scale for the skill of promoting pupil-participation can be prepared and used as given before.

## 24.6 Basic Principles of MT

They are as given below:

1. Principle of enforcement.
2. Principle of continuity.
3. Principle of Drill and Practice.
4. Principle of microscopic supervision and observation.

### *Merits of MT*

1. It is a real teaching in its true sense.
2. It focuses on training for the accomplishment of specific skills.

3. It expands the horizon of normal knowledge and feedback dimension in teaching.
4. MT enables pupil-teachers to view their own performance and provides opportunities for making self-criticism.
5. It gives guidelines for improvement in teaching.
6. It permits concentration on some specific skills.
7. It provides immediate feedback to the teacher trainees.
8. It facilitates re-planning, re-teaching and re-feedback till the desired skill is achieved.

### *Demerits of MT*

1. It needs more time for training.
2. It is really a *simulated* technique for a small group over a short period of time.
3. It is an expensive technique as it is impossible for all Colleges of Education to make such arrangement like, video recording, MT laboratory, etc.
4. The teacher educators also need the training of its procedure.
5. MT is not complete in itself. It is useful only if it is used alongwith other techniques.

### *Conclusion*

1. MT is an innovative technique in the teacher education. It is a technique of training wherein one learns the skill of teaching.
2. It is a scaled-down technique which expects reduction in class-size, in duration of period and in the size of topic/content.
3. It provides immediate feedback for teacher trainees performance.
4. MT is a group of desirable micro-behaviours which constitute teaching skills.
5. Every pupil-teacher should give a few lessons using MT.

## 24.7 Simulated Teaching

- (Definition) 'Simulated teaching is a mechanism of feedback devices to induce certain desirable behaviour among pupil-teachers by playing the role of teacher in their own group as an artificial situation of classroom teaching.'
- Simulation is defined as — 'A role playing in which the process of teaching is inacted artificially and an effort is made to practise some skill of communication.'
- Simulated teaching is a teacher-training technique which modifies teacher's behaviour.
  - Simulated teaching is also known as 'Simulated Social Skill of Teaching (SSST)'.
- In simulated teaching the pupil-teacher and the students simulate a particular role and try to develop an identity with the actual classroom environment.
  - It is not actual teaching. Simulations are learning exercises that place the pupil-teachers in roles similar to real world roles and in playing the game that requires to make decisions as if they are parts of the real situation.
  - Hence the whole simulated teaching programme becomes training in role perception and role playing.

- It is the basis of sensitivity training, role playing sociodrama and psychodrama.
- In simulated teaching, a pupil-teacher plays several roles, such as teacher, as an observer (supervisor) and as a pupil.
- It is assumed that through role perception, the psychological appreciation of the classroom problems will grow and develop in pupil-teacher, a basis for handling the problems in the classroom.
  - The feedback mechanism is used for the modification of social communication skills of the pupil-teachers.

## 24.8 Procedure of Simulation

- According to Flanders, the procedure of simulation teaching involves the following steps:

### *Step I: Assignment of roles*

Letter A, B, C ... are assigned to each pupil-teacher in the group.

The role assignments are rotated by given letters so that each individual can get a chance to be an actor or observer.

### *Step 2: Selection & Discussion of social skill for practice*

The teaching skill to be practised is discussed and topics of conversation that suit the skill are also suggested.

### *Step 3: Preparation of work schedule*

After the selection and discussion of specific social skill, it is decided — who will intervene? Who will stop the interaction? When will it be summed up? Thus, the work schedule is prepared.

### *Step 4: Procedure of evaluation*

- In this step, decision regarding the procedure of evaluation is taken.
- It includes the type of data to be recorded, method of recording, way of interpretation of data, etc.

### *Step 5: Organising the first teaching session*

- Now, the first teaching (practice) session is conducted.
- The feedback is provided to all pupil-teachers who participate in the practice session for their performance.
- The session is followed by discussion and demonstration to provide feedback to the pupil-teacher by giving the awareness of his specific social skill of teaching.
- If necessary, the procedure of the second session is altered in order to improve the training procedure.

### *Step 6: Altering the procedure*

- After the first session, necessary changes are made in the teaching procedure. The topics are changed. Also, pupil-teacher, supervisor (observers) and teaching skills are altered to present a meaningful change to each actor to keep his interest as high as possible.

This cycle goes on till the pupil-teacher is trained in the specific skill.

## Elements of Simulated Teaching

- The process of simulation (simulated teaching) consists of three roles:
  (1) Pupil-teacher
  (2) Observers (teacher-educator and pupil-teachers)
  (3) Students (pupil-teachers)
- Cruck Shank considered the inclusion of three elements:
  (1) Diagnosis (2) Prescription (3) Evaluation.

## Simulation Games

- Simulation games are introduced for the purpose of introducing the elements or qualities of competition, co-operation and conflict as they normally occur in real life situations.

  Hoover (1980) has suggested the following steps in applying simulated games to teaching situations:

  (1) Identification of the problem to be used in simulation.

  (2) Development of the outline of the simulated games.

  (3) Identification of role players (actors).

  (4) Identification of game resources.

  (5) Playing the simulation game.

  (6) Conducting post-game discussions and analysis.

### *Merits of Simulation*

1. It establishes relationship between theory and practice.
2. Some serious teaching problems can be analysed.
3. It provides feedback effectively to pupil-teachers.
4. The pupil-teachers get the opportunity to play various roles.
5. Role consciousness is developed in pupil-teachers.
6. It is useful in research work.
7. It is a useful technique for slow learners.
8. It promotes high level of critical thinking.
9. It motivates pupils by making real life situations exciting and interesting.
10. It increases interest and enthusiasm of the pupil-teachers in the classroom.
11. It helps to modify teacher's behaviour and to acquire classroom manners.
12. It helps in creating self-confidence in teacher-trainees.

### *Demerits of Simulation*

1. Sometimes it becomes difficult to practise teaching skills for many pupil-teachers.
2. It is not economical with respect to time, labour and money.
3. It is difficult to play various roles by a pupil-teacher.
4. This technique needs much preparation. So, every teacher cannot opt extra workload.

5. It is a training technique rather than a teaching device.
6. It is quite possible that during an exercise, the observer may record incorrectly.
7. It may be more effective if used with other techniques of teacher training.

## Problems in SSST

Flanders has suggested the following problems in using SSST. The ability to —

(1) ask questions (closed or open type of questions)
(2) summarise what pupils have said previously.
(3) move the discussion to the next step in a logical sequence of problem-solving.
(4) use the ideas expressed by the pupils.
(5) make the constructive use of both the positive and negative feelings of the pupils.
(6) give reasons for the use of praise/blame.
(7) guide constructive discussions.
(8) assist pupils to compare consequences of alternate actions through speculation.
(9) Organise pupils' ideas in terms of teaching objectives. These are the same problems which are faced in simulated teaching.

- Thus, ST or SSST is a powerful technique in solving some of the problems of teaching. It can also help in imparting training of certain skills which are necessary for teaching profession.

## EVALUATE YOURSELF

1. What do you understand by the term 'micro-teaching'? Discuss its nature and characteristics.
2. Write short notes on:
   (1) Need of micro-teaching
   (2) Elements of simulated teaching.
   (3) Simulation games
   (4) Problems of SSST.
3. Discuss the general procedure involved in micro-teaching by giving outlines of different steps and activities.
4. What is meant by 'Identification of teaching skills'?
5. What is the meaning of 'skill of introducing the lesson'?
6. Explain the component behaviours involved by the 'Skill of introducing the lesson.'
7. What is the skill of 'probing questions'? Explain the component behaviours involved in this skill.
8. What is meant by 'Skill of stimulus variation'? Explain the component behaviours involved by this skill.
9. Define the 'Skill of Reinforcement.' Explain fully three desirable component behaviours and three undesirable component behaviours.
10. Describe the meaning, definition and components of the 'Skill of promoting Pupil Participation.'
11. State the basic principles of micro-teaching. Also, enlist the merits and demerits of micro-teaching.
12. Explain: Simulated Teaching. Describe the procedure of simulation.
13. Bring out merits and demerits of simulation.

❋ ❋ ❋

# PROGRAMMED LEARNING IN MATHEMATICS

## 25.1 Concept and Definitions

- Generally the instructions provided by a 'Teaching Machine' or 'Programmed Text Book' is referred to as 'Programmed Learning'.
- The meaning, nature and characteristics of Programmed Learning (PL) may be revealed by the definitions given below:

Smith & Moore (1962)— 'Programmed Instruction (PI) is the process of arranging the material to be learnt into a series of sequential steps, usually it moves the pupil from a familiar background into a complex and new set of concepts, principles and understanding.'

Espich & Williams (1967) — 'PI is a planned sequence of experiences, leading to proficiency in terms of stimulus-responses relationship that have proven to be effective.'

Jacobs & others (1966)— 'Self instructional progammes are educational materials from which the pupils learn. These programmes can be used with many types of pupils and subject matter either by themselves, hence the name 'self instruction; or in combination with other instructional techniques.'

Leith (1966) — 'Programme is a sequence of small steps of instructional material (called 'frames') most of which require a response to be made by completing a blank space in a sentence. To ensure that an expected response is given, a system of cueing is applied and each response is verified by the provision of immediate knowledge of results. Such a sequence is intended to be worked at the learner's own pace as individualised self-instruction.'

Susam Markel (1969) — 'It is a method of designing a reproducible sequence of instructional events to produce a measurable and consistence effect on the behaviour of each and every acceptable student.'

Gulati & Gulati (1976) — 'PL as popularly understood is a method of giving individualised instruction, in which the student is active and proceeds at his own pace and is provided with immediate knowledge of result. The teacher is not physically present. The programmer, while developing programmed material has to follow the laws of behaviour and validate his strategy in terms of student learning.'

N.S. Mavi (1984) — 'PI is a technique of converting the live instructional process into self-learning or auto-instructional readable material in the form of micro-sequence (the segments of subject matter) which the learners are required to read, make some right/wrong response, correct wrong responses or confirm the right response and attain the complete mastery of the concepts explained in the micro-sequence.'

## 25.2 Meaning, Nature & Characteristics

- The non-traditional device/plan for instruction in mathematics is the use of 'teaching machine' or 'programmed instruction.'
- PL is, in essence, some device which directs a learner, step by step and detail by detail through a planned sequence of steps or activities which will bring the learner to a point of understanding or mastery of that which was to be learnt.
- In effect, it involves a pre-planned sequential programme of detailed learning steps and a device which in some manner automatically directs the learner's thoughts and reactions along the channel which has been prepared.
- PL represents one of the effective innovation in teaching-learning process.
- As a highly individualised and systematic instructional strategy, it is quite useful for classroom instruction as well as self-learning or auto-instruction.
- PL occupies a unique place in the teaching and learning of mathematics requiring logical and systematic study coupled with independent practice and drill work.
- It is a sort of automatic self-teacher, containing within itself both — the substance of what is to be learnt and the sequential directions for learning it.
- PL is a method/technique of giving/receiving individualised instruction from a variety of sources like programmed text book, teaching machine, computers, etc., with/without the help of a teacher.
- In PL, the instructional material is logically sequenced and broken into suitable small steps/segments of the subject matter, called 'frames.'
- For sequencing a particular unit of the instructional material, the programmer has to pay consideration for the initial/entry behaviour of the learner with which it begins and the terminal behaviour or the competent which pupil is required to achieve.

- In actual operation, the beginning is made by presenting a meaningful frame. The learner is required to read or listen and then response actively.
- PI system has an adequate provision for immediate feedback which is based on the theory of reinforcement.
- It is the interaction between the learner and the learning material (*i.e.,* programme) which is emphasised in the PI. Here, the pupil is actively motivated to learn and respond.
- PL provides self-pacing and thus learning may occur at individual rate, rather than general, depending upon the nature of the learner, learning material and learning situations.
- It calls for the overt responses of the learner which can readily be observed, measured and effectively controlled.
- It has the provision for continuous evaluation which may help in improving the pupil's performance and the quality of programmed material.
- On the bases of the above features one may define PI as:

(Definition) — 'PI is a systematically planned, empirically established and effectively controlled self-instructional technique for providing individualised instruction to the learner through logically sequenced small segments of the content by using the principles of operant conditioning and schedules of reinforcement.'

## 25.3 Principles of PL/PI

1. *Principle of small steps*
   - This principle is based on the assumption that one learns better if the content is presented in suitable small steps.
   - Accordingly, while preparing a programme, the programmer should try to arrange the subject matter into a properly sequenced meaningful frames.
   - These frames should be presented one at a time to the learner for responding.
2. *Principle of active responding*
   - According to this principle, a learner learns better if he is active.
   - In PL, the learner remains active. He is actively involved in the programme.
   - The frames are so formed that the learner, without facing any difficulty moves from one frame to another. Thus, he remains meaningfully active and acquires knowledge in small steps.
3. *Principle of immediate knowledge of result & reinforcement*
   - It is a psychological fact that one learns better if he knows the result immediately after responding. In PL, after responding each frame, he immediately knows whether his response is correct or incorrect. Thus, the provision for reinforcement is always there in a good programme.

### 4. *Principle of self-pacing*

- PI is the technique of individualised instruction. The assumption here is that a learner learns better if he is allowed to learn at his own pace.
- Here, the principle of individual differences also gets fulfilled.

### 5. *Principle of continuous evaluation*

- For better learning, continuous evaluation goes simultaneously with continuous learning.
- The learner learns a little bit and is immediately evaluated. This is the best way for giving him feedback.

## *Advantages and Application of PL in Math*

1. PL encourages and helps pupils —
   (1) in all the tasks and aspects of education.
   (2) in assisting the teachers, pupils and educational administrators for playing their roles more effectively.
   (3) in the development of integrative, judgemental and creative learning.
   (4) in individualising the instructional process.
   (5) in providing scope of self-pacing which gives opportunity to the pupils for learning with their own optimum pace/speed without obstructing the path of others.
   (6) in the enrichment of curriculum and thereby in the education of the exceptional children.
   (7) in discovering desired concepts and relationships for themselves.
2. PL provides feeding material to the self-instructional devices like computers, teaching machines, programmed textbooks, etc.

   The use of such devices —
   (*a*) helps pupils in self-learning.
   (*b*) helps in revolutionising, developing and providing techniques of mass education and self-education.
   (*c*) solves the problem of paying individual attention and of trained and effective teachers.
3. PL can be advantageously used:
   (*a*) in situations where the class is large to be handled effectively with the help of available staff.
   (*b*) in small classes to be justified the organisation of the class.
   (*c*) in providing guidance and•remedial instruction.
   (*d*) as a supplementary instructional device in classes organised along conventional lines.
4. PL provides pupils with sound sequences of developmental exercises.
5. Through PL teachers may be freed from the hard labour and complexities of routine classroom activities.

   This may help them to bear a larger load of pupils and devote their time to more creative activities.

6. The social setting of the classroom may be improved and the problem of discipline gets solved automatically with the help of PL.
7. Through PL, the power of discrimination and that of making immediate and effective responses is developed.
8. Many complex behaviour and skills can be effectively improved and mastered through PL.
9. It proves an effective teaching strategy due to the following reasons:
   (*a*) Instructional objectives can be properly set.
   (*b*) Content can be thoroughly analysed and presented into suitable small steps (frames) and in logical sequences.
   (*c*) The learner is actively involved in learning. He gets sufficient motivation and interest by sustained attention.
   (*d*) The learners get ample opportunity for self-learning and for initiating his response and for self-assessment.
   (*e*) Feedback and reinforcement are adequately and meaningfully provided.
10. It encourages and help pupils to discover the desired concepts and relationships for themselves by providing them with sound sequences of developmental exercises.
11. It permits each pupil to proceed at his own optimum pace/speed.
12. It can be used in situations where the class is large to be handled effectively with the help of available staff.
13. It can also be used in small classes to be justified the organisation of the class.
14. It can be advantageously used as a supplementary instructional device in classes organised along conventional lines.

## *Limitations/Drawbacks of PL*

1. Once the course is programmed it is inflexible. It cannot be modified either in content or in emphasis without making a new programme for it.
2. Some courses in mathematics which have been programmed are very traditional in content and organisation. They do not reflect the spirit of modern mathematical thought.
3. PL makes no provision for —
   (*a*) the feedback and interaction between teacher and pupils and between pupils and pupils.
   (*b*) the ability to communicate understanding to others.

   Teaching machines and programmed instruction make no provision for these valuable interactions and make little demand upon the ability to communicate ideas.

## *Conclusion*

- Looking to advantages and shortcomings of PL, it seems clear that it cannot be dismissed lightly as a fad.
- It seems clear that significant experimental and commercial work on PL in mathematics is proceeding on an expanding scope and at an accelerating pace.

- Mathematics teaches should watch carefully the future developments in this field and be prepared to take advantage of such benefits as it may seem to offer for making their instruction more fruitful.
- In our country, there have been attempts for the use of PL especially in providing material to the students of correspondence courses.
    - Suitable self-instructional programmed materials for different subjects and grades have been prepared and is used for self-instructional purposes.

## 25.4 Styles of Programming

- In PL, the subject matter is presented to the learner in a systematic, suitable and meaningful form termed as 'Programming.'
- Different styles of programming are as under:
    (1) Linear (or Extrinsic) Programming (LP)
    (2) Branching (or Intrinsic) Programming (BP)
    (3) Mathetics Programming
    (4) Ruleg System of Programming
    (5) Computer Assisted Instruction
    (6) Learner Controlled Instruction
- The first three styles represent the actual basic formats.

### 1. Linear Programming: (LP)

- BF Skinner was the first to advocate linear programming style.
- This style is directly related to with his theory of 'operant conditioning.'
    - This style is based on the assumption — 'Human behaviour can be conditioned gradually, step by step, with suitable reinforcement for each desired response.'
    - As a result, here, the instructional material is sequenced into a number of meaningful frames. Each frame is presented once at a time.
    - The learner responds actively at each step.
    - Immediately after responding he comes to know about the correctness of his response. It reinforces his behaviour and motivates to learn the next frame in the sequence arranged. Thus, he attains desired learning experiences.
- The sequence of frames and of learning in the PL is linear and systematic.
- Here, all the learners have to proceed through the same frames and in the same order at his own pace.
- The whole instructional procedure is extrinsically well-controlled by the programmer, hence the name 'extrinsic programming.'
- It greatly emphasises in making errorless sequence of response. The steps (frames) are made so small and sequenced that learner makes only correct responses throughout the process and receive only positive reinforcement.

- The learner is not allowed to move to the next frame unless he responds correctly to the present frame.

### *Characteristics of Linear Programming (LP)*

1. It represents a linear arrangement of frames composed of a single track. *i.e.*,

   1st frame → 2nd frame → 3rd frame → 4th frame → 5th frame → ...

2. The learning material is presented into series of small steps (*i.e.*, frames)
   - So, the chances of an error in responding are minimised.
   - The learner is not allowed to go ahead unless he correctly responds the frame in hand.
   - As a result, this style moves slowly but steadily in leading a learner from initial behaviour to terminal behaviour constituting the path of learning.

   Entry behaviour —Path of learning→ Terminal behaviour

3. The learner receives inforcement for each of his response, as he comes to know the result immediately after responding.
4. All the learners have to travel on the same path, without changing the sequence, but at his own pace/speed.
5. The learner has to: (1) compose his own answer to each frame.
   (2) actively respond to each frame.
6. The programme is so made that the learner seldom gives incorrect response. So, he gets positive reinforcement mostly.

### *Limitations/Drawbacks of Linear Programming*

1. Linear programming restricts the learner's freedom of choice. Consequently, it results in inhibiting his imagination and initiativeness for creative, integrative and judgemental learning.
2. Its use is confined to limited topics in mathematics.
3. It makes the learning process quite uninteresting and dull as —
   (*a*) the content is broken into very small pieces,
   (*b*) responding is restricted and quite mechanical,
   (*c*) the learning process is quite slow.
4. It may encourage guessing and may obstruct real learning since the learner may get some clue for his responses.
5. It does not permit differentiation amongst answers. As a result, it is unable to develop discrimination power of the learners.

## 2. Branching Programming (BP)

- Norman A. Crowder (1954) developed and advocated 'Branching/Intrinsic Programming.'
- BP adopts to the students without a medium of any extrinsic device like a computer.
- In contrast to LP, the branching style provides an intrinsic arrangement in the sense that it is not controlled extrinsically by the programmer.
- Here, a learner is free to take decisions and can adapt the instruction to his needs.

## Basic Assumptions underlying BP Style

1. Learning takes place better if —
   (1) it is presented in its totality or in the form of meaningful components,
   (2) the pupils are made to learn on the pattern of traditional tutorial methods,
   (3) a learner is allowed sufficient freedom to take decisions for adapting the instruction to his needs and abilities,
   (4) each response is used to test the success of the latest communication to the pupil,
   (5) the testing is followed by remedial instruction.
2. Multiple-choice items help more in the learning process than the forced single-choice response items.
3. The basic learning takes place during the pupils exposure to the new material.
4. Wrong responses also indirectly help the learning of a correct response.
5. In the learning process, if errors occur, they may be immediately detected and corrected before going ahead on the path of learning.

## Procedure of BP

1. The instructional material is divided into small units called 'frames.'
2. In BP, each frame is larger (one or two paragraphs or even a page) than that employed in LP.
3. The learner, after going through the frame, has to respond the MC (multiple-choice) items given in the frame.
4. If he answers correctly, he moves forward, but if he does not, he is diverted to one or more remedial frames which explains the matter afresh, ask him test items to elicit the right answer, reveal his pre-mistakes and then return him to the original frame.
5. The cycle goes on until he attains the instructional material at his own pace.

### *Advantages/Characteristics of BP*

Advantages may be summarised as under:

1. The BP is based on traditional tutorial methods.
2. In BP, frames are larger, containing much information than those in LP. The programmer enriches his style, expand his ideas and introduces correct material in a better way.
3. The BP maintains the interest and initiativeness of the learner, through —
   (1) frames containing more information.
   (2) providing more freedom to respond.
   (3) giving scope of choosing one's own path according to one's needs and interest.
4. It provides alternatives in the form of MC items.
   - Like LP, the errors are not mistaken as incorrect learning.

- The BP makes intelligent use of errors in leading the learner to see for himself where he committed error.
- Then gives him opportunity to rectify his error and learn the correct things.

5. The programmed material in BP may be employed in the form of programmed text.

- In BP, the material when presented in a book form is called 'scrambled book' as the pages do not follow the normal sequence.

6. The BP helps —
   (*a*) in the development of the discrimination power.
   (*b*) in practising problem-solving ability and creativity.
   (*c*) in learning the skill of integration and judgement.
7. It is most helpful in the area beyond facts, definitions and basic skills.

### *Drawbacks of BP*

1. Guessing without understanding the content of the frame is possible in this style, as in this programme items are MC items.
2. It proves a difficult task to set appropriate MC items suiting to the whole material of the frames.
3. To cater to the needs and individual differences of all learners requires infinite branching which is impossible.
4. The cost of preparation of a programme in a printed book form is quite high as the programme needs frequent revision.

## 25.5 Comparison

| *Linear Programming* | *Branching Programming* |
|---|---|
| 1. B.K. Skinner propagated it. | 1. N.A. Crowder advocated it. |
| 2. Theory of 'operant conditioning' is at its base. | 2. Theory of 'electic' is at its base. |
| 3. Small steps but a large number of steps. | 3. Larger steps but a small number of steps. |
| 4. It is presented by simple teaching machine having less cost. | 4. It is presented by complicated teaching machine having high cost. |
| 5. It is presented by usual text books having pages in normal sequence. | 5. It is presented by scrambled book. The pages do not follow the normal sequence. |
| 6. Fixing of learning is the purpose of response. | 6. Measure of learning is the purpose of response. |
| 7. For incorrect response no remedy is suggested. | 7. Remedial instruction follows the incorrect response. |
| 8. Error rate is less, nearly 5%. | 8. Error rate is more, nearly 20% in general. |
| 9. Useful in lower classes. | 9. Useful in higher classes. |
| 10. Useful in realising lower order teaching objectives (Kn, understanding) | 10. Useful in realising higher order teaching objectives. |
| 11. Used for normal and less intelligent pupils. | 11. Used for talented and creative pupils. |
| 12. More useful in concept formation. | 12. More useful in concept comparison. |
| 13. Best used in teaching facts, definitions and basic skills. | 13. Best used in the area beyond facts, definitions and basic skills. |

## 3. Mathetics Programming

- It was propagated by Thomas F. Gilbert (1962).
- According to T.F. Gilbert — "Mathetics is a systematic application of reinforcement theory, to the analysis and construction of complex repertories (performances) which represent the mastery of subject matter."
- This style is quite helpful —
  (1) in learning difficult skills,
  (2) in shaping desired behaviour, and
  (3) in acquiring complete mastery over the subject matters.

### Main Features and Underlying Process of Mathetics Programming

1. A mathetics programming begins with detailed analysis of what is to be taught.
2. Here, an exercise is the technical unit of learning and not a frame.
   - No restriction is put on the size of an exercise.
   - Its size is not determined by 'breaking the material into small segments' but by determining how big a step a learner can reasonably take at a moment.
3. In this programming, each exercise assumes the reinforcement value of accomplishment.
   - Thus, a different strategy of reinforcement is employed than the immediate knowledge of results as in LP or BP styles.
4. This programming makes use of the technique of *retrogressive/backward* chaining.
   - A chain is a fixed sequence of responses to be emitted, *i.e.,* steps in division, how to wear a necktie, to find the square root of a number.
   - Usually in a chain learning, the mastery step is the final step, whereas in backward chaining it becomes the first step.
   - Regressive chaining consists of three basic steps — (1) Demonstration, (2) Prompt, and (3) Release.
   - As the mastery step is to be taught first, beginning is to be done with the identification of the mastery step (most often the last).
   - Then, the programmer supplies the learner with all the steps leading up to the mastery step and prompts him to perform the mastery step.
   - Now, the programmer supplies all the steps that immediately proceed the mastery step, prompt this step and release the learner to practise the mastery step.
   - Then he provides all the steps leading upto the step immediately proceeding the last sub-mastery and mastery steps.
   - The programmer continues in this way, each time the learner is allowed to perform one additional step until he arrives at the first step in the procedure and can perform the entire task.

*Limitation/Drawbacks of Mathetics Programming*

1. This programming is more technical in nature. It demands much skill, training and labour on the part of the programmer.
2. It is certainly not suitable for learning the material of all the subjects and for achieving all the instructional objectives.
   - Only concrete material and subject material involving psychomotor skills can be gainfully programmed by means of mathetic model.
3. Inadequate provision for individual differences. All have to learn in the same way. As a result, especially to the slow learners, to start with the teaching of mastery step or end behaviour often proves more overwhelming than challenge.

## 25.6 Development of Programmed Material

- The development of the PI material in the form of programmed text or computer assisted instruction, etc., is a highly specialised job, which involves the following main phases:

### 1. Preparatory Phase

This phase includes the planning of the programme. In general, the following steps/activities are to executed during this phase:

(1) Selection of the topic/unit to be programmed.

(2) Writing assumptions about learners.

(3) Writing objectives and specifications in behavioural terms.

(4) Writing the entry behaviour of the learners.

(5) Developing specific outlines of the subject matter.

(6) Preparing a criterion test.

### 2. Developmental Phase

This phase covers the actual writing of the programme. The task of programme writing involves 3 steps:

(1) Designing the frames.

(2) Sequencing the frames.

(3) Editing the programme.

### 3. Evaluative Phase

This last stage of PL material is related with the try-out and evaluation of the edited programmed material available in the form of sequenced frames.

The main activities undertaken in this phase are as under:

(1) Individual try-out

(2) Small group try-out

(3) Field try-out/Testing

(4) Evaluation

The result of Field Try-out in the form of data are properly analysed through the process of evaluation for testing the validity and suitability and improving the quality of the prepared programme. This validation is carried out on the following two fronts:

(1) *Evaluation measures based on internal criteria*

In these measures, the data of the field try-out are evaluated in terms of:

(*a*) Error Rate

(*b*) Programme Density

(*c*) Sequence progression.

(*a*) *Error-rates are calculated as below:*

$$\text{Programme ER (\%)} = \frac{\text{Total number of Errors}}{(\text{Total number of responses in frames}) \times (\text{number of learners})} \times 100$$

$$\text{Frame ER (\%)} = \frac{\text{Total number of errors made on the frame}}{\text{Number of learners}} \times 100$$

- A lower ER does not always ensure the effectiveness of the programme. It may be the result of an easy programme or excessive prompting used in designing the frames.
- A higher ER provides red signal to the programmer for making necessary modification in the programme.

(*b*) *Evaluation in terms of programme density*

- The computation of programme density helps in the measurement of the difficulty level of a programme.
- It is usually measured in terms of a hypothetical ratio known as 'Type Token Ratio (TTR)'.
- $\text{TTR} = \frac{N_d}{N_t}$ where $N_d$ = total number of different types of responses required in a programme.

  $N_t$ = total number of responses required in a programme.
- Since TTR is a ratio, its range lies between 0 and 1 (in reality between 0.25 to 0.33).

(2) *Evaluation measures based on the external criteria*

- Under this category of the evaluative measures, the programmer can evaluate his programme in terms of —

  (*a*) Criterian test (*b*) Gain ratio (*c*) Learner's attitude.

(*a*) The level of performance of the learners can be ascertained through the criterion test.

(*b*) The effectiveness of a programme can be properly measured with the help of Gain Ratio (GR).

$$\text{GR} = \frac{\text{Mean of post-test score} - \text{mean of pre-test score}}{\text{Mean of total marks of post-test} - \text{mean of total marks of pre-test}}$$

(*c*) For measuring learner's attitude, a 3-point attitude scale as *yes, no* and *?* (agreeing, disagreeing and cannot say) can serve the purpose well.

- The programmer then computes 'Attitude Coefficient' using the formula —

$$\text{Attitude coef} = \frac{f_{yes} - f_{no}}{f_{yes} + f_{no} + f_?}$$

where $f_{yes}$ – Total frequencies of responses marked as yes
$f_{no}$ – Total frequencies of responses marked as no
$f_?$ – Total frequencies of responses marked as ?

## EVALUATE YOURSELF

1. Explain the concept and definitions of 'Programmed Learning in Mathematics'.
2. Give an account of meaning, nature and characteristics of programmed learning in mathematics.
3. State and explain the principles of programmed learning.
4. Discuss the advantages and application of programmed learning in mathematics. Also discuss its limitations.
5. Write short notes on:
   (1) Styles of programming
   (2) Drawbacks of linear programming
   (3) Limitations of Mathetics programming
   (4) Programme Error Rate (%)
   (5) Frame Error Rate (%)
   (6) Type Token Ratio
   (7) Gain Ratio
   (8) Attitude Coefficient.
6. What is linear programming? Bring out its characteristics.
7. What do you mean by 'branching programming'?
8. Explain the basic assumptions underlying and procedure of branching programming.
9. What are the advantages/characteristics and drawbacks of branching programming?
10. Distinguish between 'Linear Programming' and 'Branching Programming.'
11. What is Mathetics Programming? Give an account of its main features and underlying process.
12. How will you develop programmed material? Explain fully its main phases.
13. 'Programmed learning has a wide use and bright future' — Justify.
14. How is the programme evaluated? Discuss various means of testing and evaluation of a programme.
15. Discuss the procedure of writing a programme by a programme writer.
16. Describe in brief the various phases of developing programmed instructional material.

Even the fraction of the Supreme Being is whole and complete by itself.

— ***Shruti***

# 26 A BRIEF HISTORY OF MATHEMATICS

- There is no exaggeration in the saying that 'Mathematics is the mirror of civilisation,' because history of mathematics is the history of civilisation.
  - Mathematics is the backbone of our civilisation.
  - It has led to the development of various subjects, vocations and techniques.
  - It has been a progressive science.
  - It is an exact science which is still playing an important role in the various walks of life.
  - It is the only best friend of knowledge of ideal systematisation.
- The studies reveals that simplest process of counting might have developed passing through several stages to present systematic level.

## 26.1 Value/Utility of History of Math

- In the curriculum, the history of mathematics has not so far been given its due place, yet it has its own value not only in the subject but in the entire human knowledge.
- Generally, the syllabus of mathematics is already heavy and lengthy, too. But alongwith other topics, the knowledge of 'History of Mathematics' is also essential for learners. It can be a source of interest and pleasure to the learners.
  - Its value/utility can be summarised as follows:

1. The History of Mathematics —

   (*i*) provides (*a*) a glimpse of the role played by mathematics in various walks of life.

   (*b*) a warning against making hasty conclusions.

   (*ii*) shows the correlation of mathematics with other branches of knowledge.

   (*iii*) makes (*a*) the teaching of mathematics interesting.

   (*b*) clear that mathematics is a man-made science.

Thus, its history may become a source of encouragement to the pupils to contribute something new to it.

(*iv*) reminds us what we have. It also teaches us how to increase our fund of knowledge.

(*v*) clearly brings out at every stage the fact that significant developments of mathematics is conditioned by human needs.

2. It is easier to understand most of the mathematical topics, concepts and terms w.r.t. their historical background.
   - Many mathematical topics can be introduced more effectively and interestingly in the class by discussing their historical background.
3. The history of mathematics gives better understanding of the subject.
4. It helps in gradation of the subject matter, the topics discovered earlier were simple.
5. The knowledge of history of mathematics enables the pupils to appreciate the progress of man over the ages.
6. The history of mathematics depicts the different stages in the development of mathematics throughout the ages.
   - It shows that mathematics is a dynamic subject, not static and it should be taught as such.
   - It also shows that mathematics has been developed in the framework of well-developed urban civilisation and well-organised economic conditions.

## 26.2 Gradual Development of Math

- In the history of mathematics, one would find some very remarkable developments in the form of discovery and evolution of certain ideas and processes.
  - These ideas and processes claim special status and significance in the overall progress of mathematical knowledge.
  - They are considered landmarks in the history of mathematics. They are —

    (1) Notation of numbers (2) Weights and measures

    (3) Decimal fractions (4) Logarithms

    (5) Computer mathematics.

### 1. Notation System

- The origin of notation system is as old as the man himself.
- Number sense is something innate in man.
  - It is believed that animals and birds also have number sense.
  - The primitive man was able to differentiate one object from two objects but could not tell one as one and two as two and one plus one as two.
  - The primitive man used various ways to count. He used fingers, knuckles of fingers and thumbs, notches, cuts on the trees, lines on the ground, pebbles, etc., for the purpose of counting.

- If a shepherd had to say that he had 7 sheap, he could tell it with the same number of pebbles on the basis of the principle of 'one-to-one correspondence, *i.e.*, 1-1 correspondence.'
- If someone asks you 'what is first-numbers or 1-1 correspondence?' Obviously, your answer should be 1-1 correspondence.'

- The number-system originated and developed differently in different countries.
  - In ancient age, Babylonian, Egyptian and Greek civilisations contributed in the development of mathematics, to a great extent.
  - In comparison to middle age, mathematics developed more speedily in ancient and modern age.
  - In Mesopotamia, the Babylonian mathematics originated with the notation of numbers.
  - The origin of number-system may be considered as old as the man himself because from the very beginning the man had number sense.
  - The number sense is as primitive as civilization itself.
  - At least as back as 3000 BC, Babylonians, Romans, Egyptians, Sumarians, Greeks, Chinese and Indians tried to develop some sort of number-system for expressing numbers of different values from unit-value upto hundreds of thousands.
  - Babylonians used wedge-shaped notations. 1 was represented by $\vee$, 10 by $<$ and hundred by $\vee<$.
  - The Roman system is based on the idea of counting fingers and lines. Thus, I, II, III represented one, two and three respectively. V probably represented the whole hand. To avoid clumsiness, IIII was represented by IV.
  - These notations gave rise to the idea of *positional value*. Thus, came the notations VI, VII, VIII.
  - The notation X was perhaps the combination of two fives, IX represented nine.
  - Hebrews and Greeks used letters of alphabets to denote numbers, *e.g.*, $\alpha$ for 1, $\beta$ for 2, etc.

## Hindu-Arabic System of Notation

- The present notation system 1, 2, 3, ... was originally developed by Hindus.
  - It was transmitted to the West through Arabs.
  - Arabs also made certain modifications in the Hindu numerals.
  - During 18th century the Hindu-Arabic numerals became popular in most of the countries, all over the world.
  - In the beginning, the notations as found on stones — for one I, for two II, for four +, for six 6.
  - The following notations were also in use at some other places:

    for one –, for two =, for four ±, for seven >, for nine ?

- In this way, large numbers posed a great difficulty in writing and even in reading. This difficulty was not overcome until Indian mathematicians appeared on the scene with their two great mathematical innovations, *viz.* zero and place-value system.
- By and by certain modifications and improvement were effected and Hindu-Arabic system assumed the present stage.

In European System : 1, 2, 3, 4, 5, 6, 7, 8, 9, 0

In Dev Nagri System:

In Arabian System:

- These inventions played a miracle by making possible the writing of any number, no matter how large it could be, with the help of only the numerals 1, 2, 3, 4, 5, 6, 7, 8, 9 and 0.

- The symbol 0 was used to denote *vacuum.* The word zero came from Arabic 'sifer (*i.e.* cipher)' which was translated into the Hindu word as 'Shunya'.

## 2. Historical Development of Metric System of Weights & Measures

- The history of development of the system of weights and measures is as old as the civilisation itself.
- In the beginning there were no weights and measures. There was no need of any currency too.
  - People used to exchange various commodities as and when they required such exchange. In economics, it is known as 'barter system.'
- In ancient time, various types of units were used for measuring and weighing in different countries. Even in the same country, different units of measurement were used in different regions due to lack of communication and exchange of experiences.
- Primitive man used different stones, seeds, etc., for weighing things. In India 'Rati' (a red round tiny seed) was taken as the basic unit of weight.
  - Masha, Tola, Chhatank, Seer, Mana — all these weighing units were developed on this small weight 'Rati'.
- An English unit of weight 'Penny', was considered as equal to weight of 32 wheat seeds.
  - The unit of weight 'Pound' was used by Romans.
  - At some places, the pound was considered to be of 13 ounces, at another of 18 ounces.
  - Thus, there was a lot of confusio in the system of weights and measures.
  - These weights and measures did not have adequate reliability and validity. They were not standardised.
  - Now-a-days one of the units of weight, in metric system, is 'gramme'. Gramme is further divided into decigramme, centigramme and milligramme. Gramme is multiplied into decagramme, hectogramme and kilogramme.
  - The weight of 1 c.c. (cubic centimetre) of water at 4ºC is taken as a 'gramme'.

- Various limbs of body were used by man to measure lengths. *e.g.,* span, cubit, pace, foot, palm, digit, step, etc.
  - In England, a *yard* was fixed as the distance from nose to the thumb of King Henry I.
- In 1960 the Eleventh General International Conference of weight and measures decided to have some uniformity in the system and adopted a system of units that includes the original metric units and various other units used in science and engineering.
- The scientists took the distance from the North-pole to the equator on a line running through Paris. This distance was divided into ten million equal parts and one such part was called a *metre*.
  - As it was not very accurate, it was given up.
  - Now, the metre is defined as the length of a standard bar kept in Parsis.
  - For shorter measurements, metre was divided by tens with the use of Latin prefixes as deci-, centi-, milli-, ....
  - Similarly, for longer measurements, metre was multiplied by tens using Latin prefixes as deca-, hecto-, kilo-, ....

    *i.e.,* 1 m = 10 decim = 100 cm = 1000 mm.

    1 m = 0.1 decam = 0.01 hectom = 0.001 km.
- The metric system of weights and measures are definitely superior to other non-metric systems.
  - It is easier to remember, use and calculate.

## Superiority of Metric units over Non-metric units

- The non-metric units varied from place to place and it resulted into great confusion.
- Metric system has brought about uniformity of measurement all over the world.
  - It has facilitated trade because the trades and manufacturers can deal and bargain on the basis of the same units as these are based on the scale of ten.
  - One who knows multiplication and division by 10 can very easily remember the units — bigger or smaller — of weights, length, capacity (volume), area, etc.
  - The scale of 10 generally facilitates calculations.

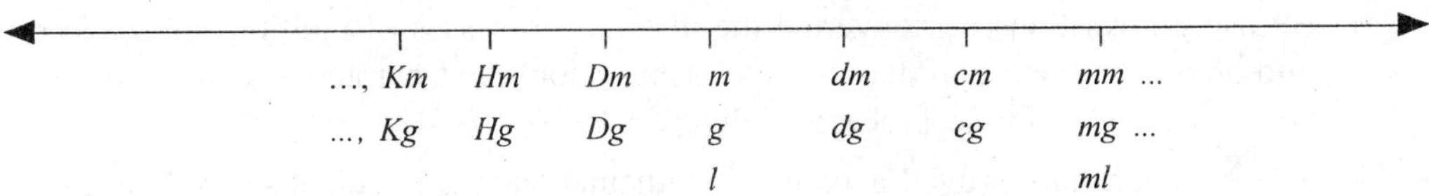


*Examples on conversion:*

(1) 4.5 m = _________ mm (Move the decimal point 3 steps to the right)

(2) 456.78 mg = _________ Kg (Move the decimal point 6 steps to the left)

## 3. Decimal Fractions

- Simon Stevin of Belgium originated the concept of decimal in 1584.
  - But the use of decimal point was invented by Napier, a Scotchman in 1617.
- In the 17th century, the decimal fractions were added in mathematical calculations.
- Government of India, for replacing non-metric system by the decimal system introduced decimal coinage in India w.e.f. April 1, 1957.
  - Rupee remained the same in value and nomenclature, but it has been divided into 100 equal parts called 'Naya Paisa'. Now, it is called 'paisa' instead of previous division of Rupee into 'Aanas' and 'Pies'.

## 4. Historical Development of Logarithms

- The word *logarithms* is derived from the Greek words *Logos* and *Arithmos*.
  - Logos means to calculate, to reason, to reckon. Arithmos means a number.
  - Thus, logarithms means 'calculation of numbers'.
- The wonderful powers of modern calculation owe their debt to three inventions:

  (1) Hindu Notation (A system of place-value with 0 as a digit)

  (2) Decimal Fractions

  (3) Logarithms.

  Lord Moulton —'The invention of logarithms came on the world as a bolt from the blue. It is a solitary exceptional mathematical invention that has resulted from the work of any one individual.'

  - Logarithms were invented by John Napier, a scotchman in 1614 after many years of hard labour.
  - He got the idea of logarithms from trigonometrical formula.

    $\sin A \sin B = \frac{1}{2}[\cos(A-B) - \cos(A+B)]$ in which the product of two trigonometrical functions can be expressed as the sum or difference of the other functions.
  - He prepared Log Tables by doing hard work for about 20 years.
  - By using logarithms he converted the difficult processes of multiplication and division into a simple process of addition and subtraction. And extraction of any root could be performed by a simple process of division.
- The use of logarithms proved a boon to mathematicians and scientists and saved a lot of time and energy otherwise wasted in longer calculations.
- To this invention, the famous astronomer Kepler remarked — 'Napier tripled the life of an astronomer.'
  - Henry Briggs, professor of Mathematics in London was so much impressed by this invention that he came to Scotland to meet Napier and discuss with him this new invention of logarithms.

- According to Briggs, Napier proceeded as below:

  log 1 = log $10^0$ = 0

  log 10 = log $10^1$ = 1

  log 100 = log $10^2$ = 2

  log 1000 = log $10^3$ = 3 and so on.
- Further he observed that (1) 1000 × 100 means simply adding log 3 + log 2.

  (2) 100 ÷ 10 means simply subtracting log 2 – log 1.
- Napier began to multiply, to divide, to square and to extract square roots of various numbers. He computed logarithms of hundreds of numbers and computed them to several decimal places and thus he prepared a first table of logarithms of numbers in 1664.

- The terms *mantissa* and *characteristics* were introduced by Briggs in 1624.
- The first table of logarithms of trigonometric functions, to the base 10 was prepared by Gunter in 1620.
- Gauss suggested the use of log-table for the fractional part of all decimals.

## 5. Historical Development of Computer Math

- Since the first acquaintance with the world of numbers, man has been trying hard to find out the possible means of computation with utmost speed and greatest accuracy.
  - In real sense, human mind is a great computer but it has also its limitations.
  - So, man has always tried to invent some or the other devices for enabling his mind to compute efficiently.
  - Electronic is the latest invention in this direction.
- The first computer used for computation was the use of fingers of hand and foot.
  - The second computer was the invention of 'Abacus'.
  - In China and Japan, abacus is still in use for carrying out the operations of addition, subtraction, multiplication and division.
- The next important development in mechanical means/calculation was that introduced by the founder of modern logarithms, John Napier, in 1617. He arranged a series of rods called *John Napier's bones*.
- In the modern calculating machine, the underlying principle is — 'all carrying is done by machine.'
  - This is achieved by mans of disc so arranged that the first has to turn units before it revolves the second one unit and so on.
- First mechanical computer based on such a principle was invented by Pascal in 1642 by attaching cylinders with the notched wheels of clocks.
  - Each wheel was divided into ten small divisions.
  - The system was so arranged that one complete rotation of unit wheel would turn one division on the tens-wheels and so on.

- Similarly with the complete rotation of tens-wheel, hundreds-wheel moved only by one notch.
- This process used to continue for all other wheels.
- Pascal used six cylinders in this first computer. Handles were fitted into these cylinders.
- It was an adding machine.
- Leibnitz introduced in this a device to calculate multiplication and division.
- The process of computation was carried out by moving the handles.
- Addition upto 1,00,000 could be carried out through this computer.

- The computer was developed from the calculating machines.
- Three great names of mathematicians associated with the development of computers are —

(1) Charl Babbage (1791-1871), Professor of Mathematics at Cambridge University. He invented a computer consisting of 18 wheels. It could compute operations involving numbers having 5 digits.

(2) Alan Turing (1912-1954), a logician mathematician of Britain.

(3) John Van Naumann (1903-1957)

## The Invention of First Electro-Mechanical Computer

- All the ideas that Babbage proposed to be incorporated in his machines are present in today's computers. Thus, Babbage can be rightly considered as the 'Father of Computers'.
- Turing did some very fundamental mathematical work in the area of computation.
- The architecture of the present day computers is the one designed by John van Neumann. To-days computers have only grown enormously in their capacity to store and in their speed.
- The Giant American Company IBM joined by the experts in Harvard university is credited for bringing the first electro-mechanical computer of the world known as 'Harward Mark I Computer' in 1944.
  - It was the world's largest calculating machine of the size 50 ft long and 8 ft height weighing 100 tons.
  - It consisted of 3500 parts in all.
  - It could add, subtract, multiply, divide and make mathematical tables.
  - It could collect 300 digits and used to take about 1/3 second in the addition of any two numbers.

## The Development of Modern Electronic Computer

### 1. The First Generation Electronic Computers

- The notable 'First Fully Electronic Computer' was developed by J. Presper Eckert and John Mauchly, USA, in 1946.
- It was named 'Electronic Numerical Integrator and Computer.'

- It required 3000 cubic feet space, weighed 30 tons and used 18,000 vacuum tubes for its electronic functioning.
- During the years 1946-59, it was labelled as 'First Generation Electronic Computer.'

## 2. The Second Generation Electronic Computers

- During the years 1959-69, came 'Second Generation Electronic Computers' in vouge.
  - They used transistor technology instead of vacuum tubes for electronic functioning.
  - There was a lot of improvement in these computers in terms of reduction in their size and weight, increase in speed and storage capacity, decrease in the amount of consumption of power and employment of high level programming language like COBOL, FORTRAN, BASIC, etc.

## 3. The Third Generation Electronic Computers

- The use of 'Integrated Circuits Technique' in place of transistor technique paved a way for the development of the Third Generation Electronic Computers, from the year 1965 onwards.
- An integrated circuit actually consists of thousands of electronic components like transistor, diodes, etc. on a single silican crystal.
- The use of such sophisticated technology brought more economy, speed, accuracy, facilities and enhanced utilities in the use of computers in so many ways.

## 4. The Fourth Generation Electronic Computers

- After 1965, came the era of the modern 'Fourth Generation Electronic Computers.' Actually, the application of micro-processor silicon crystal and large as well as very large scale integrated circuits paved the way for the development of these fourth generation electronic computers.
  - Now it is possible to incorporate millions of transistors into a single small silicon crystal. It will result into a quite drastic reduction in the size, weight and cost of the computers. Again, it will result into the increase in speed, efficiency and application of computers.
  - At present, we have computers with 16 and 32 bit micro-processors which have surprisingly reduced the size, weight and cost of the computers, alongwith an appreciable increase in their speed, reliability and applications.
- Specially in the late 1990's thee has been a tremendous growth in the manufacturing and technical advancement of the computers w.r.t. its use in mathematical functioning and business operations. It is also useful for all types of personal, social, cultural and global advancements.
- The present day computer technology has arrived at a quite advanced stage.
  - One of the modern computers 'CDC 3600' established in Tata Institute of Fundamental Research is able to perform 2,00,000 multiplication or division of numbers having 15 digits, within a second.
  - The developed electronic brain is able to solve in a few minutes, equations, which would take most brilliant scientist several months if not years.

- In our country, computer technology is growing fast day-by-day. Indian made 'IBM' computers help the country in its development in industry, agriculture, education, research and innovations, etc.
- Thus, we can conclude that a computer is basically a child of mathematics and mathematicians.
  - A very well-known mathematical problem known as the 'Four Colour Problem' which had remained unsolved for a very long time, was solved in 1975 because by then, sophisticated computers were in vogue.

## 26.3 Historical Development of Math in India or Vedic Math — A Historical Perspective

### What is Vedic Math?

- The mathematics that originated and developed during the Vedic Period (6000 BC – 500 BC) and the evidence of which are available in Vedic Literature is called Vedic Mathematics.
- With the sole purpose of helping students, teachers, parents, common people and people from non-mathematical areas of study and to discover the joy of solving mathematical problems, the vedic people invented a wonderful set of techniques called 'Vedic Mathematics'.
  - These techniques are derived from 16 'sutras' in the Vedas which are thousands of years old and among the earliest literature of ancient Hindus in India.
  - These sutras are all endless source of knowledge and wisdom providing practical knowledge in all spheres of life.
- In the studies in vedic age, vedic mathematics was given the highest position.
- It is extremely important to know significant glimpses of the contribution made by vedic mathematics to the world and the whole human civilization.
- The importance of mathematics is very much highlighted in Vedas, Upanishadas and other famous books of ancient times.
- According to the great Indian mathematician Mahaviracharya — 'In this whole world whatever thing is in existence, cannot be understood without the knowledge of mathematics.'
- Much before the European countries, India had acquired so many great achievements in the field of mathematics.
  - The Arab traders and those of other countries were used to come to India for business. They learnt many mathematical processes and methods and techniques which were commonly used in India.
  - The knowledge of Indian mathematics reached to European countries via media Arabian countries.
  - In ancient age, India was, indeed, knowledge-preceptor of the whole world in the field

of mathematics.

- The history of Indian mathematics can be well-studied by dividing it into certain time-periods as given below:

  1. Ancient Age — (*a*) Earlier Vedic Period (6000 BC – 1000 BC)
     (*b*) Later Vedic Period (1000 BC – 500 BC)
  2. Pre-Middle Age — (500 BC – 400 AD)
  3. Middle Age/Golden Age — (400 AD – 1200 AD)
  4. Post-Middle Age — (1200 AD – 1800 AD)
  5. Modern Age — (After 1800 AD)

## 1. Ancient Age

- In the history of Indian mathematics, the ancient age is very significant. In this age, the three main branches of mathematics — Arithmetic, Algebra and Geometry were firmly established.
- The ancient period can be divided into two time-periods:
  (1) Earlier Vedic Period, and (2) Later Vedic Period.

## [A] Earlier Vedic Period (6000 BC – 1000 BC)

- This period is remembered especially for its remarkable contributions in the field of numerical mathematics which can be summarised as under:

(1) Discovery of 0 and decimal system (*i.e.,* writing numbers based on 10 symbols (0 and 1—9) and place-value system was a great invention and Indian contribution to the world.

- With these 10 symbols and place-value system, any number can be expressed in a most elegant and simple way.

(2) The history of Indian mathematics starts from Rigveda. In Veda, number system, formed on the basis of place-value and decimal system have been clearly mentioned. *e.g.,*

- The use of word-numerals such as Dwadash (twelve), Trishat (three hundred), Shashti (sixty), Treeni (three) are examples of knowledge of decimal system.
- If 0, decimal system and place-value system were not invented, it was impossible to present and write numbers more than nine.

(3) More evidences w.r.t the use of developed numerals, place-value system and operations on numbers are well available in earlier Vedic literature.

(4) In Narad-Vishnu Puran, written by Ved Vyas, the following numbers have been mentioned:

Eka - 1, Dasha - 10, Shata - 100, Sahashra - 1000, Ayut - 10,000, Laksha - 1,00,000, Koti - $10^7$, Arbud - $10^8$, Abja - $10^9$, Kharva - $10^{10}$, Nikharva - $10^{11}$, Mahapadma - $10^{12}$, Shanku - $10^{13}$, Jaladhi - $10^{14}$, Antya - $10^{15}$, Madhya - $10^{16}$, Parardha - $10^{17}$.

- In this Puran, the operations of mathematics such as addition, subtraction, multiplication, division and operations on fractions, squares, square roots, cube, cube roots, etc. have been explained.

(5) While commenting on the development of mathematics of modern era, Jhunjhunwala (1992)

states — 'Hundreds of very practical and simple mathematical algorithms (Sutras) were created during this period, many of which are still in use at present. Most of these techniques and algorithms follow from a deep understanding of the place-value system in mathematics, linking back of the full Hindu understanding of the value of zero.'

## [B] Later Vedic Period (1000 BC - 500 BC)

### (a) *Period of Shulva and Vedang Astronomy*

- This period is also known as 'Period of Shulva and Vedang Astronomy'.
  - This period of Vedic mathematics is known for its development and contributions in the field of Geometrical mathematics.
- In this period, the more importance was given to the correct formation of altars (Vedi).
  - In the process of forming altars and their sub-divisions, various formulae of Geometry were developed and put into practice.
  - These formulae were termed as 'Shulva Sutras'.
  - The rope, used as a measure to prepare altar was called 'Shulva'.
- The main founders of Shulva Sutras were Baudhayan (1000 BC), Aapstamb and Katyayan.
  - The world famous Pythagoras Theorem of present time was mentioned in Shulva-Sutra developed by Baudhayan.
  - He had given the method of constructing a square equal to the sum and difference of the two other squares and found the value of $\sqrt{2}$ upto five decimal points.

    *e.g.* $3^2 = 5^2 - 4^2$ *i.e.* $5^2 = 3^2 + 4^2$

    $5^2 = 13^2 - 12^2$ *i.e.* $13^2 = 5^2 + 12^2$
- Astronomy was also progressed in this age, to determine the appropriate and correct time for performing the 'yajna'. so this period is also known as 'Vedang Astronomy Age'.
- Baudhayan was a very well-known mathematician of this age.
- Baudhayan's Sutras displays an understanding of basic geometric shapes and techniques of converting one geometric shape to another of equivalent/multiple/fractional area.
- Shulva Sutras contain geometric solution of a linear equation in a single unknown quantity, and also the solution of quadratic equations.

### (b) *Period of Surya Pragyapati (500 BC)*

- Surya Pragyapati and Chandra Pragyapati are well-known books of Jain religion. In the literature of Jainism, mathematical principles have been explained.
  - In Surya Pragyapati the concept of ellipse (oval shape) has been clearly described.
- There is significant contribution of Jain thinkers in the development of mathematics and astronomy.
  - The examples of permutation and combination, logarithms, set theory, etc. are found in Jain's religious books.
  - This indicates that logarithms was invented by Indian mathematicians long before than

Napier (1550 AD - 1617 AD).

- The knowledge of mathematics was highlighted in the literature of Buddhism. In this literature, mathematics is divided into two parts:

  (1) Computation (General mathematics), (2) Numbers (Higher mathematics).

  - The number has been described in three forms: countable, uncountable and infinite.
  - This shows that Indian thinkers had the idea of the concept of infinity.

## 2. Pre-Middle Age (500 BC - 400 AD)

- The famous books of this period are: (1) Vakshali Ganit (2) Surya Siddhanta, and (3) Ganitanuyoga.
  - Only few pages of these books are available now.
- In Vakshali Ganit, the fundamental operations of Arithmetic, Decimal system of writing the numbers, squares, cubes, rule of false positions, questions related to sale and purchase, etc., is described in detail.
  - Evidences show that this book had been written about 300 BC.
  - In this book, permutation (bhanga) and combination (vikalpa) is mentioned.
- In Vakshali Ganit, alphabets of Sanskrit were used in place of numbers 1, 2, 3, ..., as unknown figures.
  - It has been termed as 'Ishta Karma (Rule of false position). This rule of false position is considered by mathematicians as the primeval source of extention of Algebra.
- In Surya Siddhant, present Trigonometry is described. The sinc (Zya), Inverse sine (utkram zya) and cosine (kotizya) are mentioned.
  - Thus, one can say that Indian mathematics has a significant contribution in the development of Trigo.
  - Indian mathematicians used this knowledge to determine the position and speed of planets.
- In this period, the use of Algebra had got a wide extention.
- In the pages of Ganitanuyoga, the Laws of Indices in Algebra are given in this form:

First square of x = $(x^2)^1 = x^2$ First root of x = $\sqrt{x} = x^{\frac{1}{2}}$

Second square of x = $(x^2)^2 = x^4$ Second root of x = $\sqrt{\sqrt{x}} = x^{\frac{1}{4}}$

Third square of x = $(x^2)^3 = x^6$ *n*th root of x = $\sqrt[n]{x} = x^{\frac{1}{n}}$

*n*th square of x = $(x^2)^n = x^{2n}$

- It reveals that Indian mathematicians were using and extending the knowledge of Algebra.
  - Like Arithmetic, the knowledge of algebra also reached to Arab from India.
  - The famous books of Arabian mathematician Al-khowarizmi *viz.* 'Algab' and 'Al-muquabla' are based on Indian Algebra.

- This branch of mathematics is known as Algebra after the titles of these books.

## 3. Middle Age/Golden Age (400 AD - 1200 AD)

- The middle age is also called as Golden Age of Indian mathematics because many great mathematicians such as Aryabhatta-I, Aryabhatta-II, Brahmagupta, Mahaviracharya, Shridharacharya, Bhaskaracharya-II — belong to this age.
  - They contributed to all the branches of mathematics of today. (For their contribution, please refer the next chapter]
  - The formulae, principles and methods of mathematics given in Vedas in complex forms were explained by Indian mathematicians of middle age and thus the Vedic mathematics could become in use of common people.
- The heights which mathematics is occupying today and the progress which it has made through the ages is all due to the dedicated and sustained work of many great Indian mathematicians of middle age.

## 4. Post-Middle Age (1200 AD - 1800 AD)

- In 14th century, the contribution of some eminent mathematicians of Kerala State was very significant.
- They expanded sin θ, cos θ, $\tan^{-1}\theta$ in the form of infinite series and established the exact value of π (pie) to the several decimal points.
- The well-known mathematicians of Kerala State were:

  Madhav (1350-1410 AD), Neel Kantha (1500 AD)

  Shankara Parshava (1500-1560 AD), Jyeshtha Dev (1500-1600 AD).
  - Neel Kantha established the value of sin r as $\sin r = r - \frac{r^3}{3} + \frac{r^5}{5} - \frac{r^7}{7} + \ldots$

    This is known as Shregari Series.
  - Jyeshtha Dev wrote a book "Yukti Bhasha'.
  - Shankara Parshava explained the problem of 'Lilavati' in his book 'Kriyakarma Karee'.
  - Narayan Pandit wrote a well-known book 'Ganit Kaumudi' in 1356 AD, whose manuscript is preserved in the library of Cambridge University. This book includes theoretical formulation of permutation and combination, partition of numbers and magic squares.
  - Ganesh Devagya, a famous astrologist wrote a book 'Graha Laghava' in 1520 AD.
  - Kamalakar, a maharashtrian brahmin wrote a book 'Siddhanta Tatva Vivek' in 1658 A.D.

## 5. Modern Age (After 1800 AD)

- In 19th century, Nrisingh Bapu Dev Shastri and Sudhakar Dwivedi were the eminent Indian mathematicians.

- Dev Shastri compiled a book on Indian and Western mathematics.
- Sudhakar Dwivedi wrote many books on the properties of ellipses, spherical trigonometry, calculus, etc.
- Dr. Ganesh Prasad, Srinivas Ramanujan, Swami Bharati Krishnatirtha are eminent mathematicians of present era.
- Few other eminent modern Indian mathematicians are Shakuntala Devi, D.R. Kapreker, Dr. M.N. Saha, Dr. Satyendra Nath Bose, Dr. Gorakh Prasad, and so on.
- Swami Bharati Krishntirth (1884-1960 AD) was a brilliant scholar who discovered the 16 'Sutras' in the Vedas and spent 8 years in their intense study.
- He has left an invaluable treasure for all generations to come, consisting of a set of unique and magnificent methods and techniques for solving mathematical problems in areas like Arithmetic, Algebra, Calculus, Trigonometry and Co-ordinate geometry.
- These techniques are very easy to learn and encapsulate the immense and brilliant mathematical knowledge of ancient Indians who had made fundamental contributions to mathematics in the form of the decimal numerals, zero, infinity and place-value system.
- Even young children enjoy learning and using these techniques.
- The techniques reduce drastically the number of steps required to solve problems and in many cases, after a little practice, many of the problems can be solved orally.
- This will give tremendous self-confidence to the pupils which leads them to enjoy mathematics instead of fearing and disliking it.
- These techniques deal with major Arithmetical operations like multiplication, division, computation of squares and square toots, and complex fractions besides a whole lot of other techniques.

## EVALUATE YOURSELF

1. What is the utility/value of History of Mathematics?
2. Enumerate the landmarks in the History of Mathematics? Discuss in detail any one of them.
3. Write short notes on:
   (1) Hindu-arabic System of Notation,
   (2) Decimal fractions,
   (3) Superiority of Metric units over non-metric units.
4. Sketch the historical development of Metric System of Weights and Measures.
5. Give an account of the historical development of logarithms.
6. Explain fully the historical development of Computer Mathematics.
7. Give an outline of the invention of First Electro-Mechanical Computer.
8. Summarise the development of Modern Electronic computer, giving in detail its four generations.
9. What is Vedic Mathematics?

10. Discuss fully the historical development of mathematics in India by dividing it into certain time-periods.
11. Give an account of the history of Indian mathematics during one of the following time-periods:
    (1) Ancient Age — Earlier Vedic Period and Later Vedic Period.
    (2) Pre-Middle Age
    (3) Middle Age/Golen Period
    (4) Post-Middle Age
    (5) Modern Age.
12. 'The contribution of mathematicians of middle age is considered very significant in Indian mathematics.' — Justify it.

'The astonishing progress that the Indians had made in mathematics is now well known and it is recognised that the foundations of modern arithmetic and algebra were laid long ago in India. The origins of Geometry, Arithmetic and Algebra go back to remote periods. Geometry made progress in India but it was in arithmetic and algebra that India kept the lead. The adoption of zero and the decimal place-value system in India unbarred the gates of the mind to rapid progress in arithmetic and algebra.'

***— Jawaharlal Nehru***

As are the crests on the heads of peacocks,
As are the gems on the heads of the snakes,
So is the Ganit at the top of Science known as Vedanga.'

***— Vedanga Jyotish***

'I am sure that no subject loses more than Mathematics by any attempt to dissociate it from its history.'

***— J.W.L. Glaisher***

'The zero which gives to airy nothing, not merely a local habitation and a name, a picture, a symbol, but helpful power is the characteristic of the Hindu-race from where it sprang. No single mathematical creation has been more potent for the general on-go of intelligence and power.'

***— Holstead***

# CONTRIBUTIONS OF SOME GREAT MATHEMATICIANS

## I. Indian Mathematicians

### Aryabhatta (475-550 AD)

1. He wrote the book 'Aryabhatia' the first Indian Astronomical text.
2. He was the first person to present Arithmetic, Algebra and Geometry in his astronomical calculations.
3. He wrote four books on mathematics:
   (1) Aryabhatia Dasgitika — A collection of Astronomical tables
   (2) Aryastasatam — A note on numeration in Arithmetic
   (3) Kalkriya — A note on time and its measurement
   (4) Gola — A note on sphere.
4. Aryabhatia consists of 121 shlokas, divided into four parts:
   (1) Gati paadika (2) Ganit paadika (3) Kala kriyapaad (4) Ga-paad

In these shlokas, he has mentioned —

(*i*) Five basic principles of Mathematics.
(*ii*) Decimal system and its uses.
(*iii*) Methods to calculate the area of a rectangle, triangle, circle, curved surface of a cone and volume of a sphere.
(*iv*) Methods for constructing a triangle, a circle, a quadrilateral, etc.
(*v*) Principles of Algebra.

5. He pointed out that if the diameter of a circle be 20000 units, then its circumference equals 62832 units.

$$\pi = \frac{\text{circumference}}{\text{diameter}} = \frac{62832}{20000} = 3.1416 \text{ (approx.)}$$

He was the first to give the value of $\pi$ correct upto four decimal places.

6. He gave a general solution of a linear indeterminate equation by method of 'continued function'.
7. He pointed out that volume of a pyramid $= \frac{1}{2}$(base × height)

   Also, volume of a sphere $= \frac{4}{3}\pi r^3$
8. He gave almost all the formulae for knowing areas of different geometrical figures.
9. He suggested the use of letters to represent unknown number.
10. He explained the famous Pythagoras Theorem as under:

    "The square of the Bhuja plus the square of the koti is the square of the Karna."
11. He invented the notation system consisting of alphabet numerals.
12. In his aryabhatia, he had described the method of extracting square root and cube root of a given number.
13. He derived the formula for finding the sum of a given Arithmetic Progression.

    $S = \frac{(a+l)n}{2}$ where a = first number, $l$ = last number, n = number of terms
14. He gave the idea of Decimal System, properties of similar triangles.
15. He introduced the concept of 'sine' in trigonometry.
16. He was also the master of Astronomy which is closely related to mathematics.
17. He held that Earth is a spherical body and that it revolves around the Sun.

    This fact was realised by Copernicus and Galileo in 16th century after about 1100 years.
18. He had calculated the relation of Earth on its axis.
19. He had also the knowledge of gravitational pull of the Earth.
20. He revealed the identities —

    (1) $(a + b)^2 = a^2 + 2ab + b^2$ which leads to $ab = \frac{(a+b)^2 - (a^2 + b^2)}{2}$

    (2) $1^2 + 2^2 + 3^2 + \ldots n^2 = \frac{1}{6} n(n+2)(2n+1)$ where n = number of terms

    $1^3 + 2^3 + 3^3 + \ldots + n^3 = (1 + 2 + 3 + \ldots + n)^2 = \frac{1}{4} n^2((n+1)^2$

## 2. Brahmagupta (598-658 AD)

1. He wrote books on Astronomy and Mathematics. He wrote his first book 'Brahm-Sphuta Siddhant' at the age of 30.
   - It consists of 21 chapters which contain great knowledge of Arithmetic, Algebra, Geometry and Astronomy.
   - This book helped Arabs to know Indian astronomy.
   - Astronomer Kanka of Ujjain translated the book into Arabic language.
2. He gave the exact meaning of the concept of zero. He defined it as $a - a = 0$.
   - He explained operations of addition, subtraction, multiplication and division with zero. But he made an error of assuming that 'zero divided by zero is zero.'
3. In his calculation, he has used the value of $\pi^2 = 10$, *i.e.*, $\pi = \sqrt{10}$.
4. He gave the method of inversion for the first time.
5. He gave the method of squaring and cubing and also that of extracting square roots and cube roots.
6. He explained the operations of fractional addition, subtraction, multiplication and division.

   *e.g.*, $\frac{a}{b} \times \frac{c}{d} = \frac{ac}{bd}$
7. He gave the rules to deal with negative numbers.

   *e.g.* (*i*) $(-a)(-b) = ab$ (*ii*) $\frac{-a}{-b} = \frac{a}{b}$ (*iii*) $0 - (-a) = 0 + (a) = a$
8. He solved the equation of the type $x^2 - 10x = -9$. He gave this rule:
   (*a*) Multiply the constant term by the coefficient of $x^2$. Here $(-9 \times 1)$
   (*b*) Add the square of half the coefficient of x and find the square root of this sum. (Here, $(-9 \times 1) + 25 = 16$ and $\sqrt{16} = 4$)
   (*c*) Subtract half the coefficient of x and divide it by the coefficient of $x^2$. (Here, $4 - (-5) = 9 \div 1 = 9$)
   (*d*) The quotient gives the solution of the equation (Here, $x = 9$)
9. He found the formula for addition of Geometrical Progression.

   $$a + ar + ar^2 + ar^3 + \ldots + ar^n = \frac{a(r^n - 1)}{r - 1}$$
10. He elaborated upon the properties of right triangles and for the first time gave the solution of a right triangle by the following values of its sides:

    (1) $a = 2mn,\ b = m^2 - n^2,\ c = m^2 + n^2$ where m and n are two unequal natural numbers.

    (2) $a = \sqrt{m}$, $b = \frac{1}{2}\left|\frac{m}{n} - n\right|$, $c = \frac{1}{2}\left|\frac{m}{n} - n\right|$

11. He for the first time suggested the construction of a cyclic quadrilateral. Two of his formulae are in use even today:

(1) Area of a cyclic quad = $\sqrt{(s-a)(s-b)(s-c)(s-d)}$ wherer $s = \frac{a+b+c+d}{2}$.

(2) Length of one of the diagonals of this cyclic quadrilateral

$$= \sqrt{\left(\frac{bc+ad}{ab+cd}\right)(ac+bd)}$$

Length of the other diagonal = $\sqrt{\left(\frac{ab+cd}{bc+ad}\right)(ac+bd)}$

12. He was the first to apply Algebra to Astronomy.
13. He introduced the decimal system based on the incorporation of zero in enumeration. It made computation easier. Thirty eight in Roman System XXXVIII is written as 38 as per the decimal system.
14. He has given a detailed account of progression, slopes, volume of trenches and amount of grains in a heap, etc.
15. He was particularly concerned with the *series* and *permutations*.
16. In writing the fraction, the scheme of writing the Numerator above the Denominator was used by him.
17. His work on arithmetic includes integers, fractions, progressions, mensuration of plane figures and problems on volumes, simple interest and barter.

## 3. Bhaskaracharya (1114-1150⁺ AD)

1. He was very good in Astronomy and served as a head of astronomical observatory at Ujjain.
   - He wrote many books on different branches of mathematics. Some of them are: (1) Siddhant Shiromani (2) Karan Kotuhal (3) Samaya Siddhant Shiromani (4) Surya Siddhant.
   - Siddhant Shiromani is divided into four chapters. They are:
     (1) Lilavati — based on the name of his daughter – on Arithmetic.
     (2) Vijaganit — on Algebra
     (3) Goladhyaya — on sphere
     (4) Grahaganit — on mathematics of planets.
2. He is well-known for his treatment of negative numbers which he considered as debts/losses and also for his treatise on Arithmetic and measurement which he had named after his daughter 'Lilavati'.
   - The book Lilavati includes notation, the operations with integers and fractions, the rule of three, interest, series, most common commercial rules, permutations, mensuration, simple Algebra, etc.

- It also includes rules related to zero, viz., $a + 0 = a$, $a - 0 = a$, $0^n = 0$

3. He gave the value of $\pi = \frac{3927}{1250}$ or 3.1255 and suggested $\sqrt{10}$ for ordinary work.
4. He, for the first time, introduced the idea of 'infinity $\infty$' while dividing a number by zero.

   *e.g.,* $\frac{a}{0} = \infty$ where a is any positive integer.

   - He was the first to declare that the sum of any number and $\infty$ is $\infty$.
5. He contributed a lot in the field of mensuration. He revealed the following formulae:

   (1) Area of a sphere $= 4 \times$ area of a circle $= 4\pi r^2$

   (2) Volume of a sphere $=$ Area of a sphere $\times \frac{1}{6}$ of its diameter

   $$= 4\pi r^2 \times \frac{1}{6}(2r)$$

   $$= \frac{4}{3}\pi r^3$$

6. He also gave formulae related to permutation and combination *e.g.,* Number of permutation of 'r' things $= \frac{r!}{k!\,l!}$ where $k$ and $l$ are different things.
7. He had the knowledge of surds, *e.g.,* $\sqrt{13}$, $\sqrt{5}$, etc.

   - Problems like the following are found in his writings:

     'The sides of a triangle are $\sqrt{13}$ and $\sqrt{5}$ and its area is 4. Find the length of its base.'
8. He dealt with cubic equations and biquadratic equations —

   (1) $x^3 - 2x^2 - 400x = 9999$ (Cubic equation)

   (2) $x^4 + 42x = 6x^2 + 65$ (Biquadratic equation)
9. He dismissed the imaginary numbers by stating – 'There is no square root of negative quantity for it is not a square.'
10. In Siddhant Shiromani, he dealt with astronomy and he asserted the sphericity of the Earth.
11. He also gave a proof of Pythogoras Theorem.
12. His contribution in Trigonometry is also worth mentioning. He gave the formula:

    (1) $\sin(A \pm B) = \sin A \cos B \pm \cos A \sin B$.

    (2) $\sin\left(\frac{A - B)}{2}\right) = \frac{1}{2}\left[(\sin A + \sin B)^2 + (\cos A - \cos B)^2\right]^{\frac{1}{2}}$

13. He had also the knowledge of gravitational force long before Newton. He called it 'Dharnikatmak Shakti'.
14. He introduced cyclic method to solve algebraic expressions. Six centuries later, European mathematicians like Eular and Lorange re-discovered it and called it 'Enverse Cyclic.'
15. He can be called the founder of differential calculus. He gave an example of what is now called 'differential coefficient' and the basic idea of what is now called 'Rolle's Theorem'.
16. His greatest strength lay in his ability to handle problems which lead to indeterminate equations.

In journal of Royal Society, Dr. Stopwood has remarked – 'We must acknowledge the intimate capabilities of Bhaskaracharya'.

## 4. Mahaviracharya (850 AD)

- Mahaviracharya was the follower of Jain religion.

1. He I known for his famous books – 'Ganit Saar Sangraha', 'Shatrinshika' and 'Jyotish Patal.'
2. His book Ganit Saar Sangraha has been translated into English by Dr. E. Smith.
   - According to Smith – 'The analysis of oral and written questions in Trigonometry given by Mahaviracharya is far superior to that given by Brahmagupta and Bhaskarcharya.'
3. He has dealt with conversion — (1) of rectangles into squares and vice versa
   (2) of circles into squares and vice versa.
4. He also studied different properties of ellipse.

## 5. Shridhar Acharya (850 AD)

- He was the follower of Shaiva religion and later changed over to Jainism.
- He was contemporary to Mahaviracharya.

1. He wrote the famous books of mathematics 'Nav-Shatika', 'Trin-Shatika'. 'Paati Ganit' and 'Beej-Ganit'.
   - Trin-shatika consists of three hundred shlokas.
   - His book 'paati-Ganit' has been translated into Arabian language entitled as 'Saral Tarabt'.
2. His work includes treatises on square root, cube root, fractions, compound practice, progressions, areas and interest.

## 6. Dr. Ganesh Prasad (1876-1935 AD)

1. He established Agra University in 1927.
2. His first research paper was on 'Elliptical functions and Spherical Harmonics.'
3. He also detected and corrected the errors in the works of eminent French mathematician Lebesgue.

## 7. Srinivasa Ramanujan (1887-1920 AD)

- He was so bright in Mathematics that he was declared 'child mathematician' at the age of 12 by his teachers.

1. His greatest contribution to mathematics was in the field of theory of numbers.
2. He pointed out that every even integer greater than 2 is the sum of two primes, *e.g.*, $4 = 2 + 2$, $6 = 3 + 3$, $8 = 5 + 3$, $16 = 13 + 3$, $20 = 17 + 3$, ...
   - The number of primes in case of large numbers may be more than two. *e.g.*, $44 = 31 + 13 = 37 + 7 = 41 + 3$.
3. With respect to partitioning of whole numbers, he pointed out that if only integers are to be used, then —
   (1) There are 3 alternative ways to write 3. These are $3 + 0$, $2 + 1$, $1 + 1 + 1$. There are no other ways of partitioning this number.
   (2) Similarly, 4 can be written alternatively as $4 + 0$, $3 + 1$, $2 + 2$, $2 + 1 + 1$, $1 + 1 + 1 + 1$. There are no other ways of partitioning it.
   (3) However, the process of partitioning is very different but Ramanujan developed a formula that is valid for any number. This formula is universally applicable, no matter whether the number is 3 or 30,00,000.
4. He was one of the greatest masters in the field of hyper geometric series and continued fractions.
5. He wrote 120 theorems on 'divergent series' in 1913 which were sent to Prof. Hardy. Prof. Hardy writes — 'I had never seen anything the least like them before. A single look at them is enough to show that they could only be written by a mathematician of the highest class.'
6. He worked on 'Definite Integrals' and 'Elliptic Functions.'
7. He pointed out that a prime number of the form $4n + 1$ is the sum of two squares, *e.g.*, $4(1) + 1 = 5 = 2^2 + 1^2$, $4(3) + 1 = 13 = 3^2 + 2^2$, $4(4) + 1 = 17 = 4^2 + 1^2$, $4(7) + 1 = 29 = 5^2 + 2^2$, ...
8. Once, while going to meet Ramanujan, Prof. Hardy took a taxi cab number 1729 and remarked the number seemed dull to him because it is divisible by 13 and 19. Ramanujan immediately replied – 1729 is a very interesting number, it is the smallest number expressible as a sum of two cubes in two different ways:
   $$1729 = 1^3 + 12^3 = 9^3 + 10^3$$
9. Dr. Hardy, a great mathematician of England of his time, has remarked about Ramanujan's work on numbers — 'The elementary analysis of highly composite numbers is most remarkable and shows very clearly Ramanujan's extra-ordinary mastery over the Algebra of inequalities.'
   - Prof Hardy – 'Here was a man who could work out modular equations, work out thousands of complex multiplication.'
10. His work threw light on Divergent series, Hyper-geometric series, continued fractions, the theories of numbers, Definite integrals, partition functions, Ecliptic functions, Fractional differentiations, and highly composite numbers.

11. He remembered the distinctive characteristics of the first ten thousand integers to an extent that each one of them became his personal friend.
    - When Ramanujan returned to India, Prof. Hardy remarked 'Ramanujan is returning to India as the greatest mathematician India has ever produced. I hope, his country will give him a befitting reception.'

## II. Western Mathematicians

### 1. Pythagoras (569-500 BC)

- He was a pupil of Thales, the father of Greek mathematics, astronomy and philosophy.

1. He was very much interested in numbers.
   (1) He was the first to classify all positive numbers as even or odd.
   (2) He pointed out that any odd number (2n+1) can be expressed as the difference of two squares, *i.e.,* $2n + 1 = (n + 1)^2 - n^2$ *e.g.,* $5 = 3^2 - 2^2$, $11 = 6^2 - 5^2$, $25 = 13^2 - 12^2$
   (3) He found triangular numbers and perfect square numbers.

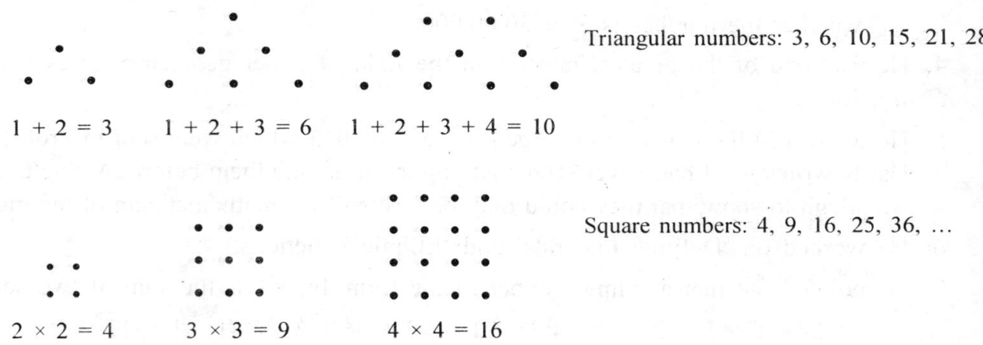


   The dots depicting triangular numbers could be arranged as triangles. The dots depicting square numbers could be arranged as squares.

2. He was the first to give a proof that $\sqrt{2}$ is an irrational number.
3. Apollonius adopted this nomenclature which is in use even today. This classification has proved to be the key to further discoveries such as irrational numbers.
4. He was the first who suggested that earth is round like a sphere in space.
5. He knew that a point in a plane can be filled by six equilateral triangles, by four squares or by three regular hexagons.
6. He proved the proposition relating to the sum of the measures of angles of a triangle.
7. He was able to construct five regular polyhedrons.
8. He is credited for the famous theorem known as Pythagoras Theorem (Although it was known to Indian and Egyptian mathematicians long long ago). This is related to the property of sides of a right triangle.

9. He stated the properties of areas and volumes of various plane and solid figures.
   - He was the first to prove that a circle (old concept) contains a greater area than any plane figure with the same perimeter.
   - He also proved that a sphere contains a greater volume than any other solid figure bounded by the equal surface (a cube).
10. He made a great progress in mathematics specially in the field of numbers, geometry of solids and area.
11. He made Geometry a science by basing it on axioms, postulates, definitions and by setting down methods of proof.
12. According to Pythogoras, 'Sphere is the most perfect of all solids.'
    - He also stated – 'There are five regular solids which are exactly in a sphere, *viz.*, tetrahedron, hexahedron, octahedron, dodecahedron and isosahedron.
13. Eardemus remarked – 'Pythagoreans changed Geometry into a liberal science, they diverted Arithmetic from the service of commerce.'
14. Pythagoras made substantial progress in the theoretical side of Arithmetic and Algebra.
    - Pythagoreans had a geometrical equivalent for our method of solving quadratic equation.
    - They studied various types of progression – Arithmetic, Geometric and Harmonic.
15. In Geometry, Pythagoras identified 1 with a point, 2 with the line, 3 with the plane surface and 4 with the solid.
16. He discovered the Harmonical Progression in the notes of musical scale by finding the relation between the length of a string and the pitch of vibrating notes.
17. To him, numbers were not attributes but have valuable meanings and they were the stuff out of which all objects we see are made — the rational reality.
18. He took interest in 'application of areas' and introduced the terms 'Parabole', 'Hyperbole' and 'Ellipse'.
19. Aristotle remarked – 'Pythogoreans first applied themselves in mathematics, a science which they improved and penetrated with it, they fancied that the principles of mathematics were the principles of all things.'

## 2. Euclid (330-295 BC)

1. Euclid wrote 'Elements', consisted of 13 books, which has influenced the teaching of Geometry for centuries.
   - Until about only a few years ago, school geometry was simply 'Euclidian Geometry'.
2. ***Elements***

| *Volume No.* | *Content* |
|---|---|
| I. | Congruence, parallels, Pythagoras Theorem<br>Area of rectilinear figures, triangles, perpendiculars. |
| II. | Algebraic identities like $(a+b)^2 = a^2 + 2ab + b^2$ treated geometrically, areas. |
| III | Circles, chords and tangents |

| | |
|---|---|
| IV | Circumscribed and inscribed polygons |
| V | Treatment of proportion (treated geometrically) |
| VI | Similarity of polygons, idea of proportion applied to similar figures. |
| VII, VIII, IX | Arithmetic (treated geometrically) giving an interesting account of Theory of Numbers, Theory of continued proportion<br>— Prime and composite members (Numbers of primes are infinite), Even and odd numbers<br>— HCF and LCM, Theories of geometrical progressions<br>— $a^m.a^n = (a)^{m+n}$<br>— Summing the progressions using equal ratios. |
| X | Doctrine of irrational numbers specially of the type $\sqrt{a} \pm \sqrt{b}$ where a, b are positive integers |
| XI | Elementary solid geometry. |
| XII | Method of exhaustion, Finding the area of a circle in the form of $\pi r^2$. |
| XIII | Constructions for the five regular solids, ends with decahedron. |

3. He introduced the idea of perfect numbers, which is far difficult to find than the rare postage stamps.
   - A number is said to be perfect when it is equal to sum of its factors, such as 6, 23, 486.
   - The largest perfect number so far discovered is $2^{126}$.
4. He carefully laid down his definitions, then his common axioms, and then his postulates.
5. Many other writings of Euclid have come down to us dealing with Astronomy, music and optics.
6. He wrote a number of other mathematical and physics work.
   - Among them (1) 'optics' and 'cataptrica' belong to Physics.
     (2) 'Phenomina' deals with the celestial sphere and contains 25 geometrical propositions.
     (3) 'Data' consists of supplementing geometrical material regarding algebraic problems.
     (4) 'Surface Loci' composed of two books, deals with loci that are surfaces.
7. A few of his works 'Book of Fallacies', 'Porisms' and 'Pscudaria' are lost and we only learn of them indirectly through some commentators.
8. Euclid thought about the then current problems of his times, *viz.*

(1) Dividing an angle into 3 equal parts,

(2) Making double of a cube,

(3) Obtaining square form of a circle.

9. He solved problems related to irrational numbers.

## 3. Napier (1550-1617 AD)

1. Napier propounded the binary system (having only 2 numerals, 0 and 1) of writing the numbers as against decimal system.
2. He discovered Logarithm – a device which replaces multiplication by addition and division by subtraction.
3. He prepared the tables of logarithm which proved very practical in other branches of mathematics and sciences.
4. He had intimate knowledge of correspondence between arithmetical and geometrical progression.
5. He devised new methods in spherical astronomy.

## 4. John Kepler (1571-1630 AD)

1. He thought of a harmony between Arithmetic, Geometry and Music which could solve all mysteries of the universe.
2. He found three laws of planetary motion:
   (1) The orbit of each plant is an ellipse with sun at focus.
   (2) The line joining the sun to the planet sweeps out equal areas in equal times.
   (3) The square of the period of the planet is proportional to the cube of its mean distance from the sun.

## 5. Rene Descartes (1596-1650 AD)

- A French philosopher, scientist and mathematician.

1. He published two books: (1) Discourse on Methods, (2) Mediations
   - Discourse on Methods contains important mathematical work.
2. He is said to be the father of modern co-ordinate geometry.
3. He carried out meteorological observations, studied glaciers and computed the height of mountains.
4. His great contribution is in applying Geometry to Algebra and vice versa.
5. His most significant contribution lies in the integration and harmonization of different branches of knowledge.
   - He first tried to show unity in different branches of mathematics and then tried to reconstruct and interrelate the non-mathematical sciences saying that all employ the mathematical reasoning.
6. He laid the foundation of Analytical Geometry, which founded differential calculus.

7. He expressed properties of curves by algebraic equations.
8. He was the first who denoted variables by x, y, z, ... and constants by a, b, c, ...
9. He framed axioms and postulates to build up the system of mathematics.
10. Decartes found the method of doubling the cube and of trisecting an angle of which enabled him to contribute to the theory of equations.
11. He discovered an interesting curve, called Cartesian Oval that led to far-reaching research in geometrical analysis.

## 6. Sir Issac Newton (1642-1727 AD)

1. Newton's valuable contribution to mathematics was discovery of differential and integral calculus.
2. He discovered and elaborated the law of universal gravitation, and applied it in Astronomy.
3. He propounded Binomial Theorem, equations of motions, etc.
4. His most famous book is 'Principia.'

## 7. Carl Friedrich Gauss (1777-1855 AD)

- Just to keep the class engaged, a teacher named Buttner gave the class a long problem of addition of numbers from 1 to 100. Within a very short time, Gauss answered it correctly. The teacher was astonished and asked Gauss how he found the answer. Gauss showed the following method:

$$\begin{array}{cccccccccccccc} 1 & + & 2 & + & 3 & + & 4 & + & \dots & + & 49 & + & 50 \\ 100 & + & 99 & + & 98 & + & 97 & + & \dots & + & 52 & + & 51 \\ \hline 101 & + & 101 & + & 101 & + & 101 & + & \dots & + & 101 & + & 101 \end{array}$$

50 pairs of 101 means $50 \times 101 = 5050$ (Ans)

The formula we use is: $Sn = \dfrac{n(n+1)}{2}$ which is derived from above.

- A mathematician like Laplace had to say – 'What to talk of Europe, Gauss is the greatest mathematician of the world.'
- At the age of 12, he was familiar with the 'Binomial Theorem', 'The Theory of Infinite Series' and 'Possibility of Non-Euclidian Geometry.'
  - He was one of the first to study the 'Non-Euclidian Geometry'.

1. He invented the process of constructing a regular polygon of 17 sides with the help of only a ruler and a compass.
2. He developed the theory of surfaces.
   - Three of the problems which Gauss considered in his work on *surfaces*, suggested general theories of mathematical and scientific importance.
3. The method of 'least squares' which is indispensable at present was invented by Gauss.
4. He was the first to give coherent account of complex numbers.
5. He gave the proofs of the following algebraic facts:

(1) Every integral rational equation in a single variable has at least one root.

(2) Every equation will have as many roots as the highest power (Degree) of the unknown, *e.g.*, quadratic equation has two roots as the highest power of the unknown is two.

6. Besides negative, positive, rational and irrational numbers, he dealt with 'imaginary numbers'.

   ⏩ For the first time, he used the symbol '$i$' for imaginary quantity $\sqrt{-1}$. *e.g.*, $5+3\sqrt{-1}$ means $5 + 3i$ was named as complex number.

7. He published his 'Theory of Motion of heavenly bodies revolving round the sun in conic section.'

8. He computed accurately orbit of some newly discovered planets and satellites.

9. In the theory of probability, he was the first to present the law: 'Gaussian Law of Normal Distribution of Errors.'

10. He also made researches about magnetism and electricity.

11. Kronecker once said, 'Almost everything which the mathematics of our century has brought forth in the way of original scientific ideas is connected with the name of Gauss.'

▸ He is popularly known as 'Prince of Mathematics.'

## 8. Einstein (1879-1955 AD)

1. He proposed the 'Theory of Relativity'.
2. In 1916, he published his book – 'General Principles of Relativity.'

## EVALUATE YOURSELF

1. What was the contribution of Aryabhatta in the development of Indian mathematics?
2. 'S. Ramanujan was the greatest Indian mathematician of modern age who revived with full glory the ancient Indian tradition of scholarship in mathematics.' — Discuss.
3. 'Euclid's 'Elements' has been regarded as the most popular and universal text book adopted so far in the world of mathematics.' Comment.
4. Discuss the contribution to Mathematics by any one of the following mathematicians:

   (1) Bhaskaracharya or Gauss

   (2) Brahmagupta or Pythagoras

   (3) Mahaviracharya or Rene Descartes.

'I am sure that no subject loses more than Mathematics by any attempt to dissociate it from its history.'
***— J.W.L. Glaisher***

'The zero which gives to airy nothing, not merely a local habitation and a name, a picture, a symbol, but helpful power is the characteristic of the Hindu-race from where it sprang. No single mathematical creation has been more potent for the general on-go of intelligence and power.'
***— Holstead***

# STIMULATING & MAINTAINING INTEREST IN MATHEMATICS

## 28.1 Stimulus/Motivation

- Teaching is a sort of stimulus to learning.
- 'How much' and 'how well' a child responds and learns depends upon 'how effectively' he has been motivated to do so.
- The motivation of work in mathematics has two aspects:

  (1) Aspect of creating interest (2) Aspect of maintaining interest.
- Motivation is nothing but providing a sort of inducement to action. It is the process by which the pupils' interest to work is maintained.
- All modern methods of teaching, attach great significance to motivation in maintaining interest in the learning process.
- Try to understand the inner motives of the pupils. It creates a learning situation and instills a thirst for learning in the pupils.
- Highly motivated pupils have a keen interest in mathematics and take up the work enthusiastically.
- Motivation may be direct as well as indirect.

## 28.2 Interest

- Interest is a key factor in achieving success in any task performed by a teacher.
- To arouse and maintain pupils' interest in mathematics is a major problem of the teacher of mathematics.

The most important task of a mathematics teacher, specially at secondary level, is the creation of interest in the pupils towards mathematics and to maintain it.

- The problem of inculcating interest in the learning of mathematics has two phases: (1) Arousal of interest (2) Maintenance of aroused interest.
- In the first place, desired interest is aroused in the learning of mathematics. The pupils are spontaneously attracted, motivated and are drawn nearer and nearer to the learning of mathematics.
- Once the pupils are attracted and motivated to learn mathematics, there is every possibility for the diminishing and vanishing of the aroused interest.

  Every care should be taken to maintain the interest in the pupils for a sufficiently long period so that the desired aims and objectives may be properly realised.

  The loss of interest is the major cause of pupils' failure in mathematics.
- Whatever one learns, interest plays a dominant role in making him learn that thing. Interest, attention and learning – all are quite interdependent.
- Interest is said to be the mother of attention and attention is the mother of learning.
  - If one wants to learn mathematics, he should try to catch hold of, from the very beginning, the grandmother, *i.e.,* interest.
  - In a mathematics class, the teacher should try to inculcate sufficient interest in his classroom teaching so that mathematics may not be considered as dull, tiresome and troublesome.
  - Unfortunately, mathematics which is an interesting subject is considered as a dry, hard and uninteresting one by the pupils.
  - The main reason behind it is —
    (1) the lack of interest in the teachers of mathematics,
    (2) tendency to memorise the content without comprehension. As a result, the content is generally forgotten.
- Problem of arousing and maintaining interest in mathematics can be overcome by applying appropriate methods and techniques of teaching.
- It may be taken as axiomatic that pupils will work most diligently and most effectively at tasks in which they are genuinely interested.
  - As a rule, pupils readily become interested in things —
    (*i*) which are new and exciting
    (*ii*) for which they can perceive —
      (*a*) practical values, or
      (*b*) application to situations in life, or
      (*c*) applications to fields of study in which they are already interested.
    (*iii*) which involve puzzle element or elements of mystery.

  Therefore, to create and maintain interest becomes one of the most important tasks of mathematics teacher.

It is also one of the most difficult problems which the teacher encounters.

  - The interest of pupils is easily caught by any new things, but it is as easily distracted to other new things.
- The elements of novelty, usefulness, relatedness and sheer intellectual curiosity – are the primary stimuli for the awakening of interest.
- It is observed that the pupils tend to 'remain interested' in those things which they can do most successfully and which they understand most completely.
  - The work should present a continual challenge, but it should be a challenge in a real sense and not mere drudgery at tasks devoid of meaning or inexcusably difficult.
- Interests are motives which serve as important influences in producing both – activities and attitudes that are favourable to learning.
  - Interests are motives that almost all teachers try to use to promote learning/
- A strong interest in mathematics would tend to produce a favourable attitude towards mathematics. Such an attitude would in turn probably lead to or enhance the desire to study mathematics in a serious and productive way.
- Genuine interest in mathematics depends basically upon the problem-solving aspect of mathematics.
  - Problems once recognised/sensed leave an individual in a state of perplexity, uneasiness or tension until they are solved.
  - When a solution has been found, tension-reduction and satisfaction results.
- If mathematics is properly taught, it presents the pupil with an abundance of problems and it also provides him with certain general modes of thought and a supply of techniques which enable him to attack these problems successfully.
  - With each successful solution he receives a dividend of satisfaction.
- Incentives may serve to build motive and thus to promote genuine interest in mathematical work. But the use of incentives cannot guarantee this.
  - Incentives are only means to an end. Unless they are used judiciously, some incentives such as marks and rewards of various kinds, even produce undesirable attitudes.
- Pupils are move inclined towards a particular subject according to their inner taste, aptitude and ambition.

## 28.3 Suggestions

Some suggestions are given below which may serve useful purpose in stimulating and maintaining interest in mathematics:

### 1. Motivation through Good Teaching

- For good teaching a teacher should prepare his lesson plan and use correct method or technique or strategy of teaching.
- The teacher should try to make the content attractive and pleasant. A teacher should himself in interested in the good teaching of mathematics. A good teacher is sure to keep pupils interested in mathematics.

## 2. Motivation through the use of Multi-sensory Aids & Devices

- Most people gain new impressions more vividly through sensory experiences than they do through reading or abstract reasoning.
  - The electronic media have been proved very effective in changing the behaviour of the people. In mathematics the use of this media is very limited because mathematics, by its nature, is idea-centred.
  - So many pictorial materials are available in mathematics for motivation.
  - Various AV (audio-visual) aids in mathematics teaching are available. The use of teaching machine and computer also help in developing and maintaining interest in mathematics.
  - The remarkable growth and public acceptance of motion pictures, radio and TV leave no doubt of the interest-getting power of this AV media.
  - Teachers of mathematics have been slower than their colleagues in other subject to take advantage of this eye-and-ear appeal as a means of stimulating interest in their pupils.
    - (*i*) This has been partly due to the nature of mathematics which is essentially one of ideas rather than things.
    - (*ii*) Not very many really good pictorial representations of mathematical topics have been commonly available.
- The AV aids provide a departure from routine teaching and help in making understanding even difficult ideas.
- Preparation of aids and applications can be a regular activity of the learners.

## 3. Motivation through Application to Other Subjects of Study

- The relation of mathematics to other fields of study often provides an important means of stimulating interest.
- Mathematics is literally indispensable in the study of Physics, Chemistry, Engineering, Astronomy, etc.
- Remarkable advances have been made through the application of mathematical procedures in advanced studies, in genetics, heredity, nutrition, growth and maturation, metabolism, fatigue, the effect of various stimuli on organisms and many other special phases of biological and physiological study.
- The social sciences are also beginning to draw heavily upon mathematics, particularly statistical and graphic methods for the investigation and interpretation of social phenomena.
- Economics and sociology deal essentially with mass phenomena and the only mathematics which is used in connection with those subjects is statistics.
  - Even industrial arts require mathematics.
- Even English, the foreign languages and the Fine Arts are enriched by an understanding of the mathematical principles of form and number, of symmetry and order, upon which they are based.

- By continually impressing upon the pupils, the relationships and applications of mathematics to other school subjects, teacher can stimulate interest in the study of mathematics.
  - Mathematics has a key position in learning other school subjects.
  - Let the pupils know that the knowledge of mathematics is extremely necessary in the study of other subjects, they take more interest in mathematics.
  - While teaching mathematics, it is desirable to take up relevant problems of mathematics from other fields of study.
- Study of mathematics is the Art of all Arts and Science of all Sciences.

## 4. Motivation through Intellectual Curiosity

- Pupils are very curious to learn something new and exciting. Their intelligence can definitely be stimulated through a challenge to their curiosity. Mathematics exhibits fully the power of man to think consistently and logically.
- The intellectual activity is governed by three motives, *viz.*,
  (1) The thirst for knowledge.
  (2) The love of truth and beauty.
  (3) The desire to interpret and control the environment.
- Do not present mathematical facts to the pupils in a readymade form, since this will encourage only cramming.
- Curiosity is the powerful urge which stimulates efforts to understand and learn new things.
  - Most pupils are persistently curious individuals and they work and work hard at things that interest them.
- Teachers need to remind themselves continuously that to bring out the best in their pupils, they must appeal to intellectual motives that are strong and that intellectual curiosity is one of the strongest, as well as the most desirable of these motives.
- The range of the potential intellectual interests of these pupils is practically unlimited.
- Mathematics is not devoid of strong appeal to the curiosity and interest of pupils.
- Pupils are interested in seeing how numbers behave and Algebra is essentially the science of the behaviour of numbers.
- As a matter of fact, it is quite possible that the presence of the puzzle element in problems is often a greater stimulus to interest than those elements of so-called reality which authors of text books try so hard to incorporate in problems.
- Pupils are curious by nature. They always desire to go deep in solving the problems.
  - So, a natural curiosity should be awakened among the pupils by presenting the things in an exciting manner.
  - This awakening of curiosity would create interest in them and develop their attention towards the subject.

- So, utilise their nature of absorption. They should not be made to cram the facts of mathematics but to learn and discover them by maintaining Heuristic attitude and problematic approach.

- Interest will be maintained if it remains challenging to their mental powers.

## 5. Motivation through Application of Math to Vocations

- Another important means of stimulating interest in mathematics is through pointing out the applications of mathematics to fields of work such as business, industry and professional fields, through which people gain their livelihood.
- Pupils are generally interested in learning something which helps them in selecting an occupation and earning a living.
  - Application of mathematics is in various vocational fields.
  - Numerous text books are found with titles such as 'Mathematics of Finance', 'Mathematics for Printers', 'Shop Mathematics', 'Mathematics for Electricians', 'Mathematics for Agriculture', etc.
  - By pointing out these applications, teachers can perform valuable service by the way of guidance to the pupils and at the same time, stimulate their interest in mathematics itself.
- Mathematics is now coming to be recognised as a necessary part of professional equipment in such fields as Anatomy, Physiology, Psychology, Psychiatry and Medicine.
- The efficient study of mathematics increases he pupils' competency in different vocations.
  - The knowledge of mathematics is now necessary for most of the vocations.
  - What to say of Trade and Commerce, Engineering, Industry, Insurance, Banking, Accounting, etc., the knowledge of mathematics is equally essential for tailoring, carpentry, masonry, etc., too.
- The most practical aim of education is to make the pupils capable to earn their livelihood.
  - Learning of mathematics serves this purpose properly as it opens ways and means for the various occupations and vocations.
  - Study of mathematics gives more guarantee for jobs in comparison to other subjects.
- So, to create interest in mathematics, vocational value of mathematics be emphasized.

## 6. Motivation through Interest in Math as a Career

- Today there are literally thousands of job opportunities for professional mathematicians. And the number is still growing both in volume and diversity.
- The demand for professionally trained mathematicians in business and industry is greater than the supply. Moreover, the demand is increasing faster than the supply.
- The capable young man/woman who wishes to make a career in the field of mathematics and who is willing to make the efforts needed to secure the necessary professional training will find a variety of opportunities open to him/her.

- The remarkable developments in mathematical statistics and high-speed computing and data-processing; and the great variety of striking applications of these developments have made these branches of mathematics more widely known and appreciated than some of the others.
- The whole spectrum of mathematics offers career opportunities to young man/woman with professional training in mathematics.

## 7. Motivation through Practical Utility/Value of Math

- Emphasise the practical value of mathematics. Utilisation aspect of mathematics enhances its value.
    - Let the child feels that the study of mathematics is going to help him in his day-to-day life, and he would automatically attracted to it.
    - Theoretical facts of mathematics should always be integrated with the relevant utilitarian aspects.
    - The realisation that the study of mathematics is going to help them in their practical life will surely make them interested in learning mathematics.
- One is always anxious for a thing which one considers more and more valuable.
    - Pupils' interest is aroused by pointing out the application of mathematics to some other fields with which he is already familiar.
    - He comes to know that mathematics is an important subject worth learning.
- When the pupil realises the utility of the subject, his interest is aroused and maintained in mathematics.
    - Make the pupils know that the knowledge of mathematics is indispensable for their future life activities.

## 8. Motivation through Practical Work in Math

- Pupils have much interest in observing and handling various objects.
- They seldom understand the subject matter presented in abstract form.
    - Teaching should be started with some related practical task.
- The handling of material and learning through experimentation should be permitted and arranged as frequently as possible.
    - Pupils should be asked to verify mathematical truths by making experiments.
    - Practical presentation of matter should always proceed its abstract form to arouse interest in pupils towards mathematics.
- Pupils may be made interested in learning mathematics by emphasising the practical aspect of mathematics, besides its theoretical aspect.
    - Theory should be properly integrated with practice.
- Project method, Laboratory method should find proper place in teaching of mathematics.
    - Pupils should have practical experience of utilising the knowledge of mathematics.

## 9. Motivation through Cultural/Educational Value of Mathematics

- By making use of cultural value of mathematics, interest in studying mathematics can be inculcated.
- This history of mathematics throws light on its various cultural aspects.
- Study of mathematics helps in preservation, promotion and transmission of the cultural heritage.
- The study of the following presents numerous opportunities to inculcate interest in the learning of mathematics:
  (*a*) The life history of mathematicians.
  (*b*) Contributions of great mathematicians and that of different races in the field of mathematics.
  (*c*) Universality of the mathematical principles and facts and their exchange among different nations.
  (*d*) Contribution of mathematics in the development of culture and civilisation.
- Aside from the technical aspect of mathematics, the *postulational* method of mathematics has a major contribution to make the cultural education of the individual.
  - If the pupils are made aware of the nature and the universal applicability of this method, it will be found to provide an exceedingly strong motive for the study of mathematics, not only from the stand point of its cultural significance but also because of its intrinsic interest.
- In addition to practical/utility value, mathematics possesses some other important educational value such as disciplinary value, cultural value, vocational value, recreational value, etc.
  - A mathematics teacher must have a sound knowledge of these values, so that he may be able to convince his pupils about the educational utility of mathematics.
- An appreciation of the significance of the 'If ... then' type of reasoning is one of the most important potential educational and cultural values of the study of mathematics.

## 10. Motivation through Principle of Change and Variety

- The persistence of same type of activity and learning for a longer time breeds monotony and dullness.
  - Teacher should try to bring some novelty/change in his day-to-day teaching.
  - It is the method or procedure which needs change to maintain interest in learning.
  - Use of varied teaching-aids, change of topics, change of branch of subject, change of methods, techniques, strategies; change of the place of teaching and learning, etc. are the sources of the means through which the desired interest may be maintained.

## 11. Motivation through Proper Learning Environment

- The presence of proper learning environment contributes towards inculcation of desired interest in learning.

- Pupils should be provided with the essential congenial environment to work and learn properly without experiencing any discomfort.
- Pupils should get all the necessary guidance and direction and essential things to learn mathematics according to their own pace and abilities.
- Teacher should adopt proper methods and techniques of teaching as an effective means.
- Teacher who teaches well is sure to prove successful in creating and maintaining interest in learning mathematics.
- Interest is very much linked with the appropriate environment and opportunity available for teaching-learning process.

## 12. Motivation through suitable physical conditions

- Provision of suitable physical conditions for study forms a good atmosphere of the study.
- In schools (*i*) spacious, airy, lighted and well-furnished classrooms
  (*ii*) moderate temperature
  (*iii*) essential teaching supplements and equipments, etc. —

  facilitates the teaching-learning process.
  - There should be no overcrowding in the class.
  - Blackboard should be well-painted
  - Room temperature of about 69°F is considered best for the study.
- At home the pupils should have the facility of a quiet, well-lighted and well-ventilated room with a table and chair for convenient work.
- The physical discomforts should be eliminated and distractors should be avoided.

## 13. Motivation through suitable psychological conditions

Besides suitable physical conditions, some psychological conditions are also necessary for study. Self-confidence, concentration, alertness, critical thinking, systematic working, avoidance of unnecessary distractors and interruptions, classification of thought by writing, discussion; verification of results, etc. are necessary psychological conditions for effective teaching and learning.

Teacher should provide appropriate psychological situations for the study of mathematics.

## 14. Motivation through Individual Attention

- Individual attention is an important factor in teaching-learning process.
- Some of the pupils may not understand certain steps and they begin to lose interest. Such pupils need special attention and guidance from the teacher. So, the teacher should pay individual attention to various categories of students.

## 15. Motivation through Recreational Value of Math

- Mathematics is generally considered as a dry, dull and hard subject. This assumption takes place in the minds of pupils from primary stage by listening the talks of senior pupils and even parents. But the fact is not so.

- Mathematics is an interesting subject and it has recreational value, too.
- The employment of mathematical games, puzzles and contests create interest in mathematics and produce recreation to the learners.
- The programme of Math Club may cover a wide range of activities including the organisation of workshops, seminars, project work, extension lectures, mathematical games and contests, etc.
- Use of AV material, mathematical games, riddles, puzzles – all may prove very useful in creating interest in mathematics.
- Establishment of mathematical association, organisation of lectures on the interested topics on mathematics may also serve the desired purpose.
- The organisation of Math Club can provide a combination of recreational activities and learning.
- An active Math Club is very helpful in developing and maintaining interest of pupils in mathematics.
- Mathematics has its own beauty. Its artistic and aesthetic value should be made known to the pupils of mathematics.
- Mathematics has all opportunities for recreation and entertainment.
- Pupils should be given opportunity to learn mathematics in a playway spirit.

- In the minds of a good many people, the concept of motivation has become identical with the idea of games, plays, puzzles, anecdotes and other interesting matters, but sometimes more or less trivial and unrelated matters referred to as 'mathematical recreation.'
    - It is a rare individual, especially child, who is not interested in games or in things which are unusual or unsuspected and which contain elements of surprise or mystery.
    - While mathematical puzzles, contests and games cannot be permitted to take too much of the time allotted to regular classroom, yet the moderate and appropriate employment of such devices add much of interest and zest to the course of mathematics.
    - The aim of teaching mathematics for fun and pastime should receive some attention of the teacher of mathematics.
- In general, the teacher should also try to understand the teaching of mathematics as well as his pupils, their general level of achievement, attitude, interest and forms of developments.
    - The knowledge about pupils helps the teacher in selecting and adopting appropriate motivational techniques to arouse and maintain the interest of pupils in mathematics.
    - A reference to historical background of different mathematical terms and ideas gives a good start for learning them.

## EVALUATE YOURSELF

1. What do you mean by Stimulus/Motivation and Interest?
2. Enumerate the factors which serve useful purpose in stimulating and maintaining interest in mathematics. Discuss in detail any one of them.
3. Mathematics is considered as a dull subject by the students. How would you cultivate interest and taste among them for mathematics?
4. How will you make mathematics interesting for pupils? Give some concrete suggestions.
5. Discuss both the possibilities and the limitations of mathematics contests as means of motivation.
6. How will you motivate the pupils through practical work in mathematics?
7. Give an illustration of how you would use the cultural motive as a basis for stimulating interest in mathematics.
8. Explain how the classroom environment and the equipment for mathematical work might affect the pupils' interest in mathematics.

An optimist sees an opportunity in every difficulty, a passimist sees a difficulty in every opportunity.

***— Anon***

Integration of logic and mysticism is the best and highest possible in human thought.

***— Bertrand Russel***

# 29 MATHEMATICS LABORATORY AND LIBRARY

## 29.1 What is a Mathematics Laboratory?

- Mathematics laboratory is a room where a group of pupils learn mathematics by actually performing experiments.
- According to E.H. Moore – 'Would it not been possible for the children in the grades to be trained in the power of observation and experiment and selection and deduction so that always their mathematics should be directly connected with the matters of a thoroughly concrete character?... This programme of reform calls for the development of a thorough going laboratory system of instruction in Mathematics and Physics?
- Laboratory is a place which serve two-fold purposes:
  (1) It provides safe and proper place for placing all the necessary material and equipments concerning the learning activities in mathematics.
  (2) It gives proper facilities and opportunity for the essential practical work and living learning experiences.
- The laboratory approach embodies the concepts of (1) active learning, (2) pupils involvement and participation, and (3) relevance.
- It is the demonstration of the concept of activity-oriented mathematics programme.
- It is true that the idea of mathematics laboratory has yet not received the same general acceptance as the science laboratory has. This is due to the fact that mathematics teachers have not themselves recognised and insisted upon its importance as the science teachers have.
  - Teachers of science, art, music, home economics and other subjects do not hesitate to ask for space and equipment for this type of work and they get it.

- But most of the mathematics teachers do not even ask for it even if to do so would be quite reasonable and proper.
- Recently, in good schools, laboratory approach for mathematics instruction is being used effectively.

## 29.2 Need and Importance of Math Laboratory

1. Mathematics laboratory helps the pupils —
   (1) in the inculcation of scientific, problem-solving and heuristic attitude.
   (2) in training for the practical application of mathematical facts and principles in their life.
   (3) in creating interest in the learning of mathematics.
   (4) in making use of all the progressive methods such as inductive-deductive, analytic-synthetic, heuristic, project, in teaching and learning of mathematics.
   (5) in providing opportunity for individualised instruction, for introduction to the use of calculators and computers.
   (6) in providing a good platform for the integration of theory with practice in mathematics.
   (7) in developing habit of critical thinking and logical reasoning, practical mindedness, problem-solving attitude, sense of keen/sharp observation, etc.
2. It is a setting within which the pupils can develop their independent study programmes and interest in learning mathematics.
3. The complex and abstract theoretical concepts may be easily clarified through suitable practical demonstrations.

   This would definitely save time and energy of both, the teachers and the pupils.
4. It satisfies creative and constructive urges of the pupils, and also the varying needs and interest of the gifted children in mathematics.
5. It definitely gives the life and blood to the activities of mathematics club.
6. It will prove a fertile ground for the germination of future mathematicians and scientists.

## 29.3 Organisation of Math Laboratory

### 1. Staffing

To start with, establishment of mathematics laboratory requires only one or two staff members, but the development of the laboratory as a mathematical learning centre requires the involvement of total mathematics staff.

### 2. Physical facilities

New schools should spare a specific area for a mathematics laboratory. Its location should be in the vicinity of other mathematics classrooms. Its dimensions should be large enough for the availability of large group instruction.

## 3. Furniture

Here, the requirement of calculatory corner, measurement corner, game corner, reading and writing corner, diagnosis and tutorial corner, chairs and tables, filing cabinets, enough shelves, a store room and one large permanent screen should be fulfilled.

## 4. Equipments

Calculating equipments, equipments for games, riddles and puzzles, multi-sensory teaching aids should be available.

## 5. Instructional Material

Math Lab should contain —

(1) computational skills development materials *e.g.,* calculators, computers, work books, etc.

(2) problem-solving materials *e.g.,* collection of real life problems, question-bank, other commercial materials.

(3) essential multi-sensory teaching aids *e.g.,* models, charts, geometrical figures, tape recorder, improvised and commercially developed materials, material for recreational mathematics (*e.g.,* various games, funs, puzzles, etc.)

(4) instruments that will assist in diagnosing pupils' needs, weaknesses, strong points, and in determining the level of performance.

(5) individual pupils records of diagnostic and progress reports.

(6) an evaluative procedure to accompany each developmental stage.

## 6. List of Instruments

1. Blackboard
2. Demonstration table
3. Tracing material (tracing papers, carbon-papers, graph papers, coloured pencils, sketch pens, inks, brushes drawing-board, flash board, card board).
4. Books (text books, reference books, magazines, old and new literature of mathematics, books containing the history of mathematics, biographies of great mathematicians).
5. Drawing instruments (Geometrical instruments, chalk, pencil, metre rule, compass, divider, sets squares).
6. Projective aids (slide projector, screen projector, step projector, sound projector, over-head projector, epidiascope, films, slides).
7. Measuring instruments (measuring tape, metre rod, sextents, balances, weighing machines).
8. Log tables, ready reckeners, slide rules, tables of constants.
9. Computers, electronic calculators, calculating machines.
10. Teaching aids (mathematical models of geometrical solids such as cube, cuboid, sphere, hemisphere, cone, cylinder, prisms, pyramids).
11. Surveying instruments (angle mirror, sextent, hypsometer, clinometer, level, transit).

## 29.4 Laboratory Work (Activities) in Mathematics

- The use of multi-sensory aids can serve a double purpose when well-coordinated with the other classroom learning activities:
  (1) It serves to stimulate interest.
  (2) It provides a most effective means of clarifying many mathematical concepts and relations through the experience of associating them directly with physical things.

  Thus, it serves as a highly important avenue for organic learning as well as for motivation.

  Such practice is often referred to as 'laboratory work in mathematics.'
- Even if mathematics teachers do not ask for separate mathematics laboratory, laboratory work in mathematics is receiving increasing attention.
- Textbooks, teachers' manuals, teachers' handbooks and professional journals for teacher are giving more suggestions for laboratory work than they ever have before.
- Special courses are being organised to equip teachers and prospective teachers for such work. Mathematics laboratory has become almost a standard adjunct of institutes and professional meetings for mathematics teachers.
- As the name implies the underlying idea of mathematics laboratory is that pupils will develop new concepts and understandings through experimental activities, dealing with concrete situations such as – measuring, counting, drawing, weighing, averaging, estimating, taking readings from instruments, recording, comparing, analysing, classifying, doing statistical calculations, graphing, checking data, obtaining original data or impressions from concrete physical situations and working with such data.
- Most work of this nature will involve the use of various kinds of physical equipment.
- Some of these works can be done in the classroom which is suitably arranged and equipped.
- Some can take the form of elementary field-work such as — determining angles and distances, mapping of small areas, etc.
- Most pupils find such work highly interesting and through it, they can develop many mathematical concepts and insights with interest and clarity often attained through a strictly intellectual approach.
- It is also likely that these concepts and principles become more enduring and more functional and meaningful when they are seen in relation to actual applications.
- To be productive of learning, the activities should be carefully planned, closely supervised and guided towards definite end.
- Responsibility for the effectiveness of laboratory work depends squarely with the teacher and the discharge of that responsibility depends upon adequate planning and supervision of activities.

## 29.5 Types of Lab Activities

The activities involved in laboratory work in mathematics fall broadly into two classes, not mutually exclusive *viz.,*

(1) Demonstrations (2) Experimental activities

1. Demonstration means the illustration and explanation of some mathematical concepts or relation by the teacher through a method using some physical equipment or device. *e.g.,*

- To illustrative operations with positive and negative numbers.
- To illustrate how trigonometric functions vary.
- To confirm the identification of the centre of gravity of a plane triangular solid with the geometrical centroid of a triangle of the same shape and size.
- To verify the geometric description of the locus of the vertex of an angle whose sides pass through two fixed points.
- To explain the difference between a square and a rhombus having the sides of same length.

Demonstration activities, therefore, are associated with the 'giving out' or 'transmitting' to others, information and ideas already acquired by the demonstrator.

Any demonstration which is well-planned and effectively carried out involves a real learning experience.

2. Experimental activities means any kind of activity which —

(*a*) is carried on individually or by a small group working together, and

(*b*) is aimed primarily at helping the experimenter themselves to clearer understandings.

*e.g.,* (1) checking the solution of simultaneous equations in two variables by accurately made large-scale graphs.

(2) verifying distances or angles first by estimating and then by measuring.

(3) checking the volume of a triangular pyramid is 1/3 that of prism in which it is inscribed.

## 29.6 What is Math Lib?

- A place or room in the institution where teaching material like books, reference books, magazines, educational journals, newspapers, etc. are kept is known as 'Library.'
- The section in the library where books and literature related to the knowledge of mathematics is kept is called 'mathematics section of the library'.
- In the depart of Mathematics, a separate room where books, literature and aids concerning the knowledge of mathematics are placed is called 'Mathematics Library'.

## 29.7 Why Separate Math Lib?

- The separate arrangement of mathematics library gives a sense of separate identity and inculcate interest in mathematics.
- It brings efficiency in the organisation.
- Mathematics teacher remains in touch with the volumes and literature in mathematics.

- The pupils get better facilities for referring the books and literature in mathematics.
- It helps in nurturing gifted and potential pupils in mathematics.
- It helps the activities of 'Mathematics Club'.

## 29.8 Organisation of Math Lib

The whole section of mathematics library can be divided into the following parts:

1. *Prescribed Text books:* There should be provision of all text books related to mathematics according to prescribed syllabus for each class of the school.
2. *Reference books:* The books other than the text books which are directed for further study, written by experts in mathematics.
3. *Books of interest and amusement:* The books which inspire the teachers and pupils for teaching and learning. *e.g.,* fun in mathematics, wonder of mathematics, puzzles in mathematics, tricks in mathematics, magic in mathematics, amusement in mathematics, mathematical recreations, riddles in mathematics, etc.
4. *Books on methodology:* Books on methodology and devices of teaching are generally meant for teacher. Remember that a teacher is a life-long learner first and then a teacher..
5. *Books on biographies and historical development:* This includes the books on historical development of mathematics and the biographies of great Indian/Foreign mathematicians.
6. *Books showing contribution of mathematics in other fields:* Books on mathematical advantages in social sciences, in biological sciences, mathematics in human affairs, mathematics for the millions, mathematical challenges, etc.
7. *Popular Math books:* Books on popular mathematics contain latest ideas about the discoveries and inventions in the field of mathematics. *e.g.,*

   (1) Reports of various committees and seminars, symposiums, etc., on mathematics education at the regional, national or international level.

   (2) Reports of publications of various mathematics clubs and associations.

   (3) Literature concerning guidance and career information related to mathematics education.

   (4) Mathematical journals, periodicals, magazines, etc.

## 29.9 Need/Importance of Math Lib

- Library is the mirror of the school. In any scheme of education, library plays a key role.
- In mathematics pupils are expected to do a lot of drill and practice work. A particular set of the text book cannot serve this purpose.
- It develops good hobby of reading in leisure time, habit of self study and self education.
- Pupils can improve their general knowledge by reading general books, magazines, periodicals, newspapers in mathematics.
- Thirst of knowledge can be quenced by reading books of self interest.

- The examiners are not supposed to set the question paper from the problems/exercises given in the prescribed text books. The pupils have to prepare themselves all sort of problems or exercises.
- It is possible only through a good mathematics library to develop various types of abilities and skills and inculcation of proper attitudes, interests and appreciations.
- It also serves the needs and interests of the teachers. Knowledge has no boundaries. The teacher has to keep himself up-to-date of the latest knowledge and skills in mathematics.
- He has to learn most effective and fruitful methods and devices for teaching. This is possible only through a good mathematics library.
- The pupils are acquainted with the different types of approaches in solving the problems. This makes them open-minded and also exercise their intellectual power.
- Mathematics library is the birth place of the future mathematicians. It inspires, stimulates and equips the pupils —

  (*a*) to take interest in the research work in mathematics,

  (*b*) to follow the footprints of great mathematicians.

## EVALUATE YOURSELF

1. What is a mathematics laboratory? Explain its need and importance.
2. Discuss the factors you will keep in your mind while organising mathematics laboratory.
3. What is 'Laboratory work/activities in mathematics? How will you provide it?
4. Discuss the type of laboratory activities.
5. Is mathematics laboratory essential for our High School? Give your views.
6. Justify the need of mathematics laboratory for effective teaching and learning of mathematics.
7. What type of material and equipments would you keep in a mathematics laboratory of a secondary school?
8. What do you understand by a mathematics library? Is it necessary to have a separate mathematics library in our high school? Justify your answer.
9. Discuss the need/importance of mathematics library.
10. What types of books will you keep in your mind while organising 'mathematics library'? Explain in detail.

❋ ❋ ❋

# 30 MATHEMATICS TEXT BOOKS

## 30.1 Mening

- Hall Quest rightly stated – 'A good text book is (*a*) a source of knowledge, (*b*) a guide, (*c*) a tool and an instrument to the pupils, (*d*) a means of interpreting truth.'

  Becon — 'Text book is a book designed for classroom use.'

  Lang — 'Text book is a standard book for a special branch of study.'

  American Text book Publishers Institute – 'A true text book is one specially prepared for the use of pupils and teachers in a school or a class, presenting a course of study in a single subject or closely related subject.'
- Education is a tripolar process. Its poles are teacher, student and content. The content/ subject matter is an intervening variable. It helps in the interaction between teacher and students. A teacher cannot proceed successfully without the help of proper content. In text books, the prescribed content is presented in a well-manner to suit the teacher as well as the students.
- Text books are standardised planned collection of the subject matter that has been prescribed for a particular grade-level or age-level.
- In a text book, subject matter is presented in a well-planned way —

  (*a*) to facilitate the learning of new concepts and skills, and

  (*b*) to maintain the knowledge already acquired.
- In a text book, emphasis is laid upon to correlate the theoretical knowledge with the practical aspects of life.
- It has became the key of knowledge. It has become a valuable aid to learning. Now-a-days, the whole education is based on text books. Text book is the pivot of modern education.

## 30.2 Significance of Mathematics Text Books

1. The mathematics text book occupies an important place in the classroom teaching.
2. A good text book of mathematics provides the content of mathematics and also determines the method of teaching.
3. It is not a master to be afraid of, it is rather a servant to be ordered.
   - It should be followed not slavishly but carefully and intelligently.
4. It is the most widely used teaching instrument. It meets all the requirements of the prescribed syllabus.
5. It is a means not an end in itself.
6. It is an inevitable instrument in teaching-learning process.
7. Mathematics text book is an essential aid and has occupied a pivotal role in educating the children in mathematics.
8. It is indeed a course of study, organised according to a set plan and a learning guide rather than a source book of information.
9. It is a potent determinant of 'what' and 'how' the mathematics teacher will teach.
10. It is regarded as strictly supporting and supplementing to the teacher's lesson on mathematics.
    - Its place can only then be real if the mathematics teacher supplements in by his oral exposition, by reference reading and by all his illustrations.
11. It is probably the cheapest and reliable source of mathematical knowledge.

## 30.3 Need/Importance of Math Text book

### [A] For Teachers

The mathematics teacher uses the text book to fulfill the following needs:

#### 1. *For reference material*

A text book serves as a reference book. It is generally written by expert and experienced teachers. A list of references is given about original source of information. So, if needed, the teacher may consult the original references given in the text book.

#### 2. *For suitable subject matter*

- Mathematics text book provide a lot of good illustrations and questions/problems for exercises.
- It also provides suitable content according to syllabus of a particular class and guidelines regarding the syllabus of mathematics.
- It helps teacher not to waste time on irrelevant details.
- A text book is usually written by the well-experienced and subject-experts teachers. A mathematics teacher can make use of their services by making use of their text books.
- It is also essential for the critical appraisal of the content in it.
- Valuable knowledge and information regarding content of mathematics collected from various sources is readily available in it.

- In it, content is presented in a well-organised and systematic form. The logical and psychological sequence followed in the text book proves very useful to teacher.

### 3. *For Guidance*

- Mathematics text book provides some important guidelines to the teachers about the presentation of topics in the class.
- It helps teacher in planning his lesson, deciding the methods of teaching and preparing suitable teaching aids.
- It provides answers to all the problems given in the text book. This helps mathematics teacher.
- It helps teacher in selecting and organising content properly according to the level of the class.
- It presents illustrative examples related to various types of problems on a particular topic. It makes the task of the teacher easy as it suggests ways and means of solving and teaching different types of problems.
- It also gives suggestions for —

  (*a*) correlated study

  (*b*) mathematical principles

  (*c*) experimental work

  (*d*) project activities

  (*e*) hints for the solution of difficult problems

  (*f*) explanatory notes for complicated puzzles.

  All these things guide a mathematics teacher a lot.
- It guides the teacher about the limits of his teaching in a particular class. It keeps him on track and thus directs all his energy for the realisation of the pre-determined aims and objectives.
- It also suggests possibilities of correlating mathematics internally and externally.
- The task of paying individual attention to the pupils becomes quite simple to the teachers by making use of the mathematics text book.

### 4. *For Planned and Systematic Teaching*

- A mathematics text book helps mathematics teacher —

  (*a*) in improving teaching efficiency.

  (*b*) in teaching in an organised and systematic way which makes teaching-learning process effective.

  (*c*) in correlating mathematics with its different branches and also with other subjects.

  (*d*) in specifying the standard expected to be attained by a particular grade/class.

  (*e*) in planning properly the unit/daily lesson.

(*f*) in systematic teaching and learning. This influences the teaching-learning situations in a class.

- It contains various topics in a proper sequence.
- It suggests the steps of planning, suitable methods of teaching and appropriate illustrative material to the teacher.
- It serves as a guide for mathematics teachers to proceed in an orderly manner according to the prescribed syllabus.

The content in it is organised according to the plan and in a systematic and specific manner.

- Mathematics teacher can use it as (*a*) a reference book, (*b*) a text book, (*c*) a means of imparting new knowledge to the pupils.

### 5. *For assigning Drill Work and HW*

- Mathematics is a subject of practice. Without practice it cannot be well understood. Till the rules and formulae are not used by the learner, they cannot be comprehended.
- Mathematics text book includes a number of good problems and sums related to different topics. They are readily available. They provide a wide opportunity to the teacher to assign pupils for drill work and HW.

A teacher has not to bother for setting of sums and problems.

### 6. *For Evaluating Pupils' Progression*

- Evaluation is an important part of education. Most of the teachers are unable to construct a good achievement test.
- Mathematics text book helps in the selection and construction of various types of sums and problems for setting a good question paper or test paper.
- Thus, it helps in evaluating pupils' progress.

## [B] For Students

### 1. *Helpful in the Self Study*

- When the pupil is eager and highly motivated, he can read and learn a topic in advance using text book by self-study.

It saves time and energy of the teacher.

- The well-illustrated examples help the pupils in self-study and in solving the other similar problems.
- Mathematics text book is also quite helpful to those pupils who remain absent in the class due to any reason.
- It helps —

(1) to complete the assigned HW at home.

(2) to do drill/practice work.

(3) to solve the problems given in the exercise by understanding the illustrative (solved) examples.

(4) to write the given assignments by collecting facts and information from the text book.

(5) to supplement class work and home study by the pupils after the topic discussed in the classroom.

(6) to revise independently the learnt content.

(7) to develop the habit of self-study in the pupils.

(8) to make up his deficiencies because of his failure to attend the class.

### 2. *Helpful in Understanding the Concepts*

- If pupil is unable to understand the concepts and certain complex matter as described by the teacher in the class, the text book helps him to understand the subject matter by reading it again and again. Thus, it makes things clear.
- If a pupil wants to understand and clear something which he could not understand in the class room, he may consult the text book.

### 3. *Developing Virtues*

- Text book develops scientific attitude in the learners.
- It also develops understanding regarding open-mindedness, co-operative attitude and scientific method, and certain mathematical abilities and skills among pupils.
- It leads to classroom discussions to accurate conclusions.
- It arouses and maintain interest in studying mathematics.
- It acquaints pupils with the wide variety of the application of mathematical knowledge.
- It helps to inculcate power of understanding and interpreting facts and ideas given in it.
- It stimulates the thinking and reasoning in the minds of the pupils over and above supplying necessary information.
- It includes sufficient material for inculcating desired interest, habits and aptitudes in learners.
- It helps pupils —

  (*a*) for systematic and speedy revision of the learnt content.

  (*b*) to form right and exact understanding of fundamental laws, principles, formulae and theorems in mathematics.

### 4. *Playing a Role of Teacher*

- Mathematics text book plays a role of teacher out of classroom.
- Text book contains illustrations which help pupils to solve other similar problems on their own.
- The text book of lower classes with coloured figures and illustrations provides an incentive to learn and attracts the young learners.

- If the pupils commit mistakes in copying the formulae, symbols, definitions, principles from the blackboard or if there remains gaps due to their inability of quick understanding or slow writing, the text book helps them a lot in correcting or supplementing the class notes.
- It supplements meagre expectation that can be performed in the classroom.
- It saves time energy and unnecessary labour of the pupils. *e.g.*,

  They need not (1) copy the illustrative examples/problems written on the blackboard.
  (2) write down problems/questions for drill and HW.

- It helps —

  (1) to acquire the required information with speed and accuracy,

  (2) to achieve the objectives set for teaching of mathematics.

5. *Useful for Gifted/Backward Pupils*

- Text book is most useful to those pupils who cannot proceed with other pupils in the class.
- Gifted pupils can learn topic in advance. This provides them a sense of satisfaction.

  Gifted pupils have more abilities and capacities to learn than mediocre pupils. They have the desire to learn more and more. So, the classroom teaching is not sufficient to them.

  Teacher cannot guide them in extra class due to work load of school. In this situation, text book helps them.

- Backward children have to learn with their own pace and capacity, because their speed of learning is slow.

  Thus, text book helps them as a teacher at home.

- In short, text book meets the requirements of the slow, average and gifted learners.

6. *Uniformity in Standard*

- A text book helps in maintaining uniformity of standard —

  (1) in the field of education throughout the state.

  (2) in different schools of a district/state having common curriculum and objectives.

  (3) in case different teachers teach in different divisions of a particular class of the same school.

This is because the same content is to be learnt by all the pupils of a particular stage or school or state.

- The public examinations and evaluation process becomes possible only due to such uniformity.
- It also helps pupils to seek migration from one school/district/state to another with least disturbances to their syllabus.

## [C] For both the Teacher and Pupils

- Text books have been criticised for numerous reasons. *e.g.*,

  (1) Text book lack challenges for pupils if the content printed is too easy.

  (2) If the text book content is too complicated for pupils to understand, the pupils fail to learn it.

- The teachers are the best judges to determine whether a text book or a part of it is too easy or too difficult. It should be either too easy nor too difficult. Such text books has many advantages.
- Mathematics text book helps in saving time and energy of both – the teacher and the taught.
- It gives suggestions regarding the use of various teaching aids and activities to be undertaken by the pupils as well as the teacher.
- It serves as a reference book for both – the teacher and the pupils, because it is the most reliable source of information to them.
- It provides certain well-illustrated examples which guide both of them.
- It helps related project activities which involve both – the teacher and the learner.

## 30.4 Main Features/Characteristics of a Good Text Book

The teacher and the pupils should know the essentials of a good text book. Following are the main characteristics of a good text book:

### 1. Get Up

- The get-up and set-up of a mathematic text book should be attractive. It should have psychological implications and have relevant, simple and pin-pointed title.
- The shape and size of a good text book should be proportional and quite handy.
- Its cover design should be appealing and attractive.
- It should have durable binding.
- The paper used in the text book should be of superior quality.

  Text book should have quality printing. Printing mistake should be next to nil. In mathematics, even the most ordinary printing mistake can play havoc.
- Proper marginal space from all the sides of a page should be maintained.

### 2. The Author

- The author should —

  (1) be well-qualified, competent and experienced.

  (2) be not only a logician but also a psychologist.

  (3) have a certain amount of experience of teaching mathematics.

  (4) consider and understand the real learning situations and difficulties of the learner.
- Author's aim of writing should be very genuine.
- For the author(s) certain main academic and professional qualifications may be prescribed.
- A good text book of mathematics should be written according to the aims and objectives of teaching of mathematics.

## 3. The Language

- The text book should be written in lucid, simple, clear, precise and scientific language. The style of writing should be comprehensive and interesting.

  If the language is within the comprehension of the pupils, it will become purposeful and the pupils will enjoy it.
- The sentences should be simple, short, correct, unambiguous and clear in expression.
- Text book should make use of national and international standard terminology in terms of symbol, formulae, principles and definitions.

  The symbols and terms used must be well recognised and authorised. The new terms introduced should be clearly defined so that there is no confusion.

## 4. The Content/Subject Matter

- The content should contain —
  (1) hints for the difficult and typical problems.
  (2) only the established facts aiming at shaping integrated modern world outlook.
  (3) valuable suggestions in the shape of assignments, project works, correlated learning and other useful practical work.
- The content should be —
  (1) presented in a very simple language with suitable examples and in a proper sequence.
  (2) written strictly according to the latest prescribed syllabus for a particular class or grade. It should cover each and every aspect of the syllabus properly and adequately.
  (3) arranged from simple to complex and from concrete to abstract.
  (4) organised on the principle of spiral (concentric) order, so that what is being taught may be correlated with the past (precious knowledge) and future learning.
  (5) consistent with the pupils' needs, interest and previous knowledge.
  (6) up-to-date and related to the daily life and experience of the pupils.
  (7) written according to the demands of modern mathematics. *e.g.*, the units of weight, length, capacity and coinage etc. should be in the SI units.
  (8) properly selected and, if possible, it should contain self-composed matter based on the author's own experience.
- The content should —
  (1) reflect the unknown and uncertainties in mathematics.
  (2) create and retain interest in the pupils for mathematics.
  (3) mention the audio-visual aids and other supplementary reading materials.
  (4) give due place to all practicable progressive methods of teaching like inducto-deductive, analytico-synthetic, heuristic, laboratory, and problem-solving methods.
  (5) suggest (*i*) the effective teaching methods.
  (*ii*) the possible aids for teaching the topic,

(*iii*) the correlation of the topics, and

(*iv*) the activities or practical work connected with the topic.

(6) meet the abilities, interest and experience of the pupils for whom it has been written.

(7) cater the needs of all types of pupils – slow, average and advanced learners.

- The statements of facts, laws, principles, terms, theorems must be unambiguous and cent per cent correct.
- The topics and sub-topics should be illustrated with suitable figures, diagrams, graphs, etc.
- The major headings and sub-headings should be appropriate to the content.
- The presentation of the subject matter should be logical and psychological, interesting and attractive.
- The variety of topics should correspond to the variety of interest which the pupils are expected to have.
- Sufficient tube of more difficult problems and project should be given for gifted children.
- At the beginning of a new unit, a brief introduction should be given.
- The day-to-day needs of the pupils and their physical, social environment should find place in the content.

The pupils should be equipped with the 'know-how' of utilising the knowledge in their everyday life.

- If necessary, at the end of the unit, tables and appendices should be supplied with.
- The new latest development and inventions in the field of mathematics should find their due place in the text book.
- All the definitions, concepts, principles, new terms given in the text book should be as clear and definite as possible. They should be accurately and neatly defined.
- Oral mathematics should find its due place in the text book.
- The correct answers should be given at the end of every chapter and not at the end of the book.
- The text book should avoid irrelevant material, not included in the syllabus.
- The content of the text book should develop the interest, sense of appreciation, power of thinking and reasoning, power of observation and genealisation, etc.

It helps pupils to develop technical skills, scientific attitude and training in scientific methods.

## 5. Exercises and Illustrations

- The text book should contain —

(1) new and thought-provoking exercises.

(2) sufficient number of examples to motivate the pupils to solve the problems given in the exercise.

- The problems should be —
  (1) graded in difficulty values at the end of each new unit.
  (2) related to everyday life.
- The problems should satisfy the demand of examination, specially objective type of tests in mathematics.
- The examples should help to develop further concepts, desirable attitudes, technical skills and creative power of the pupils. Also, they should develop thinking and reasoning power of the pupils.
- Exercises should contain —
  (*a*) provision for revision and practice work of the work done in the previous class.
  (*b*) essay type questions, short answer type items and objective type items.
- There should be a few difficult examples to challenge the gifted pupils. In some cases, hints may be given for more difficult problems.
- The text book should be well-illustrated. The illustrations, diagrams and sketches should be (1) bold, distinct, attractive and realistic and (2) at proper places.
- The illustrative examples given in the text book should be quite appropriate. They should be neither too many nor too less in number, so that pupils can get adequate opportunity of learning through initiative and independent efforts.
- The principle of 'learning by doing' and maxim 'from concrete to abstract' should be adequately followed for the illustrations of the subject matter.

### 6. Some General Characteristics

- For pupils there should be text book but for teachers there should be 'Teachers Hand Book' which contains how to introduce a particular topic and ways and means of teaching it. There should be hints for teachers about HW, assignments, project work and other related activities.
- In the text book, there should be suggestions for pupils to improve their study habits.
- Text book should be reasonably priced so that majority of the pupils can easily purchase it. Again, it should be readily available in the market.

## 30.5 How to use the Text Book?

- Text book is the most valuable and useful teaching aid. It should be used as an *aid* in teaching and not as a substitute for teaching.

  It is a means and not an end in itself in education. Teachers and pupils should not follow it blindly.
- The matter given in a text book is not for memorising it either in the class or at home.
- It should be used only as a supplementary aid. The teacher should supplement it by his oral exposition, by reference reading and by all his illustrative and objective techniques.
- Text book should be followed very carefully, intelligently, cautiously and not blindly or slavishly.

- It should be used only when pupils feel a real need of it.
- In mathematics, the aim of teaching is to help the pupils in finding out the solutions of the problems and to discover rules and formulae.

  To get this aim fulfilled, the teacher has to use analytico-synthetic, inducto-deductive and heuristic approach in his teaching in the classroom.
- However, no teacher can proceed properly without the use of text book.

### A Word of Caution

- Don't over-depend on the text book. It is not the only source of instructional material. It is only one of the means or aids in teaching mathematics.
- Text book should not dominae the mathematics teaching programme. It should be used keeping eyes open.
- The greater the capacity, professional training, knowledge and experience of a mathematics teacher, the less the need to depend only on the text book.

## 30.6 Critical Evaluation of a Math Text Book

- The knowledge of characteristics of a good mathematics text book helps anyone in its critical evaluation.
- The following criteria may be useful for the critical evaluation of a mathematics text book:

### 1. Appearance

(1) Get up of the text book

(2) Quality of the paper and printing – Type of print

(3) Suitability of the size of letters

(4) Binding of the book

(5) Figures and its detail

(6) Size and bulkness of the book

(7) Price of the book – its reasonability

(8) Year of publication

### 2. Panel of Authors

(1) Qualifications and teaching experience of authors

(2) Their specialisation

### 3. Content/Subject Matter

(1) Its usefulness

(2) Proper organisation

(3) Coverage of the prescribed syllabus

(4) Accordance with the standard of pupils

(5) Adequate presentation

(6) Figures, graphs and their nomenclature
(7) Number of problems and exercises – their sufficiency
(8) Material and devices for motivation
(9) Content whether up-to-date or not
(10) Sufficiency of illustrations
(11) Diversification and utility of illustrations
(12) Their appropriateness and correctness

## 4. Presentation of Content

(1) Use of proper methods
(2) Emphasis on problem-solving approach
(3) Writing style – its interestedness
(4) Appropriate use of italics, bold type
(5) Use of maxims of teaching
(6) Proper instruction for teachers and pupils
(7) Alternate methods of solving a problem, if any
(8) Types of questions
(9) Style of presentation

## 5. Organisation of Content

(1) Table of content
(2) Appropriateness of headings and subheadings
(3) Division of content in proper units
(4) Grading of questions/problems in exercises
(5) Inclusion of latest concepts, symbols and units of measurement
(6) Relation of problems with daily life
(7) Variety of illustrations
(8) Table of reference books

## 6. Language

(1) Its simplicity and clarity
(2) Its ambiguity
(3) Use of well-defined and authorised technical words
(4) Comprehensibility and readability of illustrations
(5) Free of errors and mistakes

## 7. Accuracy

(1) Errorless printing

(2) Correctness of figures, symbols, formulae, graphs, etc.

(3) Correctness of answers provided

## 8. Readability

(1) Clear printing

(2) Simplicity of sentences

(3) Appropriate number of words in a line

(4) Properness of paragraphs

## 9. Adaptability

(1) Utility of the book for all the pupils

(2) Its usefulness for pupils of different backgrounds

(3) Fulfillment of needs of different categories of pupils

## 10. Miscellaneous

(1) Suggestions for using proper teaching aids

(2) Suggestions for project work

## EVALUATE YOURSELF

1. What is the need and importance of text books in mathematics teaching?
2. Discuss the importance of text books of mathematics for students, for teachers and for both.
3. How can a mathematics text book be used effectively?
4. What criteria would you follow while selecting a text book in mathematics?
5. What are the functions of a text book of mathematics?
6. Write short notes on:
   (1) Place of text books in mathematics
   (2) Characteristics of a good text book of mathematics
   (3) Selection of a mathematics text book
   (4) Effective use of mathematics text book
7. What are the essential qualities of a good text book of mathematics?
8. How would you critically evaluate a text-book in mathematics? Explain in details.
9. What do you understand by the term 'text book'? Give significance of 'mathematics text book.'
10. 'Text book of mathematics should be used as a means and not as an end.' — Comment.
11. What improvement would you suggest in mathematics text book of secondary classes?

❋ ❋ ❋

# MATHEMATICS TEACHER

## 31.1 Role/Importance of a Teacher in Modern Education

- The teacher is an integral part of the process of education. If there is education in any society in any form, there must be teachers and pupils in existence. It means there is no education without the existence of teachers.
- One may argue that we learn many things by insight, by self-education. But behind the insight there is a teacher in the form of —

  (1) knowledge acquired earlier (2) gained experiences

  (3) intelligence (4) will-power

  (5) maturity (6) level of aspiration
- Again, one may argue that at present so many open-schools and open-universities impart education through correspondence or through some other media. In this system of education, the lessons, assignments and other reading materials are prepared by subject-experts and experienced teachers.

  Thus, in any form of education, teachers help pupils directly or indirectly which certainly proves that their role has a vital importance.
- A number is so important a factor in any teaching situation that all other considerations are of secondary importance by comparison.
- In this regard, let us quote some educationists.

  Rabindranath Tagore — 'A teacher can never truly teach unless he is still learning himself.'

  Henny Van Dytre — 'Knowledge can be gained from books but that *love of knowledge* can be transmitted only by personal contact.'
- In the field of education teacher's role is multi-dimensional. He is the pivot of education system.

- The progress and quality of education of any country depends upon the teachers who impart education.

## 31.2 Need/importance of Math Teacher

1. The teacher plays an important role in the system of education. Teachers are considered to be 'builders of nation'. Mathematics is an indispensable part of education. So, mathematics teacher is a must in the process of imparting mathematical knowledge in the field of education.
2. In this era of science and technology, the future of the country and in fact the future of mankind depends upon mathematics teacher.
3. The aim of education is to develop all-around development of the pupils. Different subjects of the curriculum contribute towards the achievement of this aim.

   Mathematics is one of the subjects of curriculum. So, mathematics also contribute towards the realisation of the aims and objectives of education.
4. The educative values derived from a study of mathematics are not inherent in the subject matter, they are potentialities realised by skillful teaching.
5. A mathematics teacher shapes the personality of the pupil. He has a unique opportunity and a vital role to play in contributing an overall development of the pupil.
6. Perhaps, the most critical single element of an effective mathematics programme is none but the mathematics teacher.
7. A mathematics teacher cannot be replaced by a machine or by other sources, however sophisticated that may be.
8. Thus, anyone has to believe that mathematics teacher holds the key position in teaching mathematics.

## 31.3 Functions of a Math Teacher

A mathematics teacher has to discharge the following functions:

(1) Teaching functions (2) Administrative functions

(3) Departmental functions (4) Social functions.

### [A] Teaching Functions

1. With regards to teaching, a mathematics teacher has to perform the following duties and responsibilities:

   (1) To make efforts for successful, meaningful and effective teaching.

   (2) To build up understanding and motivation among pupils.

   (3) To create interest in the pupils for mathematics through well-presentation of the topic using teaching aids.

   (4) To create positive attitude towards mathematics through proper appreciation of the achievement of pupils.

(5) To have good planning and preparation of subject matter to be taught.

(6) To have personal contact with pupils so that a good academic environment can be established in the class and in the school.

(7) To select appropriate method for teaching of the topic.

(8) To correlate the subject with the branches of the same subject, with other subjects and with daily life.

(9) To give due consideration to individual differences while evaluating teaching and learning and while assigning the HW.

2. A competent and effective teacher of mathematics should —

(1) plan the teaching of mathematics.

(2) explore new techniques and devices for teaching mathematics.

(3) collect and utilize a variety of audio-visual aids.

(4) choose/write appropriate reference books.

(5) purchase various equipments for teaching mathematics.

(6) provide suitable facilities for effective learning of mathematics.

3. The first task of mathematics teacher, in connection with teaching of any unit/topic/aspect of the subject matter is to decide just what the immediate definite objectives are. *e.g.*,

(1) Which concepts/items of information the pupils are to gain from their study of the topic,

(2) Which skills are to be mastered,

(3) Which techniques and materials will be most effective producing the desired results.

4. A good and effective teacher of mathematics —

(1) exhibits general clarity of instruction.

(2) creates a task-focused and a relaxed learning environment.

(3) demonstrates higher achievement expectations.

(4) demonstrate alternative approaches for responding to problems.

(5) teaches class as a unit.

(6) emphsises the meaning of mathematical concepts.

(7) builds systematic review procedures into his instructional plans.

5. No good teacher can do a thoroughly good job of teaching mathematics unless he is willing to make a careful analysis of his job. He has to get guidance from that analysis in making his preparations and in conducting the work of the class.

6. A poorly prepared teacher can destroy the effectiveness of any carefully selected and well-organised curriculum with inadequate and unenthusiastic instruction, inaccurate and uninformed interpretation and indifferent and negative attitude.

On the other hand, a professionally prepared teacher can use even an inadequately structured curriculum to build an instructional programme of significant merit.

## [B] Administrative Functions

1. For administrative set up of a school, co-operation of all the teachers is a must.
2. Mathematics teacher has also to serve on some administrative committee in the school, as per the requirement.
3. He may be in charge of or a member of admission committee or examination committee or sports committee or discipline committee (*i.e.,* on proctorial board), etc.
4. He should take interest:
   (1) in all administrative and co-curricular activities that are organised in school.
   (2) in framing time-table, in maintaining various records like general register, progress reports.
   (3) in organising Mathematics Club or Mathematics Corner, etc.
   (4) in setting question papers and planning other evaluative devices.

## [C] Departmental Functions

- In schools, there may be a single mathematics teacher or more than one teacher. In both the situations a teacher has to perform various types of departmental duties such as —
  1. To organise and look after the Department of Mathematics room.
  2. To organise and maintain the Mathematics Laboratory, Mathematics Library and Mathematics Club.
  3. To organise and participate in departmental meetings and discussions.
  4. To select, to prepare order for purchasing and to maintain the books and periodicals on mathematics; and the mathematics equipment.
  5. To accept and to carry out successfully any related work assigned by the head of the department/institution.

## [D] Social Functions

- A teacher has some social responsibilities.
- Dr. S. Radhakrishnan — "The teacher's role in society is of vital importance.
  - He acts as the pivot for transmission of intellectual traditions and technical skills from generation to generation and helps to keep the lamp of civilisation burning.
  - He guides the individual and the destiny of nation.
  - On the other hand, it is incumbent (necessary) on the society to pay due regard to the teaching profession and to ensure that the teacher is kept above want and given the status which will command respect from his students."
- A mathematics teacher should have a good relation and link with the community. He can perform his social responsibilities in the following way:
  1. The mathematics teacher should act as an educational counsellor of the society.
  2. He should be co-operative with parents in improving relations between school and community.

3. He should be helpful to community people in removing their problems of banking or business or of paying taxes.
4. He should actively participate in parent association or past students association.
5. He should attend some specific meetings of social and civil groups.
6. He should organise fairs, exhibitions related to mathematical topics, which should be open to all. He should explain the visitors the importance of mathematical items prepared by pupils.
7. He should explain the parents —
   (*a*) the importance of mathematics in every field of life,
   (*b*) and other community persons the facilities offered by the school for the teaching of various subjects, specially mathematics.

In the light of these responsibilities, a mathematics teacher should realise that he is not only an individual but an institution.

## 31.4 Expectations from A Math Teacher

1. Modern education is child-centred. Here, teacher is more like a gardener who has to look after and nourish each plant (child) of the garden (school) very carefully and wisely.

   So, the teacher has to study the child, to know the effect of environment on the child and to know the psychological process of learning.
2. The purpose of education is the harmonious and all-around development of the child. So, in addition to teaching in a classroom, a mathematics teacher has to look after various curricular and co-curricular activities of pupils. He should be a friend, philosopher and guide of the child.
3. It is not an easy job for a teacher to transmit his knowledge to the pupils. For that, he has to apply various methods, techniques and strategies of teaching for which special training is necessary for him.
4. He has to develop in the pupils the qualities like self-confidence, self-reliance, good habits, competency to work with speed and accuracy, good citizenship, hard works, etc.
5. He has to realise the ultimate aims and objectives of education, *i.e.*, the desired change in the behaviour of the pupils.
6. A competent mathematics teacher should realise that in system of constructive thought and the validity of the conclusions depend entirely upon the validity and consistency of assumptions and definitions upon which the conclusions are based.

   From a logical point, the basic characteristics of a set of fundamental assumptions are—

   (1) *Consistency:* No two statements should contradict each other.

   (2) *Independence:* No two statements should follow as a logical consequence from any or all of the remaining statements.

   (3) *Completeness:* It should not be possible without further extensions of the set of primitive elements to add another postulate which is independent of and consistence with the given set of postulates.

7. An effective teacher of mathematics must —
   (1) continue to investigate new mathematical knowledge and effective teaching strategies.
   (2) create a stimulating atmosphere conductive to learning.
   (3) possess the desire, passion and patience to facilitate the learning of the pupils.
   (4) always willing to learn new methods, techniques and strategies for introducing and fixing concepts in the minds of pupils.
   (5) help his pupils to erase the fear and anxiety that mathematics represents to so many pupils.
   (6) be devoted fully to his profession.
8. For effective instruction a teacher of mathematics needs —
   (1) to talk frequently with other mathematics teachers about how mathematics can be taught, learnt and assessed.
   (2) to investigate, plan, adapt and implement the mathematics curriculum as a group of mathematics teachers.
   (3) to teach each other what they know about teaching and learning of mathematics.
   (4) to support each other as they take risks.
   (5) to have both – time and access to observe the teaching of other mathematics teachers.
   (6) to implement pedagogies that elicit and build upon pupils' thinking about mathematics.
   (7) to engage continually in analytic reflection on their practice.
   (8) to have deep understanding of —
      (*i*) mathematics they teach — concepts, principles, representations, applications, practices, etc.
      (*ii*) the ways that pupils learn mathematics.
9. A teacher of mathematics must have desire to learn —
   (1) modern mathematics,
   (2) how to educate pupils in mathematics,
   (3) how to supply the optimum mathematical environment for each pupil.
10. If the objectives are to attain in an effective and economical manner, the teacher of mathematics must keep in his mind —
   (1) his responsibility to create, stimulate and maintain interest in mathematics.
   (2) the exercises and activities that contribute most effectively to produce the desired understanding and skills.
   (3) the selection and arrangement of motivating materials to be made.
   (4) the analysis of these teaching materials to anticipate the specific difficulties which the pupils are likely to encounter in attaining the objectives of the unit.
   (5) the procedure and devices that promise to be specifically helpful to the pupils in overcoming these difficulties.
   (6) the organisation of explanations and developmental discussions.

11 Now-a-days education in general and mathematics in particular is child-centred. The mathematics teacher should give the pupils varied learning experiences through mathematics—

(1) to modify their behaviour

(2) to extract their potentialities

(3) to develop their personalities.

12. A competent teacher of mathematics needs —

(1) wide knowledge of people – of their aspirations, needs, strengths and shortcomings — so that he may use his knowledge of mathematics as a means of aiding his pupils to become competent citizens in a democratic society.

(2) to know what information, skills, habits of thought and attitudes are desirable outcomes of the educational process.

13. He must be skilled in the techniques and familiar with the literature of his profession.

- He should possess the essential teaching skills/techniques appropriate to his subject matter field.
- He should keep himself well-informed about (1) current theories of child development (2) the psychology of learning (3) teaching aids and testing aids (4) techniques and procedures (5) curricular organisation, and (6) other professional knowledge helpful to the task of teaching mathematics.

## 31.5 Qualities and Characteristics of a Math Teacher

- A teacher is a teacher first and then the teacher of a special subject. A teacher of mathematics is a teacher first and then the teacher of mathematics.
- The strength and success of any educational system largely depend upon the efficiency and qualities of its teachers.

  American Commission of Teacher Education (ACTE, 1944) states —

  - 'the quality of a nation depends upon the quality of its citizens,
  - the quality of its citizens depends upon the quality of their education,
  - the quality of their education depends upon the quality of their teachers.'
- The quality of mathematics education is determined to a large extent by the qualities of mathematics teachers. The success or failure of a mathematics course rests mainly with the mathematics teachers.
- The teachers of mathematics should posses two types of qualities:

  (*a*) General qualities and abilities required in every teacher including mathematics teacher.

  (*b*) Special qualities and abilities which made mathematics teacher successful.

### [A] General Qualities

### 1. *Well-versed in his subject*

- Adequate general knowledge
- Resourcefulness

- Adequate expression (verbal and written)
- Habit of self study
- Knowledge of current trends in modern Indian education.
- Professional degrees/diplomas like B.Ed., M.Ed., D.Ed., P.T.C., etc.
- Studious nature

2. *Well-integrated and Effective Personality*
   - Qualities of leadership
   - Progressive and dynamic outlook
   - Satisfactory mental health and adequate adjustment

3. *Love and Respect for*
   - discipline
   - his profession
   - his pupils
   - his subject
   - pupils' parents
   - other members of the staff

4. *Praiseworthy Qualities*
   - patience
   - self-confidence
   - dutifulness
   - honesty
   - frankness
   - studious nature
   - hard working nature
   - strong will power
   - punctuality
   - capacity of adjustment
   - co-operation with pupils' parents and members of the community
   - feeling of common harmony
   - skill and ability to understand his pupils
   - desire to help pupils in their self development

5. *Good Behaviour*
   - sympathetic
   - affectionate
   - impartial
   - unbiased
   - justice-loving behaviour

6. *Administrative*
   - Interest in framing time-table
   - Interest in maintaining disciple
   - Interest in maintaining various records, registers, progress reports
   - Interest in all the administrative, curricular and co-curricular activities organised in school
   - Interest in setting question-paper and in planning other evaluative devices

## [B] Special Qualities

1. *Command over Math*
   - The first and fundamental requisite of a competent and effective teacher in mathematics is the thorough mastery of the subject matter.

- No teacher can teach properly with full confidence unless he has a thorough knowledge of his subject.
- Mastery of the content makes mathematics teacher confident in his teaching.
- The effective teacher of mathematics should have competency in mathematics.
- If a teacher of mathematics is poor in his subject —
  (*a*) he may afraid of being caught sometimes by the intelligent pupils in the class.
  (*b*) he may not be able to respond satisfactorily the questions raised by the pupils.
  (*c*) on the part of the pupils, difficulties will be encountered creating negative mathematical experiences which will prove unsuitable for the development of the learner.
  (*d*) the students will not be influenced by such teacher, they will not listen him attentively.
  (*e*) the problem of indiscipline may arise.

- The mathematics teacher should be well-equipped academically.
  - He should have academic qualifications like B.Sc. or M.Sc. with mathematics as a principal subject.
  - His academic level of mathematics should be much higher than that of pupils.
- Education is a tripolar process. Its three poles are — pupils, teacher and content. The teacher imparts education to his pupils by means of content prescribed for them.
  - So, a teacher should have a thorough knowledge of mathematics.
- This is a guarantee for him to be a successful teacher, and this will help him to be confident in his teaching mathematics.
- There is a trichotomy of knowledge, significant to the teacher of mathematics, which might be classified as:
  (1) General knowledge
  (2) Professional knowledge
  (3) Specialisation in mathematics.

*General knowledge:* We are living in an age in which events takes place very rapidly. This rapidity of development and its implications for future change tend to encourage satisfaction in superficiality of information.

Under these circumstances the teacher of mathematics should have a broad educational background against which to project his thinking and in which to orient his appreciation of values.

*Specialisation in mathematics:* He has need of a synthetic type of scholarship in which he seeks mastery of the fundamentals of mathematic thought and closely interwoven chain of logic and of methods making deductions and implications.

- He should have positive attitude towards mathematics. Because his self attitude directly influences the learning process of the pupils.
  - Life history of mathematicians and history of mathematics inculcate positive attitude towards mathematics.

- Every ten years, mathematics is doubling. It can be rightly called the explosion in mathematics.
  - So, the mathematics teacher should be in touch with the latest development in mathematics. He should be fond of reading journals, magazines, periodicals on mathematics. He should keep his study continuous.
- He should go on revising his knowledge of mathematics during his academic career.
  - He should attend seminars, symposiums, workshops, orientation and refresher courses, conferences etc. on mathematics organised by the Government or private institutions and thus get himself enriched in the knowledge of mathematics.
- He should know the availability of resources of teaching mathematics so that he can adequately use techniques and devices of teaching mathematics.
  - Only a resourceful teacher makes arrangement of different means timely according to their needs and thus succeed in making teaching of mathematics effective.
  - A mathematic teacher should be creative and imaginative, too.
- A mathematics teacher should be good at research work related to mathematics and mathematical application.
  - To give importance to research and experiments in mathematics he should apply scientific and discovery methods for the solution of mathematical problems.
  - Priority should be given to experimental work so that pupils may be habitual of learning by self-doing and hence the teacher can work as a scientist and researcher.
- He emphasises the clarity of meaning of mathematical concepts which are generally too abstract to understand.

## 2. *Ability to Teach Math Effectively*

- The main aspects of any profession are —

  (*a*) Significant knowledge (*b*) Effective methods and techniques of teaching. Both are equally important.

The teacher should be able to communicate the suitable knowledge and content to the pupils using various methods and techniques of teaching.

- The mathematics teacher should have some professional training so that —

  (*a*) he can perform his work successfully and effectively,

  (*b*) he can be aware of the appropriate methods and techniques of teaching mathematics,

  (*c*) he can be aware of child psychology which is essential for him to know thoroughly the child and his behaviour.

Through professional training, he acquires essential qualifications like P.T.C., D.Ed., B.Ed., M.Ed., etc., of a competent teacher.

- Only those teacher can do his job successfully who have interest in his profession.
  - In the beginning, he has to spend most of his time in improving his knowledge of teaching mathematics and its techniques of teaching. This can be done only if he has keen interest in his job and devotion to his duty.

- ▸▸ He should not take teaching work as an employment and means of money-making. In the teaching profession, spirit of social service is a must.
- ▸▸ Interest in mathematics makes the teacher efficient in teaching mathematics.

  Teacher's love and interest would help to create similar love and interest for mathematics in his pupils.

- He should teach mathematics in such a way that the aims and objectives of teaching mathematics may be realised to a great extent.
  - ▸▸ For that, he should know them at all levels of education.
  - ▸▸ The awareness of aims and objectives makes him successful in his job.
  - ▸▸ This helps the mathematics teacher to devise ways and means for imparting knowledge effectively and adequately to reach upto the desired goal.
- He should possess ability to —

  (*a*) organise Math corner, Math Club, Math Lab, Math Library, Math projects.

  (*b*) administer and score the standardised or teacher-made tests.

  (*c*) present the topic of mathematics logically as well as psychologically.

  (*d*) provide guidance and remedial teaching for slow learners and for pupils backward in mathematics.

  (*e*) know difficulties of pupils.
- One of the trichotomies of knowledge is the professional knowledge. Professional attitude is interpreted to mean all enthusiastic interest in mathematics as a chosen field of study and service.
  - ▸▸ The body of professional knowledge should be provided through courses to acquaint the individual with the place and function of mathematics education in our social order.
- According to J.B. Show — 'There are four significant methods of teaching mathematics:

  (1) Scientific Method — Leading to generalisation of widening scope.

  (2) Intuitive Method — Leading to an insight into subtler depths.

  (3) Deductive Method — Leading to a permanent statement in rigorous form.

  (4) Inventive Method — Leading to an ideal element and creation of new realms.'
- He should be fully aware of the innovations and latest trends in teaching mathematics through radio lessons, TV lessons, micro-teaching lessons, etc.
- He should not teach mathematics in isolation. He should find ways and means to correlate (internally or externally) mathematics properly and adequately with other subjects or topics.
- Self confident and patient mathematics teacher —

  (*a*) can classify and analyse the subject matter adequately.

  (*b*) can solve the problems of his pupils in an efficient manner.
  - ▸▸ Lack of self-confidence and patience make him irritative in nature and it casts bad influence on pupils. This leads him to failure in his teaching.

- He should present the content skillfully making interaction with the pupils, introducing proper methods and applying various aids.
- Every problem should be introduced to the pupils logically and psychologically in a systematic manner.
  - He should first judge the nature of the pupils. Then, he should apply different methods to make his teaching more effective and comprehensive.
- He should have knowledge to judge individual differences as every pupil is different in reading, writing, understanding and in work speed.

  Here, knowledge of psychology makes him understand interests, abilities and capacities of different pupils and thus, he can guide them properly.
- He should teach the pupils by effective teaching methods like analytico-synthetic, inducto-deductive, heuristic, laboratory, project and problem-solving methods.
  - Here, pupils get the opportunity of learning by doing which helps in retaining knowledge for a longer time.
- He should inspire and motivate pupils to do more and more drill work and practical work.
  - This will make them creative and the knowledge received becomes permanent and solid.
  - This is necessary to understand the basic concepts, principles, laws, formulae, etc., thoroughly.

### 3. *Impressive Personality*

- Mathematics teacher should possess a well-integrated and impressive personality.
  - He should be physically and mentally healthy.
  - A healthy mind lives in a healthy body.
  - If his health is not good, he cannot perform teaching mathematics efficiently as power and activeness brings prompts in teaching.
- He should possess an aptitude of sobriety and seriousness.
- He should be well-dressed, enthusiastic, energetic, cheerful and confident.
- He should have a good command on mathematics and should be able to communicate it effectively.
- He must be just, co-operative and should have a sense of humour.
- His work and behaviour should serve as an ideal to the pupils.
- Personality of a mathematics teacher influences directly or indirectly to the pupils. So, he should do his work honestly, patiently and with full dedication.

### 4. *Scientific Outlook*

- Mathematics is an exact science. In it, nothing can be accepted without logical reasoning and proof.

- Mathematics expects the mathematics teacher to have —
  (*a*) an effort to proceed on scientific approach,
  (*b*) original and logical thinking.
  This will create similar scientific attitude in his pupils.
- He should possess scientific attitude, so that he can train his pupils in scientific method of solving problems.

## 5. *Psychological Outlook*

- The present education is child-centred. This means, education should be according to needs and interest of the child.
  - A mathematics teacher has to study the child and for that he must have a good knowledge of child psychology.
- With the knowledge of educational psychology and psychological outlook, he may be able to know the psychological requirements of his pupils and he may organise his teaching of mathematics accordingly.
- He should exhibit general clarity of mathematical instruction.
- He should create a task-focussed and relaxed learning environment.
- He should demonstrate higher achievement expectations.
- He should build systematic review procedures in his instructional plans.
- He should be non-evaluative (*i.e.,* beyond praise and criticism).

## 6. *Knowledge of Application of Math*

- If a mathematics teacher has a good knowledge of the application of mathematics in real life, in various vocations, in other subjects, etc., he can communicate and transfer it to his pupils.
  - If a student knows the utility and application of mathematics in his real life, he grasps it with interest.
  - Again, this makes his teaching meaningful, successful, interesting and effective.

## 7. *Mathematical Skills and Analysing Ability*

- A mathematics teacher should possess essential mathematical skills such as computational, problem solving, skills of drawing and sketching, skills to comprehend various types of graphs, skill to tabulate data, etc.
- He should possess the ability of analysis because he has to explain in detail many things to his pupils.
- In the presentation of proofs of geometry theorems, the capacity of analysis plays an important role.

## 8. *Leadership and Organising Ability*

- The teacher is an ideal for pupils. They learn many things from his acts and behaviour.
  - Therefore, the teacher of mathematics having the quality of leadership can lead the pupils in the desirable direction.
- Teacher's leadership is totally based upon his character and personality. If he is sound in his character and personality, he can inspire the students to take part in different activities in a group.

  Students may imbibe the quality of leadership from that of the teacher.
- A teacher should be a good organiser as he is required to organise various activities related to mathematics and also some other activities in the school. *e.g.,*

A mathematics teacher has to organise Math Lab, Math Lib, Math Club, etc. Through these activities he can influence his pupils.

## 9. *Patience and Tolerance*

- For ordinary pupils Mathematics is a difficult subject. They take more time in understanding the mathematical abstract concepts.
  - Few students are unable to learn after several repetitions.
  - So, there are various chances for a teacher of mathematics to be impatient. But a good teacher should not lose his patience and tolerance.
  - He should be optimistic and should have full confidence in his pupils.
  - He should adopt alternate methods or techniques or strategies to get success in teaching-learning process. But, it can be done if he has patience and tolerance.

## 10. *Proper Habits and Attitudes*

- A good mathematics teacher is expected to possess good habits like hard work, studiousness, initiativeness, self-confidence, patience, tolerance, strong will power, systematic working, cleanliness, aesthetic and artistic outlook, sweet speaking, etc.
- He is also expected to have rational, scientific and sympathetic attitude towards pupils.
  - His approach should be rational and original.
- He should be capable in the use of 'presence of mind' and prove things by examples and not only by words.
- A mathematics teacher should be justice-loving, refined in character. Thus, he can develop in his pupil quality of justice-loving.

  It is said — 'Good teachers are inborn and not made.' But training and their self-experience bring a great positive change in them.
- With these good qualities, he can definitely influence his pupils and may be able to make them interested in Mathematics.

### 11. *Democratic Dealing*

- A teacher of mathematics must be just and fair minded.
  - He should treat all his students alike and should not favour or disfavour on the basis of caste, colour, creed, nepotism, etc.
  - He should have a sense of justice and willingness to seek the facts.
- Only a just teacher can inspire confidence in his pupils through which he can carry them alongwith himself.
- Every pupil likes such type of teachers and obey them outrightly.

### 12. *Resourcefulness*

- A Mathematics teacher should make good efforts to be equipped with resources essential for effective teaching and learning.
  - The use of multi-sensory aids help him for successful teaching.
- He should present complex/complicated things in a simple way by using the appropriate aids and thus can develop in pupils good interest for mathematics.

### 13. *Affectionate Behaviour*

- A teacher of mathematics should love his pupils as liking or disliking is a reciprocal phenomenon.
  - If the pupils like their teacher of mathematics, they will obviously like mathematics taught by him.
- Establishment of rapport with the pupils before the actual teaching of mathematics will help him to understand pupils, their interest, abilities, achievement, aptitude, etc.

  Then, he would have relatively fewer behaviour problems.

### 14. *Communication*

- Human being is a social creature and generally he lives in society, and deals with the society.
- To be a good mathematics teacher, he should have some social feelings. He should accept the social traits that help him in classroom teaching, in school and in community.
- He should possess high decision-power, courage, positive attitude, habit to accept his weaknesses and feeling of co-operation. By organising curricular and co-curricular activities, he can develop in pupils social feelings.
- He should behave equally with all the pupils.
  - He should make no difference of rich or poor, dull or intelligent, low or high, familiar or non-familiar.
  - His behaviour should be, impartial with all students.
  - Only then he can communicate well to the society.

## Improving Professional Competence of A Math Teacher

- In National Policy on Education (1986), the present teachers and their education (training) is quoted as —

  "Traditionally teachers have enjoyed a position of great respect in our country. The religious leaders and social reformers have been addressed as teachers of the people and the community.

  "However, on the whole, the status of teachers has been diminished during the last five decades. The reasons are:

  (*a*) deterioration in work,

  (*b*) phenomenal expansion of the educational systems,

  (*c*) lowering of standards of teacher-training,

  (*d*) a general impression that a very huge number of teachers do not perform their duty properly,

  (*e*) changes in value system in society, etc."

  "The status of teachers has had a direct bearing on the quality of education and many of the illustrations of the latter can be ascribed to the indifferent manner in which society has looked upon the teacher and the manner in which many teachers have performed their functions."

- To get over the above mentioned situation, the following steps may be adapted:

  1. A comprehensive and effective professional education for prospective teachers.
  2. Selection of candidate for Pre-service Teacher Education on the basis of Aptitude Test.
  3. Organisation of selective academic training programmes.
  4. In-service training and continuing education (*i.e.,* Life Long Education) of teachers.
  5. Provision for research work and innovations and implementation of their findings in actual teaching situations.

## 31.7 Professional Growth of A Math Teacher

Professional growth for a mathematics teacher is beneficial to him from the following point of view:

1. It helps to develop —

   (*a*) an alert, sensitive attitude to the advancing age of human knowledge.

   (*b*) organisations from local to state and national levels.

2. It enables him —

   (*a*) to alone ensure for him a recognition from society.

   (*b*) to identify himself with work and to fulfill his life mission through hard labour.

3. It rises the standard of education.
4. It improves the conditions of employment.
5. It maintains security and integrity of the profession itself.

6. It supplies him with facts whereby he can improve his own work.
7. It stimulates him to go on beyond existing research findings to discover additional facts for himself.
8. It gives him right and high place in society and columnity.
9. It can maintain a good and high standard of living.
10. It builds up in him faith to feel pride in his work, dignity of his profession and democratic way of life.

## 31.8 Preparation before going to Classroom

- The mathematics curriculum mainly includes different concepts, formulae, hypotheses, theorems, axioms, postulates and content based on relations. These all are abstract in nature.
- So, the work of a teacher of Mathematics becomes very difficult. He has to think over deeply while presenting any topic/content in the class that 'what' and 'how' is to be taught in a particular class.
- So, it becomes his essential duty to prepare the lesson before teaching it so as to make his teaching effective, impressive and meaningful.
- It is said — 'It is a crime to enter the class without full preparation of the lesson.' This is very much applicable to the teacher of mathematics in particular.
- He should consider the following points before going to the classroom:

### 1. *Previous Knowledge and Experience of Pupils*

- A teacher of mathematics should know well the previous knowledge and experience of the pupils before going to the classroom.

  He should link previous knowledge of the pupil to their new knowledge (*i.e.*, the use of maxim: From known to unknown).

### 2. *Selection of Teaching Materials*

To make his teaching more effective and smooth, the teacher of mathematics should select and arrange systematically the different teaching aids, audio-visual or multi-dimensional, and required apparatus in order of their requirement.

### 3. *Selection of Examples*

He should consider 'what type' and 'how many' examples he has to cover in his teaching to make it more simple and effective.

### 4. *Preparation of Lesson Plan*

The above mentioned three stages will help him while preparing his lesson plan.

- He should definitely know the order of points to be taught in the class and the skills to be developed in his pupils.

- Lesson plan should contain —
  - (*a*) objectives to be realised,
  - (*b*) points of content to be discussed,
  - (*c*) activities to achieve learning experiences through proper oral and written work,
  - (*d*) evaluation procedure,
  - (*e*) proper drill work, HW or assignment to be given.

He should previously determine what type of questions and how many are to be given in drill work.

He should divide the drill work in three categories:

(*i*) most simple problems (for below normal students)

(*ii*) some difficult problems (for normal, average students)

(*iii*) some very difficult problems (for genius/gifted students)

- If he keeps all these points in view, his teaching will be effective, impressive, meaningful and successful.

## EVALUATE YOURSELF

1. Discuss the role/need/importance of a mathematics teacher in modern education.
2. Explain fully the functions of a mathematics teacher.
3. What are the expectations from a mathematics teacher? Describe it fully.
4. What are the general characteristics/qualities of a mathematics teacher?
5. Enlist special qualities of a mathematics teacher.
6. 'Teacher is a nation builder.' Justify the statement stating the duties of a mathematics teacher.
7. 'A mathematics teacher requires much more than merely the mastery in his subject.' — Comment.
8. What type of personality should a mathematics teacher develop in himself? Discuss.
9. 'Teacher is the pivot around which the whole educational system moves.' In the light of this statement, discuss the importance of the mathematics teacher.
10. As a student-teacher what different qualities would you like to imbibe for becoming a successful mathematics teacher?
11. What measures should be adapted to improve the professional competence of a mathematics teacher?
12. Write short notes on: Professional growth of a mathematics teacher.
13. What preparation should a mathematics teacher do before going to the classroom?

> Do not leave this earth unless you have made it a little better than you found it when you were born. This is the only religion that I know of.
>
> — ***Osho***

# 32 MATHEMATICS CLUB

- In the formal classroom environment, a teacher of mathematics hardly finds time to go beyond the syllabus. He teaches only that demanded by the existing examination system.
    - Teachers, students and parents — all have become examination-minded. So, the realisation of the aims and objectives of teaching mathematics at any stage of the school curriculum, is a remote possibility through the formal classroom teaching.
- Under the circumstances, there is a genuine place for a 'mathematics club' in a present day school. It can play a significant role in the total programme of a school. In many progressive schools of today, it has become a reality.

## 32.1 Need/Importance/Merits of a Math Club

- Mathematics club can serve a number of purposes. These purposes/values certainly show the need and importance of a mathematics club. The values of it may be summarised as under:

1. Mathematics club in our school helps —
    (*a*) in arousing and maintaining interest in mathematics,
    (*b*) in satisfying interest and needs of the gifted children in mathematics,
    (*c*) in proper utilising leisure time.
2. Its activities develop in pupils —
    (*a*) heuristic and problem solving attitude,
    (*b*) and nurture the habit of self study, habit of selective study, various skills, power of reasoning and understanding, power to distinguish between relevant and irrelevant material,
    (*c*) love for mathematics.

3. Its activities provide the pupils an opportunity —
   (1) for the basic training in organising the activities and programmes related to mathematics.
   (2) of free discussion. As a result, the pupils are benefitted from good views of one another.
   (3) of leadership, active participation, co-operative working, feeling of joint responsibility.
   (4) to satisfy their needs and interest by participating actively in the club activities.
   (5) of extra reading of literature of mathematics *viz.*, mathematical journals, magazines, etc.
   (6) to translate the theory into practice and to make use of their learning in day-to-day life.
   (7) to discuss classroom topics in detail.
   (8) to listen to some distinguished mathematicians, renowned mathematics teachers and educationists.
   (9) for getting proper inspiration and incentive for independent research work and thus helping in nurturing future mathematicians and scientists.
   (10) for meeting parents and other members of the society and making them familiar with the activities of the school. It, thus, helps in bringing school close to the society.
   (11) for informal education and thus helps in making the task of formal education easy and complete.
4. Mathematics club can be a good medium —
   (*a*) of developing pupils' interest in mathematics,
   (*b*) of exchange of mathematical informations, experiences, experiments and innovations.
5. Mathematics club in our school provides a good platform —
   (1) to supplement and enrich the classroom teaching,
   (2) for the nourishment of inventive and creative potentialities of the pupils.
6. It stimulates the active participation of the pupils. This gives them opportunity to work together. They may learn the lesson of co-operation and inculcate many social virtues.
7. It helps in acquiring the pupils with the latest knowledge and developments in mathematics.
8. The club makes the mathematics education meaningful and effective.
9. It may be a suitable forum for organising various mathematical activities.
10. The club activities can link the knowledge of mathematics with actual life activities.
11. The knowledge gained by pupils through the various activities of the club supplements the classroom teaching.
12. The club can have co-operation with other associations and clubs in the school, for organising big functions.
13. The utility of mathematics club depends upon —
   (*a*) the interest shown by the teacher and the learners,
   (*b*) extent to which pupils are motivated to take part in the activities of the club.
14. It provides an excellent means of stimulating and fostering mathematical study.

15. The club makes possible an informality and a social atmosphere which the classroom can hardly provide.
16. It offers an ideal place for a free exchange of mathematical ideas and for frank, helpful criticism of this ideas.

## 32.2 Organisation of Math Club

- Mathematics club is an organisation of the pupils, by the pupils and for the pupils.
- The mathematics teacher is only a sympathetic counsellor whose main functions are:
  (*a*) to foster a continuance of interest,
  (*b*) to co-operate in guiding the activities of the club along appropriate lines.
- A draft constitution of the club is a must. It should be prepared by the mathematics teachers in consultation with the Head of the institution.
  - It should provide —
    (1) the name of the club,
    (2) aims and objectives of the club,
    (3) details regarding membership and the fees, etc., to be paid by members,
    (4) purposes for which the expenditure can be incurred and person competent to approve such expenditure,
    (5) various offices available to members and procedure for filling up these offices by other relevant details.
- The club should be given an inspiring and attractive name may be after some renowned mathematician/discovery.
- Some content of the draft constitution:
  1. The principles of organisation of the club should be neither numerous nor complicated.
  2. The objectives should be clearly stated and understood by all the members.
     - Emphasis should be on active participation of the members.
  3. Such a club should have the Head of institution as its patron.
  4. There should be a faculty sponsor (one of the senior mathematics teachers) who should be inconspicuous (not clearly visible or attracting attention) and ready to advise and help when needed.
- Membership of the club be open to all the mathematics pupils of the school.
  - Associate membership may be allowed to some other pupils interested in mathematics.
  - It is desirable that the club limits its membership to such size that there will be opportunity for all the members to participate the activities organised by the club.
  - Only a nominal membership fee be charged from the members.
  - The membership of the club should be fairly homogeneous as regards to age and grade level, so that the programmes which will be of interest to all the members, may be arranged.

- Membership in the club is usually voluntary and for this reason the club is composed mainly of pupils who have a real and earnest interest in mathematics and who desire to obtain a view of mathematics which is somewhat different from that gained in the classroom.

- The following members of the executive council should be nominated/elected from amongst the pupils.

  (1) Chairman (2) Secretary (3) Asst. Secretary (4) Treasurer (5) one or two class representatives from each class.

  - Executive council may include a Librarian, a Store-keeper and a Publicity Officer.

- The club members should tap other sources and carry out the club activities in their locality.
- All meetings be held at regular scheduled times, at least twice in a month.

## 32.3 Nature of Programmes and Activities undertaken by Math club

- The programmes and activities of the club for the whole session should be properly planned. In such a planning, the recreational and the educational aspects should be properly co-ordinated.
- The programmes and activities of the club may cover a wide range of topics many of which have been listed and discussed in numerous books and articles in periodicals like 'Mathematics Teacher', 'School Science and Mathematics.' 'Mathematics Students Journal', etc.

  - These will include topics drawn from the 'History of Mathematics', including biographical sketches as well as interesting anecdotes, the evolution and development of certain aspects of present day mathematics, topics from Algebra, Arithmetic, Geometry and Trigonometry, games and contests and applications to other subjects and fields of activity.

- In general, any criticisms that the sponsor of the club might have to make concerning programmes should be given in private to the individual pupils concerned.
- The following are some important programmes and activities which may be organised by the club:

  1. Organising —

     (1) general and extra reading in mathematics.

     (2) paper reading contests about certain important topics of mathematics.

     (3) lectures of prominent distinguished scholars and teachers on some important and useful topics.

     (4) mathematical exhibitions and fairs.

     (5) relevant seminars and career courses related to mathematics.

     (6) interclass and interschool contests, debates, workshop, symposia on interesting mathematical topics in collaboration with other subject clubs.

     (7) useful competition on mathematical games, riddles, puzzles, catch-problems and quiz competitions.

(8) visits and excursions to the places of mathematical interest.

(9) discussions about the practical applications of mathematics.

(10) film strip shows and film shows for the pupils of mathematics.

(11) recreational activities in mathematics like number-games, riddles, puzzles, catch-problems, funs in mathematics, etc.

2. Celebrating days and events of history of mathematics and man of mathematics.
3. Making or collecting charts, models, pictures, graphs, etc. for the Math Lab.
4. Conducting useful individual and group projects on mathematics.
5. Making arrangement for —

(*a*) taking advantage of radio broadcasts, TV talks and TV lessons on mathematical topics.

(*b*) wall magazines.

### Merits of Organising Activities

(1) Various activities of the club can easily be correlated with classroom teaching. Thus, the learning becomes effective and permanent.

(2) They are very much helpful in developing —

(*i*) the mathematical skills of the pupils.

(*ii*) power of reasoning, understanding and their ability to distinguish between relevant and irrelevant, right and wrong, logical and illogical, etc.

(3) They provide an opportunity to the pupils to express their talents and abilities.

(4) The pupils become self-motivated and thus the learning becomes meaningful and effective.

(5) The pupils also feel their responsibilities as a member or office bearer of the club.

(6) These activities are helpful in creating interest in mathematics and in having an idea of practical utility of mathematics.

## 32.4 Math Club and Classroom Teaching

- The activities of the mathematics club are a supplement to classroom teaching.
- Various charts, models, graphs, improvised apparatus prepared by the members of the club can be used as important Teaching Aids for teaching mathematics in the classroom.
- Various mathematics projects undertaken by the club members can be explained by them in the class.
- To make best use of the trips, tours, excursion and visits arranged by the club, the pupils be given a questionnaire to fill and supply answers to them during the trip.
  - These answers can be discussed in the classroom. The teacher can co-ordinate all the facts observed by the pupils, into a complete lesson.
- Some methods may be used to correlate and co-ordinate various club-activities with classroom teaching.
- If the club activities are properly organised, they will never interfere with classroom teaching.

## 32.5 Evaluation of the Club

- To find out to which extent a club has succeeded in achieving its set objectives, it is essential to carry out regular internal and external periodical evaluation of the programmes and activities of the club.
- For internal evaluation, the views and suggestions of the patron, sponsor, about the activities of the club should be obtained.
- For external evaluation, the sponsor of some other nearby mathematics club can be invited to visit the club and express his opinion with suggestions for the future improvement.

### EVALUATE YOURSELF

1. Justify the need of a Math Club in your school.
2. How will you organise a Math Club in your school? Suggest some programmes and activities for this club.
3. Write short notes on:
   (1) Merits of organising activities in a Mathematics Club.
   (2) Math Club and classroom teaching.
   (3) Evaluation of the Math Club.
   (4) Activities of a school Math Club.
   (5) Role of Math Club in the teaching of mathematics.
4. What is the place of Math Club in the school? Enumerate some activities of the club which provides incentive for the study of mathematics.

> This man, the product of materialistic civilisation knows the price of everything but the values of nothing.
>
> — ***Oscar Wilde***

# MATHEMATICS FOR RECREATION

## 33.1 Recreational Activities

- Generally mathematics is considered as a dull, dry and uninteresting subject. But this impression can be reversed by introducing the students a variety of recreational activities in it.
    - Recreational activities develop taste for mathematics.
- In ancient period too, people had a great interest in mathematics. Mathematics was mainly studied for its recreational value and as a leisure time activity.
    - People had a great interest in the game of numbers and other mathematical problems, puzzles and riddles.
    - Puzzles and riddles in mathematics provided fun and were quite witty. *e.g.*,

        (1) What number gives you the same result whether you divide or subtract by 5? (6.25)

        (2) What number gives you the same result whether you square it or find square root of it? (1)

        (3) What number gives you the same result whether you square it or double it or add it by the same number? (2)

        (4) How many minutes is it past 3 o'clock if 25 minutes ago it was half as many minutes past 3? (50 min past 3)

        (5) A clock strikes 6 in 5 sec. How long does it take to strike 12? (9 sec)

        (6) An oil merchant has a tank of oil and has the measures one of 2 *l* and another of 5 *l*. How will he take 8 *l* from the tank? (5+5–2 or 5–2+5)

        (7) A bridge stands on 15 pillars/supports. How many intervals/gaps are there under the bridge? (14)

## 33.2 Importance of Recreational Activities

1. Recreational activities develop taste for mathematics and pupils get motivation for further learning.
2. They bring a healthy change in the class atmosphere.
3. They prepare pupils for leisure time.
4. They provide a source of enjoyment and make the fruitful use of leisure time.
5. They help in developing self-confidence and self-reliance in the pupils.
6. If properly organised a maximum possible benefit may be derived from these activities.
7. The pupils learn to appreciate power and beauty of mathematics.
8. They sharpen wit and stimulate quick thinking.
9. They develop many abstract relationship which otherwise remain vague.

## 33.3 Organising Recreational Activities

For deriving maximum possible advantages, such activities should be properly organised.

1. The teacher should fix a period in time-table for recreational activities. Pupils should be informed accordingly.
2. An intelligent and active pupil may be made in change of these activities.
3. The teacher should ask all the pupils to come prepared with some riddles or recreational work for such activities.
4. The participants be asked to give their names to the pupil in-charge of these activities.
   - They should be asked to come to the stage turn by turn and present their items.
   - At a time only one pupil be asked to put his item before others.
5. The teacher or the participant should make clear the mathematical principle or formula underlying a riddle.
6. The teacher should choose some interesting riddles that are related to the particular topic which he is teaching. Such riddles have great motivational value.

### Some Number games:

1.

| | |
|---|---|
| $0 \times 9 + 1 = 1$ | |
| $1 \times 9 + 2 = 11$ | $1 \times 8 + 1 = 9$ |
| $12 \times 9 + 3 = 111$ | $12 \times 8 + 2 = 98$ |
| $123 \times 9 + 4 = 1111$ | $123 \times 8 + 3 = 987$ |
| $1234 \times 9 + 5 = 11111$ | $1234 \times 8 + 4 = 9876$ |
| and so on | and so on |

$9 \times 9 + 7 = 88$

$98 \times 9 + 6 = 888$

$987 \times 9 + 5 = 8888$

$9876 \times 9 + 4 = 88888$

and so on

2.

$1^2 = 1$

$(11)^2 = 121$

$(111)^2 = 12321$

$(1111)^2 = 1234321$

$(11111)^2 = 123454321$

$(111111)^2 = 12345654321$

$(1111111)^2 = 1234567654321$

$(11111111)^2 = 123456787654321$

$(111111111)^2 = 12345678987654321$

3. Multiply 142857 by 2 or 3 or 4 or 5. The product will involve the same numbers. *i.e.*, 1, 4, 2, 8, 5 and 7, and that too in order. Try.

4. $152207 \times 73 = 1111111$

5. $12345679 \times 9 = 111111111$

Write digits 1 to 9 omitting the digit 8.
Now if you want to bring in product all the digits 1, then multiply it by
$1 \times 9$ *i.e.*, 9
If you want to bring in product all the digits 4, then multiply it by $4 \times 9$, *i.e.*, 36.

Whatever digit you want to bring in product, multiply 12345679 by that digit by 9.

6. *Jugglery of 3-digit number:*

| | *Illustration* |
|---|---|
| (1) Take any 3-digit number. | 479 |
| (2) Repeat it to form 6-digit number | 479479 |
| (3) Divide the number formed by 7 | $479479 \div 7 = 68497$ |
| (4) Divide the quotient obtained by 11 | $68497 \div 11 = 6227$ |
| (5) Divide the quotient obtained in step 4 by 13 | $6227 \div 13 = 479$ |

You will arrive at the same number you started.

7. *Telling the Age of anybody*

| | *Illustration* |
|---|---|
| (1) Add your present age and next year's age | $14 + 15 = 29$ |
| (2) Multiply the sum by 5 | $29 \times 5 = 145$ |
| (3) Add the unit digit of the year in which you were born *e.g.*, 7 if the year is 1987 | $145 + 7 = 152$ |
| (4) Subtract 5 from the number you get in step 3 | $152 - 5 = 147$ |
| (5) Tell the final number | 147 |

The two digits on the extreme left of this number indicates your age, *i.e.*, 14 (check whether only two steps are sufficient or not)

8. The product and the sum of the following numbers are the same !!

$$1\frac{1}{2} \times 3 = 1\frac{1}{2} + 3 = 4\frac{1}{2}$$

$$1\frac{1}{3} \times 4 = 1\frac{1}{3} + 4 = 5\frac{1}{3}$$

$$1\frac{1}{4} \times 5 = 1\frac{1}{4} + 5 = 6\frac{1}{4}$$

$$1\frac{1}{5} \times 6 = 1\frac{1}{5} + 6 = 7\frac{1}{5}$$

$$1\frac{1}{6} \times 7 = 1\frac{1}{6} + 7 = 8\frac{1}{6}$$

and so on

The formula is:

$$\left(1\frac{1}{n}\right)(n+1) = \left(1\frac{1}{n}\right) + (n+1)$$

Put n = any positive integer.

9. The product and the remainder of the following numbers are the same !!

$$1 \times \frac{1}{2} = 1 - \frac{1}{2} = \frac{1}{2}$$

$$2 \times \frac{2}{3} = 2 - \frac{2}{3} = 1\frac{1}{3}$$

$$3 \times \frac{3}{4} = 3 - \frac{3}{4} = 2\frac{1}{4}$$

$$4 \times \frac{4}{5} = 4 - \frac{4}{5} = 3\frac{1}{5}$$

$$5 \times \frac{5}{6} = 5 - \frac{5}{6} = 4\frac{1}{4}$$

and so on

The formula is:

$$n\left(\frac{n}{n+1}\right) = n - \frac{n}{n+1}$$

10. The quotient and the sum of the following numbers are the same !!

$$1\frac{1}{3} \div \frac{2}{3} = 1\frac{1}{3} + \frac{2}{3} = 2$$

$$2\frac{1}{4} \div \frac{3}{4} = 2\frac{1}{4} + \frac{3}{4} = 3$$

$$3\frac{1}{5} \div \frac{4}{5} = 3\frac{1}{5} + \frac{4}{5} = 4$$

$$4\frac{1}{6} \div \frac{5}{6} = 4\frac{1}{6} + \frac{5}{6} = 5$$

and so on

The formula is:

$$n\left(\frac{n}{n+2}\right) \div \frac{n+1}{n+2} = \left(n + \frac{1}{n+2}\right) + \frac{n+1}{n+2}$$

11. The quotient and the remainder of the following numbers are the same !!

$4\frac{1}{2} \div 3 = 4\frac{1}{2} - 3 = 1\frac{1}{2}$

$5\frac{1}{3} \div 4 = 5\frac{1}{3} - 4 = 1\frac{1}{3}$

$6\frac{1}{4} \div 5 = 6\frac{1}{4} - 5 = 1\frac{1}{4}$

$7\frac{1}{5} \div 6 = 7\frac{1}{5} - 6 = 1\frac{1}{5}$

The formula is:

$$\left(n + \frac{n}{n-2}\right) \div (n-1) = \left(n + \frac{1}{n-2}\right) - (n-1)$$

12. *Triangular Numbers:*

Thus 1, 3, 6, 10, 15, ... are triangular numbers.

How to find them? Add n+1 to the previous number where n is the number of the term.

13. Find the pattern and complete it.

(*a*) 21, 22, 25, 30, 37, 46, 57, __, __. (+1, +3, +5, +7, +9, ...; 70, 85)

(*b*) 73, 71, 69, 67, 65, 63, 61, __, __. (–2; 59, 57)

(*c*) 70, 68, 66, 63, 61, 57, 55, __, __. (–2, –2. –3, –2, –4, –2. ...; 50, 48)

(*d*) 40, 45, 51, 58, 66, 75, 85, __, __. (+5 +6 +7 +8+... ; 96, 108)

(*e*) 65, 57, 61, 52, 56, 46, 50, __, __. (–8, +4, –9, +4, –10. +4, ...; 39, 43)

(*f*) 10, 17, 23, 28, 32, 35, 37, __, __. (+7, +6, +5, +4, ... 38, 38)

14. You can play this game with your friend — *Illustration*

(1) Ask him to think of a number — Let it be 7.

(2) Make it double — $7 \times 2 = 14$

(3) Add 8 to the product — $14 + 8 = 22$

(4) Make the sum half — $22 \div 2 = 11$

(5) Subtract your original number from the quotient — $11 - 7 = 4$

You can right away say that the resulting number is 4. Whatever number you asked to add in step 3 (here, your asked 8), the resulting number will be *half* of it.

**Explanation:** 1st step: Let it be x; 2nd step: 2x, 3rd step: 2x + 8; 4th step: $\frac{2x+8}{2}$

*i.e.,* x + 4, 5th step: 4.

15. (1) Ask him to think of a number — Let it be 15
(2) Make it thrice — $15 \times 3 = 45$
(3) Add 18 to the product — $45 + 18 = 63$
(4) Make the sum one-third — $63 \div 3 = 21$
(5) Subtract your original number from the quotient — $21 - 15 = 6$

You can right away say that the resulting number is 6. Whatever number you asked to add in step 3 (here, you asked 18), the resulting number will be 1/3 of it.

**Explanation:** 1st step: Let it be x; 2nd step: 3x; 3rd step: 3x + 18; 4th step: $\frac{3x+18}{3}$

*i.e.,* x+6; 5th step: 6

You can frame so many such number-games.

16. *Pythagoras Triplets*

(*a*) If x is odd, then first number $= x$
second number $= (x^2 - 1) \div 2$
third number $= (x^2 + 1) \div 2$ Pl. check

(*b*) If x is even, then first number $= x$

second number $= \left(\frac{x^2}{2} - 2\right) \div 2$

third number $= \left(\frac{x^2}{2} + 2\right) \div 2$ Pl. check.

*Illustration*

17. (1) Take 3-digit number, digits in decreasing order — Let it be 853
(2) Now inverse the digits and the number so formed be subtracted from the original number

$$\begin{array}{r} 853 \\ -358 \\ \hline 495 \end{array}$$

(3) Now inverse the digits of the remainder and add to the number in step 2.
The answer will be *always* 1089

$$\begin{array}{r} 495 \\ +594 \\ \hline 1089 \end{array}$$

18. Select four measures such that with the help of them you can weigh commodities upto 40 Kg. (1 Kg, 3 Kg, 9 kg, 27 Kg)

19. Kshitij sells 60 oranges at the rate of 3 oranges per ₹ 2. His brother Vismay sells 60 oranges at the rate of 2 oranges per ₹ 1. As they both were ill, they asked Ravi to sell 120 oranges at the rate of 5 oranges per ₹ 3. Considering the rate of selling price of both the brothers together, who got the profit and how much? (Ravi)

20. 14 28 57 × 1 = 14 28 57 (Keep in mind the order of digits)
" × 2 = 28 57 14 (Start with digit 2)
" × 3 = 42 85 71 (Start with digit 4)
" × 4 = 57 14 28 (Start with digit 5)
" × 5 = 71 42 85 (Start with digit 7)
" × 6 = 85 71 42 (Start with digit 8)
" × 7 = 99 99 99

21. $\frac{a^2 - b^2}{a - b}$ = --------

One intelligent boy did the sum like this:

$$\frac{a^2}{a} = a, \quad \frac{-}{-} = +, \frac{b^2}{b} = b \quad \therefore \quad \frac{a^2 - b^2}{a - b} = a + b$$

Similarly, $\frac{a^2 - b^2}{a + b} =$ ________

He did the sum like this: $\frac{a^2}{a} = a, \quad \frac{-}{+} = -, \quad \frac{b^2}{b} = b$

$$\therefore \quad \frac{a^2 - b^2}{a + b} = a - b$$

What do you think, is he logically right? (Not at all !)

22. To remember the product of positive and negative numbers, the following key will help you a lot.

Consider the sign of positive number (*i.e.,* +) as your friend and the sign of negative number (*i.e.,* –) as your enemy.

Now,

(*i*) Your friend's friend is also your friend, *i.e.,* (+) × (+) = +

(*ii*) Your friend's enemy is also your enemy, *i.e.,* (+) × (–) = –

(*iii*) Your enemy's friend is also your enemy, *i.e.,* (–) × (+) = –

(*iv*) Your enemy's enemy is your friend, too, *i.e.,* (–) × (–) = +

23. Can you find out the mistake in the following examples:

(1) ₹ 1 = 100 p

= 10 p × 10 p

Mistake: 100 p = 10 p × 10

$= \frac{1}{10}$ ₹ × 10

$= \frac{1}{10}$ ₹ $\times \frac{1}{10}$ ₹ $= 1$ ₹

$=$ ₹ $\frac{1}{100}$

$= 1$ p.

$\therefore$ ₹ 1 $= 1$ p. !!!

(2) $\sqrt{a} \times \sqrt{b} = \sqrt{ab}$

Let a = b = –1

or

$\therefore \sqrt{-1} \times \sqrt{-1} = \sqrt{1}$

$\therefore \left(\sqrt{-1}\right)^2 = 1$

$\therefore -1 = 1$ !!

*Mistake:* Remember that while extracting square root of a number, the answer may be positive negative. *i.e.,* $\sqrt{n^2} = \pm n$

24. See the fun of numbers

| | |
|---|---|
| $1^2 = 1$ | $1^3 = 1$ |
| $2^2 = 1 + 3$ | $2^3 = 3 + 5$ |
| $3^2 = 1 + 3 + 5$ | $3^3 = 7 + 9 + 11$ |
| $4^2 = 1 + 3 + 5 + 7$ | $4^3 = 13 + 15 + 17 + 19$ |
| $5^2 = 1 + 3 + 5 + 7 + 9$ | $5^3 = 21 + 23 + 15 + 27 + 29$ |
| and so on | and so on |

25. Simplify: $4^{44} + 4^{44} + 4^{44} + 4^{44}$ [$4^{45}$ as $4(4^{44}) = 4^{45}$]

Simplify: $2^{83} + 2^{83} + 2^{83} + 2^{83}$ [$2^{85}$ as $2^2(2^{83}) = 2^{85}$]

26. To tell the answer before the sum is written !!

| | *Illustration* |
|---|---|
| (1) Ask the pupil to write any-digit number on the blackboard. | 18374 |
| (2) You write now the answer (218372) | |
| (3) Ask the pupil again to write now any 5-digit number | 35269 |
| (4) Now, you write the 5-digit number (use the trick) | 64730 |
| (5) Ask the pupil to write again any 5-digit number | 28541 |
| (6) You write the number (use the trick) | 71458 |
| (7) Ask him to add all the five numbers | 218372 |

He will get the answer you wrote before hand!!

*Trick:* (1) Whatever number he gives, write 2 to its extreme left and subtract 2 for the number.

This will be the answer!!

(2) While writing the numbers in step 4 and step 6, be careful to see that the sum of every digit in the same place is 9. You write the number keeping this thing in mind.

For example 3 + 6, 5 + 4, 2 + 7, 6 + 3, 9 + 0 and 2 + 7, 8 + 1, 5 + 4, 4 + 5, 1 + 8.

## Fun with Figures

1. How many squares are there in the figure? (14 sq)

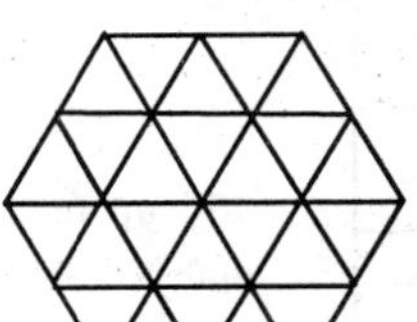

2. How many triangles are there in the figure? (38 triangles)

3. How many squares are there in this figure 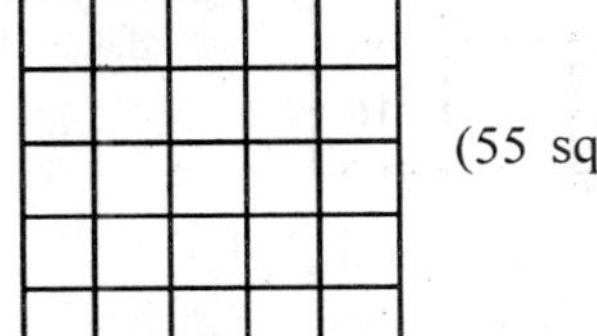 (55 sq)

4. *Magic Squares* (Odd number of boxes): Sum of the numbers in rows, columns and diagonals will be the same.

| | | |
|---|---|---|
| m + 1 | m + 2 | m − 3 |
| m − 4 | m | m + 4 |
| m + 3 | m − 2 | m − 1 |

Taking m = 5 →

| | | |
|---|---|---|
| 6 | 7 | 2 |
| 1 | 5 | 9 |
| 8 | 3 | 4 |

*Note:*
Take m = 5 or more. If you take m < 5 then also the magic square will be formed but it will include negative numbers.

Another method

| | | |
|---|---|---|
| m + 3 | m − 4 | m + 1 |
| m − 2 | m | m + 2 |
| m − 1 | m + 4 | m − 3 |

Taking m = 12 →

| | | |
|---|---|---|
| 15 | 18 | 13 |
| 10 | 12 | 14 |
| 11 | 16 | 9 |

In both the cases above, What is the relation between the sum and m? $m = \frac{1}{3}(\text{sum})$

In this way, you can form many magic squares. If each number in the magic square is added/ subtracted/multiplied/divided by the same number, then also you will get the magic square.

5. *Magic Square* (Even number of boxes)

| | | | |
|---|---|---|---|
| 1 | 2 | 3 | 4 |
| 5 | 6 | 7 | 8 |
| 9 | 10 | 11 | 12 |
| 13 | 14 | 15 | 16 |

Write diagonally opposite the numbers in the diagonals →

| | | | |
|---|---|---|---|
| **16** | 2 | 3 | **13** |
| 5 | **11** | **10** | 8 |
| 9 | **7** | **6** | 12 |
| **4** | 14 | 15 | **1** |

Fill up rest of the numbers as they are

This is a magic square

6. Find the secret trail

[Illustration]

| | | | |
|---|---|---|---|
| 9 | 2 | 4 | 2 |
| (4) | 5 | 5 | 5 |
| 5 | 6 | 6 | 5 |
| 4 | 10 | 8 | 7 |
| | | + | 49 |

(*a*)

| | | | |
|---|---|---|---|
| 1 | 1 | 2 | 3 |
| 7 | 9 | 7 | 3 |
| (3) | 8 | 4 | 1 |
| 8 | 2 | 7 | 3 |
| | | + | 38 |

(*b*)

| | | | |
|---|---|---|---|
| 10 | 7 | 4 | 8 |
| 1 | 1 | 10 | 10 |
| (10) | 3 | 10 | 5 |
| 3 | 7 | 3 | 10 |
| | | + | 57 |

By adding you should get 49.

7. Find the secret trail

[Illustration]

| | | | |
|---|---|---|---|
| 5 | 2 | 10 | 2 |
| (28) | 2 | 5 | 9 |
| 9 | 2 | 1 | 3 |
| 8 | 8 | 2 | 1 |
| | | – | 2 |

(*a*)

| | | | |
|---|---|---|---|
| 2 | 2 | 10 | 5 |
| 5 | 9 | 2 | 9 |
| 6 | 7 | 9 | 9 |
| (57) | 8 | 2 | 10 |
| | | – | 3 |

(*b*)

| | | | |
|---|---|---|---|
| (47) | 7 | 3 | 9 |
| 6 | 7 | 4 | 9 |
| 3 | 1 | 8 | 10 |
| 3 | 1 | 10 | 8 |
| | | – | 8 |

## Puzzles & Riddles

1. What did you wear the day after yesterday? [What I am wearing today]
2. There is a pink house made of bricks, a blue house made of bricks, an orange house made of bricks. What colour bricks is a green house made of?

   [A green house is made of glass or plastic, not bricks]
3. If a rooster laid 11 eggs and a farmer took 5 of them and another rooster laid 14 eggs and 5 of them were rotten, how many eggs were left? [Zero, Roosters do not lay eggs]
4. Three lawyers rent a hotel for the night. When they get to the hotel they pay ₹ 30 rent. Then they go up to their room. Soon the bellboy brings up their bags and gives the lawyers back ₹ 5 as the hotel was having a special discount that weekend. Each lawyer keep ₹ 1 out of ₹ 5 and give the bell boy ₹ 2 as a tip.

   However, when they sat down to tally up their expenses they could not explain the following details.

   Each one of them had originally paid ₹ 10 (towards the initial ₹ 30) then each get back ₹ 1 which meant that they each paid ₹ 9. The bellboy got ₹ 2 tip. After all, <u>they three paid out ₹ 30</u> but could only account for ₹ 29. Can you determine what happened?

   [The underlined phrase is wrong, they never paid out ₹ 30 at all !]
5. A farmer is trying to cross a river. He is taking with him a rabbit, carrots and a fox. He has a small raft. He can only bring one item a time across the river. How does he cross the river?
6. A sailor and his wife — each weighed 60 kg. They have two sons, each of them weighed 30 kg. Each of them knew how to boat. But the boat can carry weight upto 60 kg only. How will they cross the river?
7. If you have one kg of rocks and one kg of feathers, which one will weigh more?

   [The both weigh one kg]
8. As I was going to the fair, I saw a man with golden hair. He had 3 sons. How many people were going to the fair? [one, just me]
9. How can you add eight 8's to get the number 1,000 ? [use only addition]

   [888 + 88 + 8 + 8 + 8]
10. A beautiful pearl-necklace of a lady was torn in a quarrel and the pearls were all scattered on the floor. 1/3 of the number of pearls were on the floor, 1/6 were found by the lady, 1/10 were collected by her lover. 1/5 were found by her friend and 6 pearls were seen hanging in the thread. What was the number of pearls in her necklace? [30 pearls]
11. A scientist was studying about a type of bacteria. He found that they get double every 2 min. One day he put a bacteria on a pizza at 12:00. After six hours at 6:00, he found that the pizza was fully covered with bacteria at that time. Find at what time the bacteria would have covered 12.5% of pizza? [5:54]
12. A trader sells two T-shirts for ₹ 154 each. He gets 12% profit on the first T-shirt and 12% loss on the second T-shirt. Does he get profit or loss in this business? How much?

[Loss, ₹ 4.50]

13. Kavya and Vismay want to go from Surat to Anand. The distance between these two cities is 400 km. Vismay walks 1 km on 1st March, 2 km on 2nd March, 3 km on 3rd March and so on. Kavya starts from 6th March and every day covers 12 km. On which day they both meet each other second time? [15th March]
14. A man asked a shepherd the number of sheep he possessed. He said, "The number of my sheep is such that if it is divided by 7 and 13 the remainder is 1 and if it is divided by 4, 6 or 9, the remainder is 3. But the number of sheep is not greater than 200." Find the number of sheep he has. [183 sheep]
15. Can you tell what would be the unit digit of $4^{2005}$ ? [4]
16. An intelligent trader travels from one place to another with 3 sacks having 30 coconuts in each. No sack can hold more than 30 coconuts. On the way, he passes 30 check points. At each checkpoint, he has to give one coconut for every sack, he is carrying. How many coconuts are left with him in the end? [25]

## EVALUATE YOURSELF

1. What are recreational activities? What is their importance?
2. How will you organise recreational activities?
3. You coin some recreational items on the basis of the given items in this chapter.

Education is the sum total of all environmental influences, all training, all discipline, all culture, from the cradle to the grave.

— *T. Everard*

# INDEX

## D



## E

# BIBLIOGRAPHY


1. Aggarwal, S.M. : Teaching of Modern Mathematics, Dhanpat Rai and Sons, New Delhi, 1999.
2. Allen, D.W. (ed.) : Micro-teaching: A Description, Standard Univ., California, 1966.
3. Allen, D.W. & Eve, A.W. : Micro-teaching in Theory into Practice, Vol. 70, 1968.
4. Austin, Charles M. : Motivating Mathematics, School Science and Mathematics, 1939.
5. Bhatia, C.L. : Audio-Visual Aids in Education, Atma Ram and Sons, Delhi, 1963.
6. Bush, R. N. : Micro-teaching: Controlled Practice in the Training to Teachers in Communication, 1968.
7. Butler & Wren : Teaching of Secondary Mathematics, McGraw-Hill Book Co., New York, 1965.
8. Cajori, Florian : A History of Mathematics, MacMillon (II ed.), London, 1919.
9. Cliff, J.C. et. al. : Structure of the Skill Acquisition Phase of a Micro-teaching Programme, British Journal of Educational Psychology.
10. Espich, J.E. & Williams, B. : Developing Programmed Instructional Materials, Pitsman, London, 1967.
11. Goel,. Amit : Learn and Teach Mathematics, Authors Press, New Delhi, 2006.
12. Gulati, R. and Gulati, K. : Programmed Learning, Mahindra Capital Publishers, Chandigarh, 1976.
13. Gupta, Atul : The Power of Vedic Mathematics, Jaico Publishing House, Mumbai, 2005.
14. Howard Eves : An Introduction in the History of Mathematics, Holt, Rinchart and Winston, New York, 1976.
15. Janardhan Prasad & Kaushik, V.K. : Advanced Curriculum Construction, Kawshka Publishers, New Delhi.

16. Jangira, N.K. & Ajit Singh : Core Teaching Skills: The Micro-teaching Approach, NCERT, New Delhi, 1963.

17. John Russel : Teaching of Mathematics, Crescent Publishing Corporation, New Delhi, 2006.

18. Leith, G.O.H. *et al.* : A Hand Book of Programmed Learning, University of Birmingham, London, 1966.

19. Licks, H.E. : Recreations in Mathematics, D. Van Nostrand Co., Inc., New York.

20. Mc Alease, W.R. & Unwin, D. : Micro-teaching, New University, Ulstar, North Ireland, 1970.

21. Malhotra, V. : Methods of Teaching Mathematics, Crescent Publishing Corporation, New Delhi, 2006.

22. Mangal, S.K. : Teaching of Mathematics, Tandon Publications, Ludhiana.

23. Mavi, N.S. : Progarammed Learning: An Empirical Approach, Vishal Publications, Kurukshetra, 1964.

24. Mujibul Hasan Siddique : Teaching of Mathematics, A.P.H. Publishing Corporation, New Delhi, 2005.

25. Pepola, C. : Teaching of Mathematics, Anmol Publications Pvt. Ltd., New Delhi, 2005.

26. Paswan, N.K. : Modern Methods of Teaching Mathematics, Cyber Tech Publication, New Delhi, 2006.

27. Saxena, R.C. : Curriculum and Teaching of Mathematics in Secondary Schools, NCERT, New Delhi, 1970.

28. Sidhu, K.S. : The Teaching of Modern Mathematics, Sterling Publishers Pvt. Ltd., New Delhi, 1998.

29. Singh, L.C. : Micro-teaching: An Innovation in Teacher Education, Department of Teacher Education, NCERT, New Delhi, 1977.

30. Smith, D.E. : History of Mathematics, Dover Publication, New York.

31. Smith, W.J. and Moore, W.J. : Programmed Learning, Van Nostrand, New York, 1962.

32. Sue Jhonson-Wilder *et. al.* : Learning to Teach Mathematics into the Secondary Schools, T.R. Publications Pvt. Ltd., Chennai, 1999.

33. Sueltz Ben, A. : Drill-Practice-Recurring Experience, 21st Year Book, Washington D.C., NCTM, 1953.

34. Suneetha, E. *et. al.* : Methods of Teaching Mathematics, Discovery Publishing House, New Delhi, 2006.

35. Swami Bharati Krishna Tirthaji : Vedic Mathematics, edited by Dr. V.S. Agarwal, Motilal Banarsidas, 1965.

36. Swarupa Rani, T. : Teaching of Mathematics: Modern Methods, A.P.H. Publishing Corporation, New Delhi, 2007.

37. Vasudeva, Gurjar Laxman : Ancient Indian Mathematics and Vedha, Ideal Book Service, Poona, 1947.

38. Wadhwa Shalini : Modern Methods of Teaching Mathematics, Sarup & Sons, New Delhi, 2000.

39. Webb, N.L. (ed.) : Assessment in the Mathematics Classroom, 1993, Yearbook of NCTM, Reston.

40. Wilson, R.H. : Diagnostic and Remedial Reading for Classroom and Clinic, Charles E. Merril Publishing Company, Columbus, Ohio, 1972.


❋ ❋ ❋